MAMA LOLA

Comparative Studies in Religion and Society

MARK JUERGENSMEYER, EDITOR

MAMA LOLA

A Vodou Priestess in Brooklyn

KAREN McCARTHY BROWN

UNIVERSITY OF CALIFORNIA PRESS

Berkeley   Los Angeles   London

University of California Press
Berkeley and Los Angeles, California

University of California Press, Ltd.
London, England

© 1991 by
The Regents of the University of California

Library of Congress Cataloging-in-Publication Data

Brown, Karen McCarthy.
    Mama Lola : a Vodou priestess in Brooklyn / Karen McCarthy Brown.
        p.   cm.—(Comparative studies in religion and society ; 4)
    Includes bibliographical references and index.
    ISBN 0-520-07073-9 (cloth : alk. paper)
    ISBN 0-520-07780-6 (ppb. : alk. paper)
        1. Kowalski, Alourdes.   2. Mambos (Voodooism)—New York (N.Y.)
    3. Voodooism—New York (N.Y.)   4. Brooklyn (New York, N.Y.)—
    Religion.   I. Title.   II. Series.
    BL2490.K68B76   1991
    299'.67—dc20
    [B]   90-40070
                                                                  CIP

Printed in the United States of America
08   07   06   05   04   03   02   01   00
15   14   13   12   11   10   9

The paper used in this publication is both acid-free and totally chlorine-
free (TCF). It meets the minimum requirements of ANSI/NISO Z39.48-1992
(R 1997) (*Permanence of Paper*). ∞

TO MY TEACHERS,

ABDUL EL ZEIN, FLORENCE MIALE, AND

ALOURDES MARGAUX

The spirit is a wind. Everywhere I go, they going too . . . to protect me.

Alourdes Margaux

CONTENTS

Mama Lola is an intimate spiritual biography of a Vodou priestess and her family. Haitian Vodou is not only one of the most misunderstood religions in the world; it is also one of the most maligned. In New York City, where Mama Lola lives, prejudice against Vodou practitioners is common. Because of this reality, I have acceded to her request to change some names in the text and to use no photographs of her or her family. Given their understandable fears, I am all the more grateful for the courage that Mama Lola and her daughter, Maggie, have shown in agreeing to the publication of this book. They do not need to read these lines to know that, in addition to my gratitude, they have my love and my respect.

This book is the result of a dozen years of research and writing. Over such a long period many people have either read portions of the manuscript or heard me deliver lectures drawn from it. It is impossible to thank all those who have had a hand in shaping the final product. In fact, I do not even know the names of some of the persons who have been most helpful. For example, at Amherst College, where I did the first public reading from the manuscript, a black student who thanked me for caring enough about this woman to tell her story and for the "respectful" way I told it helped me to let go of some lingering uneasiness about questions of tone and style. And there was the student at Mount Holyoke who challenged me to look yet more carefully at Mama Lola's network of women friends.

I have taught courses on women in Caribbean religions at Harvard, Barnard, and my own institution, Drew University, and I have also given a series of lectures from the book at Princeton. Students at these institutions have had more sustained contact with the material. Their candor and their difficult questions as well as their enthusiasm have been more important to me than they know.

I also have colleagues to thank. Two women's groups, Academic Women at Drew and the New York Area Feminist Scholars, provided the safe space in which I first spoke about Mama Lola and in which the idea for the book took shape. In addition, I want to thank especially Carol Christ, Paolo Cucchi, William Doty, Christine Downing, Catherine Keller, Florence Miale, Gail Pellett, Judith Plaskow, Arthur Pressley, and Delores Williams, each of whom read and responded thoughtfully to portions of the manuscript. *Mama Lola* is also a better book because of the patient support of Naomi Schneider and Amy Klatzkin, my editors at the University of California Press, and the careful and respectful copyediting of Mary Renaud. Thanks are also due to Jerry Gordon and Judith Gleason for permission to use their photographs.

Early research for the book was funded in 1979 by a summer stipend from the National Endowment for the Humanities. Support for writing came from two grants administered by the Women's Studies Program at Harvard Divinity School. In 1983–84 I was visiting lecturer and research associate in women's studies in religion at the Divinity School, and in the spring of 1986 I was the Philips scholar in the same program. Constance Buchanan, the director of the women's studies program and associate dean of the Divinity School, deserves special thanks for her enthusiastic support of this project. I also want to thank the Board of Trustees of Drew University. On three occasions I have been given leave to work on the book. Thomas Ogletree, dean of the Theological School at Drew, must be thanked for his unflagging support of faculty research and writing and for the creative ways in which he makes those things possible. Finally, I want to thank Leary Murphy and Martha Dyson for their technical assistance in preparing the manuscript.

Haitian Creole is not a written language. The orthography of the Creole used in this book follows the official orthography adopted by the Haitian government in 1979 and interpreted and applied by Albert Valdman in the *Haitian Creole–English–French Dictionary* (Bloomington: Indiana University, Creole Institute, 1981).

I met Mama Lola in the summer of 1978 while working for the Brooklyn Museum on an ethnographic survey of the local Haitian immigrant community, a project that included photographing altars in the homes of Vodou priests and priestesses. Theodore B., a recent arrival to the United States who had befriended me during my first research trip to Haiti in 1973, offered to introduce me to Haitian spiritual leaders in Brooklyn. The home of Marie Thérèse Alourdes Macena Margaux Kowalski, also known as Mama Lola, was to be our first stop.

I had already made several research trips to Haiti, but the brief drive to Mama Lola's house was my introduction to the Brooklyn outpost of the Caribbean. As Theodore and I inched through the traffic clogging Nostrand Avenue on an intensely hot July afternoon, our nostrils filled with the smells of charcoal and roasting meat and our ears with overlapping episodes of salsa, reggae, and the bouncy monotony of what Haitians call jazz. Animated conversations could be heard in Haitian French Creole, Spanish, and more than one lyrical dialect of English. The street was a crazy quilt of shops: Chicka-Licka, the Ashanti Bazaar, a storefront Christian church with an improbably long and specific name, a Haitian restaurant, and Botanica Shango—one of the apothecaries of New World African religions offering fast-luck and get-rich-quick powders, High John the Conqueror root, and votive candles marked for the Seven African Powers. I was no more than a few miles from my home in lower Manhattan, but I felt as if I had taken a wrong turn, slipped through a crack between worlds, and emerged on the main street of a tropical city.

By the time we reached Fort Greene, a nondescript section of Brooklyn near the naval yard, the illusion had receded. Mama Lola owns a narrow, three-story row house there, in the shadow of the elevated Brooklyn-Queens Expressway. As I parked my car on that hot and muggy day, I noticed that it was the only house on the block with all the blinds down, the doors closed, and no one sitting on the stoop. Closing up the house is a Caribbean technique for staving off the midday heat. I should have guessed that this was the home of the only Haitian family living in this North American black neighborhood.

Alourdes ("Ah-lood" is the Creole pronunciation), the name by which I eventually came to address Mama Lola, took a long time coming to the door. Theodore and I were about to leave when the door opened a crack and we were scrutinized by a heavy-lidded, thick-jowled face the color of coffee ice cream. "Humph," she said as Theodore burst into a stream of nervous Creole telling her who I was, why we were there, how important our work was, and how she was the perfect person to help us. Alourdes sucked her teeth and shook her head in disgust at Theodore. "You coming here after I don't see you for six month—no, almost a year I don't see you—and you don't even say, 'Hello, how are you, Mommie Lola?' Right away you telling me what I got to do for you!" She opened the door and motioned us inside the musty, cool interior of her home. My eyes were still adjusting to the dim light when she turned abruptly and headed for the basement. As her head was about to disappear beneath the level of the banister posts running along the stairwell, she said simply, "You coming?"

Moments later, standing in the makeshift living room outside the door of her altar room (a door which remained resolutely closed on that initial visit), I got my first good look at a person who was to be central in my life for years to come. Alourdes, who also responds to the nickname Lola or Mama Lola, is a big woman—not tall, but round and solid. That day she wore a loose, sleeveless cotton housecoat. Her hair was covered by a scarf knotted tightly around her head. Floppy bedroom slippers revealed swollen feet and ankles. Even though Alourdes was then in her mid-forties, her skin looked as fresh and smooth as a child's. Yet she seemed like anything but a child to me; in fact, she made me quite uncomfortable. The fluorescent light in the basement accentuated the broad fleshy planes of her face and exaggerated the expression she wore, one I interpreted as either anger or fatigue. I quickly decided we were intruding. "Perhaps we could come back another time," I said, smiling politely at Alourdes while nudging Theodore back toward the stairs.

Alourdes looked confused. "You don't want no coffee? Theodore is my friend. Long time I don't see him. Long time. You going make him go before we even got a chance to talk? Ehhh? Theodore like my child! Even I don't see him, I know he thinking about me. Right, Theodore?" Breaking into a dazzling smile, she enfolded Theodore in her enormous arms, and the two of them did a little dance round and round to the music of their mutual laughter. The thick body was suddenly light and graceful; the sullen face warm, even beautiful. I have come to accept these mercurial changes in Alourdes, and sometimes I enjoy them. But I never know what I will find when I visit her, and I still feel vaguely guilty when she is in one of her dour moods. The observation of an anthropologist friend helped: "That look," she remarked after a joint visit some months later, "is the psychic's torpor."

I went back to see Alourdes several times before the project for the Brooklyn Museum was completed. She finally let me photograph her amazing altars: crowded tabletops with tiny flickering flames; stones sitting in oil baths; a crucifix; murky bottles of roots and herbs steeped in alcohol; shiny new bottles of rum, scotch, gin, perfume, and almond-sugar syrup. On one side was an altar arranged in three steps and covered in gold and black contact paper. On the top step an open pack of filterless Pall Malls lay next to a cracked and dusty candle in the shape of a skull. A walking stick with its head carved to depict a huge erect penis leaned against the wall beside it. On the opposite side of the room was a small cabinet, its top littered with vials of powders and herbs. On the ceiling and walls of the room were baskets, bunches of leaves hung to dry, and smoke-darkened color lithographs of the saints.

The lithographs included several different images of the Virgin Mary and one each of Saint Patrick with snakes at his feet; Saint Gerard contemplating a skull; Saint James, the crusader on his rearing horse; and Saint Isidore, the pilgrim kneeling to pray by a freshly plowed field. These I recognized as images of the Vodou spirits. Each of these spirits has both a Catholic and an African name: Mary is Ezili, the Vodou love spirit; Saint Patrick is the serpent spirit, Danbala; Saint Gerard is Gede, master of the cemetery; Saint James is the warrior Ogou; and Isidore is the peasant farmer Azaka. Vodou, the new religion that emerged from the social chaos and agony of Haiti's eighteenth-century slave plantations blended several distinct African religions with French colonial Catholicism. Dozens of the resulting Vodou-Catholic spirits continue to thrive in the twentieth century, where they reign over one or another troublesome area of human endeavor and act as mediators between God (Bondye) and "the living."

In this altar room, Alourdes practices a healing craft that has been passed down through at least three generations of her family. She is a priestess (*manbo*) in the Haitian Vodou tradition. As such, she is not unique or even rare. Rather, she is one of hundreds of similar professionals who minister to the approximately 450,000 Haitian immigrants living in New York City.[1]

Many other Vodou leaders—mostly men—operate on a much grander scale. For example, I know a priest (*oungan*) who rents the basement of a large apartment house on one of the main arteries in Brooklyn, where he stages dancing and drumming events attended by two to three hundred people. In contrast, Alourdes, like the great majority of Haitian healers in New York, works in her home. Much of her time is spent consulting with clients, one or two at a time, and the spirit feasts she holds several times a year rarely draw more than thirty people. She does not usually have drummers; they are expensive, and, more to the point, she does not want to attract the attention of her neighbors. Given the negative image Vodou has in the United States, many devotees prefer that their Vodou "families" operate on a small scale.

Alourdes does have an enviable reputation, however. She has a group of steady followers who appreciate her for being trustworthy and discreet as well as effective. It is also widely known that she adheres to a tradition that discourages making large profits from healing work. Her reputation, spread by word of mouth, has led to invitations to perform "treatments" throughout the eastern United States and Canada and in several places in the Caribbean and Central America. In these respects, there are not many like Mama Lola.

Healing is at the heart of the religions that African slaves be-

---

[1]Michel S. Laguerre, *American Odyssey: Haitians in New York City* (Ithaca, N.Y.: Cornell University Press, 1984), 31.

queathed to their descendants, and Alourdes's Vodou practice is no exception. She deals both with health problems and with a full range of love, work, and family difficulties. Like healers in related traditions found throughout the Caribbean and South America, Alourdes combines the skills of a medical doctor, a psychotherapist, a social worker, and a priest.

It can be argued that Haitians are more religious than people from many of the other former slave colonies and also that Haitian Vodou is closer to its African roots than most other forms of New World African religion. Vodou's closer ties to its African origins are primarily a result of Haiti's virtual isolation from the rest of the world for nearly a century following its successful slave revolution (1791–1804). The strength of religious belief in Haiti can be accounted for, in part, by the poverty and political oppression that have characterized life for most Haitians from independence to the present. Haiti is currently the poorest country in the Western Hemisphere, a country whose inhabitants are beset by disease and malnutrition. The wonder of Haiti is that its people seem to have responded to suffering throughout history by augmenting their stores of aesthetic and spiritual riches.

A well-worn joke claims, with some truth, that of Haiti's six million people 85 percent are Catholic, 15 percent are Protestant, and 100 percent serve the Vodou spirits. Among Haitians living in the United States, the few who have made a place for themselves in the middle class have tended to leave Vodou behind—except in times of crisis. But the vast majority of Haitian immigrants are poor, and these people maintain the habit of turning to healers like Alourdes for help with their stressful lives.

Half a dozen times a year, on or around the saints' days set by the Catholic calendar, Alourdes holds "birthday parties" for her favored spirits, or *lwa*, as they are also called. Clients, friends, and relatives gather around a decorated "niche," whose centerpiece is a table laden with food. Here they pray, clap, and sing until the crowd is sufficiently "heated up" to entice a Vodou spirit to join the party, to "ride" Alourdes. In a trance state from which she will later emerge with little or no memory of what has transpired, her body becomes the "horse" of the spirit, her voice the spirit's voice, her words and behavior those of the spirit.

These possession-performances, which blend pro forma actions and attitudes with those responsive to the immediate situation, are the heart of a Vodou ceremony.[2] The spirits talk with the faithful. They hug them, hold them, feed them, chastise them. Group and individual problems are aired through interaction with the spirits. Strife is healed and misunderstanding rectified. At these ceremonies, crucial community bonds are reinforced through the process of giving gifts of food and entertainment to the Vodou spirits.

Haitians, like their African forebears, operate from understandings of the divine and the virtuous that are markedly different from those of mainstream Catholicism. Bondye does not get involved in the personal, day-to-day affairs of human beings. "He is too busy," Alourdes told me. Instead, it is the spirits and the ancestors—neither properly referred to as gods—who handle day-to-day problems and who, if necessary, mediate between the living and God.

Although the *lwa* who possess Alourdes are often called *sen-yo* (saints), they are not saintly types in the traditional Christian sense. For example, in stories about the soldier spirit Ogou/Saint James, he not only liberates his people but also betrays them. Ezili Dantò/Mater Salvatoris, the mother, cradles and cares for her children but also sometimes lashes out at them in rage. The Vodou spirits are not models of the well-lived life; rather, they mirror the full range of possibilities inherent in the particular slice of life over which they preside. Failure to understand this has led observers to portray the Vodou spirits as demonic or even to conclude that Vodou is a religion without morality—a serious misconception.

Vodou spirits are larger than life but not other than life. Virtue for both the *lwa* and those who serve them is less an inherent character trait than a dynamic state of being that demands ongoing attention and care. Virtue is achieved by maintaining responsible relationships, relationships characterized by appropriate gifts of tangibles (food, shelter, money) and intangibles (respect, deference, love). When things go as they should, these gifts flow in continuous, interconnected circles among the

---

[2] I use the term *possession-performance* not to indicate that possession is playacting but to emphasize the theatrical quality of visits from the Vodou spirits.

living and between the living and the spirits or ancestors. In the ongoing cycle of prestation and counter-prestation, each gives and receives in ways appropriate to his or her place in the social hierarchy—an overarching, relentless hierarchy that exempts neither the young child nor the most aged and austere spirit. Moral persons are thus those who give what they should, as defined by who they are.

These days, the little room Alourdes calls her "altar" feels bigger to me than it did when I first saw it. It has become familiar, its contents no longer confusing. During ceremonies in the living room outside, I am sometimes sent into the altar room to fetch a particular bottle, image, or implement. Occasionally I sit in on diagnostic card readings and ritual treatments performed in the altar room itself. Furthermore, some of the contents of the room have changed because I have entered Alourdes's gift-exchange network. The room still contains the rock that whistled to Marie Noelsine Joseph, Alourdes's maternal grandmother, as she walked near her home in the remote mountainous interior of Haiti; but now it also contains things I have given Alourdes. The dingy skull candle on top of Gede's altar has been replaced by one I bought in the New Orleans airport gift shop, a clean white one with bright red wax-blood dripping over the face. Next to Ogou's altar hangs a photograph I took of Alourdes while she was possessed by this spirit.

It was neither an easy nor a direct path that brought me to such familiarity. During the fall and winter after I first met her, I visited Alourdes every few weeks. I usually brought some small gift, often her favorite bread from an Italian bakery near my home. During this early period, neither of us was sure why I was there, and, although Alourdes was hospitable, she never seemed especially happy to see me. More than once, I waited for hours while she talked on the phone or worked with clients, only to be told that she did not feel like talking that day.

For the first year or two, my visits to Alourdes's home and my presence at her ritual events were met with suspicion by some members of her Vodou family. Fortunately for me, Haitians usually keep such judgments to themselves, and the tension and drama that surrounded my entry into the community became known to me only later. Maggie, Alourdes's daughter, told me one story. "You know, they had a bet on you," she said. "Mommie won a lot of money!" In response to my confused expression, Maggie explained: "You remember that day I made a *manje Marasa* [a feast for the Vodou twin child spirits]? Everybody was suppose to take off their shoes and sit on the floor and eat with their hands, right? Some people tell Mommie, 'Karen never going to do that; she is too proud. White people don't do that.' But you know my mother, nobody gonna tell her who can be her friend. So when they say, 'Karen too proud to sit on the floor,' she just say, 'You wanna bet?' She won a lot of money on you." Maggie laughed. "She don't ever tell you?"

Alourdes and her family are all either citizens or legal residents of the United States, but many of the people she works with are not. Such a community is tightly knit, protecting its own and sharing few intimacies with outsiders. During the early years of my contact with its members, I felt their resistance; at the birthday parties for the spirits, I ventured no further than the edge of the crowd.

But things are different these days. Although a few still keep their distance, I now have many friends among the people who "serve the spirits" under Alourdes's tutelage. Today, Alourdes seats me near the center of the ritual action at her ceremonies, and I often assist in saluting the Vodou spirits. My change in status is a result of the initiation I underwent in the summer of 1981. Under the watchful eyes of Alourdes, I entered the initiation chamber in a small temple on the coast road south and west of Port-au-Prince. I am now one of the "little leaves" (*ti-fèy*) on Alourdes's Vodou family tree, and she introduces me as her "daughter." Her offer of initiation and my decision to accept marked the culmination of two inseparable processes. One was the growth of my friendship with her. The other was a shift in the way I understood my professional work.

The friendship grew despite our early halting and not always successful efforts to trust each other and to share the contents of our lives. Alourdes and I went through a great deal, singly and together, in the three years between the July day in 1978 when Theodore took me to her door and the July day in 1981 when she guided me through the taxing initiation rituals. We traveled to Haiti together once before the initiation, sleeping on the same pallet, talking late into the night, and discussing our dreams in the mornings. We also faced serious problems during that three-year period: I went through a divorce; Maggie was hospitalized with stomach trouble; and Alourdes's son William was arrested for purse snatching. Each of us sought to help the other when and how we could.

Like her altar room, Alourdes herself gradually became less exotic to me. As the shape of her character emerged, I began to feel considerable admiration for her. Alourdes is a strong woman who provides the main financial and emotional support for a hard-pressed family. She is also a fighter, a survivor who has had a hard life but nevertheless shows little trace of bitterness from her suffering. She is a presence to be reckoned with, someone who commands the respect of others. And her self-respect is palpable. But Alourdes is also a giver, a caring and empathic person who takes pleasure in helping others. By necessity, she has become adept at balancing this desire to help others with the need to care for herself.

Alourdes lives with her daughter, Maggie; her son William, who is mentally retarded and requires monitoring, although he is an adult; and three young children: her own son Kumar and Maggie's two small ones, Michael and Betty. Often there are others temporarily living in the house: new arrivals from the extended family in Haiti, clients from her healing practice, and family members or friends down on their luck. Except for the early, quiet hours when the adults are at work, the older children are at school, and Alourdes is babysitting with Betty, the house hums with activity. During my visits in the late afternoon and early evening, children clamber over me. Haitian music pours from the radio, and the television may be on at the same time. The doorbell rings frequently, with each new arrival raising the energy level in the house. Holidays and other special occasions fill the tables with food and the house with people a dozen times a year. I enjoy being part of this group; Alourdes treats me like family.

As Alourdes and I became friends, I found it increasingly difficult to maintain an uncluttered image of myself as scholar and researcher in her presence. This difficulty brought about a change in the research I was doing. As I got closer to Alourdes, I got closer to Vodou. The Vodou Alourdes practices is intimate and intense, and I soon found that I could not claim a place in her Vodou family and remain a detached observer.

Participating in the ceremonies in her Brooklyn home ironically brought me close to a form of Vodou older than the form I had been studying in urban Haiti. It brought me closer to the family-style Vodou of the countryside, where the patriarch of the extended family functions as priest and all those who serve the spirits under his tutelage are either blood kin or honorary members of the family. In rural Haiti and in Alourdes's Brooklyn living room, the group itself provides the content and drama of Vodou ceremonies in much more obvious ways than it does in the large-scale ritualizing common in Port-au-Prince.

My presence in Alourdes's Vodou world brought other insights. I had long been aware that Vodou priests and priestesses performed divination, administered herbal treatments, and manufactured charms and amulets, but I had initially seen their healing work as one of several priestly functions, one distinct from communal ritualizing. After some time with Alourdes, I realized that this perception was off the mark, that there is no Vodou ritual, small or large, individual or communal, which is not a healing rite.

It is no exaggeration to say that Haitians believe that living and suffering are inseparable. Vodou is the system they have devised to deal with the suffering that is life, a system whose purpose is to minimize pain, avoid disaster, cushion loss, and strengthen survivors and survival instincts. The drama of Vodou therefore occurs not so much within the rituals themselves as in the junction between the rituals and the troubled lives of the devotees. People bring the burdens and pains of their lives to this religious system in the hope of being healed. I realized that if I brought less to this Vodou world, I would come away with less. If I persisted in studying Vodou objectively, the heart of the system, its ability to heal, would remain closed to me. The only way I could hope to understand the psychodrama of Vodou was to open my own life to the ministrations of Alourdes.

I entered gradually. I accepted Alourdes's invitations to salute the spirits and pour libations for them. On occasion I brought her dreams and asked for interpretation. Sometimes I requested card readings. At one difficult point in my life, she suggested that I undergo a ritual "marriage" to two of the Vodou spirits, Ogou and Danbala. I did that. And in 1981 I went through the rituals of initiation.

No Haitian—and certainly not Alourdes—has ever asked me if I "believe" in Vodou or if I have set aside the religious commitments and understandings that come from my childhood and culture. Alourdes's approach is, instead, pragmatic: "You just got to try. See if it work for you." The choice of relinquishing my worldview or adopting another in its entirety has therefore never been at issue.

Nevertheless, I soon realized that my personal involvement in Vodou represented both gains and risks in relation to my work. The potential gains were in depth of understanding. One of the major risks involved losing the important distinction between Vodou interacting with the life of a Haitian and Vodou interacting with my own very different blend of experience, memory, dream, and fantasy. My experiences with Vodou both are and are not like those of Haitians. The stories I tell about these experiences have authority only in the territory between cultures. I have attempted to stay clear on this point and even to use these stories quite self-consciously as bridges for my readers, most of whom will be more like me than like Alourdes.

My increasing participation in Vodou also necessitated changes in research techniques. Initially, I used a tape recorder with Alourdes. In the beginning, she submitted reluctantly and tended to answer my questions about her life with portraits that were somewhat idealized, though fairly accurate. To my delight, however, she was far too spirited a storyteller to remain cautious for long. Soon she began to unfold rich stories about her early days in New York, about the difficult life in Haiti that had forced her to emigrate, and about her ancestors, the healers who had preceded her.

I eventually had to stop relying on a tape recorder, because it was unsuited to the casual rhythms of our growing friendship. Alourdes would often give me the best information when we were working together to prepare a ritual meal or when we were riding in my car. So I began to work in another way. After speaking on the phone with her, or spending an afternoon drinking coffee at her kitchen table, or passing most of the night at one of her birthday parties for the spirits, I would sit down at my desk to write. It seemed important to capture not only what she said but also how she said it. I found I could use her mnemonic devices, the repeated refrains of her stories, and some of my own memory tools—such as especially poignant visual images. Beginning with these condensation points and working myself into the rhythm of her speech, I could construct a record

by moving both backward and forward and in this way reproduce accurate, if selective, accounts of conversations that had
taken place hours earlier.

To these records of conversations I added contextual descriptions as well as some of the more traditional contents of an ethnographic journal. Unavoidably, as I brought more of myself
into conversation with Vodou, I put more of myself into my
field journal. Sometime in the early 1980s, I stopped editing out
my reactions to Alourdes. My affection and gratitude, guilt and
impatience began to appear as ingredients in her story, at least
partly responsible for evoking her expansive hospitality, infectious humor, or sullen withdrawal. Paying attention to myself
in relation to her became both a learning device (had I not
brought some of my own dreams to Alourdes, I would never
have learned as much about dream analysis in Vodou) and a
way of staying honest (when my field notes included my own
moods and motivations, I was more likely to take account of my
filters and interventions when I returned to those notes in the
future). Yet, putting myself on the line in my field journal and
in my relations with Alourdes and with Vodou was, in the end,
even more than that. It was an acknowledgment that ethnographic research, whatever else it is, is a form of human relationship. When the lines long drawn in anthropology between
participant-observer and informant break down, then the only
truth is the one in between; and anthropology becomes something closer to a social art form, open to both aesthetic and
moral judgment. This situation is riskier, but it does bring intel-
lectual labor and life into closer relation.

The academic world has cultivated in me a healthy respect for
the limits of the intelligibility of other people and other cultures. Most of the time, whether I am working in Haiti or visiting Alourdes in Brooklyn, I appreciate the wisdom of this stance
and try to operate from it. For example, because I assume that I
do not always understand what is going on, my tolerance levels
are higher when I am with Haitians than when I am with, for
example, my university colleagues. Because reaction always
presupposes interpretation, I will sit and wait longer, put up
with more delay and chaos, and generally bend more when I
am with Alourdes and her family than I would with my own
family. Nevertheless, I have thought many times that academics

have overemphasized those things that separate individuals and cultures from one another.

For Haitians, one of life's major challenges lies in distinguishing themselves as individuals in the context of an extended family. The extended family tends to take over, defining status, controlling assets, and apportioning time. As a result, in Haiti, human connection is the assumption; it is separation that requires both effort and explanation. That is why a Haitian may quiz a beggar on the street in Port-au-Prince before giving alms. What family is it that does not provide food and shelter for one of its own?

To a great extent, Alourdes is a product of her culture. She too operates on the assumption of connection. Because of this trait, she is not afraid to incorporate elements from other cultures into her own worldview. When a woman from the English-speaking Caribbean came to her for help in interpreting a dream in which "Mister Bones," a death spirit, had appeared, Alourdes did not miss a beat: "Oh, Mister Bone—that's Papa Gede!" Alourdes's universe expanded, and she now frequently refers to Gede as Mister Bone. A friend of mine once visited Alourdes with me. In her handbag were chromolithographs of the Hindu deities Krishna and Kali. "Let me see!" cried Alourdes, grabbing the images. "You going to get me some for my altar?" Alourdes did ask questions (why Krishna was blue), but she knew instantly what category she was dealing with. In a sense, her whole life is about movement between cultures and about understanding and coping with cultural difference. She does not waste much time wondering if and how such connection is theoretically possible; she gets on with it because she has to.

I recognize that there is a difference between the understanding and skill required to live in a culture other than one's own and the understanding and skill required to write about such a culture. I therefore do not want to throw away the hard-won insights of anthropologists into the limits of intelligibility and the reality of diversity. But I do want to balance them with my own experiences. I want to give full respect to my friendship with Alourdes. It is one example of the kind of connection and understanding that is possible across cultural lines. And I want to avoid substituting a theoretical picture of Haitian culture, one with firm boundaries, for the experiences I have had both in

Haiti and in New York, experiences that attest to a constant over-lapping of cultures and a good deal of routine culture mixing.

The methods used in researching and writing this book have roots in the work of other scholars. I think of myself as working within a tradition of interpretive anthropology. According to Clifford Geertz, humans are "suspended in webs of signifi-cance" they themselves have created.[3] We can speak of culture in a general sense (that is, I can talk about Haitian culture) be-cause human beings in relation, over time, tend to evolve shared styles of web-spinning. The individual life—Alourdes's life, for instance—while open to infinite variation, is nevertheless rec-ognizable as a version of one or more of these traditional web-spinning styles we call cultures. Even more to the point, such a view makes interpretation both the subject matter and the end product of ethnographic work. What the ethnographer studies is how people create meaning or significance in their lives, how they interpret objects and events. An ethnographic study such as *Mama Lola* is thus an exercise in bridge building. It is an inter-pretation within one web-spinning tradition (in this case, my own) of the interpretations of people who follow a largely dif-ferent aesthetic in their spinning (in this case, Haitians).

A corollary of this position is that the people who are being studied should be allowed to speak for themselves whenever possible, for they are the only true experts on themselves. That is why I quote Alourdes frequently and, often, at length. In passing her stories along, I also reproduce her way of speak-ing—English, wedded to the structure, rhythm, and cadence of Haitian Creole—to bring the reader a fuller sense of her and of the creative cultural mix in which she lives.

In *Mama Lola*, I am most interested in telling rich, textured stories that bring Alourdes and her religion alive. Rather than simply trying to refute the negative stereotypes often associated with Vodou, I have chosen to enter the public discussion of Vodou by another route: constructing a portrait of this religion as it is lived by Alourdes and the people closest to her. My aim is to create an intimate portrait of three-dimensional people who are not stand-ins for an abstraction such as "the Haitian

---

[3] Clifford Geertz, "Thick Description: Toward an Interpretive Theory of Culture," in his *The Interpretation of Cultures* (New York: Basic Books, 1973), 5.

people" but rather are deeply religious individuals with particular histories and rich interior lives, individuals who do not live out their religion in unreflective, formulaic ways but instead struggle with it, become confused, and sometimes even contradict themselves. In other words, my aim is to create a portrait of Vodou embedded in the vicissitudes of particular lives.

I am aware that my material connects with larger discussions going on in the academic world, discussions about such things as immigrant experience, Third World women, and even microeconomics. I have chosen, however, not to make these connections explicit. I am also aware that several of the Vodou spirits I describe have archetypal dimensions and appear in similar forms in other places. But, because I want Vodou to speak on its own terms, I have also avoided drawing these parallels.

Yet this book has in fact been motivated by some theoretical concerns. I have deep interests in how Haitian Vodou functions in relation to family, gender roles, and social change. These issues weave their way in and out of the entire book, but, for the most part, I have left my theorizing embedded in stories. To do this, I developed a style of narrative analysis in which the flow of the text is determined by story lines that from time to time evoke an analytic voice. This voice most often speaks in asides designed not to break the momentum of a story. I agree with Geertz that ethnographic writing has its greatest integrity when it stays close to the small slices of social interaction that provide its data: "Only short flights of ratiocination tend to be effective in anthropology; longer ones tend to drift off into logical dreams, academic bemusements with formal symmetry."[4]

Another sort of theoretical argument is implicit in the structure of the book, a structure designed to make its own point about the creative role that Alourdes's multiple, and often contradictory, spirit voices play in orchestrating her life. The longer chapters, those with even numbers, are organized to reflect the major Vodou spirits who possess Alourdes. These spirits, who preside over particular life domains, serve admirably to give order and definition to the different levels on which the drama of her life has unfolded. Chapter 2 deals with the Vodou spirit Azaka, a peasant farmer who reminds Alourdes of her roots

[4]Ibid., 24.

and therefore of her connections to, and need for, family. With Ogou, the focus of Chapter 4, the themes of risk taking, assertion, and anger are explored through the stories of Alourdes's move to New York and her interactions there with various officials and bureaucracies. Chapter 6 deals with Kouzinn, a rural market woman; this section reviews the economic dimensions of Alourdes's life.

The Vodou spirit Ezili, the subject of Chapter 8, provides the context and language in which the stories of Alourdes's relationships with men and her role as a mother are told. Chapter 10 focuses on Danbala, the serpent spirit. As the most ancient and most conservative of the Vodou spirits, he provides the context for stories about the efforts of Alourdes and Maggie to preserve their spiritual heritage. Papa Gede, the trickster spirit, the master of the cemetery, the guardian of sexuality and protector of small children, presides over Chapter 12, which concerns healing and other transformational arts.

I also have debts to feminist scholarship. When I began to diagram Alourdes's family tree, nearly a year after I started working with her, I realized that what she had traced for me with her family stories was a matrilineage. True, the most distant ancestor she acknowledges was a man, her great-grandfather, Joseph Binbin Mauvant. After him, however, all of her stories follow a line from mother to daughter. After Mauvant, men appear as husbands and lovers who enter the lineage as separate individuals. No stories seem to exist in Alourdes's memory about the parents or siblings of these men. Memories of sons born to the central women have also faded.

Instead of dismissing this as an accident of memory or a result of the vicissitudes of a "broken" family (after all, such sudden disappearances routinely befall women on patrilinear family trees), I chose to follow the feminist maxim that when gender is taken as a primary category of analysis it reveals levels of meaning otherwise unsuspected. In the case of Alourdes's family tree, this direction proved wise. I discovered a women's history and a parallel kinship structure buried beneath the official versions. It is "buried," because children in the family, following Haitian law and custom, were usually given their father's name, making the family tree that lives in Alourdes's mind quite different from the one documented in such things as birth certificates.

As a result of aligning my picture of Alourdes's family tree with the stories she told, I also discovered remarkable parallels between her family and larger processes at work in Haitian history. Her ancestral stories track a cycle of social change central to the past century of Haiti's history. Her great-grandfather, Joseph Binbin Mauvant, was a rural patriarch who presided over a large extended family of the sort Haitian slaves reconstituted after they gained freedom. When Alourdes's grandmother left her family land, a sizable rural outmigration, caused by depleted soil, overpopulation, and corrupt politics, was just beginning. Alourdes's mother, Philomise, was sold into a form of domestic servitude in Port-au-Prince at a time when the flow of displaced peasant farmers into Haiti's urban areas was escalating. In her late teens, Philomise escaped to the Dominican Republic, only to return a decade later to live in one of the rapidly growing pockets of Haiti's urban poor. And in 1963 Alourdes followed the first large wave of emigrants to New York. Each stage of this cycle has carried with it shifts in gender roles as well as changes in the way men and women relate to each other and to their children. Attention to the gender dynamics in Alourdes's family stories yields considerable insight.

Alourdes's matrilineal family tree provides a second organizational scheme for the book. Short chapters, those with odd numbers, tell the family stories through five generations, beginning with Joseph Binbin Mauvant and ending with Alourdes's daughter, Maggie. I debated for a long time about the appropriate form in which to tell these ancestral tales.

Alourdes is a superb storyteller, but her stories, as she tells them, do not lend themselves to reproduction in a written text. Each story has a theme—better, a refrain—with which she opens and to which she returns time and time again as the story is woven, never in a simple logical or chronological fashion. Each time the refrain is repeated, it signals a new attempt to tell the story. Each attempt seeks to capture that story whole. Yet none succeeds, because the connections, the meanings, and the layers of possible interpretation are too dense to be caught in a single telling. Thus Alourdes moves in a spiral fashion over and over the same ground when telling an important ancestral story. Each pass over familiar turf creates redundancy, but it also brings out some additional nuance or detail. To listen, it is necessary to relax with the rhythm and to trust that it will eventually bring her around to fill in the gaps. Questions about details or attempts to locate the action precisely in time and space only derail the process and produce long digressions.

When other family members are present, they add their own versions of the stories, twisting their word spirals in and around those of Alourdes. If Maggie is there, and especially if we are talking about the recent past, the two of them speak simultaneously, around and on top of each other like voices in a fugue. Family memories are held collectively; some persons know much more than others, but no one knows it all. The full story, or, I should say, the real story, cannot be written down. The full story can only be performed by a noisy family group, with each member adding his or her versions. The real story exists only for the transitory period in which the family takes pleasure and finds meaning together in bringing their past alive.

Stories about the recent past tend to be full and detailed, whereas stories from the distant past are sparse, almost mythic in feel. Yet in all the stories the material of dream, vision, and faith holds equal ground with the drama of politics, jobs and housing, food and hunger, suffering, illness, death, love, birth, and luck. Nor are these strands kept separate. In Alourdes's family stories, neglected spirits often bring on illness, just as spirits send cures or winning lottery numbers through dreams. Virtually no story is unrelated to the *lwa*, and thus none can be told without including the role they play.

If the full stories exist only in the transitory context of family performance, how could I render them? One day in 1984 I sat down to try to reproduce one of these stories in three or four well-honed paragraphs. When I got up from my word processor several hours later, I had written a twenty-page short story based on Alourdes's tale of Joseph Binbin Mauvant's mysterious disappearance. The story was true to Alourdes's telling, but I had also invented dialogue, supporting characters, and details of location.

Turning Alourdes's family history into fictionalized short stories allows me to tap a reservoir of casual and imagistic knowledge, which all people who have done fieldwork have but do not ordinarily get to use. As Alourdes's people sit together contributing shards of memory to a larger mosaic, they do so in the context of a great deal of shared but unarticulated information. For example, when they talk about Joseph Binbin Mauvant, they remember the sound and smell of an early morning in the mountains of Haiti, the way a cooking fire is kindled, the graceful dance of bathing with only a few cups of water. I too have some of this contextual information, and I want my readers to share it.

Some of the fabrication in these short stories has larger goals than merely creating ambiance. For example, if I had not invented sour, scrawny, ageless Jepete, how would the reader know that, as poor as Joseph Binbin Mauvant and his family were, there was surely someone with even fewer resources who served as their *bòn* (maid)? I have seen many versions of Jepete in rural Haiti, and she seems somehow deeply true to me. Readers will have to judge for themselves what they think of her. In deference to the problematic character of such ethnographic invention, I have kept these fictionalized stories separate. They are discrete, short chapters that alternate with the longer ones focused on individual Vodou spirits in which I do no inventing and adhere to more standard methods of ethnographic reporting.

In Great Atlantic culture (that is, white Euro-American culture), we expect history to be written with as much accuracy as possible. We are very concerned with "what really happened," and we are anxious that stories of our ancestors be both "true" and "verifiable." Yet, as current feminist criticism shows, the canons of historiography have not prevented the omission or misrepresentation of women in most accounts written about virtually any period of Western civilization. Memory apparently works for those who do the remembering, even for the professional rememberers, in ways more self-serving than generally admitted.

Haitians acknowledge this quality of memory more directly. Whereas we are anxious that our history not be false, their anxiety centers on the possibility that their history might become lifeless or be forgotten. Whereas in our eyes truthfulness is the paramount virtue of any historical account, in theirs what matters most is relevance and liveliness. We write history books to remember our ancestors, and the Haitians call on Gede, the playful trickster who is the spirit of the dead. Mercurial Gede appears in many forms and speaks through many voices. His special talent lies in viewing the facts of life from refreshing new perspectives.

I am part of a culture that seeks to capture experience, historical and otherwise, in books. So I write a book about Mama Lola.

But in doing so, I try to remember that she is part of a culture that serves Gede. Therefore I have tried to make up true stories, ones that are faithful to both Gede and Alourdes. I have tried to create her story through a chorus of voices, much as she creates herself through a chorus of moods and spirit energies. One of the voices that speaks in the book is hers, as carefully recorded and respectfully edited as I could manage. Yet another is my scholarly voice, distanced enough to discern patterns and relationships but not so distant as to create the impression of overall logical coherence. No person's life or culture is, in the final analysis, logical. A third voice is also my own, but this one risks a more intimate and whole self-revelation. The fourth voice is perhaps that of Gede—the one who tells the ancestral tales in the form of fictionalized short stories and in so doing plays with truth, seeking to bring it alive for its immediate audience.

CHAPTER ONE

Joseph Binbin Mauvant

Joseph Binbin Mauvant did not die. Not him . . . no. He simply disappeared. They would still be searching for him if he had not come to his wife in a dream. He said to her, "Don't try to look for me. You are never going to find me. I have gone back to Ginen, to Africa, where I came from."

It was early morning in Jean Rabel in the mountainous northwestern corner of Haiti. Deep shadows clung to the feet of the *mapou*, mango, and sour orange trees, while it was still night on the narrow footpath running through the dense canebrake behind the Mauvant family compound. The woman called Manman Marasa, mother of twins, had breakfast on her mind. There was water to boil for coffee. "The cassava that's left is a little piece, real little," she thought. "What are we going to give those boys? They're clearing land today. They need food. Oh, well," she sighed, answering her own question, "we have coffee. We have sugar for that coffee. We have *kleren* [rum]. That will do. We are cooking later, God willing." It was not unusual for men who worked in the fields to start the day with nothing in their stomachs but heavily sugared coffee or a shot of sugarcane rum with salt added or perhaps some *sowosi* leaves, but Manman Marasa still worried about them from habit. The last thing she wanted to hear was the babbling of a crazy husband.

Emerging from the door of the hut in which she had borne and reared her "little people," Manman Marasa threw a rag around her shoulders to ward off the morning chill. She did not even break stride to respond to the old man reclining on the mat inside. With a disdain common to women accustomed to hard work and childish men, she dismissed Joseph Binbin Mauvant:

◄ A ritual beggar dressed as Azaka in blue denim and a straw hat, clothing typical of a peasant farmer. Saut d'Eau, Haiti, 1981. Photograph by Jerry Gordon.

"You are going today? Well, good! I will see you when you are back." Hunkering down beside the charcoal brazier in her yard, she blew on splinters of pine kindling and muttered to herself, "He says he is going today. Humph! Where is an old man like that going to go? That man has lost his head, truly."

Inside, Joseph Binbin Mauvant rose slowly from his pallet. Seventy-nine years of living had put a stiffness in his legs that did not leave him until the sun was high—no, not until the chickens' beaks drooped all the way to the ground in sleep and the donkey ceased to twitch when black flies grazed on its eyelids. When the heat of midday descended like a heavy woolen blanket to muffle the yelping and crowing of the early morning, when this diverse community of animals and people was reduced to a drowsy murmur interrupted only by the squeal of a mangy dog caught pilfering or the cry of a child needing solace, Mauvant was at his best. But at dawn, the intense heat that would warm his old bones was a long way off.

Joseph Binbin Mauvant slid the wooden bar from the only window in the one-room hut where Manman Marasa "slept behind his back," displacing the gunnysack that had been tucked in the space beneath the rotting shutters. Because of the happenstance tilt of the wall, the shutters swung open of their own accord, letting in the grey-pink dawn and the sharp smell of smoke. In the remote mountain villages of Haiti, night is taken seriously. People treat it with respect. No one wants to take the chance that bad air or, worse, bad spirits (which, as everyone knows, wander freely at night) could find their way inside. So doors and windows are barred and, where possible, chinks and cracks are stuffed with rags.

Mauvant had slept in his clothes, as he did habitually, for nights could be cold in the mountains. Most mornings, the rising sun found Mauvant sitting in the courtyard on the short-legged chair with the woven sisal seat, rumpled from sleep and smelling of the day before, drinking his thick, sweet coffee, and waiting to receive the respectful greetings of his family. But on this morning he behaved like a different man. This morning he ignored the polite queries directed toward the window of his house: "And the night, Papa?" "You're not any worse today, Papa?" In short, instead of playing his accustomed role of patriarch to the ragtag crew, Joseph Binbin Mauvant began to prepare for a bath.

"Jepete [Eyeless One]," he called out the window to a scrawny, ageless woman who stood by Manman Marasa, "fetch water for me. I'm going to bathe." Jepete, who had an angry pink hole where her left eye should have been, showed no sign of having heard the command and continued to feed a sugarcane stalk slowly into her mouth. Time passed. A sharp voice came from within the hut: "Jepete, *fè vit* [speed it up]!" With a shrug, the eyeless one bent to one side to spit the depleted cane fibers from her mouth and, in the same sideways motion, swept up a large gourd with a corncob plug that sat on the ground near Manman Marasa's fire.

It was a ten-minute walk to the well, and Jepete's foot-dragging step raised angry cries from scavenging fowl all the way across the courtyard formed by the circle of small thatch and wattle-and-daub houses that made up the Mauvant family compound. To get to the narrow, rutted path leading to the well, she had to pass behind Marie Claire's house, on the far side of the yard. The path ran for a short distance through the canebrake before opening onto an almost treeless field, part of which served as the family cemetery. The well was just beyond the cemetery.

Although Jepete would never have let on, her foot dragging came from more than the lethargy that is the constant companion of the hungry. The sun was barely above the horizon, and she did not like to go near the cemetery at these in-between times of day. But that was not the worst of it. The worst was that she had to go by Marie Claire's house.

Everyone said Marie Claire was Manman Marasa's favorite child. Whether or not Manman Marasa actually loved her more than she loved her other children, one thing was certain: that girl got everything she wanted. Jepete's marginal position in the family—a foundling who ate meagerly from the pots of Manman Marasa in return for meager labor—made her suspicious. But a person did not have to be sour old Jepete to wonder if Manman Marasa was not simply afraid to say no to Marie Claire. Everyone knew Marie Claire had "eaten" her twin sister while they were still in their mother's belly. During more than one long night, as Jepete slept on the porch of this or that person's house, she was sure she heard strange noises coming from Marie Claire's. Whatever that woman did at night, Jepete did not want to know about it. And, as Papa Mauvant sent her for water that early morning, she was not sure there was yet enough light for the awful events of the night to be over. Her fears made Jepete appear sullen.

It was nearly half an hour before Jepete's skinny body with its distended belly came around the corner of Marie Claire's house. Straight-backed and curiously graceful, she carried the heavy container of water balanced on her head. Drops of moisture condensed on the outer surface of the gourd and, in spite of the chill in the air, fine beads of sweat showed on Jepete's upper lip.

Mauvant had spent the time staring absently out the window at the dawn, humming to himself, and watching the early-morning flurry of fowl and family as if from a great distance. Jepete placed the tin basin, which was the family's prized possession, in an open area dappled by the morning sun, just behind the little house where Mauvant stood lost in thought. She poured in two inches of cool well water. Then she shoved the stopper into the gourd and left it on the ground beside the basin. On her way back to Manman Marasa and the warm breakfast fire, she passed the window where Mauvant stood and, without raising her eyes, she said in a small voice, "The water has come." "I'm going today," Mauvant said. But he said it too softly and too late for Jepete to hear.

Like a man moving under water, Mauvant reached into a sack that stood in the corner of the hut and retrieved a pair of pants made from coarse blue cotton. He located a shirt of the same fabric and pulled it out as well. Mauvant stood for a moment with the shirt dangling from his fingertips. "*M'ap prale jodi-a, m'ap prale, wi* [I'm going today, I'm going, yes]." He had just picked up a ball of dense yellow soap when Manman Marasa came back inside.

"I'm going today, Manman," Mauvant repeated. Though he was her husband and the father of her children, he still called her "Mother." "Crazy man," she said, not looking up as her busy hands struggled with a knot in the piece of cloth where she had hidden a fragment of cassava bread. "Fool," Jepete had murmured when she returned to the fire after pouring the bath water, "he takes a bath when there is dew everywhere. That man is going to fall sick." "He does what he wants," Manman Marasa had replied.

Shivering in the cool morning air, Mauvant nevertheless bathed slowly, rubbing the stiff soap into a rich lather before addressing his life-scarred, work-scarred body. When he was coated with soap, he called Manman Marasa. Using gestures centuries old, she cupped her right hand and poured water deftly in tiny rivulets across his shoulders and down his back, then across his chest and down his thighs. Each trickle of clear water was followed by a quick pass of her free hand, which took away the last traces of soapsuds. Then with sudden gentleness—these mountain women could treat their children or their men with such gentleness as easily as they could dismiss them with disdain—Manman Marasa took a small amount of fresh water in her hand and in a single, circular motion wiped the soap from the old face she knew so well.

As Mauvant's eyes blinked open, her hand still cupped his chin. She pulled his face close to hers and asked softly: "How are you feeling today, Papa?" Her tendency to call him "Papa" was even more fitting than his preference for addressing her as "Mother," for even though he was the father of her children, he was more than three decades older than she was. In the way of rural women, Manman Marasa had always understood and accepted that she was somehow the child of her husband, as were all the people who lived in his compound. "I'm going today," Mauvant said, "I'm going." Apparently still in the gentle mood of the moment, Manman Marasa simply nodded her head and smiled. But if the truth be known, she did not hear him. Her mind had already turned back to the cooking and to the grandchildren who were in her charge that day.

There was Georges, Nicole's little one. Nicole was the wife of her son Didi. According to local custom, Georges was old enough to work with the men. But his gimpy leg and his ten-year-old refusal to let it slow him down made him accident-prone. When the men were wielding the machetes and heavy hoes they used to clear land, it was deemed better to leave him under the watchful eye of Manman Marasa. And there was baby Clairice, Marie Claire's last born. The poor thing had had diarrhea for three months out of the five she had passed on this earth. And there were Keke's twin toddlers, Alphonse and Joseph. Those boys were hard to tell apart, so both were simply called *ma moun* (my man). Finally, there were Marie Noelsine's little girls, Gloria and Philomise.

Marie Claire may have been the favored daughter, but everyone agreed that Marie Noelsine, her sister, was the great beauty of the family. She had "good hair"—flat, flat, long hair—and, most amazing, green eyes. Philomise, her youngest child, had inherited traces of Marie Noelsine's beauty. Along with these external signs, there were also marks of another, deeper legacy that set Philo apart from the other children. Manman Marasa worried about the personality traits that made Philomise different, and she showed her concern by teasing the child, calling her "Madame Adult" and "Lady Serious." All these particular small lives, and probably several more as well, if the full story could be known, were in the hands of Manman Marasa that early Wednesday morning in the last year of the nineteenth century.

Wednesday was market day in Port-de-Paix, down the mountain from Jean Rabel. The mothers of these children (all save Marie Claire, who was still sound asleep) had left in the middle of the night, balancing oversized baskets of vegetables and fruit on their heads. Manman Marasa had not made this trip in a long time, although when she was younger she had been one of the most canny of market women. How well she remembered the feeling of strength and energy with which the trip down the mountain began, the fast pace and the quiet banter among the women, which held at bay the time further down the trail when feet slowed, loads became heavier, and the sun rode hot on their backs. It would be late afternoon the next day before aching legs carried the market women back up the mountain path with loads of oil, salt, cloth, and whatever other provisions their immediate families needed.

In the crowded cacophony of the town market, a woman had to have an eagle eye—and a sharp mind, too!—to avoid being cheated by her customers. By the time the women returned, some would have spent every penny they had earned for a long, hot day's work. Others would carry away a few coins in grimy double-knotted kerchiefs tucked into their bosoms or in small sacks pinned to petticoats beneath their ragged skirts. Food, tools, and labor were shared freely among the family members, but money was different. The woman who managed to earn a little beyond what she had to spend protected it by silence and magic. "Never tell a person how much money you have! Jealousy makes people do terrible things. Jealousy can kill." Even the husbands of these women rarely knew how much money they had.

The women from his compound were only minutes away

from the market in Port-de-Paix when Joseph Binbin Mauvant put on his blue pants and his blue shirt. He took a scarf—also blue—from a peg on the wall by the door. He had worn this scarf around his neck for so long that it could no longer let go of the creases it had learned from his body. He had worn it every time he healed a member of his family or eased a difficult birth for a neighbor or took away the bad luck attached to a parcel of land. On his head Mauvant placed a broad-brimmed straw hat. He always wore such a hat, as did every farmer who knew what it was like to pry cassava from the hard earth when the sun was high and hot.

The old man picked up his chair from its place just outside the door, where he left it at night. Since he had grown old, Mauvant spent the entire day, most days, sitting on that chair in the shade of the giant *mapou* (cottonsilk) tree in the center of the courtyard. Always choosing the same spot between two massive roots of the tree, Mauvant would position his chair just a few inches from the trunk. That way, if he had to lean back to assert his authority or laugh at a timely joke, the tree would keep him from toppling over. One hand rested on a carved walking stick; the other was usually occupied with a cigarette. Most mountain men used snuff, but Mauvant smoked hand-rolled cigarettes. Like his exclusive claim to one of the two chairs in the family compound, cigarette smoking was a sign of his prestige and of the leisure that came with it. When he was not smoking, Mauvant was drinking. Most mountain men of his station in life had an earthenware jug as their constant companion. Following a recipe he would share with no one, Mauvant filled his jug with an extravagant mixture of leaves and hot peppers before topping it up with *kleren.* Male friends and clients were offered a swig from the jug as a gesture of hospitality, and many a country cousin had his manhood tested by the way he reacted to his first taste of Mauvant's brew.

Endless laughs on endless hot afternoons began when someone turned red in the face and started to choke after drinking from Mauvant's legendary jug. The joke continued long after the unfortunate visitor was gone, for Mauvant was an excellent mimic. The whole family loved those evenings when he would entertain them by recreating the small dramas of the day or, even better, by telling them tales of life in Africa. On very special occasions, he taught them powerful African words.

Most days passed the same way, with Joseph Binbin Mauvant holding court from his private office between the roots of the *mapou* tree. There he was consulted about what and when to plant and when to harvest. Sitting on the short-legged chair, he taught the younger men in his family how to repair tools. He allocated land for new projects to enterprising sons and sons-in-law and settled disputes among family members. And, in the same shady spot, he worked as a healer.

Everyone knew that Joseph Binbin Mauvant was no ordinary man. He was *franginen,* as they said, a true African. When he had healing work to do, he had no need to call the spirits as others did, using drums, candles, and other ritual parapher-nalia. Joseph Binbin Mauvant was *franginen nèt*, completely Af-rican, and he had the spirits "on him" all the time, all kinds of spirits. When he treated someone, he did not read cards to find out what was wrong. He could look at a person and know. Most significant, he did not work with an *ason*, the beaded rattle priests use in the south of Haiti to give them leverage in the spirit realm. Papa Mauvant needed nothing at all in his hand. Nothing. He cured people using only *fèy* (leaves) and his own natural power. And he never took money for what he did, not a penny. He did things the old way. The old way was the simple way. Joseph Binbin Mauvant said that in Africa everyone could do it. Mauvant said, and everyone agreed, that a long time ago many Haitians could do it too, but this was no longer true. They had lost the knowledge. But there were stories about one or two among the mountain folk who, like Mauvant, were powerful enough to heal the natural way. They were always described as living a long way off, and no one seemed to have actually met them.

Not a single person gave the old man much thought that day when he picked up his chair and carried it in the opposite direc-tion from the ancient *mapou* tree. They were too busy with other things to pay attention to an addled old man muttering: "I'm going today. Hear! I'm going." Their blood was diluted by generations of living an ocean away from Africa. But Mauvant had been born there. He was a real African, which to these mountain people brought him as close to the spirits as a living being could get. Even so, the family sometimes teased him by calling him *blan* (whitey). The truth was that Joseph Binbin Mauvant's father had been white, a Frenchman. His mother had been black, but little Joseph had "come out white," as the country folk put it. Despite the teasing, Mauvant was held in high regard for his light skin, and the unlikely combination of being a *blan* from Africa ensured his authority wherever he went.

The identity of Mauvant's mother is unclear. Some say she was a North American black; others say she was Haitian. Wherever she came from, she traveled to Africa in the early nineteenth century, where she met and married her Frenchman. There, in Africa, Joseph Binbin Mauvant was born. The family later moved to France, to Bordeaux, where Joseph grew to young manhood. But the youth left France after a narrow escape in "the war" and eventually made his way to the northern port town of Jean Rabel in Haiti. There are two Jean Rabels—Jean Rabel on the sea and Jean Rabel in the mountains. It was in the latter that Joseph Binbin Mauvant settled down and lived out his full life right up to its miraculous end.

Settling his chair in the semi-private space behind his house, in the same spot where he had bathed earlier in the morning, Joseph Binbin Mauvant set about kindling a small fire. The fire caught easily. Before long, the smoke was gone, and it burned clean and bright. Mauvant sat gazing into the flames with his back straight and his hands resting lightly on his knees. *"Bon!"* he said, "at noon we won't be seeing you anymore, no." Then he began to sing:

> *O Manman Ginen, O Papa Ginen,*
> *M'kri, ago!*
> *O Manman Ginen, O Papa Ginen,*
> *M'kri, ago!*
> *M'ape rele Bondye nan syèl.*
> *M'ape rele Jezi, Mari, Jozef.*
> *O Manman Ginen, O Papa Ginen,*
> *Mwen kri, ago!*
> *O Manman Ginen, O Papa Ginen,*
> *Mwen kri, ago!*
> *M'ape rele Jezi, Mari, Jozef.*
> *M'ape rele lasent Vyèj Mari.*
> *O, mwen kri ago!*

O Mother Africa, O Father Africa,
I cry *ago!*[1]
O Mother Africa, O Father Africa,
I cry *ago!*
I am calling God in heaven.
I am calling Jesus, Mary, Joseph.
O Mother Africa, O Father Africa,
I cry *ago!*
O Mother Africa, O Father Africa,
I cry *ago!*
I am calling Jesus, Mary, Joseph.
I am calling the holy Virgin Mary.
O, I cry *ago!*

From eight o'clock in the morning until noon, Joseph Binbin Mauvant sang. He sat looking at the fire, and he sang and sang and sang. For the most part, those in the courtyard ignored him. Manman Marasa and Jepete shelled beans. Jepete pounded corn in a mortar that stood waist-high, with a pestle thicker than her arm. In spite of herself, she moved the pestle up and down to the rhythm of Mauvant's song. Salt, parsley, shallots, and hot peppers were thrown into a much smaller mortar Manman Marasa held between her knees, and, as she pounded them to a fragrant pulp, she unconsciously hummed along with the old man's song.

The older children collected pebbles and dug two rows of shallow holes in the packed earth of the courtyard. Georges and one of the twins settled down to a game of *kay*. The other twin hung over his brother's shoulder, telling him what to do on every move. Mercifully, baby Clairice slept. Manman Marasa had placed a mat beneath the breadfruit tree at one side of the yard, and the baby lay there, bobbing on waves of heat and dreams, while little Philomise sat motionless beside her. Although the sun rose higher and higher and the heat became

[1] *Ago* is a word from the Fon of Dahomey, used to mean Hey! or Hey, you! The specific African origins of such words are not common knowledge among those who serve the spirits.

more and more intense, no one even thought of sitting in the deep, cool shade of the old *mapou.*

Distracted for a moment as she stirred the huge pot of beans bubbling over the fire, Manman Marasa failed to notice Philomise slip away. Philo went around the corner of Didi's house and made her way quietly by the back route to a place where she had a good view of Granpapa Mauvant and the fire. For a time she simply watched—a scruffy little mountain child of no more than three or four, with dusty brown legs. Without taking her eyes from her grandfather, Philo raised her faded calico dress, the only garment she wore, and began to chew thoughtfully on its hem. Joseph Binbin Mauvant sat straight in his chair, with a hand on each knee, and he sang. His singing was neither casual nor energetic; it simply was. His voice rose and fell through no choice of his own. The song poured through him, singing itself.

Reaching the end of a verse, the old man looked up and beckoned to Philo. Had he known she was there all along? After some hesitation, the child approached. Mauvant said nothing. A slight convulsion passed through his body, and then another and another. He moved one hand to his mouth and vomited up a small, smooth stone. He stretched out his hand toward the child and said, "Here, little one. Eat this." Philo's dark eyes traveled from the moist black stone in the palm of the outstretched hand to the face of her grandfather and back again. Then, like the child she was, she cried, "Yuk!" and, pressing both hands over her mouth, she ran away. When Philo was one of the ancients herself, she would tell her daughter how much she regretted not having swallowed the stone. "That was his power. He wanted to give me his power. But I was just a little girl. I didn't know anything."

When the sun stood directly overhead and the mat under the breadfruit tree was filled with sleeping children, when the bean pot no longer needed a constant watchful eye, it occurred to Manman Marasa that it was quiet—completely quiet. She rose wearily and wiped the moisture from her brow with the same rag she had used to cover her shoulders in the early morning chill. Then, knotting the piece of cloth loosely around her hips and under her belly, Manman Marasa walked with the soft slapping sound of bare feet on hard earth. She walked around her house to the yard behind. The next sound was her cry: "*Woy!* . . . *Woy-woy-woy!*" There was no fire. No chair. No blue kerchief. No Joseph Binbin Mauvant! People say that if he had not come to Manman Marasa in a dream that very night and told her he had gone back to Africa, the Mauvant family would be looking for him to this day.

CHAPTER TWO

Azaka

One of the Vodou spirits central to Alourdes's life and religious work is a mountain man, a peasant farmer like her own great-grandfather, Joseph Binbin Mauvant. Like Mauvant, the spirit dresses in blue denim, wears a broad-brimmed straw hat, and keeps a jug of rum laced with herbs at his elbow. This spirit's humble demeanor, that of an illiterate peasant, actually reveals his importance: he functions to remind devotees of their roots, of their need for family (a group that includes the ancestors and the spirits), and of their connection to the land. Haitians call him Azaka Mède or Papa Zaka. More frequently, they refer to him as Kouzen (Cousin).

In Haiti, in contrast to other former slave colonies in the New World, many farmers own the land they work, and they bury their family dead on that land. In the countryside, inheriting land thus also means inheriting relationships with the spirits served by the ancestors buried there. In a traditional Vodou view, the land, the family, and the spirits are, in a way, one and the same. But for many contemporary Haitians the three legs of this tripod on which their world rests have been wrenched apart. Poverty, drought, soil erosion, and overpopulation have placed large numbers of people in a position similar to that of their slave forebears. They have been forced away from their land and away from the extended families that sustain life and give identity. Refugees from the countryside swell the urban centers of Haiti. Alourdes's story is typical of this recent chapter in Haitian history, for she is a member of the first urban-born generation of her family.

Like the African slaves who worked the giant plantations of eighteenth-century Haiti, Haitians today experience the loss of land and family as a spiritual crisis, and, like their African an-

◀ A rural family. Gros Morne, Haiti, 1980.

cestors, they turn to religion to bind up the wounds caused by this loss. Vodou temples in urban Haiti keep worshippers ritually in touch with the earth. No matter how prosperous the temple, it has an earthen floor ready to receive libations poured for the spirits. But even this symbolic comfort is denied the many Haitians (Alourdes now among them) who keep their religion alive in the modern cities of North America.[1]

Despite this attachment to the land, cities have played a central role in the preservation and enrichment of African religion in the New World from the earliest days of slavery to the present. Haiti, with an extensive peasant culture that developed following its early independence in 1804, is a somewhat special case; but, in the final analysis, even in Haiti the importance of the urban milieu is clear. Thus it would be a mistake to see Vodou as an agrarian religion that becomes precarious when transported to a city. Although the Vodou spirit Azaka points to the importance of roots in the land, other spirits (Ogou, for example) make the long urban history of the religion more apparent. It is probably more accurate to view Azaka's as one voice in an age-old and creative dialogue. He places urban tendencies toward the elaboration of ritual and the creation of religious hierarchies in tension with a viewpoint that most strongly values simplicity and immediacy. And he also reinforces enduring social bonds in an urban context where there is an inevitable tendency to break old relationships and seek out new and more profitable ones.

Urban Vodou may have retained only a symbolic tie to the earth, but it has been both more successful and more practical in providing families for rural migrants. In urban temples, the *manbo* (priestess) is called *manman* and the *oungan* (priest) is called *papa*. Those initiated in the temple are called "little leaves," or "children of the house." Along with these titles go all the privileges and responsibilities of family membership. Urban initiates are obligated to contribute money, time, and energy to the temples, and in turn they can draw on temple resources for practical assistance as well as spiritual comfort. Temple leaders are obligated to give children of the house help with such prob-

[1]The importance of the land—both the earth in general and the Haitian homeland in particular—is explored further in Chapters 6 and 12.

lems as unscrupulous landlords, difficult employers, and errant spouses. In a pinch, they even provide child care, food, and lodging. Similar processes of family creation and maintenance are now at work in makeshift Vodou temples in New York, Miami, Montreal, Boston, and a dozen other North American cities with less populous Haitian immigrant communities. This work goes on under the watchful eye of a Kouzen Zaka who, in the adaptable fashion of the Vodou *lwa*, has adjusted quite well to his role as the country cousin of far-flung city folk.

In Haiti, as elsewhere, the title *kouzen* is liberally applied. A cousin is not only the son or daughter of an aunt or uncle but also any person with whom there is a familylike connection. Kouzen Zaka thus reminds contemporary Haitians such as Alourdes of the importance of holding the family together— even if it is, by default, an ersatz family. For urban Haitians, the Vodou spirit Azaka is more than a country cousin to whom a sentimental debt is owed. He is a *lwa*, a Vodou spirit like other spirits, a model for a particular way of being and acting in the world, a typical character in the social drama, both rural and urban.

AZAKA'S BIRTHDAY PARTY, 1984

On May 26, 1984, the Saturday of Memorial Day weekend, I found myself nursing my fourteen-year-old Volvo along the clogged interstate highways between Cambridge, Massachusetts, and Brooklyn. The great-granddaughter of Joseph Binbin Mauvant had commanded my presence—not to celebrate Memorial Day, a holiday that understandably has little meaning for Haitian immigrants, but to participate in the "birthday party" of the Vodou spirit Azaka. As a member of the fictive kinship network, a "little leaf" (*ti-fèy*) grafted onto Alourdes's family tree, it was important that I be there.

I was exhausted by the time I reached Brooklyn. My loft in lower Manhattan and Alourdes's row house in Fort Greene are twenty minutes apart, and ordinarily I had only the time it took to make the quick trip across the Brooklyn Bridge to accomplish the considerable shift in worldview necessitated by movement between these two centers. In contrast, the trip in May 1984 took six tedious hours. Responding to Alourdes's telephone summons ("We going to have a birthday party for Kouzen Zaka. You coming? You got to come!") had taken a lot more energy than usual. I was on sabbatical leave from my teaching position and had sublet my New York apartment and moved to Cambridge.

"You know I'd love to come," I had said when Alourdes called, "but that's a holiday, and there will be a lot of traffic on the highways." "Yes," Alourdes had replied in a small voice, "a lot'a car . . ."

Uncomfortable in the silence that followed and ever eager to please this momentous force in my life, I had taken a deep breath and committed myself: "But of course I'll come anyway." "Good!" she responded. Then, forgetting which world I was occupying at the moment, I asked, "Can I stay at your—" "Karen!" she cried. "How come you ask me that? Aw, come on! Karen, what's the matter with you? You always asking me can you stay. Why you got to do that? This is your house. You stay any time you want. Karen, what's the matter with you? Don't do that to me! Okay?"

"Well, Alourdes," I replied, in the tone of a child unjustly accused, "I just thought you might have a lot of other people staying there since . . ." "I don't care!" She cut me off again, but this time with warmth in her voice. "I don't care. Even you got to sleep on the floor, even I got to make a bed on top of my closet . . . I always find a place for you, sweetheart. Don't you worry!"

Kumar and Michael, Alourdes's and Maggie's young sons, were jumping around the car before I even turned off the engine. Betty, Maggie's baby, in a pink sunsuit and with a dozen different colored barrettes at the ends of as many tiny braids, bobbed in concert from her safe place on the curb. Kumar poked his head into the open window on the driver's side and kissed me on the cheek, a standard polite greeting from a Haitian child, an instance of Old World manners that have carried over to the first generation born in this country. "How you doin', Karen? Maggie said you was comin'. We been waitin' for you."

Alourdes's daughter, Maggie, was leaning on one arm in the open front door, wearing a sundress with an elastic top that failed in its effort to cover the full-support bra she wore underneath. In spite of the makeshift attire, she looked sassy and beautiful. "Hi, baby. I thought you was never going to come. I was getting worried about you. Come on inside. I just got home myself. We don't even start to make the altar yet. Come on. You can help. Give me that suitcase. Mommie's downstairs." Basking in the warmth of their greetings and still spinning from the road, I went down the dark staircase to the basement level, the center of family operations.

The rooms in Alourdes's home are arranged like a string of railroad cars. Her kitchen, with one small window looking out on a modest yard, is in the back of the basement, and her "altar," the tiny room in which she does consultations, reads cards, and prepares herbal treatments, is in the front. A combination living and dining room fills the space between kitchen and altar. A new dining-room set—a table and chairs, a glass-front china cabinet, and a massive sideboard—takes up every foot of space in front of the door to the altar room. Shelves holding shiny trinkets and floor-to-ceiling strings of multicolored beads separate this surprisingly formal dining area from the random collection of chairs and tables that defines the social center of the basement floor. A large color television, rarely turned off and rarely adjusted to remove the green hue it imparts to human skin, presides over this section of the room where the family gathers, where guests are received, and where clients wait their turn in Alourdes's inner sanctum. This is also the room where birthday parties for the spirits are held.

Downstairs, I found Alourdes looking morose, slumped at a small table, her chin cupped in her hand. She noted my arrival only by blinking when I walked between her and the television set. I kissed her on the cheek and offered a standard Creole greeting: "Long time I don't see you. Give me news of yourself." Alourdes raised her great round shoulders and let them drop with a sigh.

"I'm okay," she responded in barely audible English. "Alourdes," I said, also switching to English, "what's the matter?" "Karen!" she snapped, "I don't feel good! Okay?" Then, after an awkward silence, she added, "Maggie say I eat too much salt. I don't taste it, but she tell me I put too much salt in my food. So I got too much salt. That's what I got. Look!" She displayed her right ankle, swollen beyond its usual girth.

Not until ten o'clock in the evening did the construction of the altar for Kouzen Zaka begin. A low cabinet pushed against one wall was cleared off, and a smaller table placed next to it at a right angle. These two "altars" were then covered in white sheets. Wielding a heavy staple gun, Maggie attached more white sheets to the walls behind the tables and the ceiling just above. Someone brought in an armful of leafy branches from the backyard, and the branches were stapled in small bunches to the sheets behind and above the altars. Because this was a feast for an agricultural spirit, one closely tied to the curative powers of leaves and roots, it was appropriate that his tables were decorated with greenery.

Next, familiar battered suitcases were dragged out of storage so Maggie and I could search among their contents—scarves of many colors, paper streamers, cardboard leprechauns and skeletons, bells, balls, and shamrocks—for decorations that would please Kouzen Zaka. We selected accordion streamers in Azaka's favorite colors, blue and white, and draped them in graceful, crisscrossing arcs across the ceiling of the niche. Then we pulled out a dozen scarves in the colors of Alourdes's other major spirits, those who were also likely to make an appearance that evening, and pinned the scarves to the front of the altar cloths. From meager materials we had begun to create the impression of dense opulence, the mood of Vodou altars.

Bottles of Haitian cola and liquor (rum, gin, tequila, scotch) were lined up across the back of the tables. Plates of cookies and candy were added, and a few pieces of wrapped candy were strewn across the tables. Bananas, grapes, apples, and cherries formed a mound around a plump pineapple in the corner of the largest table. Three fancy cakes from a Brooklyn bakery were also placed on the altars. One was frosted in blue and carried the message "Happy Birthday P. Azaka." The abbreviated version of Papa Azaka's name did not entirely please Alourdes.

The action soon shifted to the kitchen. Corn was dry popped and mixed with freshly shelled peanuts, pieces of cassava bread, and a few hard candies. This mixture was gathered in a large flat basket, the kind Haitian peasants use for winnowing grain, and placed on another white cloth beneath the smaller altar table where Azaka's special food was kept. Several simple boiled puddings were prepared and given time to cool. It is a rule that nothing hot can be placed on a spirit's altar.

Vodou altars are texts, there for the reading. They contain a wealth of information about the nature of a spirit or group of spirits, as indicated in food preferences. At the simplest level,

A meal for the spirits. Alourdes's home, Fort Greene, Brooklyn, 1979.

some like their food very spicy, whereas others consume only sweet things. Some drink liquor, some do not. The central theme for Azaka's table was composed from the favorite foods of the Haitian peasant farmer: among other things, Azaka loves sugarcane and cassava bread.

In assembling a table of humble foods for Azaka, Haitians in New York seek to evoke the cuisine of a simpler time, when the spirits pervaded everyday life and were readily accessible, as they were to Joseph Binbin Mauvant. Ironically, in New York, the sugarcane stalks and cassava bread used as mnemonic devices are both difficult to find and expensive. The immigrants' attempt to ground memory in the concrete details of a simple economy has actually led to the creation of an arcane food language. When Maggie's son, Michael, was given a piece of the prized *kasav*, he quickly spit it out. At five years of age, he was not old enough to be attracted to the arcane for its own sake, and the taste of cassava bread contained nothing of the magic of memory for him. It was simply a tasteless substitute for the potato chips he had been munching earlier.

Before long, two large pots, one of rice and black beans and another of cornmeal and black beans, were bubbling away on top of the stove. A pot of *chaka*—a thick, delicious peasant dish made from large-kernel corn, kidney beans, pig's knuckles, and coconut—had been made earlier in the day. When I lifted the pot lid to look at this favorite dish of Kouzen's and mine, Maggie cautioned me: "The thing about *chaka* . . . you don't never say, 'Mmm, that look good,' and look at it like you going to eat some, or the whole pot turn sour. After you give it to Kouzen, he can give you some and then you eat it. No problem! But if you taste it first or say, 'Oh, boy, I'm going to eat some of that,' then the first time you put it in your mouth it going to taste awful! The whole thing going to be spoiled."

Food, Feeding, and Family Service

Craving food that is not actually on your plate—or, better, in your mouth—is risky business. It can cause all sorts of things to happen. The first time Alourdes saw the birthmark on my back, she surmised that when my mother was pregnant she must have thought about liver as she scratched herself on that very spot. Alourdes went on to tell me that her own craving for a dessert called *krèm kay* during her pregnancy caused Maggie to be born with a faint mark on the left shoulder and that her son Jean-Pierre was born with his penis looking like the head of a chicken because, during that pregnancy, she had scratched her crotch while smacking her lips over some chicken she smelled cooking next door.

Food there for the eating is another matter altogether. Food is the major marker of the success of parties, the length of journeys, the passage of time and of life. Few stories about important events in the near or distant past do not include catalogs of what was eaten. I once watched a television soap opera with Alourdes, an episode in which a couple, seated at the dinner table, discussed the imminent death of their child. "They eating?" Alourdes asked, leaning closer to the set. "What they eating?"

Eating is more than a practical, life-sustaining activity. It is the means of identifying the in-group. "She eat in my house," Alourdes said, introducing me to people in Haiti. And it is the means of maintaining the same group. "You eat with people, you always have food," Alourdes says. "You eat by yourself, you don't have nothing." On the other side of the coin, fear of being poisoned by taking food from the hand of strangers or persons who harbor ill will is a pervasive theme, especially among rural Haitians.

Few people in Haiti grow to adulthood without knowing hunger intimately, and Alourdes is not in that minority. The fact of hunger has had no small influence in shaping Haitian culture in general and her life in particular. Thus it is not surprising that food has become a metaphor for happiness and well-being. It took me years to realize that when Alourdes announced, "I don't eat today," it meant that she was upset or depressed and not that she had forgotten the half-loaf of French bread with margarine I had just seen her consume. When I travel with Alourdes, it is easier to see the connection between food and anxiety. When she is anywhere but home, Alourdes obsesses about food. She seems to be constantly hungry and constantly worried that no one will feed her. When food is provided, she picks at her meal and rarely admits that she enjoys it.

Food is also an issue in how Alourdes relates to her spirits. She feeds her spirits on a grand scale once a year at their individual birthday parties and, on a lesser scale, daily with libations and other small offerings. Without this nourishment, the spirits would not, and perhaps could not, work for her. Providing food and creating the elaborate ritual contexts in which that food is presented to the spirits constitutes the most important work Alourdes does for them.

Spiritual Labor

"*Travay, travay-o* [work, oh, work]" is the single, repeated line of one Vodou song. Alourdes's birthday parties for the spirits are hard work, requiring a considerable expenditure of time, money, and effort. In the midst of the high-pressure life of New York City, where the survival of Alourdes and her family depends on a constant juggling of scarce resources, ritual duties sometimes become onerous. The party for Kouzen Zaka in 1984 was one occasion when the demands of life in New York came into direct conflict with the demands of the Vodou spirits. In fact, this conflict, and not an excess of salt in the diet, was eventually revealed as the source of Alourdes's illness.

Sunday afternoon, after Kouzen Zaka had been called to direct the dismantling of his festive table, after the floor had been swept clean of the last trace of ritualizing from the night before and every pot in the kitchen had been washed and put away, Maggie and I relaxed with a cup of coffee. She told me:

Kouzen made Mommie sick because he think we not going to give him no party. Because now I'm working, I don't got no time to be running around buying thing for birthday party for the spirit. Before, when I wasn't working, we start two . . . three days before. We buying, buying, buying: fruit, candy, all kind'a thing for the party. But now I work, we didn't buy nothing 'til I get back this afternoon, and Kouzen just think we not going to do nothing for him this year. So he made Mommie sick.

"What he think she gonna do?" Maggie continued, with real anger in her voice. "Taking care of those kids all day long, she can't even go outside!" Then, with a smile and a shrug of her shoulders, Maggie added, "When we build the altar and Kouzen see what we do for him, then Mommie start feeling okay right away. But it was him that made her sick!"

More than two years earlier, at another Vodou feast, Alourdes had made an impromptu speech. Standing in front of elaborate, food-laden tables, she began by noting how tired she was and how much work these parties were. She said that she had originally decided not to have a birthday party for Ogou, the guest of honor that evening, thinking that it would be enough to arrange for a mass to be said for Saint James, the Catholic saint identified with Ogou. In fact, she had planned to stop having parties in New York altogether and to hold one large feast for all the spirits every three, or maybe every seven, years in Haiti. That was what she had decided, but the spirits said, "No! Make a table." And so—once again!—here she was. And it was just too much!

Ceremonies for the spirits do require a great deal of work. Yet it is also true that those who stage Vodou parties have a vested interest in broadcasting and sometimes exaggerating the amount of effort and money involved, for the size of the undertaking determines the value of the gift being offered the *lwa*. I was aware of this tendency, and it was initially difficult for me to recognize the genuine frustration from which Alourdes spoke.

Her soliloquy that night moved into a somewhat romantic version of how much easier things were in Haiti:

New York is not Haiti. When you have a party for the spirit in Haiti, you have people to help. I just sit. Someone say to me, "Mommie Lola, can I get you a Coca-Cola?" You send him out to get ice. He keep the five *santim* left over, but that don't make no difference. You got somebody who sweep up after . . . make everything nice. All you got to do is give that person something to eat. You don't even got to pay. You can find whatever you need, things not so expensive, and you always got people to help. Here, I got to make the table, make the food, then clean it myself. Here, somebody say, "Can I have some soda?" They take the glass and just put it under the chair. And they say again, "Give me some soda." No, I don't like that!

In addition to "sending the point" to thoughtless guests and advertising her own efforts, Alourdes was speaking to a real tension in her life. A crisis that same evening in 1982 underlined the way she was caught between opposing forces.

Preparations for Ogou's party had gone on amid more chaos than usual. Maggie was pregnant with Betty and was having difficulty with the pregnancy. The summer day had been hot and sticky. With no school, the children had been constantly underfoot. In the hubbub, no one had remembered Legba, the guardian of doorways and barriers.

A small statue of Saint Lazarus, representing Legba, stands near the door at the end of the narrow hallway leading from the foot of the basement stairs to the front of the house. In preparation for ceremonies, this door is opened to allow passage for the spirits. A candle is lighted, and small offerings for Legba are left at the threshold. But all this had been forgotten. When Alourdes and her ritual assistants processed to the Legba shrine, singing, "*Papa Legba, ouvri bàryè* [Papa Legba, open the gate]," as they do at the beginning of every such event, they found a dark hallway and a closed and locked door.

Alourdes retreated into stony silence. Tension quickly spread through the group and, before anyone knew what was happening, Legba had possessed Alourdes. Her tremendous frame plunked itself down in the middle of the narrow hallway, and the venerable spirit riding her cried and whined about his mistreatment in the thin, cracked voice of one of the ancients. Tears sprang to Maggie's eyes, too, but she quickly covered them with a brusque take-charge attitude. With one arm around the whimpering Legba, Maggie sent people scurrying to fetch the things needed.

In short order, the large votive candle beside Lazarus was lighted; the door was opened; gin and molasses were poured at the threshold; and an egg was broken there. Legba was reduced to sniffling and trembling as he watched these frantic attempts to recover from an inauspicious beginning. It took some time before the small group of ritualizers returned to the crowded area around the tables and continued with the business of formally greeting the spirits, one by one. It took even longer before the ominous feelings generated there gave way to the more celebrative mood that usually characterizes these events. After this, in spite of her desire to simplify, Alourdes actually redoubled her efforts around the individual spirit feasts.

One of the problems she confronts is assembling a large enough group to serve the spirits properly. An enormous amount of energy and anxiety is involved in building and maintaining the core group that attends these ceremonies and thus constitutes Alourdes's Vodou family. In rural Haiti, the group that ritualizes together generally also lives and works together on the land. There, family is a given. In New York, however, family ties must be earned and carefully maintained. Work pressures, distance, the problems of late-night travel in New York City, even a different sense of time, now calibrated like money in order to be spent wisely—all these elements make it difficult to maintain the group necessary for effective rituals. Vodou rituals are events that cement community, but daily life in New York bombards the Haitian immigrant with messages that counsel self-interest and self-reliance. Alourdes has several blood relatives living in New York, but even the bonds with these persons are not as durable as they would be in Haiti.

To balance the centrifugal force North American values exercise on the Haitian community, Alourdes moves in two directions at once. Through her service to the spirits, she retraces the pathways back home in order to shore up weakening bonds of blood and friendship. But at the same time she reaches out to new people such as myself. She uses her spiritual skills to pull us into the family, into the network of gifts and obligations that constitutes her survival strategy. "New York is not Haiti," as she said. Events must be planned far ahead of time, and still no more than a handful of people may show up to sing and clap their hands for the spirits.

Having enough participants is not the only problem. Some of the foods necessary for the Vodou feasts can be obtained only with considerable effort. For example, the Puerto Rican markets in the Bronx are among the few reliable sources for live poultry, and a trip to the Bronx from Brooklyn can easily take four or five hours. Alourdes is constantly juggling debts and favors among the members of her Vodou family in New York—those she has healed, those she has initiated, and those friends and family members who regularly enjoy her parties for the spirits. Who can bring flowers? Who can bring rum? Who has a car and can drive to the Bronx? "You can't carry no live rooster on the subway!"

Such difficulties had prompted Alourdes's decision to reduce her ritual labor. But the spirits said, "No!" She knew they were saying no, because as soon as she made the decision to cut back, everything she put her hand to went wrong. Bad luck is understood as an expression of the displeasure of the spirits. Bad luck can be anything from a serious illness to problems with money, love, or work. A string of bad luck means something serious is wrong. Until the situation is clarified and steps are taken to remedy it, everything feels threatening.

In the final analysis there is one major threat, one overwhelming fear—that of being alone, of being without family. For Alourdes, family is a continuum running from the disparate group who attends Vodou parties at her home to the most elemental family, that of the ancestors and the spirits. When connection to the latter group is threatened, the accompanying fear accelerates. Alourdes keeps altars for the Vodou spirits in her home and expends considerable effort in feeding and nurturing them because she needs their love and protection around her daily. Relationships with spiritual families, however, are not any easier or less complicated than those with human families.

As long as persons live and breathe, they stand in the position of children in relation to the spirits. In this, Alourdes, though a *manbo*, is no different from anyone else. In Haiti, small children are extravagantly loved and indulged. But this indulgence ends when the child is old enough to make a contribution to the ongoing life of the family. Children's work soon becomes necessary to the family, and disobedient children are disciplined. In many families, children are beaten, at times severely. Showing respect for the elders and complying with their will are the only ways a Haitian child can remain in good standing within the family. In an illustration of the negative side of food symbolism, unruly children are threatened with destruction by evil spirits: "The *lougawou* [werewolf] going to eat you!" Children are deemed more likely than adults to "catch" a malevolent spirit sent against a family; only the continued spiritual vigilance of the elders protects them from such a fate.

Because the work Alourdes performs for the spirits is as essential to their well-being as the contribution of Haitian children is to the well-being of their families, the spirits also deal with her through dire threat and severe punishment. The same standards of respect and obedience that define the relation of Haitian children to their elders dictate the terms on which Alourdes must relate to the spirits. She never talks about "worshipping" the spirits; rarely does she speak of "believing" in them. Existence and essence are the theological preoccupations of Great Atlantic culture. Alourdes speaks about the spirits in the way common to Haitian people: "I serve the spirit," she says.

Gathering to Call the Spirits

On that Memorial Day weekend in 1984, it was nearly midnight when the cooking was finally done and the food for Kouzen Zaka arranged in several *kwi* (calabash shell bowls). The cornmeal with beans was poured into one and left to congeal to a hard-crusted top. A mound of rice and beans filled another. A third held large chunks of firm white yam and golden sweet potato topped with wedges of avocado. The *chaka* was poured into a fourth, and into the last went another stew, this one made from meat and several kinds of vegetables cooked to a fragrant rosy mush. Once these were cool, they were placed beneath Azaka's altar, where they stayed until early the next morning when most of the ritualizing was over. Only then were the bleary-eyed people slumped in chairs in Alourdes's basement-turned-temple fed from Azaka's ample stores.

At eleven-thirty, Maggie and I were still clattering around the kitchen. The early arrivals for Kouzen's feast were quietly watching television with Alourdes. An outside observer of this sleepy domestic scene might have thought it the end of an uneventful evening rather than the beginning of an all-night ritual drama. But around midnight, things began to happen quickly, and by ten minutes after the hour, every chair was full, the television was turned off, and events were under way. Maggie was checking and rechecking the tables, the altar room, the kitchen, to be sure nothing had been forgotten. Twenty-five people were talking, laughing, greeting one another, and catching up on the news of their lives.

About two dozen people took part in this feast. The first to arrive were other *manbo*, Alourdes's older women friends with whom she routinely exchanges support and assistance in ritual activities. Madame François and Gladys are regulars at her parties, and as usual they arrived laden with contributions: a bunch of basil leaves, a cake, flowers, a package of candles, more cassava bread. Robert and his family are the other most frequent participants. Robert is a North American black man in his mid-thirties, for whom Alourdes performed a preliminary initiation in the summer of 1981, at the same time Maggie and I went through other stages of the initiation process. After this, Maggie continued to function as Alourdes's main ritual assistant, and Robert became a regular second-level helper, often spending the entire day before a ceremony running errands for Alourdes and lending a hand wherever he was needed.

Other guests at Azaka's 1984 birthday party included Marjorie and her boyfriend, Kevin. Kevin is a drug counselor at a high school. Marjorie, who has the primary connection to Alourdes, is a native of Grenada in her late thirties who works for the New York City public school system as a teacher for emotionally disturbed children. An attractive woman with a hefty, solid body that suits her forceful personality, Marj first came to know Alourdes when she turned to her for help. Marj's husband had left her and had taken their two children back to his native Ghana against her will. It took Alourdes two years of practical as well as spiritual labor to see that the children were returned to their mother.

Gertrude, or Mrs. LeGrand, as she is almost always addressed, arrived soon after Marj and Kevin. A woman in her late forties, she has a middle-management position in one of the city social service agencies and is thus held in high regard. She speaks with the exaggerated diction of the upwardly mobile, and she dresses conservatively and with great care; shoes and handbag always match, and she sometimes carries gloves of the same color. Gertrude, who was born in the United States, became Mrs. LeGrand by marrying a Haitian, and it was her husband who introduced her to Alourdes. Mrs. LeGrand, still a close friend of Alourdes's family, is now divorced. I knew this proper woman for quite a long time before she was willing to talk to me about her growing involvement in Vodou.

Soeurette, a friend of Alourdes's from Haiti, came not long after Mrs. LeGrand. Soeurette is chunky, good-humored, and shy. She is also a Protestant. Theoretically, this affiliation should have prevented her from attending a Vodou ceremony. In practice, however, such rules, laid down by most Protestant groups active in Haiti, are not always observed. Soeurette speaks little English, yet I imagine that she copes well in New York nonetheless. She probably handles landlords, clerks, and bus drivers, as well as her co-workers in the nursing home, with the same determined pleasantness that marks her presence in this group. Soeurette brought along her ten-year-old son. Heavier and even shyer than his mother, Michel spent most of the evening sitting quietly in a chair by the refrigerator, his hands folded in his lap.

Jean-Pierre, Alourdes's oldest child, drove his family in from their apartment in Lefrack City, Queens. Just over thirty, Jean-Pierre is a handsome man, more Americanized than any of Alourdes's other children. He wore an Yves St. Laurent shirt in dark red, with tight-fitting jeans. His knuckles are heavily callused from years of karate. Defying a pattern of short-term, dead-end jobs that has been pervasive in the Haitian community, "Johnny" has worked at the same place for years, selling dry goods at a shop on Manhattan's Lower East Side. Other family guests included Frank, Alourdes's oldest brother, nearing retirement from his maintenance job at a high school, and Frank's Haitian wife.

Two teenagers, American black women, also attended. Both were magnificently tall, dressed in blue jeans, and wearing their hair in a wealth of bead-encrusted braids. Poupette, a young Haitian woman with a flirtatious personality, joined the group. She had just arrived in the United States and was looking for work. On this cool May evening, she wore two sweaters over a light cotton dress and had heavy wool socks on her feet. Aileen, a woman to whom Alourdes rented a small top-floor apartment, was present also. Scrawny and defiant, with a gift for sudden flashes of ironic wit, Aileen is an American and a welfare mother. Alourdes wanted to help her, but there had been several arguments about unpaid rent and wine bottles that had disappeared from the basement refrigerator, and Alourdes's patience was wearing thin.

Big Daddy was a late arrival for Azaka's birthday party. Fritz, his proper name but one by which he is rarely addressed, is a big, balding bear of a man who loves women—or at least loves to talk about them. Big Daddy works in a warehouse in Long Island City. Alourdes said about him, "I know him long, long time, since we little children. We grow up together in Haiti. We good, good friend. It like we come from the same place, you know . . . the same belly. We not have the same mother, no. But sometime it feel like that."

Just after midnight, and without calling attention to herself, Alourdes plunked down on the low stool by Kouzen's table and abruptly launched into the series of Catholic prayers and hymns that opens these Vodou ceremonies. People took a while to realize what was happening. Talk died out by dribbles, some of it continuing after the ceremony had begun. Then, midway through a hymn, Alourdes interrupted herself: "Maggie, don't forget Kouzen's hat!" Maggie hollered the length of the basement: "Robert, get the hat out of the altar room!" And then Alourdes quickly returned to the hymn.

The Catholic prologue to Vodou ceremonies is virtually the same no matter which spirit is the guest of honor. It begins with standard songs and chants. One of the first calls on Saint Peter (like Lazarus, a Catholic counterpart of Legba) to "open the door, the door to Paradise." Others beg Mary, Jesus, and various saints for grace and forgiveness.

New arrivals from Haiti, such as Poupette, often become the vehicle for learning new songs and recalling old ones, Catholic and Vodou. Alourdes's frequent trips to Haiti also accomplish the same kind of liturgical checking and enriching. One of the songs sung for the Virgin Mary at this party was an example of this process. Alourdes had heard the song in a friend's temple on her last visit home; she had sung it as a child but had since forgotten it. When Alourdes returned from that trip, she imme-

diately introduced it into the Catholic prologue to her own ceremonies. She especially liked its ritual details. At a certain point
in the hymn, everyone was supposed to drop to their knees,
facing the altar.

> The palm tree thumps, the palm tree knocks.
> Virgin Mary, pray for us.
> We are on our knees at your feet. . . .

That night, Alourdes noticed that I had missed the signal and
was not on my knees with the rest, and she abruptly stopped
the singing. "Come on, Karen, come on, come on, come on! On
your knees! Oh-oh, no excuse!" Then, without even taking a
breath, she finished the song:

> On the ground, on the ground,
> To pray to you.

As the last line died away, Alourdes continued to question
my lax behavior: "How come you don't know that song?" "I
know that song," I anwered defensively. I am never at ease
when Alourdes publicly exhibits her authority as my Vodou
mother, although I know that such displays are a routine part
of the discipline for any initiate in a Vodou family.

Perhaps catching my discomfort, Alourdes softened. "You
was singing?" she asked. "I was singing," I replied. "You singing, but I don't heard you," she observed. I laughed self-
consciously and latched on to the first excuse that presented itself: "I don't have a good voice, so I don't sing loud." In a more
natural tone, I added: "Alourdes, you don't want me to sing
loud!"

A great guffaw exploded from her, and, with one hand planted
on each thigh, she threw her head back: "Karen, you too smart
for me!" There was laughter all around. Our little contretemps
(one of several that added informality to the otherwise staid prologue) made a natural transition between the Catholic segment
of the ceremony and the part with a distinct African flavor.

Picking up the *ason* (the beaded rattle that is the emblem of
the Vodou priesthood) lying at her feet, Alourdes began to

shake it softly. The Creole songs that followed were also introductory. Taken collectively, these two standard opening se-
quences—one European in flavor, the other African—are called
the Priyè Deyò, the Outside Prayers.[2] The Priyè Deyò usually
last from forty-five minutes to an hour.

When these Outside Prayers were completed, the mood eased,
the social and ritual tempo picked up, and the main part of the
ceremony commenced, the part in which the most important
Vodou spirits are saluted, individually and in strict ritual order.
The first to be greeted is always Legba, guardian of crossroads
and doorways. Standing in front of the food-laden tables,
Alourdes held her *ason* in one hand; in the other she had a large
white enamel cup of a sort common in Haiti. On either side of
her were ritual assistants, one holding a candle and a bottle of
gin, the other a bottle of molasses. These elements were lifted
up to each of the cardinal directions in turn. Alourdes shook the
ason sharply each time the group dipped at the knees and
changed direction. Then, facing the larger of the altar tables, all
three stepped to the right, bent their knees in a quick movement like a curtsey, stepped to the left, and turned all the way
around, then repeated the same gestures in reverse, with an initial step to the left. A third time, again starting with a step to the
right, the small band of ritualizers dipped and twirled. Then they
headed out the door and down the narrow hallway to the Legba
shrine. Throughout the salutation, all the people present sang:

> *Papa Legba, ouvri bàryè-a.*
> *Ouvri bàryè Atibon,*
> *Pou nou pase la.*

> Papa Legba, open the gate.
> Open the gate Atibon,
> To let us come in.

The next greeting was addressed to Ayizan, the ancient female spirit who is the guardian of ritual purity within the temple.
Ayizan was saluted in much the same manner as Legba, al-

---

[2] The Priyè Deyò are discussed in detail in Chapter 10.

though gin was not used (Ayizan drinks no alcohol) and the entire salutation took place in front of the altar tables. Libations offered to Ayizan were poured into an enamel basin on the floor in front of one of the tables, a North American accommodation to the fact that ceremonies can no longer take place in temples with beaten earth floors thirsty for the gifts offered to the spirits. After Alourdes and her assistants had each knelt before the altar, kissed the ground, and poured water three times in small dollops into the basin, the cup was passed to two or three guests so they too might honor Ayizan. Other priests and priestesses are usually chosen to pour libations, but individuals who have a personal bond with the spirit being saluted may also be appropriate choices.

At all ceremonies, each spirit called must be offered either three or seven songs, which must follow a definite order dictated by the type of drum rhythm that would ordinarily accompany them. The verses of each are repeated until Alourdes judges that the spirit has been properly honored. The atmosphere is informal. For example, at Alourdes's Vodou parties, songs for the spirits are sometimes aborted by a knowledgeable guest's comment: "That's a Zepòl [a rhythmic type]. You can't introduce that one yet." Before "sending" a new song, Alourdes often checks with the gathered faithful: "How many we sing? That song, second or third?" At times, she cannot think of another song for the spirit being greeted and will turn to a guest, usually one of the older women, and say: "Come on, Madame François, send a song for Kouzen for me." Together, the people possess a memory more complete than that of any individual. Consultative ritualizing, like the constant flow of ritual information between New York and Haiti, helps the community guard against forgetting.

After the third of Ayizan's songs ended with the sound of the *ason*, the Marasa, the sacred twins, were saluted, and then it was time to turn to Loko, patron of the Vodou priesthood. First, however, came a short interlude devoted to "baptizing" the table, a moment in which Catholicism reasserted itself. In ideal circumstances, baptizing the table is the job of the *prètsavann*, a type of ritual functionary who appeared in Haiti during the period following the revolution when the Vatican refused to send priests to the new black republic. A *prètsavann*, who is used in Haitian temples as a stand-in for a Catholic priest in the portions of the ritualizing that reiterate Catholic rites, is only infrequently involved in Alourdes's New York ceremonies. But the shadow of his presence persists in the rule that only men can perform rituals such as baptisms. Usually a *oungan* in the crowd is asked to fill this role, although any other man can be pressed into service when needed.

There was no priest at Azaka's 1984 birthday party, and the responsibility fell to Robert, who is an enthusiastic and faithful supporter during Alourdes's rituals. He speaks only English, but he is uninhibited about imitating the sounds of French, Latin, or Haitian Creole in the ritual context. Standing in front of Azaka's niche, Alourdes coached him in the proper formula for baptizing the table. Handing him a shot glass filled with holy water taken from a local Catholic church and a leaf plucked from one of the bouquets on the altar, she instructed him to dip the leaf in the water and sprinkle it over the tables while saying, *"Je te baptise au nom de Kouzen Zaka Mede. Credo, credo, abonoche* [I baptize you in the name of Kouzen Zaka Mede. I believe, I believe, *abonoche*]."[3] Everyone mumbled several quick Hail Marys before moving on to sing three hymns for Mary. During the last one, actually addressed to Mary Magdalene, Robert was directed to pass a collection plate. Moving from person to person, he held out a plate, and each of us dropped in a few coins. This money was placed beneath Azaka's table.

The group then launched into salutations for Papa Loko, chief Vodou priest. At these ceremonies, it is rare that anyone other than Alourdes is "ridden" by a *lwa*. But this evening was an exception. Irma, Alourdes's half-sister (they have the same father) is a regular participant. On this occasion, she had come with her mother, a strikingly beautiful, even regal, eighty-year-old woman, who was visiting from Haiti. Loko was the first spirit to arrive that night, and he possessed Irma's mother. As the third and final song for Loko was sung, the spirit announced his presence in the old woman's head through long trembling moans. Alourdes laughed out loud, obviously delighted that Loko, and especially this particular woman's Loko, had chosen to come to her feast.

As Alourdes protectively circled her arm around the body of

---

[3] *Abonoche* is apparently a transformation of a Latin word, no doubt from a Catholic liturgical context. None of the scholars of Latin I have consulted has been able to recognize the word, however.

Irma's mother, she said with real conviction, *"M'kontan anpil ou vini. Gwo, gwo Loko* [I'm very happy you come. Great, great Loko]." Opening her arms wide, Alourdes added, "The house is for you." Then, dropping her voice to the tone of a child begging from a parent, she murmured: "Papa Loko, my dear, pass your hand over my body. Life is not good for me." The spirit responded to her in a breathy, cracked voice indicative of Loko's advanced age: "I don't give luck." "I know you don't give luck, Papa. I know that not your way," Alourdes said, sounding only a little disappointed.

She recovered quickly and began to introduce the people standing nearby. Pointing to Robert, she said, "This person a child of the house. He never desert the house. Never." Indicating a woman who had gone through the Vodou "marriage" to Loko, she proclaimed, "This woman your wife." Then, sweeping her arm across the room, Alourdes announced, "All the women here your wife!" Speaking in his whispery old voice, Loko asked for someone whose name I did not catch. Alourdes responded, "She could not come. She got nobody to watch her kids. I going tell her you ask about her."

"You are *family* spirit," Alourdes crooned, gently stroking the side of Loko's face. "Me, I'm going do everything you want me to do. When you tell me work, I'm going work. When you tell me sit, I'm going sit. When you tell me run, I'm going run. When you tell me stand, I'm going stand. My house is for you!"

This possession-performance, like most in Vodou, was a complex event. Alourdes was not only relating to one of the most venerable Vodou spirits; she was also relating to an elderly woman who had once saved her life. Just after Alourdes's birth, when her mother was suffering from "black fever" and unable to breastfeed her, Irma's mother, who had just had a baby, stepped in as Alourdes's wet nurse. Alourdes feels she owes this woman a great debt. The social drama is never far from the surface in the religious drama of Vodou. Furthermore, in a small Vodou family such as this one, people know one another well enough to grasp, even without words, the multiple meanings of what is happening.

After Loko's short visit and the saluting of such key spirits as Danbala and Ezili, the main events of the evening began with the calling of the guest of honor, Azaka. To entice him to come to his birthday party, song after song was sung for the shy and awkward country bumpkin Kouzen Zaka. There was a song

Azaka

based on his title, "Minister of Agriculture," and one on his character, "timid man." Another song laid out the basic rules of family functioning, on one level, while on another it suggested that poor country cousins would do better financially by not marrying one of their own kind:

> *Kouzen pa pran kouzinn, o,*
> *Kouzinn, o, Kouzinn, o.*
> *Senkann santim pa lajan;*
> *De goud pa dola.*

> A male cousin doesn't take a female cousin, oh,
> Cousin, oh, Cousin, oh.
> Fifty cents is not money;
> Two *gourd* not a dollar.[4]

Another of Kouzen Zaka's songs was a sort of riddle, a form of oral literature loved by country people. Only a careful listener would have realized that it was the ravaged earth who spoke in this song:

> *M'malere, m'malere vre;*
> *Se defòm m'genyen.*
> *M'konnen m'malere, vre;*
> *Se defòm m'genyen*
> *M'malere, m'malere.*
> *Se pa achte m'achte;*
> *Se Bondye kreye-m malere.*
> *Moun-yo bale sou do mwen.*

> I'm unfortunate, I'm truly unfortunate;
> It's crippled I am.

[4] Two *gourd* are the equivalent of forty cents of U.S. currency. Haitian currency is one of the few in the world kept at a fixed official rate of exchange with the U.S. dollar. The exchange rate, five *gourd* to one dollar, is printed on the *gourd* note. Black-market exchange rates, however, often devalue the *gourd* in relation to the dollar.

I know I'm unfortunate, truly;
It's crippled I am.
I'm unfortunate, I'm unfortunate.
It's not something I brought on myself;
God created me unlucky.
People sweep on my back.

That song must have had a special poignancy for many in the
room, for a significant number of them had been driven toward
their new life in New York by the devastation of the land in
Haiti. Today the border between the Dominican Republic and
Haiti is actually visible from the air, because of the widespread
deforestation and soil erosion on the Haitian end of the island
of Hispaniola. Poverty, the ravaged earth, and the peasant life
are indissolubly wedded in the figure of Azaka, who also exhibits the peasant's characteristic resignation to life's tragedies.

As Alourdes pushed the energy in the room to new heights in
an effort to *echofe* (heat things up) sufficiently to bring the spirit
into our midst, she introduced a new song:

Kouzen Zaka,
M'pral prepare mwen,
Pou regle zafè mwen.
Nèg-yo pa Bondye.
Zaka, li pa vle wè mwen.
Li di ou etranje,
Li di ou etranje.
Fanmi pa vle wè mwen.

Cousin Zaka,
I'm going to prepare myself,
To set my affairs in order.
People aren't God.
Zaka, he does not want to see me.
He says you are a stranger,
He says you are a stranger.
The family does not want to see me.

Goats to be sacrificed to Azaka. The temple behind Alourdes's mother's home, Port-au-Prince, Haiti, 1989.

This song, whose uplifting, almost joyous sound plays counterpoint to its somber ambiguity (is it Kouzen himself who "does not want to see me," or am I seeking his help because a human family has rejected me?) was sung over and over, louder and louder. Alourdes jumped to her feet and began to dance, *ason* in hand. She was playing on our energies as if we were her musical instrument. Sensing the moment was ripe for Azaka's arrival, she was stirring the room into a spiraling intensity. In the instant just before our collective energy would have peaked and headed downward to refuel, Alourdes began a second round of salutations to Azaka. She was only halfway through the dips and turns that preceded the moment when she would prostrate herself before the altar when Azaka arrived.

Her body shuddered and jerked, went lax for a moment, and then jerked again rapidly. These movements mark the struggle between the *lwa* and Alourdes's *gwo bònanj* (big guardian angel), who ordinarily presides "in her head." When the spirit wins the contest (it almost always does), the *gwo bònanj* is sent from the body to wander, as it does routinely during sleep, and Alourdes becomes the *chwal* (horse) of the spirit. Several people moved around Alourdes to help her, but there was no urgency in their movements; no one thought she was in danger. Indeed, many people in the room seemed to take no special note of her, as if the events were in no way unusual or remarkable.

Her shoes were removed, and, with one person supporting her under each arm, Azaka's blue scarf was tied around her neck. The first sign that Azaka was seated firmly on his horse was his high-pitched nasal chirp: "Whooooo, whooooo . . . whooooo . . . whoooop!" Maggie reached for the voluminous blue denim shirt made especially for Azaka and struggled to put it on him. Then she put his straw hat on his head and hung his *makout* (straw satchel) over one shoulder.

Pants and shirt made from *karabel,* a sturdy blue denim woven in Haiti; a *makout;* and a broad-brimmed straw hat—these make up the standard costume of Azaka, as well as the traditional garb of the peasant farmer in Haiti. It is partly because of such similarities in clothing that Azaka came to be identified with the Catholic Saint Isidore. In a chromolithograph widely distributed in Haiti, Isidore appears in blue pants and cape, a sack slung over one shoulder. The two are also connected by the agricultural theme: in the lithograph, Isidore kneels in prayer while, behind him, an angel plows the land with a pair of white oxen.

"*Bonswa, Kompè. Bonswa, ti Kouzinn* [Good evening, Brother. Good evening, little Cousin]," Azaka said, speaking in the highly nasal voice characteristic of peasant speech. Then he looked timidly about the room from beneath the brim of his straw hat.

Maggie was the first to address him. She whined: "*Mezanmi!*

Woy! Ti Kouzen, m'pa bon . . . malad [My friend! Oh! Little Cousin, I'm not well . . . sick]." "Eh, Kouzinn," Azaka replied, cocking his head in a manner that communicated both sullenness and studied timidity, "I think I'm going to go now."

"No! Oh, no, Kouzen," Maggie broke in, quickly changing to a placating tone. "I'm going to give you food." Other voices joined Maggie's in pleading for the bounty of the table: Didn't he want to stay? Didn't he want to have something to eat? Kouzen replied truculently, "I didn't come all this way for a banana . . . no!"

"Kouzen, don't go!" Maggie begged, with a touch of panic in her voice. Kouzen continued to pout: "Not for a yam . . . not for an avocado." "Because—let me tell you," Maggie sputtered, "you don't see all the work I do for you!" It had been an exhausting day for Maggie, and she was on edge. She had left for work at seven that morning, and when she got home, just after five that afternoon, she had begun preparations for Kouzen's feast immediately. Furthermore, she had been on her feet all night, singing enthusiastically for each spirit. "I know you come a long way, Kouzen dear," Maggie croaked. "You don't hear my voice? You don't come 'til I got no voice!"

Kouzen responded like a stereotypic peasant to Maggie's efforts to placate him. His body language communicated stubborn passivity. His objections came out as whining complaints, the thin voice rising and falling, first a little screech, then a pouty whisper. *"Manman ou dwe'm* [Your mother owes me]," Kouzen said, crossing his arms and staring at his feet. To this picture of wronged innocence, Kouzen added a definitive "Humph!" and turned his back on Maggie.

Maggie walked around in front of him to continue pleading. Anger rising in her voice along with desperation, Maggie explained the financial difficulties of the moment: "Kouzen, you don't understand. Mommie has not paid the mortgage in two month. She has telephone bill. They shut off her HBO. She tried to turn on a movie for the kids, and it was gone!"

"All my business is written down," Kouzen said with a trace of smugness, adding another "Humph!" for good measure. This statement was met by snickers from the crowd, and some laughed out loud. Kouzen became defensive: "You are trying to cheat me because you know I don't know how to write. You know how to write, and you cheat me!"

"How many tree leaves does your mother owe me?" Kouzen demanded of Maggie, using his characteristic expression for paper money. "Find my list!" he whined. "All my business is written down. I told you that! I always find somebody who writes for me."

Maggie sent Robert searching deep in Azaka's *makout* for a grubby little denim sack with drawstrings. When it was located, Maggie pulled out a rumpled scrap of paper. Sitting down in a chair near Kouzen, she smoothed it out on her knee and began to read: "Fanm Alourdes . . . five dollar, fifty cent. Gason Robert, five tree leaves. Ti Bob—"

Azaka interrupted the reading: "Listen, that man took a lot of tree leaves from my hand. A lot! A lot! He was going to buy an acre of land. How much does he owe me?" "Sixty dollars," Maggie responded and then added quickly, "My mother is looking for him, but she don't find him. He give her a telephone number, but it was no good." "I'm going to get my money this year, you hear?" Kouzen announced with unusual force.

"Get my purse," Maggie said to Robert. "I'm going to pay for my mother." Money was appearing all over the room as debts to Papa Zaka, most of them accumulated at last year's birthday party, were paid. It was unusual for Azaka to be conducting his own financial affairs. This role is usually filled by the female country cousin who "walks with him," Kouzinn Zaka. Three years earlier, Kouzinn had come to Alourdes's feast to handle Azaka's debt collection, and Maggie had explained to me: "Kouzinn is his secretary, his banker, whatever. She the one who have business, deal in money. Azaka don't have no business; he work on the plantation. Whatever money he make, he give it to her."

This version of the relationship between Kouzen and Kouzinn reflects traditional gender arrangements in rural Haiti, where, following a West African pattern, market women are the only ones who handle money. Recently, however, an entrepreneurial class of men has been steadily growing in the countryside. It is made up of farmers who have managed, often through political machinations, to amass large tracts of land and wholesalers who buy such products as coffee from small farmers and sell them to large exporting companies. Perhaps Azaka's role change was sparked by this social shift, although it seems more likely that his behavior that night in 1984 was a result of either Alourdes's fatigue (one possession is easier than two) or the pressing financial needs of her family. What followed was even more surprising, however, for Alourdes's Azaka also took over Kouzinn's market role.

Content that he had settled his outstanding loans, Azaka decided to sell the items on his altar tables. Suddenly animated and sounding like a true *machann* (market woman), he called out to people: "Come on, Brother. Come on, Cousin. Look at the big market! Come, come, come. You can choose. Pick it up. Go on, pull it right out. Hehhhhh! You don't have to be afraid! Gason Didi, you going to buy a little thing, just a real little thing, yes? Fanm Linda, you going to buy for the children? You can't tell me you don't want to! Come on! Come, come, come!"

The young man called Didi approached the table as Kouzen pattered on: "What do you want in the market, Cousin? What are you going to buy?" "How much for that cake?" Didi asked, pointing to the one frosted in blue. "Two hundred tree leaves," Kouzen responded. First, people gasped, and then they laughed. "That's too much," Didi said, laughing himself. "How about that one?" and he pointed to an unfrosted sheet cake that Irma and her mother had brought for Kouzen's altar.

"Myself with you, we are going to negotiate!" Kouzen said with real relish in his voice, and he broke into a little song about how much he loved people to gather around him. He abruptly ended the song in mid-phrase and announced that the bargaining session was open: "Forty-seven tree leaves!" Didi laughed again and came back, "How much of it will you give me for five dollars?" "Half for seven tree leaves," Kouzen replied, then quickly qualified his answer: "The half of a half." Didi agreed, and Papa Zaka balanced the sheet cake on his knees, cutting it in half and then in half again. Lifting the chunk of cake in his hand and moving it slowly up and down as if weighing it, Kouzen looked to the crowd: "*Bon mache* [A good buy], eh?"

There were polite murmurs of agreement, and Azaka nodded his head, well pleased with himself. Then he lopped off about a third of the piece and hid it in the corner of the cake plate behind his free hand, while he extended his other hand toward a chagrined Didi with a piece of cake in it no larger than an ordinary serving. The entire cake was sold in this fashion, with Kouzen at the last moment slicing off a corner of the piece just sold. Finally, he sold the resulting pile of chunks and crumbs for two dollars. "Put another tree leaf on it," Azaka said to the amused buyer, "and you can take a piece of candy, too."

With no more cake to sell, Azaka turned to hawking pieces of fruit and candy, bottles of cola, and small fragments of cassava bread. He leaned hard on the unfortunate Robert, who was pressured into buying for his three children as well as himself. "You going to buy, Cousin?" "Yes," replied Robert. "*Chwazi* [Choose]!" urged Kouzen. "*Wi*," said Robert. "*Ou poule anpil, wi Kompè? Se pa pou poule—chwazi bougay* [You talk a lot, yes, Brother? It's not to talk—choose something]!" responded Azaka, using the distortions of Creole common to the speech of the spirits, distortions in which *pale* (to speak) becomes *poule*, and *bagay* (thing) becomes *bougay*. Robert chose a banana, some cookies, and some hard candy. He began to peel the banana, but Kouzen stopped him short: "Don't eat yet. Finish bargaining first!" Despite language barriers, Robert finally got the message and handed the spirit seven dollars.

Earlier, Kouzen had appointed Robert treasurer, and throughout the evening he handed over money to him whether it came from debts repaid or from the sale of items from his "market." Every now and then, he ordered Robert to count the proceeds out loud. On the first count, Azaka had collected seventy-one dollars; on the second, the total rose to eighty dollars; and on the third, it was one hundred ten. Not long after, even Azaka tired of these games. "Now I'm finished with business!" he announced and directed Robert to count the money one last time and divide it into three piles, being sure to hide them in different places, for safety.

"No matter what *vivan* [living person] comes who needs money, you may give to them. You don't have to call me, no," Azaka declared. Then, in one last demonstration of character, he cut his eyes at Robert: "What about the pennies? You sitting on some?" "Cousin," Azaka whispered to Maggie, "check for me. What's he got in that hand?"

The market was closed at last, and Maggie spread a clean white cloth at Azaka's feet, in front of the now-depleted altar tables. She pulled the brimming bowls of food from beneath Azaka's altar and placed them before him. It was nearly four in the morning as large portions of *chaka*, rice and beans, cornmeal, avocado, yam, and sweet potato were scooped out of the homely calabash bowls and onto plates for each guest. No one was allowed to refuse, and we were all expected to eat with our hands—the child's way of eating, the only appropriate way for the *vivan*, who are all children in relation to the spirits. No longer operating in the dangerous territory of finances where competitiveness, guile, and suspicion are unappealing but useful character traits, Azaka became the generous host, urging food on all his guests: "You going to eat, Brother?" "What do you want, Cousin?" "Take some *chaka;* it's good!"

Expansive hospitality is characteristic of Haitian peasants. An American friend who lived for several years in the Haitian countryside put it this way: "If you are a guest in their house, they will break their backs to feed and entertain you. Even if they have only a cup of rice left, you will get half. Haitian peasants are incredibly generous. They will give you anything, as long as it's not money you ask for. You can't even ask questions about money!" The problematic nature of this contrast between hospitable family patriarch and canny businessman showed itself in a surprising way during the remainder of Alourdes's birthday party for Kouzen Zaka.

When Azaka left, Ogou, Alourdes's major spirit, made his expected appearance. The first words out of his mouth were inquiries about what had transpired with Azaka: "Did he ask for money? Did you buy? Do you owe him? You, too?" Receiving affirmative responses all around, Ogou, the loyal warrior known for his integrity, sighed with disgust and shook his head, "No, no, no, no. I don't like that." Then he consigned Azaka to his place with an uncharacteristically colorful epithet: "*Kaka bandit!*"

The conflict was not resolved with Ogou's appearance. Just after seven that morning, as the last of the guests were making their way out Legba's still-open door, Alourdes collapsed in a chair, completely fatigued by the succession of spirits. First it had been Azaka, then Ogou, and finally Gede, the trickster spirit whose habit is to come last and stay long, his comic performance serving as a buffer between Vodou and the outside world. Sitting slumped over, barely able to keep her eyes open, Alourdes bid her guests good-bye. She also thanked them profusely for their help in serving the spirits. In the course of several parting conversations, she mentioned that she did not approve of Azaka's behavior.

Alourdes and Maggie, Robert and his family, and I fell into our respective beds. (I had been assigned the sofa bed in Alourdes's rarely used upstairs parlor, amid a menagerie of ceramic tigers, dolls, and stuffed animals.) We slept until noon, when the noise of a Brooklyn street in early summer made further rest impossible. After cups of good strong Café Rebo, Alourdes settled herself to call Kouzen one last time, so that he could direct the dismantling of his tables. For this truncated ritual, the Priyè Deyò were shortened to two Hail Marys, and there was one quick pass through the song calling on Legba to open the gate. After the third Vodou song for Kouzen, the mountain man arrived. He was complaining as usual.

Where was his *karabel* shirt? Where was his bottle of gin? He did not want to use them; he just wanted to be sure they were put away properly. Kouzen also told Maggie what to do with the remaining food—some was to be shared with friends, some was "for the house." His directions were suddenly interrupted by a commotion at the basement door. "What's going on? The police!" shrieked Kouzen Zaka.

One of the neighborhood children had come to warn me that a police officer was about to ticket my car. I made excuses to Azaka and went out to explain that my registration had not really expired but that I had simply neglected to attach the new sticker. After assuring himself that I sufficiently acknowledged his authority, the officer proved to be reasonable, and within five minutes I was back inside, only to find Azaka cowering. "I don't like police! You see police, you run! They beat people! I've spent too much time in jail; I'm going now." All around him, voices soothed: "You don't need to go, little Cousin." "He's gone, he's gone."

After making a small private loan to one of the past night's participants, Azaka now had ninety-eight dollars in bills and a sizable handful of change left in his three small sacks. Three times he ordered it counted in front of him. The loose change, he said, was to be distributed among the boxes on the various spirits' altars in Alourdes's altar room. Then he asked if anyone in our small group wanted to borrow the "tree leaves." On the first attempt, he found no borrowers; but the second time around Maggie said she would take it.

That was the signal to begin bargaining over interest rates. Maggie repeatedly referred to the ninety-eight dollars she would borrow, and Azaka persisted in calling it one hundred dollars. After several exchanges, Maggie suggested that she was willing to pay back one hundred fifty dollars on the first of May next year. "One hundred fifty-*seven!*" Kouzen countered, and again

Maggie agreed. In an aside to me, Maggie explained: "I don't care. I know I can go to the bank, pay ten percent, maybe twelve percent interest, but why should I let some stranger come here and then borrow the money and just go out, never come back! Remember that guy last year? Ti Bob? Humph! He owe Kouzen sixty dollars. Now Mommie cannot even find him. Besides, this is not just money. This is special. Anything you put this money in going to have good luck. I need some luck!"

"If you don't pay May first, it's going to climb to three hundred dollars!" Kouzen warned. "Okay," said Maggie, "one thing only I got to say—I better be working from now until the first of May 1985. You take care of that for me!" Kouzen responded nonchalantly, "You are going to find my money works. Don't you worry."

With his financial affairs finally laid to rest for another year, Azaka gave a personal message to each member of our small group. He told Robert that he would continue to come to him in his dreams. He assured me that he was going to give my book project "a little push." Robert's wife was suffering from an annoying skin rash, and she was given a bottle of *medikaman* (medicine) made from Azaka's herb-laced gin and cornstarch. After mixing the brew, Kouzen held the medicine bottle up to each of the four directions and blew sharply across its open mouth. He then set it on the floor in front of him and instructed Robert's wife to pick it up with both hands—but only after leaving seven cents on the floor beside it. Maggie explained to her: "Some thing you can't just take. Even you just put a penny, that don't matter. You got to pay, or it don't work."

"YOU IN, YOU IN. YOU OUT, YOU STAY OUT."

Each of the Haitian Vodou spirits, in his or her own way, is a character defined by conflict. Azaka is no exception. He fed his children from the feast laid beneath his altar table, but only after he had cajoled and coerced them into buying the items on top of it. Kouzen Zaka straddles two worlds: family and business. The currencies are different in these two worlds. Within the family, food and its metaphorical extension into all that feeds and nurtures is the means of exchange. Relationships last a lifetime, and although reciprocity is expected, no one keeps strict accounts. In the business sphere, the means of exchange is money. Money is for counting; it lends itself to precise reckoning. Unlike ongoing family relations, business deals are abbreviated exchanges with, more often than not, a loser and a winner. These are worlds in tension, a tension endemic to the life of the Haitian peasant who moves between farm and market, the country and the city. It is also a tension easily translated into the life of a New York immigrant.

In Vodou, the tension between these antithetical worlds, and the very different values and behaviors that each engenders, is commented on and transformed in many ways. "Don't put money on the bed!" Alourdes yelled at me once as I started to dump out the contents of my change purse to look for a subway token. "Why?" I wondered and then remembered one of the few hard and fast rules to emerge from my initiation: "Don't put the *ason* on the bed. Never, never, never." The *ason*, like money, is an instrument of coercive power. It exercises control over the spirits, who are thought to be compelled by its sound to come and go, more or less at the will of the *manbo* or *oungan*. Neither money nor the *ason* can be placed on the bed, for such distancing power implements do not belong in the place where children are made and born, the place where family begins.

Azaka straddles these worlds in tension, and, to some extent, he also mediates them, reconciling the irreconcilable. The value of money is ordinarily equal to its quantity. One five-*gourd* note is as good as another. But in Papa Zaka's hands, money takes on quality as well as quantity. Robert's wife had to pay for her medicine, but the payment was only symbolic. And Maggie knew she could borrow from a bank more cheaply than from Kouzen, but she borrowed from him anyway: "This is not just money. This is special." Azaka's money brings luck.

Kouzen Zaka portrays the generosity and concern that prevail within a family group, but he also portrays the suspicion, even paranoia, that characterizes the attitude of such a tightly knit group toward all those who fall outside the protective circle. Participants in the dense drama of a Vodou ceremony play roles on both sides. Outsiders by definition at Kouzen's market, they are cheated and suspected of pilfering his profits. Insiders at the family table, they are fed and given boons. Such role playing is a rehearsal of and for life, and the lessons learned ricochet through the community. The challenge lies in learning these roles well enough to recognize the characters, values, and behaviors that clearly belong to each realm.

Distinguishing between those who are inside and those who are outside the family group is far easier in the rural world of Kouzen Zaka than it will ever be for a Haitian immigrant living in New York. This task highlights the significance of one part of the legacy of Joseph Binbin Mauvant. When he passed on to his children the most effective medicine he had, the medicine was African words that cast a clear and indisputable boundary between these realms: *"Sim salalam, sa salawu. Pa salam, pa salawu* [You in, you in. You out, you stay out]."[5]

In discussing her healing work, Alourdes cites her matrilineage more readily and more frequently than her patrilineage. Over the generations, the men in Alourdes's family have been less constant and less caring than the women, and they are less clearly models in her day-to-day operations as a healer. Their genuine power, however, will not be denied. When every other skill fails to heal a client, Alourdes turns to the legacy of Joseph Binbin Mauvant. Pumping her left leg up and down and slapping her thigh each time it rises, Alourdes shouts, as her mother and grandmother did before her: *"Tonnè* [Thunder]! *Sim salalam, sa salawu. Pa salam, pa salawu."*

"And that person get well, baby!" she tells me. "They have to. They have to! That was my great-grandfather who left that word. It from Africa. Sometime I'm in trouble, and I repeat that word, *'Sim salalam, sa salawu. Pa salam, pa salawu.'* And everything okay! That word mean, 'You in, you in. You out, you stay out.'"

AZAKA'S CALL TO REMEMBER

When Alourdes was in her twenties, she had three children and lived on her own in Port-au-Prince, the largest city in Haiti and its capital. Life was hard, and on more days than she cares to remember she and her children went to bed hungry. So she jumped at the chance when her brother suggested she join him in New York. Philomise, the granddaughter of Joseph Binbin

---

[5]I have not attempted to track down a specific African origin or a more precise translation for this "word from Africa." Rather, I have chosen to let it stand here as it exists in Alourdes's memory.

Mauvant, reluctantly supported her daughter's plan. Philo hated to see her favorite child leave, but she was too well versed in the sufferings of life in Haiti to deny Alourdes this chance. So Philo did what a mother could do: she sought to send her daughter on her way surrounded by the protection of the spirits.

Alourdes frequently recounts for her own daughter, Maggie, the story of this momentous departure and the subsequent problems in New York.

Let me tell you something. That day I go to New York, my whole family going with me to the airport. We got a car, a taxi, you know, and everybody in that car. Then my mother come out, and she start to get in that car too, and she say, "Oh, boy! I forgot something. Alourdes, come inside." And I say, "Why, Mommie?" 'cause everybody in that car, and everybody saying, "Come on, let's go, let's go!"

You know, that time, things was different. You going on an airplane, everybody nervous, and you had to dress nice. I had a new dress, red dress, and a red hat. And I was nervous too, so I say, "Why, Mommie? What you want me to do inside?"

She say, "Come in, make some prayer in front of the altar." And I say, "No." My mother say, "You don't want to do it? Let me do it for you." I say, "Thank you," and she go inside the house, she pray for me, and she come into the car. I say, "You pray good?" She say, "Yes, I pray good for you."

I don't want to do it, 'cause I tell my mother, "I'm going to that city—lot'a star! Beautiful! Oh, boy! I don't think I'm going to need no spirit in New York."

And I was wrong!

Alourdes came to Brooklyn in 1962, a date she holds in her mind by remembering that it was "before Kennedy die." Her early years in the United States presented greater difficulties than anyone could have expected. The first sign of serious trouble was a sudden and frightening illness.

That happen in 1963, December 1963, before Christmas. I feel sick—my stomach, my chest. Oh, boy! I can't sit down. I can't lay down. I can't stand up. I can't breathe also. I feel I'm going to die. I say, "God please save me! Oh, God, what happen to me?" Then I think about my three children in Haiti . . . my mother . . . my family.

They bring me in Jewish Hospital, in Prospect Avenue. I got fever one hundred and six, and they put me in emergency room. You know what they do for me? They ice me! They come in with bucket, ice, alcohol. They take off all my clothes, and they rub me. They rub me with the sheet. It was so cold! Like they put me in the freezer. I yell! I cry! I cry! After I cool down, I get hot. Just when I was quiet, sleepy, then they unwrap me, take another sheet, and wrap me again. I was so sick, and I don't get better.

January eight, I see priest coming. He ask me, "Are you Catholic?" I say, "Yes," and he give me last rite. Oh, yeah! One o'clock, I see three men coming in. They take me to the operate room. Doctor say I got infection in my intestine. They operate me, and when I wake up I was *so* scared. I ask that doctor, "Did you put a thing in me?" 'cause somebody tell me when they operate you . . . down there, you know . . . they put a thing in you, and you don't do it natural no more. Then I don't speak English too good, but I try, and I just say to him, "Please, can you tell me, did you put that thing in me?" And finally he understand, and he say, "No." I pass almost one month in the hospital. Yeah! Then I feel all right, and they put me out.

You know, when you come from the hospital, you suppose to go back for treatment. But I don't go back, because they ask me, "Bring your passport and alien card." They ask me, "Where your family live in Haiti?" They ask me that! Uh-huh, they ask me that. And I give the address, but when I tell my friend Carmen, she say, "Oh, yeah, if you go with your alien card and your passport, they going write the government in Haiti, make them pay." 'Cause when you operate is very expensive, and I don't have no money to pay. She say, "They going send you back to Haiti." I get scared. I never go back.

That time I don't know what is welfare. I don't know about welfare at all, and nobody don't tell me. No, nobody don't tell me, if you sick, you not working, you can go someplace, they can help you. Nobody tell me that. But everybody' friend help me. You see me, you give me two dollar, three dollar. If I come in your house, you give me plate of food, you know. That's the way I survive!

The communities that surround newly arrived Haitian immigrants today are much larger and more experienced than they were in the early 1960s when Alourdes came. They have become effective clearinghouses for practical information as well as for more tangible forms of assistance such as food, clothing, and shelter. Now, as before, however, the communities also process rumor. Lacking both access to accurate information and a feeling of entitlement that would allow them to question authority, Haitian immigrants rely instead on countless anecdotes about what works and what does not work, what is legal and what is not, what will arouse the attention of the dreaded authorities (a fear deep in the bones of those who lived under the Duvalier family rule) and what will allow a person to slip by unnoticed. Many, unlike Alourdes, are illegal immigrants, for whom living discreetly is an essential survival strategy.

When I leave Jewish Hospital, I'm okay. I eat until I got my strength back. That time, I go back to work. But three months after, I get sick again. I get sick *again!* Same system! Second time, they bring me to Wycoff Hospital. They call priest again. They give me last rite again. That's twice I got last rite. Twice! This time they tell me I got bad heart, I got all kind'a sickness. But that not true.

When I come from Wycoff Hospital, I got no place to live, because I don't have no money. I can't pay no rent. So I meet a lady in the street. Yvonne Constant. She know my family in Haiti. She say, "How come you so skinny? Oh, poor girl! Come into my house." That lady give me a big plate of food when I reach her house. *Woy!* Rice and bean, a big fish, a boiled plantain—I eat, sweetheart! She give me food, she give me place to live. I sleep in her house, and she give me food. But I don't know what happen. I always sleeping. I can't work.

One day somebody tell me, "Beatrice want to see you." Beatrice my sister-in-law. Sunday afternoon, I got clothes on me, and I go there. When I first come to New York, I live in her house. But we don't get along too good, and I don't see her for a long time. Long time. You know me, I don't go to people I know to ask or beg for nothing! So I see her, I just say, "Aunt Bebe, people tell me you was asking for me. What happen . . . my mother? . . . Something happen in my family?"

She say, "No, nothing don't happen in your family. I want to see you because I got a dream about you." I say, "Oh, yeah? It very serious?" She say, "I don't know if it serious or not."

She say, "I dream I see a mountain man on Forty-second Street." She say, in that dream, she have to cross that street, and everybody standing, just waiting for the light. She look at that man. She say, "They got mountain man in New York, too?" When they give the green light, she just walk. And one lady walking behind her say, "Hey, Madame! Madame! Madame! That man call you." Bebe say, "What man?" When she turn her head, she see the mountain man.

She went to the mountain man, and she tell the mountain man, "Hi," and he say, "Hi, Cousin." And Bebe say, "You want to speak to me?" And he say, "Yes, Cousin." And he tell Bebe, "Did you know Philo?" Bebe say, "Philo? Yeah." "Did you know Alourdes?" Bebe say, "Yes, I know Alourdes. She my sister-in-law."

And that man say: "When she come into New York, why she don't dress like me, jean pants and jean shirt? If she dress like me, she was well dressed, right?" And Bebe say, "I don't know." And the mountain man say, "Tell Alourdes if she dress like me, everything going to be beautiful!" Bebe say, "Really?" and that man walk maybe three or four step, and Bebe don't see him no more, and boom! the clock—rrrrrrrrrrrrr—and she say, "What time is it?"

It was six-thirty in the morning, and when she wake up, Bebe say, "Ahhhh! I understand that dream. I understand. I have to see Alourdes to explain her that." Because she know my mother have spirit, you know, so she say maybe Alourdes's mother' spirit come and talk to me. Maybe that man . . . maybe that Kouzen Zaka.

When Alourdes heard her sister-in-law's dream, she understood what she had to do. She had to go back to Haiti for the kind of treatment no hospital in the United States could provide. But going back to Haiti, even for a short trip, required money, and Alourdes had none. For a time, she continued to live with Yvonne Constant, her family friend, and gradually the proud Alourdes took that woman into her confidence. Alourdes told her she did not think she had the strength to work even if she found a job. She told of her conviction that it was the spirits who were troubling her. She needed to go back to Haiti, and she worried day and night about how she would find the money to do that.

Yvonne listened, day by day, until the full story was out, and then she promised to help. She told Alourdes that she would use a credit card to buy her a plane ticket and that she would also loan her the necessary pocket money. Yvonne promised to give Alourdes three hundred dollars in cash as soon as her turn came around in "Hands." When Alourdes first told me this story, she had to explain: "You don't know what is Hands? The Spanish call it 'Blood.' Say you got ten people. Then every week each person give thirty dollar. So every week somebody got three hundred dollar! That is Hands!"

Alourdes returned to Haiti with no advance notice to her mother. In fact, she had not written home for months. "You know, I got nothing to put in that letter; I don't even got money for myself! And I don't like my mother worry all the time on account of me." When Alourdes swung open the gate to the little yard on Avenue Oswald Durand in Port-au-Prince, Philo fainted.

Alourdes told her mother about Kouzen Zaka's message, and Philo said that even though she had not heard from Alourdes, she had known something was wrong. She also had had an important dream. In Philo's dream, Alourdes came back home with her arm in a cast, as if it had been broken. In the dream, Alourdes entered the house and, without saying a word to her mother, went straight to the altar to pray. After some time, she arose, turned her back on her mother, and, still silent, walked out the door. Philo had this dream about a month before Alourdes's return to Haiti, and it bothered her so much that she even discussed it with the neighbors.

On one of the first days Alourdes was home, the warrior spirit Ogou possessed her mother, and the message he delivered was not one Alourdes wanted to hear. "Papa Ogou come in my mother' head, and he tell me I'm suppose to see with card, you know . . . do spirit work . . . help people. That I don't like!" Although Alourdes's mother was very poor, she had quite a reputation as a *manbo* in Port-au-Prince. For a short period, Philo had even served as a counselor to François Duvalier, before he became president of Haiti and the ugly parts of his character revealed themselves. Nevertheless, Alourdes believed that little of her mother's healing knowledge or talent had rubbed off on her. "I say, 'Oh, boy! How I'm going to do that?' Because to help people you got to know a lot'a thing. I say, 'How I going to put all that in my head?' My mother tell me, 'You'll manage; don't you worry!'"

Initiation into the Vodou priesthood involves an elaborate set of rituals, the core of which is a long period of seclusion in which a person is said to *kouche* (literally, to lie down or go to sleep). These rituals are commonly referred to as "taking the *ason*," that is, taking up the beaded rattle that is said to give priests and priestesses a certain amount of leverage in working with the spirits.

> Papa Ogou in my mother' head say I have to take the *ason*. You know, my mother don't have no *ason*. But Papa Ogou say I have to, because my father' family serve with the *ason*, so I have to take the *ason* for protection. I serve two kind of spirit, from my father' family and from my mother' family.

The initiation rituals for Alourdes could not take place right away. Money had to be saved for drummers, sacrificial animals, food and drink for the spirits. Several sets of ritual clothing had to be sewn. Thus on this first visit only a simple ritual called a *lave tèt* (a headwashing) was performed. The headwashing was a *pwomès* (promise) Alourdes made to the spirits, indicating that she had heard their request and intended to honor it. The ritual also "cooled" the restive spirits in Alourdes's head and "fed" and strengthened them. After two weeks, she returned to New York. But before she left, she promised the spirits that she would return to Haiti to *kouche* as soon as she had seven hundred dollars.

The spirits eased their discipline, and, although life in New York continued to be demanding, there was a noticeable turn in her "luck" after this first trip back to Haiti. Before she left New York, Alourdes had been unable to find employment. But on the day after her return, she found a job in the laundry at the Brooklyn Hebrew Home, a position she held for two years. During this interim period, Alourdes also moved step by step into the role of healer.

> I start to help people, you know, little by little, start to do thing. You my friend, you got trouble—you know, anything . . . love, sickness—you come to me, I help a little bit. I try to help. Everything I do for them is good. No complaint. People

start to give me money, you know, five dollar, ten dollar, because they grateful. So one day I say to myself, "I don't have no time to go to that job." So I quit that job and I just work in my house. I read card. I help people.

During this time Alourdes drew on skills acquired during the short visit with her mother, on her awakening memory, and on the help of the spirits, who began to speak to her more directly through her dreams.

My mother teach me a lot'a thing. She show me how to read card. My mother start to show me; then, after that, I dream and the spirit finish . . . they finish show me how to read card in that dream. She teach me about *senmp*—you know, herb. My mother know a lot about herb, a whole lot! Also, I begin to remember. Since I little girl, I watch her, and now I remember a lot'a thing.

My mother tell me, "Now you going to see the real person. Somebody come in your house, they happy—you know, dancing, drinking—even they do that, you going to see if they sad. If they got something bad inside them, you going to see that."

Finally, when Alourdes had saved seven hundred dollars, she returned to Haiti to take the *ason*.

Second time I go back to Haiti, my life was not good. Not *real* bad like before, but not good. Second time I go, I pass one month in Haiti . . . nine day inside that little room where they *kouche* me. Then I a *manbo*. When I come back to New York, people pouring all over me! People who lose job, I make them find job. People who sick, I treat them. Their husband or wife leave them, I make that person come back. After I come back from Haiti second time, I did not have to work outside again.

Alourdes's reputation as a good woman and a strong *manbo*, fair to her clients and effective in her treatments, has grown steadily since then.

My mother show me how to do good, never do bad in your life. Because when you do bad to people, that return to you, that return right on your back. I remember every single thing she tell me, because that's in my family! My great-grandmother serve spirit, and my grandmother, then my mother, then me.

"Some people got spirit in their family," Alourdes concluded, "but when they grow up, they think they too big-shot to serve that spirit. They too ashame about that. But I'm not ashame at all, because I love spirit, because they help me. That's my belief!"

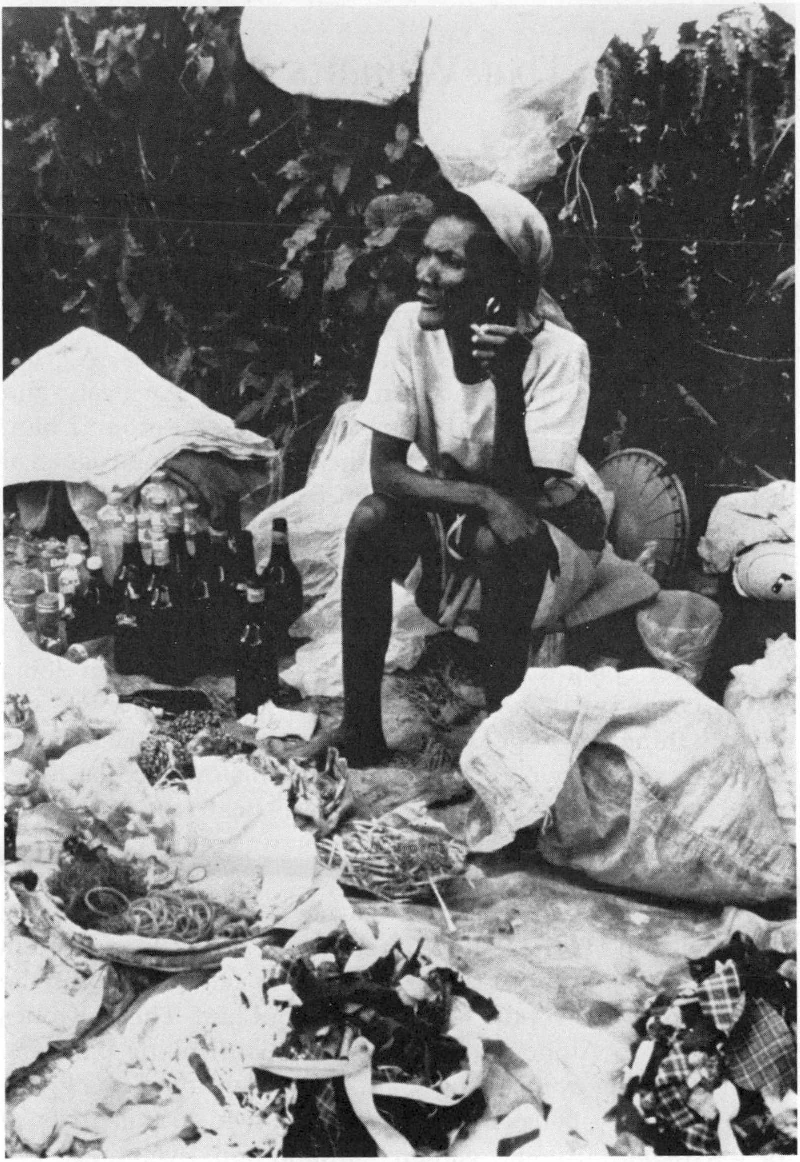

CHAPTER THREE

Raise That Woman's Petticoat

Alphonse Macena had an air about him that made people painfully self-conscious. A *grimo* (light-skinned man), tall and lean, with the grace of a cat—and so well dressed! Children became suddenly shy around him, and women patted down their Mother Hubbards and tugged at their headrags when they saw him coming. When Alphonse Macena came to the northern town of Port-de-Paix and took a room in the only pension there, people talked. Not to his face, of course.

"What's this handsome man doing here? Surveyor, you say? You are not going to find a single person who saw him doing any surveying work around here." Macena's inactivity was not the only thing that kept tongues wagging in Port-de-Paix. Some people wondered what he was doing on his own, so far away from family. The maid in the pension was heard to say that she knew someone who knew someone who was certain he had left a wife and children down south.

The mysterious stranger from Jacmel (a bustling neocolonial coffee port on Haiti's southern peninsula) stayed long enough in Port-de-Paix for the rumormongers to fall silent, but the people in town never did learn much about him. The only ones who talked to Alphonse Macena were his drinking partners. During the long evenings he spent on the balcony of the graceful—if shoddy—pension in the center of town, a small group of the town's hard drinkers gathered around him. Even these self-styled *gwo nèg* (important men) were realistic enough to know that most of what passed as conversation among them was pure swagger. Yet some stories were told more often than others.

There was the story Macena told of being forced off the family land in Jacmel by an unscrupulous older brother, a story that

◄ A *machann* selling herbs. Saut d'Eau, Haiti, 1981. Photograph by Jerry Gordon.

changed only in the details of how Macena would one day get even. Many years after the event, he still smarted from his brother's parting words: "If you ask me for that land again, I am going to kill you!" And there was the story of the surveyor in Port-au-Prince who took on an apprentice rejected by his family. There were hints that even this relationship, which had saved Macena's life, went sour in the end. But, in this case, Macena did not speak of revenge; he just called the old man a "donkey."

Macena liked to be thought of as an educated man. Many evenings before the sun set, he could be seen sitting on the balcony of Pension Hubert ostentatiously flipping the pages of a newspaper, shaking his head, and bemoaning the stupidity of the powerful. Hubert, the innkeeper and one of Macena's constant drinking companions, knew this to be a sham, but he never said so. The only time that old déclassé mulatto ventured any judgment of his own was at the bottom of a jug of rum shared with Macena, and at such times he was far more likely to ridicule his wife than to ridicule Macena.

Time passed. No one remembers how much time. It was 1888 or 1889 when the dapper young Alphonse Macena with the sharp eyes—at times seductive and at times cruel—arrived in Port-de-Paix. At least a year passed before Macena got a job as a surveyor in the mountain village of Jean Rabel, and it is likely that he worked there for a while before he met Marie Noelsine Joseph. But meet her he did.

Marie Noelsine, daughter of Joseph Binbin Mauvant and Manman Marasa, was fifteen years old when she and Macena saw each other for the first time. The attraction was sudden and mutual. Years later, when Macena grew drunk and sentimental rather than drunk and mean (his more common state), he would say that when he first saw her he thought she was an Indian. "She was real little and real black, but she had flat, flat hair . . . long, too . . . and green eyes!" She was so beautiful Macena almost fainted. That is what he said.

A small part of Macena was a hopeless romantic, and it was this part of himself he brought into full play, perhaps for the only time in his life, when he was courting his "Sina." He was a man of the world who wore a panama hat purchased in Port-au-Prince. She was a protected child who had never owned a pair of shoes and who never thought that meant anything until she met Alphonse Macena. At one and the same time, Macena robbed Marie Noelsine of a child's acceptance of the world in which she lived and brought more excitement into the life of this pubescent mountain girl than she had ever thought to hope for. The rising tides of Macena's ambition coincided with her own biological tides, carrying the young girl into a place of profound agitation and discontent. It seemed to happen overnight.

Before Macena's arrival, Sina had been a dutiful daughter. She had risen from her bed before dawn without complaint, to carry stacks of crisp, round cassava bread, baked the day before, to the roadside market her family ran at their front gate. She had taken simple pleasure in the small talk of her peasant neighbors who stopped to buy from her each morning. It was only after she met the stranger that she preferred to stay in bed in the morning, dreaming wistful, indefinite dreams. On those mornings, Manman Marasa had to call her more than once and by more than one name: "lazy," "ungrateful," "*malelve* [badly reared]."

Life was all intrigue in the months after Sina met Alphonse Macena. Each errand, each task was evaluated solely in terms of whether or not it could produce a meeting with him. More times than anyone knew or would have thought possible, Sina managed to bring a gourd of cool well water or a plump avocado to the place where Macena was working.

On those hot afternoons, which never came frequently enough for either of them, even the trees cooperated, casting a welcoming circle of shadow for the lovers. Macena would push his panama hat back on his head and begin to talk. At first, talk was slow and punctuated by pauses in which the two were more conscious of each other's presence than of what was being said. But gradually Macena would warm to his subject, and his hands would begin to dance through the air, shaping dreams and fantasies he preferred to call "things I have seen with my own eyes." Sometimes he would hear himself saying things he did not know he knew, and he would think to himself, "That's right! That's good!" Macena liked being with Sina. She was like a quiet mountain lake—a good place to gaze at his own reflection.

Macena came away from these clandestine meetings full of resolve, and impatience as well. The impatience he directed at the laborer who held the stick he eyed through his surveyor's level. And thus it was that passion grew out of words. Both Alphonse

Macena and Marie Noelsine Joseph desperately wanted worlds they did not possess and, furthermore, knew little about. Each came to believe escape was buried somewhere in the body of the other.

Mountain girls do not dream of weddings; only one in a hundred has a legal marriage. Sina was no exception. At the furthest reach of her dreams, she had an image of a "good man," someone who would protect the children he fathered and the woman who bore them for him. A good man built and repaired a house for his family, cleared the land, and even did the harvesting. Sina accepted that the rest was women's work: cooking, planting, routine gardening. Women also ran the markets, big and small. They sold the excess produce from the family land along with goods made with their own hands: bread, candy, herb teas, cooked food. In the economy of mountain life, sexual access was one of the most valuable commodities women traded.

Late one afternoon, during the early days of their courtship, Macena walked hand in hand with Sina along a tunnel-like path through the canebrake behind the Mauvant family compound. As they walked, Macena talked about a guinea hen—a beautiful, fat guinea hen a woman had offered to sell him that morning. They talked of other things while they walked, but the conversation kept coming back to the hen. When the failing light of early evening forced them back to the open road and eventually to the rickety old gate leading into Mauvant's property, the guinea hen was still being discussed. With her big toe, Marie Noelsine traced lazy circles in the soft brown dust beneath the gate. Without raising her eyes, she said quietly, *"Ou met achte* [You may buy]." Macena knew what she meant. He walked away from her that day toward a vermilion sky at the end of the country road, with his panama hat pulled down over one eye.

Before long, Sina was pregnant. For weeks after her father found out, the mere mention of Macena's name was sufficient to throw Joseph Binbin Mauvant into a fit. These men were enough alike—and different enough—to thoroughly dislike each other with integrity and with reason. Then one day Mauvant saw his daughter's swelling belly and watched her absentmindedly rub her lower back as she rose from squatting by the cooking fire. That was the moment when reality came hard up against Mauvant's stubborn pride and refused to surrender. It was not that Macena had made love to his daughter that bothered Joseph

Binbin Mauvant. What bothered him was that she had gotten pregnant, forcing Mauvant into a lasting bond, a family bond, with a man he did not trust. The old African feared that Macena was an opportunist who would soon forget that he had to give—and a lot more than guinea hens!—if he expected Marie Noelsine to tend to his needs. This fear proved well founded.

Not long after his grandson Mèdelice was born, Papa Mauvant sent word that he wanted to talk with Macena. The two sat for most of the day in the shade of the giant *mapou* in the center of the yard. Mauvant sat on his short-legged chair, tilted back against the solid, ancient tree. At first, Alphonse Macena hunkered in front of him, his panama hat resting on one knee, dark circles of perspiration forming under his arms. By noon, another chair had appeared, and the two men were trading drinks from Mauvant's jug of *kleren*. The next morning, word went out to the neighbors that a *kombit* (a cooperative work group) would be called together one week hence to pound the earth floor and thatch the roof of a new house on Mauvant's property. Sina never knew which of the men in her life had to convince the other of the wisdom of this arrangement.

Romance died quickly between Marie Noelsine Joseph and Alphonse Macena. Within months of the time they began to live together, the daily routine included at least one good fight between them and, for her, hard work from before sunrise until after dark. Macena stopped surveying, and, worse, he refused to form any attachment to the land in Jean Rabel. He spent his days drinking with his buddies, betting on the fighting cocks, and bitterly complaining about the far superior land in Jacmel that rightfully belonged to him. Their third child, Philomise, was born in 1896. By then Sina had given up hope. The only pleasure in her life during that period came from the company of the market women in Port-de-Paix.

Each Wednesday, Sina and a handful of other women from the family made the long walk down the mountain to sell in the town market. They rose in the middle of the night and gathered, whispering, in the yard. When the first among them heaved a sigh and moved toward her basket, the others quickly followed her lead. Each woman placed a circle of braided leaves on her head to cushion the weight of enormous baskets overloaded with fruits and vegetables. The first steps were always the hardest. As the band of six or seven headed down the dark path to the compound gate, a hand went out here and there to steady a cousin's load. Yet, by the time they were out on the main road, each had become familiar enough with the pitch and roll of her burden to find the compensating rhythms in her own body that provided balance on the long trek down the mountain.

Sina said she thought her luck was best when she sold at the far end of the Port-de-Paix market, near the crafty old herbalists and their odorous wares. The other women from the Mauvant family feared these women and their awesome reputations for revenge. But they let Sina go where she wanted.

Sina did not fear the old market women. She was fascinated by them and loved nothing more than listening to their gossip. The time she liked best came after sunset when she settled in to spend the night with them under the wide market portico. By the flickering light of a small fire, she could see only their wrinkled, toothless faces floating in a sea of blackness. Sina found this strange disembodied company conducive to careful listening and deep thought. She could attend for hours to story after story without saying a word. The old women liked Marie Noelsine from Jean-Rabel-in-the-Mountains, and they took care of her. She never had to worry about having something to eat on market days. They gave her soft juicy mangoes and cornmeal mush with hot peppers. On those nights after the Port-de-Paix market closed down, they shared their lives and hard-won wisdom with the young daughter of Joseph Binbin Mauvant.

A hand would emerge from the darkness to poke the fire under an oil tin in which they brewed lettuce-leaf tea. (Gargling with the tea helped to soothe sore spots in the mouth caused by the pipes they all smoked.) This slight movement or one like it was the signal that a new story was about to be launched. A quick dip with a metal cup; a quick swish and a gargle; a jet of liquid directed toward the gutter in front of the portico—a story.

Poverty and suffering were the threads of the tales they wove, but these women never whined or complained. The spice in their stories came from reports of lovers told to move on and children told to shape up or expect no food. Exploitative landowners, greedy market managers, and the real human *fatra* (garbage), the soldiers who collected spurious taxes from market women—all were threatened with the dire consequences of the women's magic. Sina let these stories brew in her heart. But time had to pass—years, in fact—and many things had to happen, including the mysterious disappearance of Joseph Binbin Mauvant, before the morning Sina rose from the company of sleeping hags and climbed the mountain to Jean Rabel, firm in her conviction that, if Alphonse Macena could not be pried from the house on her family land, she would simply leave.

Sina moved herself and her daughter Gloria to Gros Morne, about fifty miles south and east of Jean Rabel. Mèdelice, the oldest child and the only son, she left behind under the watchful eyes of Manman Marasa. She had already given Philomise, her youngest, into the care of the child's godparents, the Fouchards, storekeepers in Port-de-Paix. Sina departed before dawn without waking Macena to say good-bye. The end of the first day found her traveling on muleback along the dry riverbeds of the flat northwestern coastal plain with seven-year-old Gloria behind her, perched on a lumpy bundle strapped to the mule's broad haunches. For long stretches, the trip was hot and shadeless. Sina was forced to stop frequently to beg drinks of water from a succession of peasants like herself, whose huts dotted the road. She always addressed them respectfully as *komè* (sister) or *kouzen* (cousin). More than once, these gentle folk inquired in a polite and friendly way about the nature of her trip, and she left them shaking their heads over a man who had no respect for his family.

The journey took three and a half days. On the last and longest leg, Sina walked with one hand holding the mule's rope and the other resting lightly on Gloria's shoulder. The road to Gros Morne seemed to go straight up in places as it paralleled the reckless cascade of Les Trois Rivières. The mule stumbled along, exhausted and bleeding from ropes securing the sack that contained Sina's iron cooking pot and her modest bag of silver, accumulated during years of Wednesdays in the Port-de-Paix market. That old mule collapsed and died shortly after their arrival at the home of the cousin Sina sought in Gros Morne.

Marie Noelsine purchased a few acres of marginal land across the stream from the town center. With her own hands and the occasional help of her cousin's family, Sina built a one-room house, tight to the night's damp chill, the rain, and the wind. And then she built a brick oven in her backyard and began to make French bread from refined flour. Gradually, life improved, and before long Sina and Gloria were making regular trips to the big market on the bay of Gonaïves. They carried baskets brimming with sweet-smelling bread and heavier loads of sour oranges they had harvested from trees on their land. Just when things began to go well, Alphonse Macena showed up. In the end, it was simply a question of family loyalty. He was the father of her children; what else could Sina do but let him stay?

Alphonse Macena soon gained a reputation in the Gros Morne area for being rude, stingy, and malevolent and for having the meanest and luckiest fighting cocks on the mountain. Of all the roosters he ever owned, his favorite was named Leve Jipon Fanm-nan (Raise That Woman's Petticoat). People say the day that rooster died was the only time in his life Macena ever cried. He even gave it a real funeral, which was fitting because he loved the rooster more than any human being.

Six days out of seven, if anyone wanted to find Macena, they knew where to look: under the thatched pavilion on the far side of town where the cockfights took place. Down on his haunches, oblivious to the circle of denim-clad, sweating male bodies pressing in on him, Macena would speak to his rooster in the crooning voice of a lover. At the same time, he would hold the bird's tense body firmly between his hands and thrust him repeatedly toward the opponent on the far side of the ring. "Beautiful cock . . . Ayeee! . . . Strong cock . . . Haaaaa! . . . Earn for me. . . . Yesssssss . . . for me! For me!" Then, in a final good-luck gesture, Macena would put the whole head of Leve Jipon Fanm-nan into his mouth and draw it out slowly before throwing the bird into the quick and violent flurry of razor-sharp spurs and feathers. People said that if Macena's bird ever seemed about to lose, all he had to do was shout, "Leve Jipon Fanm-nan!" and within seconds the other cock was a bloody, twitching mass of dying bird flesh. Some said Macena always won because he used magic.

Although Leve Jipon Fanm-nan won consistently, Alphonse Macena never made money at cockfighting, for he wagered high stakes recklessly on other men's battles. Some of the more clever farmers from Gros Morne understood that they had only to challenge his courage to lure Macena into a foolish side bet. But they had to be careful because everyone knew Macena was the kind of man who could carry a grudge.

Shortly after his arrival in Gros Morne, Macena built a little house for the spirits some twenty yards from the back edge of his wife's property, where the land fell away, fast and steep, to the river below. He built it under the *labapen* tree where the two-headed serpent lived. The spirit house and the *gildiv* (rum distillery) were the only tangible contributions Macena ever made to the Gros Morne homestead. He allowed no one, not even members of the family, to go in the spirit house. In fact, if the truth be told, he rarely went in himself. Macena went to see the spirits only when he needed something.

One day the unexpected happened: Leve Jipon Fanm-nan died in battle. Rumor held that somebody had "done something" against Macena. Alphonse Macena strode back from the cock-fighting ring that day with the legs of the old fighter clenched in his fist, the bird's milky eyes fixed in a blank stare on the road churning inches beneath its lax beak. Macena drank in silence until midnight and then took the dead rooster to his spirit house. For a long time he sat unmoving. The only light in the hut came from a candle stub burning on one arm of a large red wooden cross planted in the earth floor. Thick ropes knotted here and there extended from the ceiling and corners of the room, binding the cross like an animal caught in a snare. The flickering candle flame multiplied the ropes through sevenfold shadows until it would have appeared to an observer—had there been one—that Macena was a spider lying in wait in the center of his web.

That was July, the last week of the month. For five months, Macena did nothing and said nothing against any of his neighbors. He had never been a big eater, but, after the death of Leve Jipon Fanm-nan, he consumed so little food and so much rum that the skin on his face began to sag like an old shirt hung from a peg in the middle of his forehead. Only the intensity of his eyes betrayed the inner man. Some people said he looked as if he had the spirits on him all the time. During these months, one of the neighbors saw Macena accidentally drop his tobacco pouch down the well. The oath that exploded from his mouth was still ringing in the air as Macena's body willed itself into the shape of a crab, which then scuttled down the well to retrieve the lost pouch.

Late at night, on the last day of December of the year Leve Jipon Fanm-nan died, Macena walked a half mile down the road. Without knocking, he entered a little house where a family of ten sat laughing and spinning tales. A hush fell on the group when they saw Macena's hard face. "This year was yours.

The next one is mine." That was all he said. He turned his back and walked home.

Back at his own house, Macena took a bottle of ginger beer and shook it up. Bam! It exploded, shooting its cork at the ceiling and spattering drops on all four walls. One second of silence followed. Then the soft chirping of the mountain night was split open once more, this time by a long, piercing cry from the house down the road: "Ayeeeeeeeeeee!" Bad medicine is simple like that. The wail was heard at midnight. By the next morning, men from that house were sawing wood for a tiny coffin.

After that, no one in Gros Morne tried anything against the sharp-eyed surveyor from Jacmel. In the end, it was Macena who did himself in. Macena had access to the spirits. In Jacmel, he had been given the *ason* and taught how to heal. He was a man with a lot of power; some said he could even raise the dead. What Alphonse Macena lacked was good manners. If a neighbor came by when food was cooking on the fire, Macena saw to it that the lids stayed on the pots until the visitor left. He did not like to feed the spirits, either. Macena had things backward—he had come to believe that the spirits, like his wife, were there to serve him.

One day, the family of a very sick man came to Macena as a last resort. Every other healer in the area had tried to bring the man back to health and had failed. Macena usually would have nothing to do with other people's problems, but this case was too much of a challenge to refuse. He yanked up the machete stuck in the earth floor of his spirit house, grabbed a dusty old straw sack filled with dried herbs, and went straightaway to the sick man's house. Macena summoned the spirits, but they told him to do nothing. They said, "This one is supposed to die."

When Macena emerged from the deep waters of trance and heard the message the spirits had left for him, he flew into a rage and whacked his machete so hard against the door frame that his patient screamed in fright and jumped from bed. His face pale with anger, Macena proclaimed: "I don't need the spirits. What do I need those spirits for? I am going to do it myself." And Alphonse Macena did just that. He healed that man. Macena was the one who died. The first sharp pains of the awful sickness that took Alphonse Macena's life began deep in his belly that very day, before he was halfway home.

As for Sina, she continued to work from before sunrise to long after sunset. With Macena no longer around, the neighbors began to stop by more frequently, and after a while some of the men started to court her. One offered to fix her leaking roof, another to clear a new field. Both meant to exchange their labor for her company at night, and Sina was tempted. But it soon became apparent that the spirits had another plan for her life.

The day after Macena's death, the water in Sina's well took on a strange taste and a foul odor. More than a year passed before the water was drinkable again. During that time Sina was forced to descend the steep bank to the river and carry water back up to her house. A strange thing happened one cloudy afternoon as she returned from the river with a heavy bucket balanced on her head. She was halfway up the bank when she heard a whistle: "Wheeeeeee . . . ou. Wheeeeeee . . . oooooooooou."

At first it seemed that the sound was coming from far away, but, in the next moment, it was right next to her. The whistling pierced Sina's eardrums and whipped round and round in her brain. Her hands flew up to cover her ears, and before she realized it, she dropped the bucket of water, and it tumbled down the embankment. A profound silence followed. Sina listened carefully and looked all around, but she could hear nothing, and she saw no one. After a minute or two, she simply shook her head and trudged back to the river to refill her bucket. On the second trip, when Sina reached the same spot, she heard the whistle again. This time she fainted.

Gloria became alarmed that her mother had been gone for such a long time, and she set out to look for her. She found Sina lying unconscious on the river embankment. Gloria panicked. "Manman . . . Manman . . . Manman!" she cried as she shook her mother and slapped her cheeks. Sina's eyes fluttered open. She gestured weakly to one side.

"You see that rock, Gloria?" she asked. "What rock? . . . Wha . . . wha . . . what are you talking about?" Gloria stuttered. Then she noticed a large, round, shiny rock inches from her mother's head. And at that very moment Ezili Dantò mounted Marie Noelsine Joseph. Sina's body snapped upright. Her eyes bulged, and her breath came in harsh gasps. The spirit reached out for the rock and shoved it toward Gloria. Then she gestured urgently toward the house.

Gloria understood. She ran to the house and returned in minutes with a plate of cornmeal and a candle. She lit the candle and set it on the ground. Then she took small pinches of corn-meal between her thumb and finger and traced a delicate heart around the rock. She put scallops around its edges and a cluster of arcane signs around its perimeter. Ezili Dantò watched this process carefully. When it was done, she opened her arms wide as if she wished to gather up the beautiful drawing, and she smiled broadly. Then Sina's head fell forward onto her chest. Dantò was gone.

When Sina felt strong enough to walk, she and Gloria picked up the rock and carried it back to the house. They placed it in one corner, and that night they surrounded it with tiny oil lamps flickering in twenty-one fragments of coconut shell. Throughout the night, the lamps burned, their light dancing over the walls of the hut. Sina and Gloria lay side by side on their mats. Neither one could sleep. Sometime in the middle of the night, Sina spoke. "It is better this way," she said. "I know the spirits want me. Before, I always said no. Now everything has changed. Now I will serve the spirits. They will take care of me. I do not need a man."

CHAPTER FOUR

Ogou

On July 21, 1979, Alourdes Margaux, the granddaughter of Alphonse Macena, held a feast for Ogou, the proud and powerful warrior who is her chief counselor from the spirit world. To protect herself from disapproving neighbors, Alourdes ordinarily keeps her doors and windows closed during Vodou events, but this proved impossible on that muggy summer evening. Vodou songs spread like soothing syrup, covering over the noise of restless rats in the ceiling and restive neighbors on their front stoops. Around two o'clock in the morning, Papa Ogou was presented with a fine, fat, red rooster. Before Ogou wrung the neck of the arrogant beast, it was given a "point name," as is the custom in Vodou ceremonies.[1] Ogou's rooster was solemnly baptized as "Leve Jipon Fanm-nan . . . Tonnè [Raise That Woman's Petticoat . . . Thunder]."

When Ogou came to ride Alourdes, he was outfitted in an impressive, red velvet military jacket with gold buttons and gold epaulets. Ogou's possession-performance began with a series of familiar gestures. Taking his ritual sword in hand and slicing the air in broad aggressive strokes, Ogou first attacked an invisible enemy. Then he took more controlled, menacing jabs at

---

[1] In the Vodou context, the word *pwen* (point) refers to a charm or talisman. A *pwen* may consist of words, gestures, ritual objects, or herbs rubbed into a small cut in a person's skin. In all cases, the point represents the condensation and appropriation of spiritual powers. During Vodou baptisms, sacred objects and sacrificial animals, as well as persons, are baptized. These baptismal "point names" are condensations of powerful truths. Ogou's rooster is therefore endowed not only with Alphonse Macena's considerable spiritual power but also with a cautionary coda against its misuse.

◀ A *manbo* offers a rooster to Ogou. Bedford-Stuyvesant, Brooklyn, 1979.

those members of Alourdes's Vodou family standing nearest him. Finally, in a gesture full of bravado that also hinted at self-wounding, Ogou turned the sword on himself. Lodging the point in one hip, he bent the rapierlike blade into an arc. Ogou performs his dance with the sword at nearly every public occasion on which he makes an appearance. Its elegant gestures are to body language what proverbs are to spoken language, a condensation point for complex truths: power liberates, power betrays, power turns on those who wield it.

Ogou, the warrior, condenses and re-presents the lessons of Haitian history. Haiti's military heritage is more convoluted than that of many nations. Although there is one grand and untarnished hero, Toussaint L'Ouverture, the leader of the successful slave revolution that began in 1791, Haitians are also accustomed to military liberators and political advocates who turn on them. In an attempt to restore economic and social stability, for example, Jean-Jacques Dessalines, the first Haitian head of state, forced people back into a life of servitude little different from the slavery they had just escaped. He was assassinated in 1806, after only two years in office. This story of promise and betrayal has been acted out many times in Haitian history. The occupation of the country by U.S. Marines from 1915 to 1934 and the continuing influence of the United States in Haitian political affairs provide material for many such stories.

In some ways, the most poignant morality tale of popular power gone awry is that of François Duvalier. Duvalier presented himself as a man of the people and a proponent of the philosophy of negritude. He was, among other things, a Vodou priest, and the grassroots political organization that put him in office was built partly through Vodou networks. After Duvalier became president, however, he used Vodou to intimidate people and control them.[2] He also continued the longstanding practice of utilizing the army as a domestic police force. To check the po-

---

[2]Stories are told about Vodou ceremonies in the National Palace during which Duvalier was possessed by his *gwo* Baron (big Baron). (Baron Samdi is the keeper of the cemetery and the head of all the Gede, spirits of the dead.) With his Gede riding him, Duvalier made a great show of knowing intimate details about the lives of those who worked closely with him—information that had in fact come from a network of spies.

litical ambitions of military leaders, he further compounded the forces of tyranny and oppression by arming community leaders, many of them Vodou priests, to form the civilian militia that became the dreaded Tonton Makout.

Through the countless Ogou possession-performances that occur in Haiti and in Haitian immigrant communities each year, many around Ogou's feast day in late July, Haitians remember their paradoxical military and political history. They preserve and analyze its lessons and apply them to the places in their own lives where power is the issue. To explore these issues as fully as possible, Ogou has subdivided. As Sen Jak Majè (Saint James the Elder), Ogou is a "man of war" who fights for what is right and just. As Ogou Panama, he is a *pèsònaj* (an important person) who demands to be treated with ceremony and deference. As Ogou Feray, he is fierce and uncompromising. As Ogou Badagri, he is shy, handsome, brave, and loyal. Yet, as Ogou Yamson, he is an unreliable drunkard who finds power in booze and swaggering talk; and, as Agèou, he is a liar and a beggar. And when Ogou is called by the names Achade or Shango (the two are sometimes conflated into one character), he is said to be a sorcerer.[3]

At times, Alourdes says there are seven Ogou, all of them brothers. At other times, she says there are twenty-one. In fact, I have encountered more than twenty-one in the temples of Haiti and New York. Ogou's tendency to subdivide indicates the pivotal position he occupies in Haitian traditional religion. The grand episodes of history and the small events of everyday life have brought such pressure to bear on Ogou that he has had to multiply in order to carry the weight. Haitians have loaded him with so much life experience that Ogou has cloned a small army to sort the lessons of that experience, package them, and re-present them to the people. Only one other Vodou spirit, Gede, master of the cemetery and grand arbiter of death, has subdivided to such an extent. (Gede is the subject of Chapter 12.)

[3]For a full discussion of the Vodou spirit Ogou, see Karen McCarthy Brown, "Systematic Remembering, Systematic Forgetting: Ogou in Haiti," in *Africa's Ogun: Old World and New*, ed. Sandra T. Barnes (Bloomington: Indiana University Press, 1989), 65–89.

Of the various Ogou, Panama is a particularly interesting example of how history is taken up in the Vodou temple and shaped into lessons for the lives of the faithful. Ogou Panama takes his name from the fashionable panama hat that was the trademark of President Florvil Hippolyte. In 1896 Hippolyte set out from Port-au-Prince on a punitive military mission designed to quell resistance—especially that of a certain Vodou priest—in the town of Jacmel. He vowed to burn the town and kill all the inhabitants except one man and one woman, who would be left to repopulate the region. As Hippolyte mounted his horse to leave, his panama hat fell off. The president's family took this as a bad omen and pleaded with him not to go, but Hippolyte persisted. Before he was out of Port-au-Prince, he fell from his horse, unconscious, and never recovered.[4] In Vodou temples today, people sing: *"Papa Ogou se nèg panama ye* [Papa Ogou is a panama man]." In songs of secular political satire, the falling panama hat has also become a cryptic reference to power that destroys the one who misuses it.

Through such "deep play" with character and context, Haitian Vodou brings the lessons of politics and war to bear on everyday life. Ogou teaches that to live one must fight. Pride, endurance, self-assertion, discipline, and a firm commitment to justice are qualities that bring success. But in one turn of the screw, pride can become lying braggadocio, endurance can become stubbornness, self-assertion fades into mere bullying, and discipline is transformed into tyranny. An overly developed sense of justice, one that is tempered neither by humor nor by graceful resignation, can lead to suicidal rage, especially for people whose life circumstances are as difficult as those of Haitians. In the Ogou who are alcoholic and indigent, one can still see the fierce soldiers who thought themselves invulnerable because they knew their cause was just.

Because the constructive and destructive parts of Ogou's character are so close together, none of the various Ogou is good or evil, right or wrong, in a simple, unqualified way. Each contains his own paradoxes of personality, which are teased out in

[4]See Harold Courlander, *The Drum and the Hoe: Life and Lore of the Haitian People* (Berkeley and Los Angeles: University of California Press, 1960), 150–52.

possession-performance and in song. In July of 1979, for example, Alourdes's community sang a lively song for all the Ogou:

> *Ki-ki-li-ki, o-ewa!*
> *Papa Ogou, tou piti kon sa.*
> *Papa Ogou, anraje.*

> Cock-a-doodle doo!
> Papa Ogou, all children are like that.
> Papa Ogou, enraged.

Such lean phrasing, replete with double and triple entendre, is characteristic of Vodou songs. From one perspective, Ogou is counseled in this song to show forbearance toward his children, his followers. From another, Ogou himself is a strutting banty rooster who throws childish tantrums when he cannot have his way.

Vodou spirits, unlike the Catholic saints whose names they borrow, are characters defined by contradiction. The Vodou spirits represent the powers at work in and on human life. The wholeness of the spirits—their ability to contain conflicting emotions and to model opposing ways of being in the world—gives Vodou its integrity as a religion.

Haitian Vodou is not a religion of the empowered and the privileged. Haitians have not had the choice of living with comforting fantasies about the forces that structure their lives and determine their fate. An open-eyed acceptance of finitude, which is central to the religion, is one reason the Vodou spirits have emerged as whole, three-dimensional characters. The oppressed are the most practiced analysts of human character and behavior, and Haitian traditional religion is the repository for wisdom accumulated by a people who have lived through slavery, hunger, disease, repression, corruption, and violence—all in excess.

The African slaves brought their religions with them, religions whose wisdom and insight operated on many levels in both the social and the natural worlds. Slaves were drawn from specific population subgroups, and they therefore had selective

Detail from an altar for Ogou showing Ogou's sword and the chromolithograph of Saint James. Alourdes's home, Fort Greene, Brooklyn, 1980.

memory. But, once on the other side of the ocean, they also had selective needs. Slaves in the New World reground the lens of their religion to allow it to focus in exquisite detail on the social arena, the most problematic one in their lives. The spirits they brought with them from Africa shifted and realigned in response to their needs. Some were forgotten; others were given a centrality they never had in the homeland.

As a result of this shift, the cosmos became thoroughly socialized. Ancient African spirits submerged their connections to the natural world and elaborated their social messages. Ogou is a good example. This Yoruba spirit's association with ironsmithing and his roles as the protector of hunters and clearer of forest paths are barely detectable in the Haitian Ogou. In Haiti, his connection to soldiering has come to define his character, because this is the role in which Haitian slaves and their descendants have needed him most. Few arenas of life are as problematic for Haitians as the military, and few Vodou spirits receive as much emphasis in contemporary urban Vodou as Ogou.

In some parts of the Haitian countryside, distinct "nations" of Vodou spirits can still be found. These nations generally have names indicating their African origins: Ibo, Nago (Ketu Yoruba), Mandang (Mandingo), Kongo, Wangol (Angola), and Rada (probably for the Dahomean principality of Allada). In Port-au-Prince, however, two pantheons have come to dominate, generally by absorbing the others. These two are Rada and Petwo.[5] Ogou is an exception to this binary scheme for ordering the Vodou spirits, and his altars and his rites are kept distinct in urban Vodou temples.

A look at the contrasting moods of the Rada and Petwo spirits helps to explain why Ogou cannot be easily classified as one or the other. The Rada spirits are sweet-tempered and dependable; their power resides in their wisdom. If a promised sacrifice cannot be offered to them now, they can easily be convinced to wait until later. The Rada spirits are called *lwa rasin* (root *lwa*, root spirits). They are intimate, familial spirits who are given

---

[5] The latter is a name of uncertain origin, but its iconography is clearly Kongo. For a discussion of the Kongo origins of Petwo ritual vocabulary, see Robert Farris Thompson, *Flash of the Spirit: African and Afro-American Art and Philosophy* (New York: Random House, 1983), 179–84.

family titles such as Papa and Kouzen. They are offered libations of water, sweet liqueurs, herb-laced rum, and perfume.

The Petwo spirits, in contrast, are hot-tempered and volatile. They must be handled with care and precision. Debts must be paid and promises kept, or they will badger and harass those who serve them. The power of the Petwo spirits resides in their effectivity, their ability to make things happen. They are especially good at dealing with money matters. They are offered rum mixed with ingredients such as coffee, hot pepper, blood, and gunpowder. Small charges of gunpowder are set off in the temples for the Petwo spirits, and they are served with cracking whips and shrieking police whistles. Theirs is the iconography of slavery. Whereas Rada drum rhythms are sensual, elegant, and playful, those for the Petwo spirits are harsh, rapid, and exciting.

A case can be made that the contrast between Rada and Petwo is that between two archetypal social groups: family members and foreigners, insiders and outsiders, the oppressed and their oppressors.[6] Ogou cannot be easily assimilated into either group because, as a soldier, he must necessarily be in between, defending the one from the other. He carries swords and guns, Petwo implements; but he does so in the name of Rada values. Ogou can be both merciless and righteous. His location between family members and foreigners, furthermore, makes Ogou the ideal champion of the immigrant. In New York's Haitian communities, he seems to be served more frequently and more lavishly than any other Vodou spirit, with the possible exception of Gede. It is therefore no surprise that Ogou is Alourdes's main spirit.

Ogou's rich and complex lessons about power and its uses and abuses wove in and out of the many stories exchanged between Alourdes and the internationally known Nigerian (Yoruba) scholar Wande Abimbola during a late-night visit nearly two years after the July evening when Ogou had been presented with a rooster named for Alphonse Macena's fighting cock. I

[6] For a full discussion of the Rada and Petwo pantheons as representatives of the archetypal social groupings of insiders and outsiders, see Karen McCarthy Brown, "The Vèvè of Haitian Vodou: A Structural Analysis of Visual Imagery" (Ph.D. dissertation, Temple University, 1976), 80–112.

had met Wande Abimbola at Amherst College in the fall of 1980, when he was a visiting professor. He attended a lecture I gave at Amherst on Vodou in Brooklyn, and he expressed an interest in meeting Alourdes, whom I frequently quoted in the lecture. When he came to New York City the following spring, I offered to take him to her home for a visit.

A VISIT FROM THE AFRICAN OGOU

Abimbola was in New York to give a talk at the staid and proper Liederkranz Club on Central Park West in Manhattan. The event ended late, and it was almost midnight when we arrived at Alourdes's door in Fort Greene. Anticipating an important guest, Alourdes had unlocked the seldom-used sitting room on the first floor of her house. Plates of crackers and bottles of various drinks had been set out on the coffee table, amid the usual array of stuffed animals and plaster nymphs. At first, we were stiff and formal, perched on the edge of Alourdes's plastic slip-covers. Yet Abimbola treated Alourdes with the respect due a priestess of his own tradition. And when they began to exchange stories, Abimbola's tales were as honest, poignant, and self-revealing as those Alourdes told. Wande Abimbola seemed to find relief in her presence, and she seemed to draw energy from his.

Alourdes was understandably tired when we arrived, but in less than an hour she was wide awake and in top story-telling form. To enact events from her family history, she jumped from her place on the couch next to the professor. Sometimes she slapped him lightly on the knee to emphasize a point. Abimbola matched Alourdes story for story. Both Alourdes and Maggie would later say that they liked and trusted Wande Abimbola. As Alourdes put it: "That family business. He don't have to tell us that stuff." Maggie had her own way of affirming him: "These African priests, I've met them before. They are good men . . . not always . . . but I can tell from him that he was."

One of Alourdes's first tales concerned the fatal hubris of Alphonse Macena, which led him to undertake a cure the spirits had forbidden. Abimbola jumped in eagerly when her story was finished. "The very same thing happened to my father!" he cried. And he told a story about his father, a priest of Ogou and an excellent midwife. When the wife of a family member had difficulty giving birth, Abimbola's father intervened, against the wishes of the spirits. Her baby was delivered safely, but on his way home the old Ogou priest contracted a fever that marked the onset of a long and painful illness. "I know, I know," Alourdes murmured several times. "Your father a priest," she said, "my mother, too."

"I know you have Ogou, too . . . ," Abimbola began. "Papa Ogou my husband!" Alourdes cried. "I love him very much. He very, very special. He always help me—and my family . . . my family, too. He help everybody!"

"I am a priest of Ogou," Abimbola said, "because my father was. Even the people who live in the cities, even those who go to the university, their deep connections are to a rural village. That is still the place we call our home. No important decision can be made without going back to consult our elders. That is the way we are. Also, in my country it is a little different. Ogou has his own priests. And Ogou is not just a soldier. He is the one who clears the way. He opens a path through the forest, you know."

Abimbola took a sip of his 7-Up and continued: "Ogou also works with iron. So all the people who work with iron, even those young men who work in the big oil fields, they follow Ogou, too. Ogou is important to us because he teaches us how to handle the modern world—arms, machines, trucks, all that. Without Ogou, we could forget that the things man creates can turn on him, even destroy him. In Nigeria, in my country, Ogou is very important to the people."

Wande Abimbola was warming to his subject, and his voice became more and more animated. "Why, crime could be reduced to almost nothing if people were made to swear on iron! They go to a court of law and have to swear on the Bible, and they think, 'Well, what does it matter what I say? This is a book, just another book.' But if they had to swear on the sword of Ogou, that would be another thing!"

The mention of Ogou's role in ensuring justice triggered another story from Abimbola. "For a long time my father was head of all the Ogou priests. The Ogou priests had the responsibility of guarding the cities. One night, there was an accident. The priests killed a cook. They had seen him wandering outside the city gates late at night and had mistaken him for a robber.

They were charged with murder and set for trial. By accident, my father had not been on guard that night and so was not charged. But my father told the court that he ought to be charged instead of the others, because it was on his order that they had been sent to guard the town."

"Your father a good man," Alourdes quietly observed. Abimbola acknowledged her comment with a smile. "When the authorities would not listen, my father summoned all the Ogou priests from a wide, wide area to come and surround the court. He told them, 'Go ahead and convict these people, and my priests will destroy this town!' The men who had been charged were given light sentences and probation."

Alourdes suddenly rose from the couch and spun around to face Abimbola. She moved her feet in a light and lively step, spread out her arms, and sang, full voice:

> *Aye, Aye,*
> *Lapolis a rete mwen,*
> *Jij pa kondane mwen.*

> Aye, Aye,
> The police will arrest me,
> The judge will not condemn me.

Her burst of song passed like a summer shower. In another moment, she was seated next to a smiling Abimbola. "Sometime we sing that for Papa Ogou," she explained. "It mean even . . . even the police arrest me, the judge can't do nothing; the judge can't, you know, . . . *kondane* me." "Condemn," Maggie whispered, "the judge will not *condemn* me."

"My family don't have nothing to do with the court. Not in Haiti, not my family. Only one time my mother have to go before that judge. But that not her fault. That not because of something she do." With that preface, Alourdes began her story.

"My mother have a friend, a good friend, name Carline. Carline' mother very sick. My mother don't have no money to help her, but she say, 'I going to give you the deed to my house. You can borrow some money and take your mother to the clinic.'"

A long time passed, Alourdes said, and when Philo asked for

the deed, Carline at first claimed she had lost it. Then, after a while, she said she never had it in the first place. Eventually, Carline took Philo to court, claiming the house belonged to her. Bribes were made to the lawyer and to the judge. Philo lost the case—and her home. Adding insult to injury, the judge told Philo she would have to pay for the court costs. Because she had no money, they put her in jail.

Alourdes jumped to her feet again, acting out the drama of her mother's misfortune. "Before they put her in that jail, she just turn"—Alourdes turned toward Abimbola—"and she tell that lawyer, she tell that judge: 'Okay, go ahead and put me in jail, but I going to see you both dead. In three day you both going to dead. If it happen tomorrow, that not me! If it happen in forty-eight hour, that not me! In three day, that me!'"

Philo spent the weekend in jail, where, Alourdes told us, Papa Ogou paid her a visit. "He say to my mother, 'Come on! Let's go! That lawyer, that judge—they dead!'" Ogou told Philo to make a charm from two bricks, parsley, and a leaf from the *veritab* (truthful) tree. She was to bind the bricks together with the leaves between. On the top, she was to fasten a wick from a bit of twisted cotton soaked in oil. Then she was supposed to light the wick and drop the whole thing into a latrine. As soon as Philo was released from jail on Monday, that was exactly what she did.

That same day, she also went to the Church of Saint Andre in the nearby town of Leogane, and there she laid her case before the divine court. "My mother don't beg," said Alourdes, her voice rising. "She tell those spirit what to do. She say, 'That lawyer got to dead now! That judge too!'" And that very day, the judge keeled over in his courtroom, vomiting blood. As for the lawyer, he had a *kriz* (an attack) while walking down the street later the same afternoon. After his collapse, he was taken home to die in his own bed.

After a few moments of silence, Abimbola commented that Philo was "righteous" and that was why she could call down the powers of the spirits and command them the way she did. "But," he added, "you have to be very honest and always tell the truth . . . even to yourself. That is what makes it hard, always telling the truth."

"My mother teach me how to stop the rain," Alourdes responded, so quickly she seemed to have missed Abimbola's thoughtful comment. I was disappointed. I would have welcomed a discussion of the philosophy of magic, but Alourdes places little confidence in such abstract talk. Her attitude is typical of those who serve the spirits. Vodou seldom halts its kinesthetic and sensory drama to force its wisdom into concept or precept; proverbs, anecdotes, ancestral tales, and songs are the only vehicles subtle and flexible enough to cradle the messages when the truths of Vodou are put into words.

Alourdes had in fact caught the conversational ball Abimbola tossed to her, but, rather than playing at a philosophical game, she chose to run with it through her own experiential terrain. "My mother teach me how to stop the rain. You can't just do that all the time. But it very simple. If you only know, it so easy. But you not suppose to just do that . . . for just any reason. I only do it once, when I just a little girl—for my birthday party. Everybody going to come, and it raining, raining all day long. So I go out, and I just do that thing, and the rain stop. The cloud separate and the rain stop. Later, I tell my mother what I do, and she mad! She say, 'Why you do that thing for such a silly reason?' You can do it once, twice, but it no good if you do that all the time and not for good reason—just because you having a birthday party or something. Anybody who do that, you have to die by water. You have to!" Alourdes added that it is also possible to stop the wind; again, the magic is very simple.

Abimbola responded to Alourdes by talking about good medicine and bad medicine. Good medicine is a complicated thing, he said. It must be carefully prepared. But "bad medicine is very simple." "In my country, do you know—?" Abimbola started to use a Yoruba word and then thought better of it and started anew. "This is a thing made from maize or millet. You make it into a thick paste, and then that paste is wrapped in leaves. Everyone eats that all the time, especially for breakfast. All you have to do, if you want to harm someone, is get the wrapping from one that person has eaten. You put some things inside. You put it under your foot like this," Abimbola said, raising the toe of his left foot. "You step down a little bit, and they feel pain in their intestine." The toe of Abimbola's fashionable ankle-high boot moved halfway to the floor, and then his foot went all the way down. "You step down hard, and they will die because their intestine will rupture."

The conversation between Alourdes and Wande Abimbola lasted for more than two hours. From the beginning, it was clear that Maggie and I were meant to listen. We were the children, there to learn from the elders. As if to underline this role, our names were occasionally injected into a story: "Karen, you know that, right?" "Maggie, you remember I always telling you that." Such stories are never told idly. Surprisingly, the small amount of verbal instruction that accompanies Vodou initiation ceremonies pales in comparison to what is articulated in situations such as this.

It was late, and I drifted away from the conversation for a moment. My eyes moved sleepily over the walls of Alourdes's sitting room. Shelves covering one wall were filled with souvenirs from her clients: ashtrays, dolls, feather flowers, miniature dishes. On the opposite wall were color photographs of Maggie and Alourdes's oldest child, Johnny, along with pictures of movie stars and Catholic saints. Over the door a Vodou charm to protect the house hung next to a horseshoe entwined with a Palm Sunday cross. Dominating the room was a colorful plastic cut-out of the word *love*. Vodou and Catholic, American and Haitian—the elements were disparate, but the aesthetic was unified. The homes of Haitian immigrants in New York City share a common style. They are crowded but deeply hospitable places, sending the message that there is always room for one more: one more guest to spend the night; one more relative to stay until things get better; one more pretty object, regardless of the message it carries in another context—one more point of view on a complex world.

When I turned back to the conversation, Alourdes was telling Abimbola about the little black stone Joseph Binbin Mauvant vomited up and offered to the child Philo. Abimbola's response to this story made me think that perhaps Alourdes was more comfortable in a pluralistic world than was the distinguished professor from the University of Ife.

"I know," Abimbola said, "I know. I have seen these things with my very own eyes. It is sometimes difficult to believe the things that I saw as a child." He told a story about an Egungun he had seen several times during his childhood. (Egungun is a Yoruba masking cult.) "This was a hunter's Egungun, not like the others. He had a mask with just two horns sticking up from the top of the head. And the man who danced that mask came from another town. Every year he would come and dance, and then he brought up from his stomach three little iron pots, the kind with three legs, and they would dance on the ground. I saw that! Before he brought them up, he would move this way and that, and you could hear them clanking inside of him. And then he would go r-u-uuuuuup and take one out, and r-u-uuuuuup and then another, until there were three, and he would put them on the ground, and they would dance by themselves. Sometimes it is difficult to know how to think about that." For the first time Alourdes looked at Abimbola with genuine puzzlement.

As we rose to leave, Alourdes invited Abimbola to see her altars downstairs. The African professor stood aside to let Maggie go through the living-room door. As she passed, he asked her if she was learning all these things from her mother. It was the first time he addressed her directly all evening. There was a touching urgency, concern, and even sadness in his voice. Maggie assured him with equal sincerity that she was indeed learning many things from her mother and that she had learned a lot from her grandmother as well.

A year earlier, I had taken another professor, an American with a longstanding interest in Haiti, to meet Alourdes. We picked up Alourdes and then went to a Vodou ceremony at the home of another *manbo*. When the event was over and the two of us were driving back to Manhattan, the professor fussed and fumed about the "uselessness of it all." Early in the evening, before the rituals began, the group had briefly discussed the upcoming national elections. The year was 1980 and Ronald Reagan was making his first bid for the U.S. presidency. Everyone was concerned about the cuts in social services they knew would come if Reagan were elected. "Lot'a people going to suffer," Alourdes observed.

But a substantive political discussion proved too uncomfortable for this group to sustain—especially with two *blan* (whites) in the room. So the group quickly moved to a ritualistic, although not entirely unrelated, argument about Haiti's first head of state, Jean-Jacques Dessalines. Everyone acknowledged that he had forced recently freed slaves back into servitude in an attempt to restore the country's economy. But he had also exacted swift and satisfying revenge on the whites left in Haiti. Was he a demon or a savior? Some saw it one way, some another. The men postured and yelled and acted out. Before long, Alourdes threw her arm over the back of the chair next to her and set her eyes on the ceiling with studied disdain. The rest of the women quickly followed her into superior silence.

"Why do these people spend their time doing this?" my professor friend asked, referring to both the homemade little Vodou party we had just seen and the pretend politics that had preceded it. "What would you have them do?" I shot back. "Well," he said, "they could get together and learn how to make Molotov cocktails."

VODOU AND POLITICS

People often ask if I think Vodou keeps the people of Haiti poor and oppressed. I respond that although Vodou, like every other religion, has sometimes been misused by tyrants and scoundrels alike, guns and money have far more to do with perpetuating the suffering of Haitians than religion does. Vodou comments on and shapes life, but it hardly creates it ex nihilo. If the Haitian army were not thoroughly corrupt, if little Haiti were not in the backyard of one of the world superpowers, if Haitians in New York were not regularly losing jobs because someone fears that they have AIDS or practice "black magic," then perhaps a question could be raised as to whether Vodou is a positive force in Haiti. But if those things were different, Vodou would also be different. Vodou works within the realm of the possible and practical.

At times in the distant past, and once in the recent past, revolutionary change seemed possible. In the war that eventually liberated the Haitian slaves, traditional religion played a key organizational role. It also played a role, although it is not yet clear how large a one, in the freedom movements surrounding Jean Claude Duvalier's ouster in 1986. Yet, for the great majority of Haitians, their experiences of repression at home and racism abroad have been far too tangible, persistent, and effective to nurture revolutionary ideas. When the use of force seems suicidal, Vodou introduces Ogou Badagri to teach the lessons of pride and endurance. And there is also Agèou, the liar, who teaches people how to duck, how to bob and feint. These are the practical survival skills Haitians use every day of their lives.

Bobbing and feinting come naturally to adults who have lived under the severe political repression of Duvalierist Haiti. For example, even legal immigrants in New York use a variety of names for themselves—one for family, another for co-workers, yet another for the telephone company. Secretiveness is a lesson taught by example and one that children learn early. Although the young children in Alourdes's household were born in the United States and have no firsthand experience of Haiti's repressive political climate, they too have come to recognize the usefulness of Ogou's skillful deception. No one has to remind them that the drama of Vodou that goes on regularly within their home is not to be discussed outside.

Alourdes and Maggie are convinced that their well-being, even their survival, depends on service to the spirits. The depth of their commitment explains the fierce pride with which they hold on to their controversial religious practice. Maggie once told this story: "When we just moved in the neighborhood, my brother William told his friends that my mother does Vodou and stuff like that. And then all these people have in their mind that she is a Vodou lady, she is bad. Most of the neighborhood people don't bother talking to us . . . which I don't care about anyway! We just keep ourself to ourself."

Sometimes even the people Alourdes successfully treats remain ambivalent about Vodou. They come alone and at night; they ask her not to tell anyone they have been to see her. Alourdes accepts the attitudes of her clients and neighbors without agreeing with them. And, to some extent, she adjusts her behavior to take account of such prejudice. She does her healing work in a small basement room that can be locked against the prying eyes of strangers. When I first met her, the altars in that room were on tables, in the open. Over the years, the tables have gradually been exchanged for cabinets with doors that can be closed. Reactions to prejudice have also shaped Vodou rituals in New York. "Here, you just invite couple people. They come in, sit down, clap the hand," Alourdes said. "But in Haiti, they have big yard. You can invite a lot'a people. They beat the drum. Here, you cannot do that because of the neighbor."

American popular culture dwells on images of Vodou's malevolence, an attitude as nonsensical as equating Catholicism with Satanism. The understanding most North Americans have of Vodou is derived mainly from its portrayal in novels, films, and television, where images of sorcerers, *zonbi*, snakes, blood, and violence abound. In the United States, the word *voodoo* is used in a casual and derogatory way to indicate anything on a spectrum from the deceptive to the downright evil. If it were not so clear that racism underlies these distortions, it would be hard to understand why this kind of stereotyping is tolerated for an African-based religion when it would not be tolerated for other religions.

The negative portrayal of Vodou in the press, in novels, and in travelers' accounts began in earnest shortly after the Haitian slaves won their freedom, a period in which slavery was still practiced in the United States and in many European colonies. The argument was often explicitly made that the barbarism of their religion clearly demonstrated that Haitians were incapable of governing themselves—an argument used by the United States and several countries in Europe to justify their refusal to recognize the fledgling black republic. Racism is more covert and convoluted these days, but the same stereotypes of Vodou still serve its purposes. One of the central ways such propaganda works is by characterizing Vodou as in every way the opposite of "true" religion, that is, of Christianity. This description is ironic, for people who serve the Vodou spirits consider themselves good Christians.

Haitians see no conflict between practicing Catholicism and serving the spirits, whom they never refer to as deities. "They have only one God for everybody, and I think everybody love God," Alourdes said. "I love God plenty. I got confidence in God. But I love my spirit, too, because they help me. If God don't give that help, that strength—spirit can do that for you."

Bondye (God) is singular and supreme in Haitian Vodou. He is a deity with roots in the Christian god as well as in the so-called high gods of West Africa. Yet in the Haitian view of things, Bondye, like his African models, rarely gets involved with individual human lives. Attention to the everyday drama of life is the work of his "angels," the Vodou spirits. Of course, equating Bondye and the Christian god and calling the Vodou spirits his angels are also political strategies that have roots going back to the time of slavery.

Ogou

Vodou is different for each person who deeply engages with it, because each person concentrates on his or her own particular spirits. Although Alourdes routinely honors all the major spirits, she has half a dozen on whom she focuses most of her ritual activity. It is understood within Vodou that the spirits select their special devotees, not the reverse. The spirits Alourdes concentrates on are those who have "chosen" her, who "love" her, and whose "protection" she has inherited from earlier generations within her family. They are the ones featured on her altars and routinely called on for assistance in her healing practice. Singly and in relation, these spirits, who give their names to the chapters in this book, shape and guide her professional and personal life.

Alourdes makes no major decision without consulting one or more of these spirits. All significant events are filtered through the sieve of their personalities, and their character traits and patterns of behavior frame her choices. But the spirits are not moral exemplars. Nor do they dictate exactly what she is to do, although from time to time some of the spirits give advice. More commonly, through possession-performance, the spirits explore all the potentialities, constructive and destructive, in a given life situation. In this way they provide the images that allow Alourdes to reflect on problems and to make her own choices about the most appropriate and effective ways of dealing with them.

Within Alourdes's group of special spirits, one stands out. He is her *mèt tèt* (the master of her head), Ogou Badagri. But the dominance of Ogou Badagri in her life and in her character does not go unchecked. The other spirits with whom she has a close relationship counterbalance Ogou Badagri's weight. For example, even if a situation has called out the aggression of the Ogou in Alourdes, Gede can possess her and put the matter in an entirely different light through his iconoclastic humor. Thus her view of the world and the moral choices she makes within it emerge from the chemistry of the interaction among her spirits.

The personality of the *mèt tèt* and that of the devotee tend to coincide, an intimate tie hinted at in the occasional identification of the "big guardian angel" (*gwo bònanj*), one dimension of what might be called a person's soul, with the Vodou spirit who is his or her *mèt tèt*. Diagnosing which spirit is a person's *mèt tèt*, something that is not determined by inheritance alone, amounts to a kind of personality typing. Thus, someone with Ogou as a *mèt tèt* is expected to be brave, assertive, loyal, and so forth. The specific Ogou identified as the master of the head adds nuance to this general portrait. For example, all the Ogou are quick to anger, and some mete out stiff punishment to offenders. Alourdes once said that Ogou Feray has been known to bang his sword on his own head—that is, on the head of his horse—when that horse had made him mad. But Badagri, Alourdes's Ogou, handles his anger in another way: he withdraws and withholds. "When he angry, you just don't see him. You feel it, but you call him . . . he don't come," Alourdes said. The way she herself deals with anger reflects the Badagri "in her head." Tempered by life, she is never frivolous with this potent emotion. I have seen her sulk and withdraw many times, but I have never seen her rant and rave.

Ogou Badagri possesses Alourdes more frequently than any other spirit, with the possible exception of Gede. He is almost always involved in treating the problems her clients bring to her. Because Alourdes has gone through the Vodou marriage to Ogou Badagri, she calls him her "husband."[7] She sets aside one night a week for him. On this night, she receives the handsome soldier in dreams, and no human lover shares her bed. On Wednesday, Ogou's day, Alourdes always wears his color, red.

In describing Ogou Badagri, Alourdes could well be describing herself. Badagri will not tolerate injustice. To illustrate this trait, Alourdes gives a homely example: "If you nagging people—you know, teasing—when they don't do nothing, he can get mad about that." Disloyalty is equally intolerable: "If you do something, like, you make money for him and you spend it for no reason—that make him very angry."

Badagri is also known for his good looks, his generosity ("he love to give—even he angry, he give; he like to spoil people"), his expertise in treating people's problems ("he just father for everybody; he love to make treatment"), and his penchant for hard work ("he *love* hard work"). But the most striking part of

---

[7] The *mèt tèt* is not the only appropriate candidate for marriage. Alourdes, for example, has also married Kouzen and Danbala.

Ogou Badagri's character is his ability to endure in the face of trials that would break many others. This quality is portrayed in Alourdes's favorite song for him, depicting a conversation between Ogou Feray, head of the army, and Badagri, the loyal soldier who stands guard:

> *Ogou Badagri, sa ou ap fè la?*
> *Ou sèviye; m'ap reveye.*
>
> *M'ta dòmi, Feray; m'envi dòmi, o.*
> *M'ta dòmi, Feray; m'pase dòmi, o.*
> *Se nan lagè mwen ye! Ou mèt m'reveye!*
> *O Feray, o.*
> *Gason lagè mwen ye! Yo mèt m'reveye!*

> Ogou Badagri, what are you doing there?
> You are on watch; I am going to wake you.
>
> I would sleep, Feray; I need to sleep, oh.
> I would sleep, Feray; I am beyond sleep, oh.
> There is a war going on! You must wake me!
> O Feray, oh.
> I am a soldier! They must wake me!

Forsaking attack, Alourdes, like Badagri, chooses watchfulness. She draws her power around her like a cloak, holding it close to her body. She does not dream of extending herself outward and conquering the world. Rather, she controls what experience has taught her she is able to control—herself. As it does in Ogou Badagri, Alourdes's fighting spirit comes to a keen focus in her pride and self-respect. Her current life strategy is to follow the rules, conserve her energy, and practice constant vigilance. This strategy has gotten her through both short-term crises and long-term hardship. Like Badagri, Alourdes endures.

"THE POLICE WILL ARREST ME"

In March of 1981, Alourdes's strategy was challenged. Her son William was arrested for purse snatching. Her first response was disbelief that anyone in her family could do such a thing. Then came anger, which quickly gave way to fear, as she was forced to deal with the police and the courts, institutions she deeply distrusted.

Alourdes has four children, three of whom were born in Haiti; William is the youngest of these three. William suffered brain damage from a bout of meningitis in infancy. Years later, testing by the New York City public school system indicated that his IQ was between 55 and 57. In the tradition of Haitian families, there has never been any thought of putting William in an institution. His place in Alourdes's household is guaranteed; and in the event of Alourdes's death, Maggie would assume the same commitment. Underlying this stance is an unarticulated belief that ignoring family responsibilities endangers the care and protection of the spirits. In providing the considerable care William requires, Alourdes and Maggie do not consider themselves martyrs. Neither do they infantilize William. He can be difficult, and Maggie and Alourdes do not spare him when they are annoyed.

William was twenty-one when he was arrested. He had the tall, strong body of a man, although his mind and heart were still those of a child. He vacillated between cloying eagerness to please and stubborn resistance to rules. Entrusted with two subway tokens and money for lunch, William made his own way each day to the trade school he attended in Greenwich Village. If he got in trouble, it was usually because he gave his lunch money away or got sidetracked on his way home. William could not say no. He would do anything for anyone if it would earn him a thank-you or a moment to bask in the glow of friendship. Although the full story was not known at first, this need to please had led to his involvement in the purse snatching. Another young man from the trade school had actually taken the purse. He had given it to William to hold, and William had complied. Because the other boy was too young to face criminal charges, William went through the frightening experience of jail and court appearances alone.

The police advised Maggie and Alourdes to be at the courthouse at ten o'clock on the morning after William's arrest. I arranged to pick them up in Brooklyn at nine-thirty. Snow was coming down fast and thick that day. The roads were slippery and the driving difficult. Maggie answered the door, looking dreadful. She wore no makeup and had done nothing with her hair but comb it to a stand-off. She paced the hallway in her overcoat, shaking. Maggie had not slept. "I am too nervous," she said. "You got to get those name for me. I cannot do it. We got to know the police officer' name . . . the judge' name . . . the name of that woman with the pocketbook. If we got those name, my mother can fix it."

I found Alourdes sitting on her bed watching television. Although we were running late, she said we could not leave until her friend Soeurette arrived. Insecurity had generalized itself, and Soeurette had been called to watch the empty house while we were gone. With her back to me, Alourdes kept a dispassionate eye on the television. After a time, she began to talk in a small, tired voice.

"I hope," she said (meaning "I wish"), "my mother is here and I just a little girl, and I don't have no responsibility. I just eat . . . I sleep . . . I play. When I was little girl, I say, 'Oh, boy, when I am going to grow up?' Now I am sorry. You give them everything they want, a bed to sleep in, food to eat. If they need shoes, you give them shoes, clothes, everything they want. . . . Oh, boy, I hope my mother is here. When I little girl, she give me everything . . . well, maybe if I could not get shoes right now, I get them next year! Same thing."

Then, in a more desperate tone, Alourdes continued: "Why they not call me and tell me William is dead? Just tell me come down to that place where they keep dead people and get him. Then I call you, Karen. You help me. We sad. Then it's finish. Why he not just dead?" I stood staring at Alourdes's back, unsure whether these words had offended my sense of compassion or my sense of propriety.

Soeurette bustled in the door shortly after ten. Alourdes greeted her with a sullen stare, followed by accusations. Like a nervous, clucking hen, Soeurette responded, "It not my fault, *cheri*. The car had no heat, and we had to drive slow." Excuses are mandatory; it is not mandatory that they have any logic.

The snow continued to fall in huge feathery flakes. The wind on the Brooklyn Bridge blew the snow up, down, and sideways all at once. The tension inside the car mounted. Alourdes withdrew into herself. Sitting in the front passenger seat, she hunched her shoulders and hung her head, staring at her fingers as she braided and unbraided the fringe on her wool scarf. Maggie was more anxious than depressed, talking nonstop. She made occasional brave attempts at light conversation, but more often she fell into blaming either William or herself for the crisis. Throughout the short trip, she scrambled around the back of my station wagon using her mittens to wipe off the windows.

We soon confronted the imperial architecture of the criminal courts building in lower Manhattan, at 100 Centre Street. The heavy revolving door could have accommodated a person ten feet tall. Inside, the marble was cold and endless. Feet wet with snow made us feel even more precarious. This was purgatory, the ultimate in liminal places. The hallways seemed wider than the offices that clung along their edges, yet these huge hollow spaces were not waiting rooms. There were no chairs or benches, no ashtrays. People smoked furtively, getting away with something each time they put out a cigarette on the floor. Purgatory did not provide public restrooms. We had to get directions, negotiate a maze, and then ask permission to use a toilet that seemed to be there for someone else. The building overwhelmed Alourdes. "Oh, boy, this building solid . . . yes!" she said, craning her neck at a massive marble pillar. "Look at that staircase—iron!" "Tel-e-phone," she read, tracing her finger over brass letters set in marble. "Telephone in there? Oh, boy, this building . . . everywhere gold . . . beautiful . . . yes."

A few basic rules, quickly learned, helped us sort out the social parade moving through the halls of the building. The accused were black or Hispanic and wore scruffy clothes. Lawyers were white and wore suits. Anyone dressed like the Marlboro man in jeans, a flannel shirt, and a down vest was a police officer waiting to testify. Although we had been told that in 90 percent of the cases no family members showed up, dozens of them were roaming the halls. A slender Puerto Rican woman with tight jeans and red, brimming eyes yanked her daughter's arm and screamed: "You better behave or—!"

Officer Reese flinched and instinctively backed off when Alourdes greeted him with the question: "You the man who arrest my son?" Reese was short and kind, paunchy and puffy-eyed. As the day wore on, the smell of alcohol came on his breath, yet he never seemed drunk, only tired. He told us what to do to move things along, and he waited patiently outside the doors of the crime bureaucracy. "It doesn't bother me," he said, "I get paid for it." Later, he offered an indirect apology: "I've seen too many things. I'm suspicious. I didn't know if William—that's his name?—is retarded or just putting me on. I thought maybe he was making fun of me. That happens, you know." Reese's partner was a tall black man named Matthews, who took the time to talk with William and uncover his innocence of spirit. He described William as "hurt by a night in the slammer" and a long day in the "holding pens."

Hours passed as we moved from office to office checking on the progress of William's case. We made the rounds from the room on the second floor where papers are compiled, to the docket room where each case is assigned a number, to the little window with bars on the first floor where a list of the next cases to be heard is available. My white face, my polite requests, and the right clothes (I was wearing my grandmother's old rabbit coat, which, if not inspected too closely, could pass for something finer) got me quicker and more courteous responses than others seemed to be receiving. The face behind the barred window asked: "Are you the attorney?"

When there was nothing more to do but wait, I looked at Alourdes and said, "Aren't you warm? Don't you want to untie your scarf . . . open your coat?" "Yes," she replied but made no move, so I untied her scarf and unfastened the top button of her coat. She suffered my attentions in an unprotesting, even grateful, way, as a child might. Alourdes gave herself over to me much as she surrendered to the legal system, trusting that she would be told the right way to do things.

Maggie, however, was filled with venom from the moment we first found ourselves dwarfed by the pillars of justice. "You know what I am going to do? I am going to beat him with a *resiyòl. Resiyòl* is a thing like . . . a . . . a . . . whip. In Haiti they use that on animals. They use that on people, too!" And moments later: "You know what I am going to do? I'm going to kick him in the knockers," she said, jerking her knee up sharply. "You see how I am going to do it?"

When Alourdes talked, which was not often, she also blamed William. "Why he got to do that? He know he can't bring no pocketbook back to my house." But she also questioned: "William not like that. You know me, Karen. All the time, I just leave my pocketbook. Also I got two big jar full of dime and quarter. He never take nothing." In her mind, William's major offense was disloyalty. "When he do something like this, he not just do it hisself. He got family behind him. We got to come down here.

We got to talk to policeman. When I little girl, sometime I bad— but not like this. I never do nothing serious. I know I got my mother . . . my father to think about."

It had already been a long day, and I was finding it difficult to think of anything to say to Alourdes. I searched lamely for an encouraging word: "You know, someday we will laugh about all of this. It will be funny." Alourdes, who had been dry-eyed all day, began to cry. Her crying was more movement than sound; she bent over and covered her face, and her body quaked like a mountain about to erupt.

Eventually we learned that William would be arraigned in night court, which did not convene for several hours. Alourdes would have stood in purgatory and waited patiently for her turn. Maggie, however, wanted to go back home, "pick up the children, do the laundry." Given the chill inside and the weather outside, neither idea seemed practical to me, so I talked them into going out to eat. Snow and wind were driving in our faces as we walked toward Baxter Street and Forlini's northern Italian cuisine. Alourdes, like an oversized elf in her brown coat and peaked hood, bent into the wind and cried: "*Woy! Woy!* I can't walk! Help me!"

It was early, and Forlini's was virtually empty. White cloths were spread on all the tables except one, the booth in the back of the restaurant, closest to the kitchen. Stifling her initial impulse to seat us there, the hostess directed us to the booth in front of it. Alourdes tucked her napkin under her chin, "so I don't get no food fall on my clothes," and told me to order for her. We each had a glass of red wine. Maggie had soup, and Alourdes and I split an order of stuffed shells with a green salad.

Alourdes commented on her inability to drink: "One little glass of wine and my head begin to spin." Picking up her wine glass and swaying from side to side, she demonstrated how alcohol affects her. (I had a brief but alarming fantasy of having to move Alourdes's unconscious body the length of a restaurant in which waiters carried folded linen napkins over their arms.)

"But what I don't understand," Alourdes said, sitting up straight and looking chipper for the first time all day, "is how the spirit can drink. Papa Ogou come, he drink a lot of rum. He drink but . . . when he gone, I don't feel nothing." "You don't smell no alcohol on your breath, nothing!" Maggie added in an

animated voice. The waiter checking accounts at the booth behind us turned to look at us over the banquette. Switching from
English to Creole, we continued the conversation in our private
language.

Maggie and Alourdes seemed grateful for a moment in which
to act as if tragedy were not lurking around the corner. But before long William was once again the topic of conversation. So
far, there had been no opportunity to talk with him, and no one
had been able to give us any answers about what had happened. (Later, we would all be surprised that we assumed
William took the purse.)

"Why he got to do that?" Alourdes fumed. "Dummy," Maggie interjected. Hesitantly, I entered the fray. "I don't want to
interfere in your family life . . . ," I began. Simultaneous pro-
tests came from Maggie and Alourdes: "Don't say that! You are
family." And so I talked about my fear that William would close
down if they were too hard on him. I suggested that maybe that
night they should simply tell him they loved him; tomorrow
they could tell him that what he had done was wrong. "He has
already had enough of a lesson for today," I concluded. The
wine had made us earnest, and I was vaguely aware that the
rhythms of our speech (often shifting into English mid-sentence
and then back to Creole before the thought was complete) were
careening around the restaurant.

Maggie became painfully self-reflective. "You know, you are
right. Just now I am thinking about some things. I call William
'dummy,' and all the time he wanting to kiss me, and I am busy
and I say to him, 'Don't do that.' I should not be like that." More
quietly and using English, as she usually does when talking
about her life in New York, Maggie continued: "You know I am
sitting here with my college degree [an associate's degree in
early childhood education from Brooklyn College], and I take
all these classes, and I don't know nothing. Maybe if I could just
go back and get my books. . . . If I could read, maybe, Piaget—
and there was another book, I cannot remember that name—if I
could read, maybe I could understand. I could set up a program
to help William. I am his sister!"

Alourdes reflected, too. "I am always saying to William, 'Why
don't you just get out and leave me alone?' And I mean that."
We finally settled on a comparison between William and the
children, Kumar and Michael. William was like a child who

needed both punishment and love. The conversation seemed important, and things seemed clearer. The wine helped to sustain both impressions.

While we were in the restaurant, darkness fell and the snow stopped. Alourdes was more relaxed on the walk back to the courthouse, and, after two glasses of wine apiece, Maggie and I were even looser. Impulsively, I leaned over backward on the trunk of a car, into a virgin crust of snow with two inches of powder beneath. Flapping my arms up and down several times, I made a snow angel for Alourdes and Maggie. They had never seen one.

The arraignment happened quickly. The Legal Aid Society had appointed an attorney who was soothing but not very interested in giving or receiving information. He rushed into the courtroom only minutes before William's case was called. After shaking hands all around, the attorney drew us outside for a hasty consultation. When Maggie launched into a stream of explanations and questions, he hushed her with a question of his own: "Did any of you know the woman whose purse was stolen?"

"What was her name again?" I asked, catching Maggie's eye and winking. "Pointer," he said, "Laura Pointer." Back in the courtroom, I took out the envelope from a telephone bill received that morning. I wrote "Laura Pointer" beneath the names of the judge and the arresting officers, folded the envelope, and handed it to Maggie. Accessory to magic!

William came through the door beside the judge's bench, a uniformed officer holding his left arm. The official procedure passed in largely inaudible tones at the front of the courtroom. The only comment from the lawyer that drifted our way was about the other boy taking the bag and handing it to William. A court date was set, March 26, and William was released without bail.

Outside the courtroom, the attorney explained that there had been an offer of a misdemeanor charge, but he had advised William not to plead guilty to anything. "Stay in touch," he said, handing me his card, and then he ran off toward another courtroom and another case. We stood in the now-familiar hallway for several minutes more: William, Alourdes, Maggie, myself, and the two arresting officers. The relief we felt at William's release was palpable. Everyone was thanking everyone else profusely—everyone except William, who looked dazed.

In the midst of the hubbub, Maggie grabbed the lawyer's card from my hand and said to Officer Reese: "See! See, I will show you if I was lying. I was not lying, you will see. Here, William. Read this! Read this line!" The line on the card read "Associate Attorney." William made a good guess. "Lawyer," he said. Officer Matthews shoved aside the awkward moment with a comment as unrealistic as it was caring: "I used to have trouble with reading, too. I understand. You can do it, William. Don't you ever believe that you can't. You just have to work at it."

Maggie had not cried all day, not until the moment it was clear that William would be released without bail. Then she had turned to me with a hoarse whisper: "Get me out of here!" Her muffled sobs had accompanied us out of the courtroom. In the hallway, Maggie's emotional spin began again. The talk came faster and faster; things were said too many times and too loudly. Whatever restraint Maggie intended to exercise with William was gone by the time we cleared the door and felt the cold air in our faces.

"Did you take that pocketbook?" Maggie snapped. William started to protest, but no one listened. Then Maggie linked her arm with William's and struck up another tune. "Anything you ever want, you just come to me. I will give it to you. You know you always got your sister." William said nothing.

"THE JUDGE WILL NOT CONDEMN ME"

Maggie took charge after that first day in court. She kept track of the details of William's case, making regular telephone calls to the Legal Aid office. Her calls were not always returned. In fact, as the hearing date of March 26 approached, it became more and more difficult to get anyone there to speak with her. The evening before William was to appear in court, the lawyer finally called. He did not know how the district attorney intended to proceed with the case; the prognosis was "anybody's guess." The family was nevertheless to show up at ten o'clock the next morning. And, oh, yes, he would not be able to be there, but the new attorney assigned to the case would have a complete set of his notes.

When I went to pick up Alourdes and Maggie this time, the mood was different. They were both dressed up and looking good, both wearing new wigs. Alourdes met me at the door, all sugar: "Karen, *ba'm nouvèl ou* [give me news of yourself]. Did you dream about me last night?" Her question caught me off guard: "Well . . . er . . . uh . . . I really don't know. I dreamed a lot last night, but I can't remember." I tend to take Alourdes too literally. In fact, her question was simply the prelude to telling me about her own dream. She launched into the account before I was in the door.

"I dream my mother last night . . . like I just forget she dead. In that dream, it like my mother sleeping, and she just wake up and hear me talking. My mother say to me, 'What that you say?' I say 'I don't say nothing. I just sitting here.' She say, 'Who that you talking with? I don't believe you!' She take a flashlight and shine it all around, and she say, 'I see you talking to somebody . . . I see that!'"

Alourdes's dream made me smile. If only in sleep, she had succeeded in becoming a young girl again, with no responsibility. I had heard many stories about her clandestine courtships as a young woman, and I also knew that, with little or no electricity in the poor sections of Port-au-Prince, using a flashlight would be one sure way for anxious mothers to ascertain what was going on in the yards that serve as living rooms in these areas. "Whenever I dream my mother," Alourdes concluded, "I know everything going to be okay. She come to me like that and I know." Although good luck was clearly in the air, Alourdes hedged her bets by stopping in her altar room to splash herself with specially prepared perfumes.

This time, we waited in the wide marble halls of 100 Centre Street for only two hours. Just after noon, we learned that William's case had been postponed until April 20 and that the judge had excused William from appearing then. The new lawyer told us that he hoped to have the matter resolved before the hearing date. He explained that we might not know anything definite until the last minute.

"Is anybody listening to me?" he hollered with good humor. "You are going to get a letter. It will look very official. It will say: 'If you do not show up in court on April 20, a warrant will be issued for your arrest.' You can ignore that letter because the judge has excused William. The computer will go ahead and send out the letter anyway. But you do not have to come. Do you understand?" Without a moment's hesitation, Alourdes responded, "I get a letter like that, say they going to come arrest me, put me in jail, I going to come!"

Maggie's attitude was different. "I am tired of all this trouble!" she shouted as we pushed through the revolving door of the courthouse into a clear sunny day. "This stuff going to be finish! It better be, or I am going to kill them. Papa Danbala! He is number one on my list. Then come Papa Ogou. I am tired of trouble. All the time, trouble! But, Karen," she said, moving her speech rapidly from high notes to low, "I really think everything going to be okay. Last night, for the first time, I sleep. You know I don't sleep. I don't eat. And now I just want to sit down and relaaaaaaaax! So now I know my guardian angel is quiet, and everything going to be okay. You know, before, when we was here, *tèt mwen boulvèse* [my head was turned around], and my angel got no peace. Then I don't sleep. No dream. I could not even think. Now I am coming along. If I sleep enough, I will conquer the world! But I don't got to tell you that. You know that, right?"

Maggie suddenly shouted: "You know too much, Karen!" Seeing my startled response, she laughed and continued in an ordinary conversational tone, "You my friend and you around a lot, and sometimes I just tell you things. You see thing, you hear thing. I think those spirit say, 'Karen know too much.' It is like the Mafia—once you know too much, then they got to Christian [baptize] you. I think you going to have to go to Haiti like me, get your head washed . . . you know." She grinned mischievously.

In another lightning change of mood, Maggie turned to William: "When we get home, I got to call the police. They say we got to keep them informed, what you are doing. 'Cause if you don't behave, they going to put you in jail." She gave me an exaggerated wink and whispered: "I am just trying to scare him lately."

Sometime in mid-April, the telephone call came. No one seemed surprised, and no one made much of it. With the help of school records and test scores procured by Maggie, the district attorney had finally been convinced that William was retarded. All charges against him were dropped.

DIFFERENT KINDS OF OGOU POWER

Alourdes and Maggie have each carved out a place in the New World, in New York. Their roles and attitudes differ, in part because they have lived different lives. One way to capture this difference would be to say that Alourdes is a Haitian who lives in the United States, whereas her daughter is an American who spent the first twelve years of her life in Haiti.

One afternoon in 1983, Alourdes was dreaming aloud about going back to Haiti. "Nobody don't like New York! If I got money, I be gone right back to my country. I take the front room of my mother' house, open a little boutique. Nothing big . . . just a little place. I sell hat . . . dress."

"You do that! Not me," was Maggie's quick retort. "I don't care what anybody say about New York. It is better here. I am staying. You can have your Baby Doc, your Duvalier, your Tonton Makout. Not me!" "Tonton Makout don't bother me," Alourdes said simply. "I just mind my business. I don't have nothing to do with them."

Alourdes avoids all public authority structures in the United States, as she did in Haiti. When William got in trouble with the police, there was no question that Maggie would be the family's frontline representative. Once Maggie was clear about William's actual role in the incident, she took on this task in a fighting spirit rooted in the assumption that a mistake had been made and that, furthermore, she was not powerless to do something about it. It would not have occurred to Alourdes that she could call the police and the courts to account on a matter of principle or law. In her mind, they represent a force as irrational as nature itself. She challenged them instead through the intervention of the spirits, just as Philo had when the courts took away her home. It was Alourdes who would not leave for the courthouse until she visited her altar room, and it was she who first asked for the names of the people involved in the case. She did not want to harm them, but she did want to ensure that they could not harm her.

Alourdes's attitude toward those who have authority is based in experiences that go far back in her life. One early lesson concerned her older brother Jean, who had to leave Haiti when he was nineteen. A colonel in the Haitian army had his eye on Jean's girlfriend. Philo heard through her network of loyal clients that soldiers were plotting to kill her son to get him out of the colonel's way. By calling in favors wherever and however she could, Philo managed to short-circuit the lengthy emigration process, and she had Jean out of the country in days.

"That's the way it is," Jean said to me on one of his rare visits to Alourdes's home in Brooklyn. "Any government official. Get a mistress, build her a house, give her a BMW. Whatever they have to do to get what they want, they do it."

Since the days of Dessalines, the Haitian army has functioned with few checks on its power. Around soldiers, violence erupts in arbitrary and shocking ways, sparked as often by their own greed or fragile pride as by crime or political dissent. Anyone who has spent much time walking the streets of Port-au-Prince has seen examples. These streets were Alourdes's world until she was in her late twenties. Experience has led her to conclude that survival depends on slipping through the cracks in the system. Specifically, it is necessary to cultivate invisibility around anyone who may be threatening. Alourdes credits her Vodou spirits with granting her this invisibility: "All my life, I'm walking in the street . . . I'm walking very proud and healthy and protected. Even . . . I . . . I a woman—that don't make no difference! They cannot talk to me. I pass near those people, they don't see me. Because I got protection, I got a *gad* [guard, a protective charm]. Spirit put that *gad* in me for protection. I got protection from awful people, *ennviyou* [envious] people, violent people."

Yet Alourdes acknowledges that this spiritual gift has limitations. "Let me tell you something, protection don't mean you can go fight. No, no, no, no, no. That not protection. Protection mean people can't harm you for no reason, just because you don't do nothing. But you got to protect yourself, too. You got two eye to look. If a car coming, I not going stand up in front of that car just so I see if I got protection. No. If I stand up in front of that car, that car going hit me."

Now middle-aged, Alourdes has begun to exhibit a conservatism that would not have been possible for her as a young woman, when she was still struggling to make a place for herself in the world. Her work as a *manbo* enables her to confine herself largely to her house, a place where she is in control. Alourdes seldom leaves home. When she does go out, careful planning ensures that her transit will be smooth and that the reception at her destination will be consonant with her well-developed self-esteem. The sources of Alourdes's conservatism, her current tendency to make a fortress of her home, could be examined in terms of a lesson Ogou teaches. One of his songs seems to describe the wounds to the heart and to the will that can result from too much life experience, too much pain and struggle. This song, addressed to the battle-seasoned chief of the Ogou, Sen Jak Majè, consists of the name of the spirit and one other line: "*M'blese, m'pa wè san mwen* [I'm wounded, but I don't see my blood]."

The early part of Alourdes's life was a constant struggle. She is still bruised and has reason to be wary of the larger world. For a brief period when she was a teenager, beautiful and high-spirited, Alourdes thought she had escaped forever from the hunger and demeaning poverty of her childhood. She talked her mother into letting her audition for a place in Haiti's Troupe Folklorique, and, to the surprise of everyone but the self-confident fifteen-year-old, she was successful. In no time, she became the lead singer with this group, which performed both popular and traditional religious music and dance.

But the excitement and glamour of her career soon ended, as did the brief marriage that followed it. Before long, Alourdes found herself on her own and responsible for three children. It was impossible to find steady work, and there was never enough money. At times, she fed her children salt water, as her own mother had done with her, so they would feel they had something in their bellies. "That time was awful for me. My mother have to pay my rent. When my mother don't have nothing . . . if she don't have money, she don't cook—nobody eat that day."

These hard times eventually made Alourdes decide to leave Haiti. And yet, during her first years in New York, things were not much easier. It was difficult to find a good job, her health failed, and it took a long time to save enough money to bring her children from Haiti. Then, not long after the family was reunited, another crisis hit, in 1965.

Alourdes was getting ready to make the trip home to undergo initiation into the Vodou priesthood. It was winter, and the tiny apartment she was renting had no central heat. Her landlord provided an electric space heater, but its defective wiring started a fire in the middle of the night. The fire took everything—her refrigerator, a new television, even the hundred dollars in cash a friend had given her to take to his family in Port-au-Prince. Half asleep and scrambling to get his pants on, Jean-Pierre, then fifteen, sustained burns on his back and neck from a flaming curtain. He was sent to the hospital, while Alourdes, Maggie, and little William were taken in by friends. The Red Cross gave them new shoes, warm clothing, and coupons for food.

These days, Alourdes can say proudly that she owns her own home and requires no outside help to feed and clothe her family. In the row house in Fort Greene, she and Maggie support a lively, three-generation household. Alourdes credits her chief protector, Ogou Badagri, with the security she now enjoys, and she can detect his presence throughout her early life as well. "Let me give you a story about me," Alourdes once offered. "Wednesday is Papa Ogou' day, right? I born on Wednesday. I married on Wednesday. Maggie born on Wednesday. Jean-Pierre born on Wednesday. I come to New York on Wednesday. If I got an appointment with somebody, I have to do any business, I have to go out for any reason—I go on Wednesday. I don't have no luck on Monday."

Maggie's story is different. She knew hunger and poverty as a child, but she simply accepted them as children are wont to do. For Maggie, the real struggles began when she came to the United States. It was in New York that she learned to fight. When Maggie tells stories about her first few months in school in New York City, she reveals a twelve-year-old self more frightened and more aggressive than the worldly wise and resilient mother of two who is now my friend.

"I had just come to that school, and they look at me, they think, 'That black girl!' They think I'm ugly. And I don't speak no English. We got all kind'a people in that school: white, black, Puerto Rican. Each one have some kind'a gang. These white girls jump on me and beat me up. I did not even start it, and they expel me for that! But you should of seen me, Karen; I was big then." Maggie's solemn face broke into a huge grin. "I was sooooooooo big." She planted her feet wide apart and took big thumping steps across the room. "I just walk like this. My stomach stick out to here, and my rear end just stick out like this."

In a matter-of-fact tone, she completed the story. "They took that girl to the hospital. I cut her here and here," Maggie said, vaguely gesturing toward her face and upper arm. "When I first come, I always carry a little knife, like a penknife—right here." She snapped the waistband on her skirt. "When all them white girls jump on me, I just cut one. So they put me out for three weeks. But when I come back, everybody like me! I was the leader, the leader of everybody—black, white, Puerto Rican. I was sooooooo big!"

One day, when Alourdes was singing Ogou songs for my tape recorder, we came to one for Ogou Achade:

> *Baton pase nan men mwen, Achade,*
> *Pou chyen raje mòde mwen.*

> The club passes into my hand, Achade,
> For the mad dog bites me.

When she finished singing, Alourdes exclaimed: "That's me! That's my protection. Nobody can't touch me." Maggie could have made the same point and meant it more literally, although the adult Maggie would never wear a knife in her waistband.

As an adult, Maggie, like Alourdes, has learned the value of knowing how to slip by unnoticed. Like Alourdes, she cites the spirits as the source of this talent: "When I'm on the street, it's like people don't see me. Or if I'm talking, they don't hear me. I'm like the wind . . . just passing by!" But Maggie is not Alourdes, and she will still take on a good verbal fight with bill collectors and Vodou spirits alike. Fighting with the spirits was Maggie's first response to the arrival of serious trouble in January of 1981.

For several months before this, Maggie had been preoccupied with financial problems. She and Alourdes were nearly ten thousand dollars in debt, and Maggie's annual salary was not much more than five thousand dollars. She was constantly scheming and juggling scarce resources. Lying awake one night in mid-January, she conceived a plan. Early the following morning, she and Alourdes made a trip to the bank. Maggie intended to borrow a thousand dollars on her Visa card to pay their overdue fuel bill, but the bank teller informed her that there were new credit rules. She could have only three hundred fifty dollars. "Why is that?" Maggie demanded. "I got a two-thousand credit line, and once before I got seven hundred on that Visa card."

With indignation rising in her voice, Maggie later described her reaction: "I got so mad, 'cause I don't know anything about no new rules! When I hear that—only three hundred fifty dollars!—I get so upset. I'm so mad. I just go. My mother and I walk and walk. We left the house, it was nine o'clock in the morning, and by the time we get back, it was one-thirty. We just walk and walk. We nearly freeze to death! And then when I get home, I come in, put another sweater and my hat, and go out again and walk. We don't know what we doing to do! I was gone all day. My head ache, my body ache. I take two Sinutab and go to bed."

While Maggie was lying down late that afternoon, Alourdes went to the basement. She found the entire lower floor filled with steam. Maggie said later, "I'm upstairs, and I hear that scream. . . . If Mommie was the kind'a person who have heart attack, she would be dead!" The fuel tank for their furnace had been nearly empty that morning, and the suppliers had refused to deliver more oil until the bill was paid—prompting Maggie's rush to borrow money. During the long, troubled walk, the fuel tank had gone dry, and the heat went off. The pipes froze and burst, and Maggie and Alourdes were now faced with expensive furnace repairs.

Late the same day, Maggie recounted the story for me over the phone. When she finished, there was a long silence. Then she said defiantly: "You know what I did, Karen? I talk to my people. I talk to Papa Ogou. I tell him, 'I'm going to give you one month! I need one thousand dollar. By two month from now, I'm going to need two thousand. I want it now! I'm tired of waiting! We always borrowing money from this one . . . Visa or something . . . to pay someone else. I'm tired of that! I've had enough! I want my own money!' I tell Papa Ogou I'm going to give him one month, and then I'm going to go downstairs to the altar and break everything up. I tell him, 'You better shape it or ship it! That's right! You better shape it or ship it, 'cause I am tired of waiting.'"

Sounding more depressed than angry, Maggie continued: "I don't know, Karen. Mommie say to me, 'Look, you know everything going to be all right.' But I don't know, sometime I just don't think there is any God up there." I had never heard Maggie say anything like that, and I could think of nothing to say in response. Through the long silence on the telephone, I could feel her groping for her customary strength and ironic humor. At last, she laughed.

"You know, all this time, I'm just buying thing, buying thing. All the time buying." She giggled conspiratorially and asked if I knew what she had done just the day before. "Some man come to the house, and I bought an encyclopedia for the kids. Just a little encyclopedia, but two hundred and fifty dollars! I give him a check for fifty dollars, and now I'm going to have to call him and tell him to hold that check until next Tuesday. I want my own money, Karen. I'm tired of just having other people's money. Those spirit got to help me! But all the time they just giving me trouble. I am tired of it, Karen. I am tired!"

The broken furnace was only the first in a long list of things that went wrong in Maggie's life throughout the opening months of 1981. She contracted chicken pox; she lost her job; William was arrested; and, just a few days after that, Maggie's floor of their home in Brooklyn was robbed. "Now that robber! All my jewelry! My camera—I just buy that camera! I don't even make one payment to Mastercard yet."

Maggie decided the spirits were harassing her, as they had done before, because they wanted her to become a *manbo* like her mother. By the time William's problem with the court was resolved, the other crises had receded into the past, and Maggie had become philosophical: "This bad luck, it begin with me when I get chicken pox, and it end with me, with that robber. That's it! Now those spirit know I know what they want." Ogou provides the weapon to fight mad dogs. But at times the source of trouble is Ogou himself.

> *Sen Jak pa la.*
> *Se chyen ki la.*

> Saint James's not there.
> It's a dog who's there.

When I first met her, in 1978, Maggie said, "Work with the spirit run in my family—my grandmother, my mother. People coming in here to see my mother all hour of the day and night. She never too tired to see people. She just like my grandmother, always helping people." Maggie hesitated before she continued with this train of thought. "My mother, my grandmother—they don't ever have no money. They just giving . . . always giving. I don't want to be like them!" But then, with resignation in her voice, Maggie added, "Seem to be each time I say I don't want to be like them, something pulling me back . . . saying, 'You can't do that!'"

In the summer of 1981, Maggie finally gave in to the will of the spirits, much as her mother had done a quarter of a century earlier. She went to Haiti to take the *ason*. She did not do so with dreams of wealth and success. She went out of the conviction that initiation would reinforce her bonds with her family and that bonding with family, living and dead, represented her best hope for peace and security.

Vodou does reinforce family ties. In the presence of Ogou, however, this statement must be qualified. Alourdes and Maggie discuss family with great warmth and feeling; there is no question of their deep commitment to each other and to their children. And they both speak lovingly of the extended family, a good part of it still in Haiti. Nevertheless, although they expend considerable energy nurturing family roots, both acknowledge that these links no longer sustain them the way they should.

Their fears are often apparent in discussions of what they would do in the case of a real crisis—a serious illness or a death in the household. With characteristic exaggeration, Maggie once said to me, "I don't have no friend. Even if my mother die . . . I could call Madame François. I could call her, and after that the very next person I call would be you. I don't got nobody to ask." Alourdes's complaint is not very different: "I use to got so many friend in Haiti. Now . . . nobody! I go to Haiti, everybody happy, happy, happy. I see my daddy. I see my sister. Then what I going do? You know, me and my father never get along together. After one week, they tired with you. Where my friend? They in Miami. They in Chicago. They in New York. And I even don't see them."

When this mood sets in, Maggie and Alourdes seem more willing to lay their bets on new friends and new ways of handling the challenges of life than to count on family. Such judgments do not mean that they have rejected their family any more than that they have rejected their Vodou roots. But both family and religion have been redefined. Relative newcomers in their lives, people such as myself, carry fictive kinship titles— Alourdes calls me her daughter, and Maggie calls me her sister. And the family of spirits has been rearranged as well. Azaka, the rural country cousin, is faithfully honored once a year, but he is seldom called at other times. Papa Ogou is the most frequent spirit guest in their home. He is the one who clears a path through the social forest and generally assists in taking on the challenges of the new.

"PAPA OGOU, DO YOU TAKE THIS WOMAN?"

Early in the summer of 1980, Alourdes read the cards for me, as she does from time to time. That day we were considering whether or not I should undergo the Vodou marriage to Papa Ogou. My first trip to Haiti had been in the summer of 1973. Starting with that trip, every priest or priestess who chose to make a diagnosis told me that Papa Ogou was my *mèt tèt*. In 1977 a *manbo* I had never met before made her way across a crowded temple dance floor just to tell me that she could see Papa Ogou "around my head."

A person's *mèt tèt* can be identified in several ways, most often through divination or consultation with the spirits during possession. *Manbo* or *oungan* with the intuitive powers called

A ceremony for Ogou in a temple located in the basement of a large apartment house. Crown Heights, Brooklyn, 1979.

"the gift of eyes" are said to see protective spirits directly. Diagnosing someone's *mèt tèt* is more than a surface labeling of personality types. It often works at a deeper level, where it zeros in on significant latent characteristics. Even though the diagnosis of Ogou as my *mèt tèt* did not fit easily with my own self-image, I could see the wisdom of it.

Although I had witnessed many Vodou marriages and been fascinated by them, I originally had no intention of going through the ritual myself. Then, one day in 1980 when I was alone in my apartment and full of rage (I had some things to be angry about in that period of my life), I found myself muttering, "Stop trying to make the anger go away. It only makes it worse. It's yours. Marry it!" I picked up the phone and called Alourdes.

This spontaneous decision marked a new stage in my relation to Haitian Vodou. It also brought new and deeper understandings of how Vodou actually works in the lives of individuals. The contents of Vodou rituals—from private healing consultations to public dances and possession-performances—are composed from the lives of the particular people performing them. When I began to bring my own life to the system for healing, I began to understand more of what it meant for Haitians to do that. But there were also new risks. In a way, I was setting out to do fieldwork on my own psyche. I remain convinced that this was the best and perhaps the only way for me to move my understanding of Vodou beyond external description into the deep places where it takes up the dreams and fears, hope and pain of an actual life. I try to exercise caution in not claiming more authority for my experience than it can bear. What I have gained from participating in Vodou is a kind of knowledge that exists in the seam between two cultures, where the various strands of the fabric can never be disentangled.

As Alourdes laid out the cards for my reading, we talked. She said to me, "Karen, you very intelligent person. Only thing about you, you don't push yourself. You just stay right where you are." In two quick gestures, her hands framed a small, tight box. "You could push faster . . . yes." In Vodou, there is a pervasive contrast between being immobile and blocked and having a life of energy and flow. The goal of all Vodou ritualizing is to *echofe* (heat things up) so that people and situations shift and move, and healing transformations can occur. Heating things up brings down the barriers, clears the impediments in the path, and allows life to move as it should. When Ogou discussed Maggie's initiation with her, he used another metaphor for energy and movement, telling her that if she would make the commitment to take the *ason*, then *"dlo klè va koule devan ou* [clear water will flow in front of you]."

The opposite of this openness, heat, and flow is the state of being arrested or stopped (*rete*) or, worse, of being bound (*mare*). Charms and amulets made by every Vodou healer, which are designed to control the behavior of others in limited ways, are *mare*, bound or tied, round and round with thread, wire, or rope. Slave chains are even kept in some temples, where they are part of the iconography of "left-hand work," a type of Vodou ritualizing directed at much more extreme forms of control. When Alourdes said, "You just stay right where you are," she was not suggesting that I was the victim of left-hand work; instead, she was suggesting that my own behavior boxed me in.

After Alourdes delivered this verdict, the room was quiet save for the tapping noise her middle finger made as it descended two or three times in quick succession on a card here and there in the four neat rows of eight cards in front of her. "Karen, you got to fight. You got to be a fighter," she said. More silence and tapping followed. "Look, if you decide you going marry Papa Ogou, you got to do it for yourself. Don't do nothing for me. Do it for yourself." More silence. More tapping. "Karen, you think too much!" "What?" I asked. "Drink too much?" Alourdes laughed. She told me to come back the next Wednesday and she would call Papa Ogou for me.

It was eight-thirty on a hot summer evening when I returned. Maggie was in the living room. All the lights were off except a tiny one on the portable sewing machine where she was working. The door between the living room and Alourdes's bedroom was open. Alourdes lay on her stomach on the bed. I sat on the edge of the bed, and we talked. The conversation moved in fits and starts, focusing mainly on a familiar topic, money problems. Alourdes yawned repeatedly. So did I. After almost two hours of labored talk and long silences, I began to think that Alourdes had forgotten her promise to call Ogou. Or perhaps she had concluded that it was too hot to work.

I decided not to press the issue, to wait for another occasion when she was more in the mood. But I was annoyed. I had traveled from Manhattan at the end of a busy day and in weather that sapped my energy and fogged my mind. Ending an especially long silence between us, I stood up and said I thought it was time to be on my way.

Alourdes rolled over slowly onto her back, a questioning look on her face. "You don't want to talk with Papa Ogou?" she asked. This is often how it works: Alourdes pulls through just when I am thoroughly frustrated and ready to give up. Our attitudes toward time are very different. I hoard it and spend it like a miser; she rides the rhythms of the day like a surfer. She lets things happen when the time is right for them to happen. Alourdes recognizes the right moment only when it is upon her.

Together, we went to the basement. Alourdes knocked three times on the door to the altar room, and we went in. She struck a match and pushed the wick of a candle stub into the flame. She anchored the small white candle on the edge of her work table and settled herself on a low stool next to the table. I was asked to reach into Ogou's altar cabinet for a bottle of rum. She poured a dollop or two of the amber liquid onto a red metal plate and then dropped matches on the thin film of rum until it ignited. Alourdes sat staring into the fire while tipping the plate from side to side to keep the blue flames dancing across its surface. Her free hand was held to her forehead like a sunshade, which paradoxically kept the light in rather than shutting it out. Narrowing her eyes, Alourdes sought the focused state of mind that creates a portal through which ordinary consciousness slips away.

For a *manbo* as accomplished as Alourdes, the struggle that marks the onset of trance is usually pro forma. During community rituals, when energetic singing and hand-clapping bring on possession, the struggle between her *gwo bònanj* and the spirit who seeks to possess her is over in minutes. First, her eyes narrow. Then her head bends forward as if she had a weight on the back of her neck (the spirits are said to ride on the back of the neck), and her facial features go slack. She often loses her balance and requires support from bystanders. Assistants remove her shoes and take the *ason* from her hand. Soon, the personality of the *lwa* is in full control of her body and voice. When Alourdes does not have the energy and support of a crowd to push her along, this process can be slower, as it was on this night.

As she concentrated on the slippery blue flame, a light tremor passed through her body from time to time, and she squeezed her eyes shut. Once, she jerked her left hand away from her forehead and shook it vigorously as if it had gone numb. But, like a restless sleeper, Alourdes seemed to wake with a start each time she dipped below the surface of the waters of consciousness. At one point, her body shook so much I was sure the spirit had come. But the crisis passed.

Alourdes sighed and reached for the rum bottle to refuel her small fire. Again, there was intense concentration, and this time it worked. Barely perceptible tremors became intense shaking, and then the energy shot out her arms and legs, making them do a stiff staccato dance in the air. When the shaking stopped, Alourdes's body was drawn up straight, and keen black eyes were staring at me with interest. Papa Ogou had arrived.

"*Bonjou, bèl ti fi* [Hello, pretty little girl]," Papa Ogou said in the nasal speech of the spirits. "*Ba'm nouvèl ou. Sa ou genyen? Kouman ou ye, pitit?* [Give me news of yourself. What's going on with you? How are you, little one?]" Ogou asked with paternal concern. Then, without waiting for answers, he requested his red scarf and his *shouga,* spirit talk for *siga* (cigar). He tied the scarf tightly around his head and lit the cigar. Then he leaned back and eyed me from head to toe.

When I asked if he thought I should marry him, Ogou continued staring and did not respond. I put the question in another form, and Ogou still said nothing. I began to tell him about the things that made me angry—my marriage breaking up, packing, moving, too much work, tension on the job. Ogou nodded sympathetically but without comment. Things went on like this for a long time. I felt like a chicken senselessly flapping its wings, unable to take off. The room was full of my clucking. He was as unmoveable and silent as a mountain.

When I was close to the end of my patience, Ogou spoke. He asked quietly: "What can I do for you?" "Tell me what to do," I sputtered. "Should I do the marriage or not?" Ogou's body snapped forward, and a thick cloud of cigar smoke shot into my face along with his forceful reply: "*Pran tèt ou* [Get ahold of your head]! Do what you want! Do you want to marry me?" I had tried to get Ogou to tell me what to do, and he had been waiting for me to say what I wanted. In the end, I said I wanted to have the ceremony. I had made the decision, and I intended to carry it through.

"*Bon!*" Ogou said and sat back, puffing contentedly on his

cigar. "You have the spirit all around you," he observed. "Did you know the Ginen spirit can love a white person? You don't know that? I think you have a *rasin* Ginen [an African root] in you . . . an Indian root . . . Jewish, too! You are a very intelligent woman. You could be a doctor, a lawyer. But no, you choose this. You don't have to come here. But you are searching . . . searching. You are digging. Why did you choose this? Because you have an African root in you! Do you understand what I am saying to you?"

The marriage took place the next month at Ogou's regularly scheduled July birthday party. Around two o'clock in the morning, when the songs summoning Ogou began, I excused myself from the twenty-five or so people gathered around Alourdes's sumptuous altar tables. I went upstairs to change into my wedding clothes—a bright red sundress purchased especially for the occasion and, on my head, a red satin scarf. When I came down the stairs half an hour later, everyone oohed and aahed over my fine attire. Everyone, that is, except Papa Ogou.

He had mounted Alourdes in my absence, and I found him decked out in his own finery, his red velvet military jacket with the gold epaulets. But Ogou ignored me. I stood by patiently while he talked to one person after another without even acknowledging my presence. No matter how I maneuvered, he always managed to keep his back to me.

Everyone was getting nervous. One woman said, "Papa Ogou, your beautiful bride is here, behind you. Don't you want to talk to her?" Ogou ignored the question. Then a man whispered in my ear, "Go on!" and gave me a shove in front of Ogou. The spirit looked me over with a cold eye. "What do you want?" he asked. I found my voice: "I am here to marry you. You promised me you would marry me. You have made me wait a long time. I am ready." Papa Ogou threw back his head and laughed. It was a deep, rich laugh. "Begin the ceremony!" he shouted, and, taking my arm, he propelled me toward the largest of the altar tables. Once again, Ogou had taught me the warrior's lesson: know what you want and fight for it.

Two chairs were placed in front of the table. Papa Ogou and I sat, and the four people who were "godparents" for the wedding gathered behind us. Willy, functioning as *prètsavann,* stood in front of us. *"Liberté, égalité, fraternité,"* he began, reading from a paper bearing the official stamp of the Republic of Haiti.

(Blank forms are available near the big Iron Market in Port-au-Prince for four cents apiece; my Acte de Mariage had been written out in ballpoint pen on the first page of the folio sheet.) "In the year one thousand nine hundred and eighty in the state of New York . . ." Willy continued in French.

"Make it fast!" Ogou snapped. Willy laughed, put the paper down, and began to ad lib in Creole. "Do you, Ogou Badagri, take this woman, Karine . . . uh . . . uh . . . Brown, as your wife? And do you promise to give her protection?" "Yes!" answered Ogou, thumping his sword on the floor for emphasis. "Do you take Monsieur Ogou Badagri as husband?" Willy asked me. "To be faithful . . . to give him one night each week?" "Yes!" I said.

From the altar Ogou took a saucer holding the ring with a small red stone that I had purchased earlier in the week. He doused the ring in Florida Water and rum and set it on fire. While the ring was still warm, he slid it over the middle finger of my left hand. He held my hand up to each of the four directions. Four times he blew a fine mist of rum over my hand and the ring. Then Papa Ogou plucked a red carnation from a bouquet on the table and doused it in the mixture of rum, perfume, and cool blue fire. He handed me the flaming flower, as Willy intoned the final words in French: "Maître Ogou Badagri and Mademoiselle Karine are united by marriage!"

People cheered. A champagne cork popped. Ogou refused champagne, preferring a long swig from his rum bottle. He also refused to eat any of the wedding cake, but he did cut it. With his sword, he removed a circular piece from the center of the cake and instructed me to take it home to feed friends, family, and spirits. Everyone present signed the marriage document, including Ogou Badagri, who scratched a big "O.B." with a red felt-tip pen.

CHAPTER FIVE

The Baka Made from Jealousy

Around the turn of the century, not long after Joseph Binbin Mauvant sang his way back to Africa, a mysterious event occurred in Port-de-Paix that dramatically changed the life of his granddaughter Philomise Macena. It happened in the middle of the night when a wild, unlikely wind roamed the broad, dusty streets of the small port city. The wind shook the massive wooden doors of the closed shops and rattled the bones of mongrel dogs huddled beneath their wide, deserted porches. The wind gave off a high-pitched whistle. Doors struggled to escape the hold of iron bars. Dogs bared their teeth and snarled.

Madame Fouchard lay beside her husband in their comfortable quarters behind the well-stocked shelves of Magasin Fouchard. Because of the wind, she had been sleeping lightly and was instantly awake when a perfectly ordinary voice called out: "Wake up! Wake up! An old man has died. I need sugar, cinnamon, black cloth, *malfète* leaves." Even the urgent pounding on the door seemed common enough—another crisis, another chance to turn a profit.

Elsa Fouchard answered the summons without alarm or resentment. It was not unusual for the shopkeeper to open her door in the middle of the night. Magasin Fouchard was the biggest store in Port-de-Paix, and mountain people and townspeople alike came to her when there was an emergency. There was no way she could have known what waited behind the door: a *baka* called into being by a neighbor who could no longer bear the jealousy he felt toward the Fouchard family. They were too prosperous and, more to the point, too self-sufficient. Elsa and Claude Fouchard asked for no charity, and they gave none. It was unnatural.

◀ *Machann* in front of a gingerbread house. Port-au-Prince, Haiti, 1973.

When the *baka* made from jealousy turned up at Madame Fouchard's door, she knew it was time to close up shop and leave town. *Baka* are evil incarnate. Sometimes called *kombinay-son* (combinations), they bring things together that ought to be kept apart. The *baka* Madame Fouchard confronted, hours before the first light of dawn, was a two-legged horse—a horse standing straight up like a man! She caught just a glimpse of it before she slammed and barred the door. The wind had sent her kerosene lantern swinging. It took only one upward swing to reveal bulging black eyes the size of lemons, a heavy wet snout resting on a hairless chest, a gnarled human hand fondling a velvet ear. Only later did she remember the rotten-sweet breath that had enveloped her. When Elsa Fouchard recalled the odor years later and many miles from Port-de-Paix, her stomach churned.

The Fouchards had been in Port-de-Paix for fifteen years before the *baka* appeared. Yet, behind their backs, they were still called *etranje* (foreigners). They moved into town in 1886 and opened the *magasin* shortly thereafter. At the time, it seemed like a good idea. There were fewer than two thousand residents in this isolated port on Haiti's dry and inhospitable northwest-ern coast, but Port-de-Paix had the only sizable market for many miles around. Every Wednesday, the mountain people flooded in to sell vegetables, tobacco, and coffee and to buy supplies such as cloth, tools, and kerosene. Before the Fouchards opened their store, finding such supplies was a matter of chance. But after they came, those who had money or goods to trade could find anything they needed. While Claude pursued ephemeral busi-ness deals from his favorite table at the local bistro, his tough-minded wife did the real work. She ran the store.

No matter how hot it was, Elsa Fouchard, a substantial woman, wore a corset beneath her neatly pressed cotton frock. It was impossible to enter the store without first encountering her, sitting ramrod straight at her desk beneath the portico, a leather-bound ledger open before her. She was a daunting pres-ence, but she was also capable of considerable charm when her keen business sense told her charm could be profitable.

Not long after the shop opened, Marie Noelsine Joseph from Jean-Rabel-in-the-Mountains became the object of Madame Fouchard's attention. The produce Sina carried to the Port-de-Paix market (especially the tobacco leaves—some as long as your arm!) was of superior quality. So Elsa Fouchard made it her business to befriend Sina. "When you come to town, pass by here first. You will find coffee waiting for you," Elsa said warmly. Sina welcomed the chance to rest before plunging into the chaos of the market. And she knew the value of a connection with such an important, wealthy woman.

One day, Elsa pressed a piece of bread into Sina's hand along with the usual cup of thick, sweet coffee. "You must eat, my dear," she crooned. "I can see you have a baby in your belly." Sina, a businesswoman herself, responded: "I'm going to give my baby to you to baptize. You are going to be the godmother."

Elsa Fouchard knew she was bartering over more than congo peas and tobacco, but for the moment she only smiled. It would not do to appear overly eager. She simply watched while the strikingly beautiful mountain woman with the long hair and green eyes tied up her bundles and replaced them in an enormous basket, which she then hoisted and settled on her head. Sina was already out the door when Elsa called after her: "Don't forget, I'm going to baptize that baby!"

Five years later, on the night the *baka* came, when Madame Fouchard's heart was still jumping around like a panicked rodent, her first coherent thought concerned her goddaughter, Philomise. "I'll need a maid in Port-au-Prince," she said to herself. "It would be nice if I did not have to pay her."

After the *baka* appeared, Magasin Fouchard was never again open for business. The decision to move was made in an instant, and within days most of the merchandise was packed in barrels and giant baskets and sent to the harbor to await the next boat bound for Port-au-Prince. On the following Wednesday, when Sina made her customary stop, she found the shop closed. She was about to leave when a snaggle-toothed charcoal merchant seated near the door hissed: "Madame Fouchard asked me to wait for you. She needs you. Knock three times on the back door."

Marie Noelsine squatted on the floor at one end of the nearly empty shop, and Madame Fouchard paced around her, talking of things of little consequence in a supple, sweet voice. Sina listened carefully, but she did not look at this woman whose favors she had come to depend on. She knew her debts were about to be called in, and she could not imagine what Madame Fouchard could ask of her that would fill her with such foreboding as she felt at that moment.

Finally, Elsa Fouchard came to the point. She wanted to take Philomise to Port-au-Prince. Sina said nothing; she did not even look up. Behind her stoic mountain woman's face a storm was raging. Not long before, Sina had reached a decision to leave her ne'er-do-well husband and move from Jean Rabel. Madame Fouchard's plan would make this easier. But . . . oh, what a price! She knew that starting a new life with three small children would be more than she could handle, and she had already decided that Mèdelice, her son and firstborn, could be left in Jean Rabel. But Philo, her baby! Sina had never allowed herself to think they might be separated.

The next morning, on the long, hot trek up the mountain, Sina consoled herself with images of Philomise as the beloved goddaughter of a wealthy family, walking the streets of a big city, schoolbooks in her arms, shoes on her feet. Sina's imagination could take her no further, but she felt certain that whatever Philo found there, it would be better than what she could provide. By the time Sina reached the gate of the Mauvant family land, the sun was gone and with it the meager comfort of fantasy. She dragged her protesting feet the last quarter of a mile to the rhythm of a muttered apology: "Women have got to do all kinds of things . . . all kinds of things . . . all kinds of things." When Sina lay down on her sleeping mat and curled her aching body around her tiny daughter, she was already saying good-bye.

Philomise Macena became a *restavèk* (literally, a stay-with) in the Fouchard family. The fortunes of these borrowed children vary greatly, and Philo was among the least fortunate. She became a servant who was treated like a slave. In the early days, she fetched water and ran small errands for the cook. By the time she was eleven, Philo was responsible for all the cleaning and laundry in the rambling gingerbread house the Fouchards owned in the Bois Verna section of Port-au-Prince. She also did most of the marketing.

Philo slept on a thin mat in the servants' quarters behind the house. She shared a room, six feet by ten feet, with four other people. Her clothes were tattered hand-me-downs, and she was never given a pair of shoes. Although the Fouchards sent their own children to expensive private schools, they did not send Philo to school at all, not even to the public school for maids, held late in the afternoon.

Perhaps the worst of the evils of Elsa and Claude Fouchard

was their refusal to talk to the little girl about her own family. At first, whenever the topic came up, they became evasive. Then one day, Madame Fouchard sought to end the annoying questions once and for all. "They are dead. They are all dead," she said. "Fresh little girl! You are lucky to have someone to give you food and a little corner to sleep in!" Vast need and deep knowing made the child doubt these cruel words. Philo hugged to herself a distant memory of a beautiful, green-eyed mother with gentle loving hands. In her mind's eye there was an indelible image of Sina heading off to market, her hair falling down her back, a basket filled to overflowing balanced on her head. In her memories, Philo was always saying good-bye to her mother. In her fantasies, the situation was quite different. Philo vowed that one day she would have lots of money and would find her mother and shower her with love and wonderful gifts.

Early one morning when Philo was seventeen, she told Madame Fouchard she was going out to buy laundry soap. Barefoot and with only twenty cents in the pocket of her faded cotton dress, Philo walked away and never returned. Once out of sight of the Fouchard house, Philo turned her back to the sea and to the busy commercial center of Port-au-Prince and headed up the mountain. She walked steadily for nearly four hours on a steep road that curved through thick forests before it broke open to the wide paved streets, the steepled churches, and the wealthy homes of Petion-Ville with their red tile roofs and deep porches designed to catch the mountain breezes. Keeping her head down and her step firm, she walked on through Petion-Ville.

On the other side of town, the road narrowed to a dirt track, and thick stands of pine came right up to the edge of the road. Energized by her sudden freedom, the altitude, and the cool air, Philo hurried to the big rural market at Kenscoff near the top of the mountain. Here, by prearrangement, she met a sizable group of friends, discontented young people like herself, her companions in escape. They planned to walk together across Haiti's southern peninsula, over three high mountain ranges, following a narrow, slippery path worn by the bare feet of market women, a path that ran from Kenscoff to Marigot on the far shore. Then they would turn east and follow the coast across the border of the Dominican Republic and beyond to the fabled city of Santo Domingo.

And that is what they did. The journey took one month—thirty long days. During the daylight hours, they slept and performed small jobs for local people in exchange for food. At night they walked, a short distance inland, keeping the sound of the ocean on their right and using the moon as light and the stars as guides. The area around the border proved the hardest to negotiate. For two days they slept in the forest, and at night they walked softly and spoke in whispers to avoid attracting the attention of patrolling soldiers. Twenty had started out, but by the time they crossed the border, several had turned back, and the group had shrunk to a dozen.

Eight women and four men made it to Santo Domingo. The ragtag band of adventurers wandered through busy urban streets for nearly a day before they discovered a cool and inviting park in the center of the city. Here they put down their homely bundles, sat on the grass, and talked among themselves: "Where are we?" "Look at that building! Beautiful!" "Cars! So many cars!" "Look at that woman! Did you ever see clothes like that? She must be a *pèsònaj* [a very important person]." "I'm so hungry!" "Where do you think we are? Do you think this is Santo Domingo?" "I'm scared!" "Me too!"

In time, fatigue took its toll, and Philo and her friends fell silent and waited. An hour passed, and then, just before sunset, the air was suddenly filled with the mad chattering of the small black finches Haitians call *madansara*. A dense cloud of these hyperactive creatures landed in the royal palm above the refugees. Philo craned her neck to look with gratitude on a scene that made a small piece of this strange new world seem familiar and safe.

Throughout the afternoon, passersby had cast a curious eye on the group of Haitians so clearly out of place in the metropolitan center, but no one said anything. Even Haitians who happened by pretended not to understand their Creole. Many Haitians resided in Santo Domingo in the early part of the twentieth century, but they lived and moved cautiously. Dominicans were happy to have Haitians around to do menial labor, but they gave them little respect. In Santo Domingo in 1913, a young Haitian woman was assumed to be a prostitute, and a poor Haitian man was a candidate for what amounted to slave labor on the vast sugar plantations along the Haitian border. From time to time, the police in Santo Domingo rounded up Haitians and imprisoned them, eventually sending them back to Haiti or, if they were in good health, to work in the cane fields. Philo and her friends were in a precarious position.

Luckily, a good-hearted woman came to their rescue. Sylvia, a tall, thin, no-nonsense Haitian woman came striding into the park just after sundown. "My little friends," she called out in Creole while she was still ten yards away, "don't you know you cannot sit here? The police will arrest you. Come with me. You are going to my house."

Sylvia had heard about the Haitians from a friend who had seen them and had sought to turn their naïveté into an amusing story. Sylvia did not think it was funny. She had removed her hands from the wash tub, wiped them dry, and set off for the park. Soon, she was leading the weary travelers to her modest home, where she fed them and convinced two friends to provide extra places for them to sleep. Philo and three other women were taken to the home of Madame Victoir Suffrant.

Madame Victoir was a *machann* (a market woman) who sold combs, mirrors, and costume jewelry in the big covered market in Santo Domingo. This practical, generous woman took an instant liking to Philomise Macena and offered her a job. It soon became the pattern for Philo and Madame Victoir to rise at two in the morning and make their way to the torch-lit, chaotic Santo Domingo market. Here they spread cloths on the ground and artfully arranged their baubles, most fashioned from cow horn by Haitian artisans: delicate little combs, mirrors with scalloped frames, bracelets, and necklaces. The market opened at three and ran until ten in the morning. It was both the wholesale market for the city's boutiques and restaurants and the poor people's shopping center. Anything could be found in this sprawling market, if a person knew where to look and how to barter. Entire sections of the market were run by expatriate Haitians who spoke little Spanish but managed nevertheless to strike hard bargains with their Dominican customers.

A successful market woman communicated with her eyes, her hands, her body. She had to be a superb actress. No matter how hungry or needy she was, she could never appear too eager to sell. She had to strike just the right posture between reasonable self-confidence and outright disdain for her customers. The trick was to intimidate prospective buyers and flatter them at the same time.

Timing was crucial. A *machann* began by quoting a high price. When the customer offered half, she responded by splitting the difference. But then she had to hold her ground long enough that even a small reduction in price felt like a triumph for the buyer. A talented *machann* knew when to deliver an insult, in a mixture of Creole and Spanish, and when to let customers walk away. When they came back a half hour later, she knew she had them. But a clever *machann* did not rub it in. She often concluded a sale by complaining in a good-natured way that if every customer were as sharp as this one, she would soon be out of business.

Philo had these talents in her blood. She was descended from a long line of rural market women, and for more than a decade she had carefully observed the Port-au-Prince market women when she shopped for the Fouchard family. Madame Victoir's little business prospered under Philo's hand, and, when men began to notice the young girl with the intense eyes, she bartered with her sexuality in the same sure-footed way.

Thirty-two-year-old Luc Charles was a Haitian who had lived in Santo Domingo since the age of twelve. The first time he saw Philo, when she was barely eighteen, he knew he wanted her. Like so many poor Haitian women accustomed to hard physical labor, Philo's body was lean and graceful, and she moved with an unstudied economy of gesture. She stood out from the crowd because she was a *grimèl* (a light-skinned woman) and because her hair was longer and straighter than most. But perhaps the most compelling thing about the young Philomise Macena was her pride.

Luc Charles was the head chef in a big restaurant in Santo Domingo, but he did not care for the bland upper-class cuisine he prepared on his job. When Luc was hungry for Haitian food, he would drop by the home of his friend Victoir Suffrant. On one such visit he discovered Philo. "Where did you find that girl?" he asked. "She is beautiful!"

"Luc Charles says he loves you," Madame Victoir later told Philo. "I don't know that man," Philo responded. "I only said hello to him." "But he doesn't have a wife," Madame Victoir persisted, "and he's healthy, and he has money." "That's his problem," responded Philo. "I didn't come here for love. I came here for work."

Luc Charles staged a six-month campaign to win Philomise

Macena. It became his habit to show up late at night after the restaurant closed and before the two women left for the market. He usually brought gifts: pastries from the restaurant, cloth for a new dress, and, one day, a bottle of real French perfume. Philo warmed up slowly. They became friends. Good friends. The day Philo told him she was pregnant, he promised to rent a place where they could live together.

This was a secure and happy period in Philo's life. Luc Charles treated her like a queen. She had everything she wanted, and she no longer had to work so hard. Their son Frank was born on January 19 the next year, a fat cherub with a big head and large wide feet. He was so big and fat everyone referred to him as Toto. The child's appetite was also legendary. Sometimes they called him Toto Six Eggs, sometimes Toto Six Cakes. Philo and Luc cheerfully spoiled their child. When he padded through the streets behind Philo, he would suddenly reach his arms up and say, "*Toto bouke* [Toto is tired]," and tiny Philomise would lift her chunky child and carry him. "Your grandmother should see how you are big and strong," Philo cooed and nuzzled him affectionately. Older women in the Haitian community in Santo Domingo shook their heads at such parental folly.

The good times were undercut only by Luc's jealousy. After they had been together for two years, the trouble began with playful accusations about an imagined lover, and it escalated to protracted arguments, which at times grew violent. The neighbors called the police at least once. The tension grew much worse when Philo went back into the jewelry business. When Frank was two years old, she began a small operation like Madame Victoir's. With Luc's backing and her natural business acumen, the enterprise quickly expanded. Soon Philo was taking the boat to Kingston once a month to purchase gold and silver baubles, which she then sold in Santo Domingo. She began to buy her own dresses and shoes, and occasionally she gave money to friends.

Philo's independence threatened Luc. One day they had a quarrel about it, so violent that Philo announced her intention to leave him. A desperate, frightened Luc Charles countered by offering his precious Philomise the one thing he knew would surely win back her affection. "Even though you have not seen your mother since you were five years old, you talk about her every day. You dream about her every night," he said. "I'm going to give you money to go and find her." Luc put four hundred dollars in Philo's hand and put her and little Frank on a cargo boat bound for the northern ports of Haiti.

Philo and Frank disembarked in the hot and smelly harbor of Port-de-Paix and headed immediately for the market, the information hub of every Haitian town. Here Philo learned that most of her family had left Jean Rabel long ago. Mountain people remembered Marie Noelsine Joseph, and they were certain she had moved somewhere near Gonaïves. All they could tell Philo was that it must have been a long time ago, because Sina's daughter Gloria had been only six or seven at the time.

Philo hired a local guide, and, sitting astride his scrawny horse with Frank strapped behind her, she retraced the path her mother had taken more than fifteen years earlier. When Philo arrived in Gonaïves, she checked into a small pension and then went to the police station. The police were no help. "This is a big *seksyon* [section]. We cannot be expected to keep track of everybody," they told her. Philo gave the police chief fifty *gourd* (ten dollars), an enormous sum of money at the time, but it did no good. He said only that he would get in touch with her as soon as he finished his "research."

The Gonaïves market was one of the biggest in Haiti, and it operated full-tilt six days of the week. All day Tuesday, Wednesday, and Thursday, Philo wandered through the market stalls, questioning everyone she met and peering intently into the face of each passing stranger. No one had news of her family. By the end of the third day, Philo was ready to give up. She sat down at one end of the market, between piles of plum tomatoes and neat mountains of rice. Seated in her lap, Frank played contentedly with a new wooden top. Philo was tired and very depressed. No longer able to attend to the chaos around her, she withdrew into herself.

The business day was almost over. Those who had come to sell were gathering up their wares and either heading home or searching out a comfortable place to prepare a little food and bed down for the night. Dusty-footed burros and dusty-footed *machann* streamed past the place where Philo sat. She did not even notice when one of the market women pivoted, put a hand up to steady her basket, and looked hard at the woman and her uncommonly fat child. Then the *machann* shook her head, turned back, and kept walking. But after four or five steps, she once again reversed direction, and approached Philo.

"*Se pa sè-a mwen* [Isn't that my sister]?" she queried in the high-pitched nasal voice of a mountain woman. Philo looked up in disbelief. "What is your name?" she asked. "My name is Gloria," the woman said. "Gloria Macena?" Philo asked in a small, hopeful voice. "That's me!" was the robust reply. "Take off your shoe," commanded Gloria, and the clean, soft foot of the Santo Domingo jewelry trader was placed next to the dirty, callused foot of the sour-orange merchant from Gros Morne. "Look at that toe!" Gloria screeched. "It's the same! My grandfather always told me, if you see a foot like that, you know that person is family!"

The next day, Gloria and Philomise packed two burros with market baskets, citified suitcases, and the chubby toddler and headed up the mountain to Gros Morne. Sina, now a nearly toothless old woman of forty, was grilling coffee beans in the front yard. She sat on a small chair before a charcoal brazier, her knees akimbo, her long grey hair tied up in a bit of rag. Using a small wooden paddle, she was slowly coating the beans with viscous black sugar, pooled in the center of her pan, and then spreading them out along its broad, sloping sides. Sina was so absorbed in her task that she glanced up only for a moment when the two women entered the yard.

"*Bonswa, Madan*," said Philo quietly. "*Bonswa, pitit mwen* [Good evening, my little one]," Sina responded with a polite greeting mountain folk commonly use to address younger people. "But I am your little one, truly," Philo answered. "You don't remember me?"

"I had a little girl who died a long time ago," Sina responded, "but that's not you." "Oh, yes," came the answer, "it is me, Philomise." Sina fainted.

Philo stayed in Gros Morne for a month. She gave her mother a beautiful gold bracelet and a wristwatch (the first one Sina had ever seen) and more than three hundred dollars. When she left, Philo promised that she would be back before long to build her mother a new house that would keep her safe and dry for many years. During her short stay, many tears had been shed, tears of joy and of sadness, and many family stories had been passed on to Philomise. She learned about her father and his famous fighting cocks and about how he died because of his stubborn pride. And Philo also lit a candle and prayed before the whistling rock that held the spirit of Ezili Dantò.

Not many years later, back in Santo Domingo, Philo woke in a cold sweat. She had had a nightmare. In her dream, she saw her mother's face. It did not look right—the lips were pulled back in a harsh grimace that showed all her teeth, and she laughed in a way that chilled Philo's blood. "My mother is dead. I know it," Philo told Luc Charles. Luc, who was only half-awake, could not hide his annoyance. "Go back to sleep! I give you money to find your mother, and now that you find her, you still can't leave the worrying. Women are all *loco*," Luc pronounced. Now too agitated to sleep, he got up and left the room. In less than a week, Philo was on a boat headed for Gonaïves. The day she reached Gros Morne was the ninth, and final, day of prayers for the death of Marie Noelsine Joseph.

Two weeks earlier, Philo's mother had taken to her bed with stomach pains. On the day Sina died, she foamed at the mouth and spit up blood—a sign of poisoning. Everyone knew who had done it. Alphonse Macena had had twin daughters by another woman before he met Sina. Sina had not known about these stepchildren until after she moved to Gros Morne and Macena followed her there. But when she found out, Sina had opened her heart and her home to the twins. One was good and one was bad; one loved her very much, and the other hated her. The bad twin, with the help of her own mother, had conceived and carried out the plan to poison Sina. Both mother and daughter were jealous of Sina's beauty and of the attraction she held for Alphonse Macena until the day he died.

And so it was that Philo twice lost her mother on account of jealousy. The visit of the *baka* made from jealousy had occasioned their separation when she was only five years old. And now jealousy, the most destructive of emotions, had taken her mother away a second and final time. This was too much! Philo ceased to feel safe in the world. For the first time, she felt like an orphan. She knew she could no longer count on hard work and ordinary good luck to sustain her.

This realization led Philomise to accept her inheritance without hesitation. Gloria told her that Sina had expressed the wish that the whistling rock and the other things on her spirit altar pass to Philo. Such a legacy brings with it heavy family responsibilities. Philo had never served the spirits before, and she was not sure how she would manage. But, in anguish over her mother's death, she knew she must try.

Before leaving Gros Morne, Philo gave the family enough

money to cover the funeral expenses, and she built her mother a fine concrete tomb. On the last day, Philo struck a deal with the spirits. Lacking the habit of prayer or easy access to its ancient ritual forms, Philo could say only what was in her heart: "Take care of my mother. Protect me and my family. I will serve you well. I promise." It would be many years before Philo felt the full weight of that bargain. Family spirits can be patient, but they never forget a promise.

✳

CHAPTER SIX

Kouzinn

Kouzinn, the female counterpart of Azaka, is different from the other spirits described in the main chapters of this book. Alourdes cites no Catholic counterpart for Kouzinn and does not hold an annual feast especially for this female spirit. Kouzinn usually makes an appearance at Azaka's May birthday party, but she does not possess Alourdes on other occasions. Unlike Ezili Dantò and Ezili Freda, Alourdes's primary female spirits, Kouzinn is always paired with her man, and, in the ceremonial context, she is clearly ancillary to him.[1]

Her minimal place in Alourdes's spirit work and her supporting role on the ritual stage are all the more surprising given that, with the exception of Ezili Dantò, who focuses on childbearing and child-rearing, no other spirit deals with issues as close to the center of Alourdes's life or the lives of the women who make up the majority of her clients. Like Alourdes's grandmother, Marie Noelsine Joseph, Kouzinn is a market woman, a *machann*. The keen business sense that is part of the popular image of the *machann* is a key survival skill for poor Haitian women.

In the patriarchal extended families of the countryside, the market woman on whom Kouzinn is modeled is often the only person who deals with money. A *machann* must buy family provisions with her earnings, but whatever is left over is hers. A market woman's capital gives her what leverage she has in otherwise male-dominated families. This leverage is especially important because rural men can have more than one common-

---

[1] Ayida Wèdo, the wife of the rainbow serpent Danbala, is another spirit whose identity tends to be subsumed in that of her mate. There are very few of these wifely types in the Vodou pantheons.

◀ A young *machann* selling chickens. The road to Saut d'Eau, Haiti, 1981. Photograph by Jerry Gordon.

law wife. In times of natural or personal disaster, a market woman's savings ensure her survival and that of her children. In the countryside, men's power is thus in tension with and to some degree modulated by that of women.

The situation is very different in the city and in immigrant communities, where extended families are either absent or in some state of transformation. In New York, as in Port-au-Prince, many families are headed by women, a situation mirrored in the large number of urban Vodou "families" headed by *manbo*. In urban settings, much of the wage labor available to the poor is either piecework or domestic service, and, on average, women fare better than men in this job market. The resulting independence of women threatens Haitian men. But it also threatens women, who tend to experience the situation more as an onerous responsibility than as liberation.

Ironically, along with the rise in women's power in the cities has come a new emphasis on the ideology of romantic love, including reassertion of the belief that men should be in charge. Thus urban men and women, each in their own way and for their own reasons, often argue that male dominance is both traditional and ideal. Both Alourdes and Maggie have expressed this view, although their statements are tinged with irony.

In Alourdes's Brooklyn community, Kouzinn's deference to Azaka appears to take on the flavor of gender politics. In this context, its raison d'être may be the need to soothe male egos and to blunt the threat posed by the centrality of women's roles. Representing the notoriously strong and assertive market women, who nevertheless defer to the men of their *abitasyon* (rural homestead), the Vodou spirit Kouzinn is well suited to convey such complex and contradictory messages. In Chapter 8, questions of sexual politics will be explored more directly through the two Ezili, Dantò and Freda. Here, in Kouzinn's chapter, the emphasis is on the economics of women's lives.

HAITI'S MADAN SARA

Market women are called Madan Sara, after the raucous and busy little black finches found throughout Haiti.[2] The nickname

[2] The term is often used to refer more specifically to women who travel from place to place conducting fairly large-scale wholesale trade.

is usually understood as a caricature of market women's loud voices and aggressive sales techniques. Yet there is another, even more revealing, interpretation of the label. Some say the *machann* is named after the *madansara* bird because the female of the species will work herself to exhaustion hunting for food for her young.

In Brooklyn and in Port-au-Prince, men and women have different ideas about what constitutes dignified labor, and these differences affect their economic and social roles. Whereas women draw on the Madan Sara model for a style of earning a living that depends on constant work, high energy, and the ability to exploit several small and often erratic sources of income simultaneously, men usually find it demeaning to emulate the Madan Sara, and they consequently have less flexibility in weaving an economic safety net than women do.

Virtually all poor women are forced to be Madan Sara in one way or another. For years, Alourdes's grandmother, Marie Noelsine Joseph, carried produce, which she had also planted and harvested, from the fields of Jean Rabel to the market of Port-de-Paix. When her irresponsible husband forced her to leave Jean Rabel and the security of her extended family, she moved to Gros Morne and purchased a small piece of land with the savings from her market money. She planted vegetables and harvested them along with sour oranges and other fruits, all of which she sold in the big market in Gonaïves. With the profits, Sina bought the ingredients to bake bread in a backyard brick oven. Some of the money she made from selling this bread was reinvested in sugar and peanuts, from which she made candy. On those days when Marie Noelsine did not make the trek down the mountain to the Gonaïves market, she sat by the road, at the gate to her land, selling sweets to passersby.

There is a line that stretches through three generations, from the board across Marie Noelsine's knees holding dollops of peanut candy to Alourdes's bed in Brooklyn, where she once laid out for my inspection a dozen pretty nightgowns in various colors that had been given to her by a client of her healing practice. The line between these two makeshift markets runs through the endless varieties of small-scale commerce that women in Alourdes's family have pursued in order to survive.

The large open-air markets, both in the countryside and in Port-au-Prince, are almost exclusively the province of women;

only butchering, woodcarving, and a handful of other occupations are under male control. Women also walk the city streets selling from baskets carried on their heads: bread and eggs, Chiclets and mints, cigarettes singly and by the pack. Some carry yards of cloth folded on their heads and draped for display across outstretched arms. Others balance pyramids of aluminum pots and pans three feet above their heads.

In the center of Port-au-Prince, many corners are filled with merchants, mostly women. Women crouch by pots of stew or hot oil in which they fry plantain, fritters, and chunks of meat. Beneath the porticos of downtown buildings, stretching along entire blocks and taking up most of the sidewalk, are small tables displaying shoes, powder, soap, underwear, chromolithographs of Catholic saints, nail clippers, and mirrors. Many, but not all, of these merchants are women. Whenever the value of the merchandise (and the size of the profits) rises, so does the percentage of men doing the selling.

Poor Haitian women who have relatives in the United States or Canada introduce rich variations into the themes of commerce. If ten yards of fabric or a dozen pairs of children's shoes can be passed through customs without paying duty, they become the seed for another business enterprise. *Kòmès* (commerce) goes on everywhere, not only in the markets or on the streets. A casual visit to a friend's home may include examining a toaster, a lacy half-slip, and six packages of Bisquick—all for sale. A woman friend stopping by to deliver a message carries a small plastic bag containing red and black men's socks, two pairs of scissors, and a few infant T-shirts. "If you don't need the T-shirts, perhaps you will remember to tell Carline about them. She just had a baby." Successful *machann*, those with energy and an eye for a good price, may save enough to open a small shop.

Such was the case with Madame Alphonse, who was living with Alourdes's father when I met him, in 1980. She had worked hard as a young woman and had eventually opened her own *boutik*. But success can be dangerous, spawning jealousy and revenge. Madame Alphonse lost her business through magic. Someone sprinkled powder at the threshold of her house, and, when she stepped on it, she developed a debilitating swelling in her feet. Her illness forced her to retire, which in turn forced Alourdes's father, her estranged husband, to provide a place for her to live. When I met Madame Alphonse, she was in her eighties and had numerous physical problems—angina, dizziness, pains in her feet, ankles, and legs. But she still carried on a bit of *kòmès* on the side.

Alourdes's father owned a refrigerator, which was the necessary and sufficient cause of the little business Madame Alphonse ran from a shady spot in his side yard. She sold Haitian soda for thirteen cents, Coca-Cola for twenty cents, and corn muffins for two cents apiece. For those in the neighborhood who knew enough to make their way down the narrow alley, she was the source of tin cans of ice and rum bottles filled with cold water. She also sold cigarettes. Money from each enterprise was kept in its own ancient cigar box, all of which had fallen apart and been repaired with string, a large needle, and precise stitches. From her chair beneath the grenadine tree, Madame Alphonse kept a sharp eye on customers to be sure no one walked off with a bottle or a can. It was not clear whether the profits belonged entirely to Madame Alphonse or were shared with Alourdes's father, who was also known for his keen business sense. Whatever the case, like most Haitian men, he would never have engaged in such small-scale selling himself.

The Madan Sara is a well-known character in Haitian jokes, stories, and folktales. Like Kouzinn, she is known to drive hard bargains and keep careful accounts. Alourdes has inherited this sensibility and uses it well when she can. In 1980 Alourdes and I traveled together to Haiti. On the plane from New York, Alourdes showed me a list of things she had to get in Haiti. On her list were items such as plants and herbs. (Haiti remains the medicine chest of healers operating in New York.) Most of the items had to be purchased, however. Some were for herself and some for friends; some were to be used in Haiti, but most would be carried back to the United States. The list began with soap, coffee, and *kleren*—ingredients for a ritual feeding of the poor that would take place toward the end of our stay in Port-au-Prince—and moved on to items needed for her spirit work in New York, including gourd rattles, a whip, two bottles of almond extract, three pinches of earth from the center of the market, three more from the cemetery and three from in front of the church, baskets, small chairs for the dolls that sit on her altars, glycerin-phosphate (a dietary supplement), tobacco leaves, and *afiba* (dried beef tripe).

From the moment we arrived, Alourdes began to carefully in-

A *machann* selling fruit juice on a main street in Port-au-Prince, 1980.

quire about the going prices and the best places to find what she needed. When she decided what constituted a good price, she wrote it on her list. Then, when she asked someone to buy the item for her, she told that person exactly where to make the purchase and handed over exactly the sum she had decided to spend.

This amount of financial control is possible in Port-au-Prince, which is, after all, a relatively small town where most prices are still open to bargaining. Financial dealings are a different matter in New York, where Alourdes's small income and lack of mobility often force her to pay premium prices for substandard goods. Myrtle Avenue, for example, a main shopping street in Fort Greene, is notorious for the high prices charged for poor-quality meats and vegetables. Or, to give another sort of example, Alourdes and Maggie once purchased a small freezer on the installment plan. The freezer stopped working after three weeks, but the store owner refused to fix it or take it back. Then he harassed them with bill collectors and eventually intimidated them into continuing to make payments. Haiti's economy is rife with graft and corruption, but it is nevertheless easier for a poor woman to be a good Madan Sara in Haiti, exercising caution and control in spending money, than it is in New York.

Money falls through one's fingers in New York, a lesson Alourdes learned the hard way during her early years in the United States. Her first job was as a cleaning woman in an art school in Brooklyn. She was fired just before she was due to receive health care benefits. To justify the firing, her boss accused Alourdes of sleeping on the job. Alourdes went to his office with a Haitian co-worker to refute the charge, but her friend fell mute in the face of authority.

After leaving the art school, Alourdes turned to an employment agency in Brighton Beach, which placed domestic workers on a daily basis. This work was quite an adventure for Alourdes, who at first knew only three words of English: mop, pail, and vacuum. Her English rapidly improved, but other problems plagued her career as a domestic. On one occasion in 1963, she had to ask the police to intervene in order to collect the ten dollars (plus thirty cents for carfare) she had earned for eight hours of housecleaning. Alourdes had vacuumed, scrubbed, dusted, and polished three floors (each with its own bathroom) of a townhouse on Manhattan's Upper East Side. Finding the condition of one of the bathrooms less than perfect, the owner of the house announced that Alourdes had to stay until the job was done correctly or leave without her money. "I got my children at home. They waiting for me," Alourdes objected. The woman then began to rant about Haiti and Haitians. She "knew all about them." She had once taken a cruise that stopped in Haiti, and there were beggars in the street—beggars everywhere!

"Maybe you were one of them," the woman concluded. "Lady," Alourdes responded, "I don't come here to discuss my country with you. I come here to clean. Eight hours for ten dollars. Pay me. My children waiting."

For a short time, Alourdes also did piecework in the garment industry, first as a trimmer and later as the operator of a large pressing machine. She was not happy with this job. Most of all, she hated the pressure of having her wages depend on the speed with which she worked, so she soon found a position in a large commercial laundry. This was a better fit. Her laundry experience enabled Alourdes, shortly after her first trip back to Haiti, to obtain steady work at the Brooklyn Hebrew Home. She stayed there two years, the longest she has held any position other than that of *manbo*. Although Alourdes has not worked in a laundry for nearly twenty years, she still lists "laundry" as her occupation on travel documents. "I love laundry," she says. "Laundry is good work!"

Maggie's job history is somewhat different. Even though she holds a two-year college degree in education, that field has remained closed to her. But she has held jobs that are at least marginally more responsible, more long-term, and better-paying than those Alourdes held in her early years in New York City. When I first met Maggie in 1978, she was working behind the counter in a fast-food restaurant in Newark, New Jersey. For a short period after that, she worked as a receptionist at a Catholic rectory. Things improved when she moved into health care work, a field that employs many Haitian women. First she became an assistant in a gynecological clinic on Manhattan's Upper East Side. Now she works as a nurse's aide at a city hospital and is taking a course in emergency medicine to advance her standing. But there is little of the Madan Sara in Maggie. During the 1987 Christmas season, the shopping channel on cable television enticed her to spend most of one month's salary.

BARTERING WITH SEX

In the spirit of the *madansara*, poor Haitian women sell whatever they have to in order to survive and to feed and care for their children. A *machann* I encountered on a 1987 trek across Haiti's southern peninsula had her own irreverent way of describing her assets. "Where are you going?" I asked her. "To the market in Kenscoff," she replied. "What do you have to sell?" I queried. "Beautiful tomatoes. A few beans," she said, "and my land." "You are going to sell your land in the market?" I asked, uncertain I had heard her correctly. *"Wi!"* she hooted and grabbed her crotch. "I can sell my land anywhere!"

After Jean Claude Duvalier was forced into exile in February 1986, the first well-organized public demonstration was a women's march through the streets of Port-au-Prince, in part protesting the widespread practice of women being forced to exchange sex for jobs. During a difficult period when Alourdes was still in Port-au-Prince and solely responsible for supporting two children, she sought and eventually obtained employment as an inspector in the government-run tobacco industry. Many years later, she described her job-hunting experience in this way: "Let me tell you something. When you go to the office and ask for job, that man—the inspector, the one in the head office—if he say, 'Yes, I'm going give you that job,' you have to make love first!"

"What happens when you say no?" I responded naïvely. Alourdes quickly shot back: "You say no, you don't have no job!" And then she added, "Sometime they make love to you, and after, you still don't have no job. They just want to make love to you. For nothing!" "Don't you get angry about being treated that way?" I asked, still wishing to avoid the harsh conclusion that some types of self-respect are only for those who can afford them. "Sometime," Alourdes sighed. "Sometime when I think back, I get angry. But that's life! I can't help it. That's life."

Alourdes's first job, at age sixteen, was as a singer in Haiti's Troupe Folklorique. She earned what was, for her and for that time, an enormous sum: sixty-two dollars a month. Her singing career ended when she married. From the time this brief marriage broke up until she came to the United States, Alourdes's financial situation deteriorated steadily. When she lost her job as a tobacco inspector, she was driven to sell sexual favors more directly and more frequently. There was no other way to buy food, pay her rent, and manage her children's school fees.

Alourdes began to work as a "Marie-Jacques," a method of selling one's "land" that is considered several steps above the occupation of *bouzen* (street prostitute). At first, she dressed up in her best clothes and visited offices throughout Port-au-Prince. She flirted and made small talk until one of the male workers asked her for a "date." It was understood that she would sleep with him after going dancing or to the movies, but it would have been a major breach of etiquette for either party to have mentioned a price. At the end of the evening, Alourdes accepted whatever the man gave her. "I don't charge. I go bed with them, and they give me whatever they want. I don't have no courage to charge. They give ten dollar, fifteen . . . twelve . . . five dollar sometime."

After several years of this, Alourdes arranged with a chauffeur to refer tourists to her when they asked for "a good person . . . not a public lady who have some kind'a disease." She explained, "They was private tourist. . . . Businessman who come to Haiti . . . they want a good lady. You have to dress up like you going to a wedding. I meet them. I go to club with them . . . you know." Alourdes paused in her painful story and suddenly laughed: "Lot'a time, he don't speak French. When we go bed, I don't know what he talkin' about! I just say yes, yes, yes." In a more serious mood, she added: "Sometime you find a good man, and they see you poor, you got children, they give you fifty dollar, one hundred dollar. But you don't find good man every day."

When I asked if she had any bad experiences working as a Marie-Jacques, Alourdes responded not with stories of physical or psychological abuse but with tales of those few times when no money was forthcoming at the end of an evening. "I party all night, and I go bed with him, and the next day I don't have no money to feed my children! Sure, I have bad experience. Everybody have bad experience." When a man failed to keep his end of their unspoken bargain, Alourdes's pride forbade her to say anything. She said good-night and went home from "visiting a friend" (the way she described her absences to her children) with nothing in her hand to compensate for the shame she never stopped feeling.

Miraculously, Alourdes did not become pregnant by any of these men. "When I say, 'I don't want to get pregnant,' a friend tell me: 'Don't get lazy! As soon as you finish make love, get up, and sit down in the bathroom, on the toilet seat. You drink one aspirin, plus a glass of water, and you take that finger [the index finger] and you put it in your belly button, and you press it while you drink that water with the aspirin. And all the sperm coming. Nothing don't stay inside!' When I go to work, I always got aspirin with me. Always!"

Alourdes did become pregnant by a friend during this time, but their lovemaking was not a business arrangement. René was a man she cared for, and he hurt her badly, deserting her when he learned she was going to have their child. This third child was William, who suffered brain damage from meningitis that went untreated because Alourdes had no money. "When William five month old, he get very sick. He get meningitis, and then pneumonia. Both of them. I have no penny that time. He get so hot, like he going to burn up. Middle of the night, I go to the hospital, they give me a prescription and I can't even buy— fifty-two *goud!* Ten dollar, forty cent. I can't buy that medicine. They cut my electricity, and I don't even have gas to put in the lamp. I just sit in the dark, William in my arm."

A short time after this trauma, Alourdes met and fell in love with Gabriel. The economic security this relationship provided allowed Alourdes to stop dating for money. Gabriel was a taxi driver, and although his income was not large, it was steady. They had been living together happily for nearly three years when Alourdes arranged to have a letter written to her brother in New York, asking for one hundred dollars that would allow her to begin a little *kòmès* to supplement Gabriel's income. Her brother's response was surprising. He offered her a choice. He would send either the money or a notarized letter stating he would be her sponsor if she chose to emigrate to the United States.

Alourdes once said: "Poor people don't have no true love. They just have affiliation." Ever the good Madan Sara, Alourdes broke off her relationship with Gabriel and decided to go to the United States. But the first time she applied at the U.S. embassy for her visa, her past came back to haunt her. The American consul said: "How do I know you are not going there to work as a prostitute? Maybe this fellow Jean is not your brother, maybe he is your pimp." It took a full year for Alourdes to convince him that Jean was her brother; only then was she allowed to start the emigration process.

THE MARKETPLACE OF THE SPIRITS

Service is one of the things the Madan Sara trade. For a few, their trading partners include the Vodou spirits. Serving the spirits is a lifelong commitment and a heavy responsibility. The decision to serve has never been made quickly or easily by the women in Alourdes's family. There are several ways to understand why a woman would make such a move; one is to see it as an economic strategy. For Philo and Alourdes, this is particularly clear. Their decisions to work as healers came in the midst of financial crises, and both eventually found steadier income doing spirit work than they were able to generate in the job market.

It is a truism that for poor Haitian women issues of money and love cannot be separated. Thus another way to understand the decision to work for the spirits is to see it as an alternative to inadequate love relationships. Vodou spirits are ideal lovers—protective, constant, powerful, and, if treated right, benevolent. From this perspective, a decision to serve the spirits becomes a decision to stop serving men. The fact that lovers, human and divine, are pitted against one another in the volatile mix of love and money is made plain by both Philo's and Alourdes's stories.

Agèou, who eventually became Philo's main spirit, made a surprising appearance in her life when she was caught in a dilemma created in equal measure by love and by money.[3] On her way back from Gros Morne after her mother's death, Philo stopped in Port-au-Prince. She had spent or given away all her money, and she had to wire Luc Charles for funds to return to Santo Domingo. Luc Charles, angry with her for staying away so long, sent nothing. Instead, it was Agèou who presented Philo with a solution.

Philo was staying with a friend in Port-au-Prince. The friend's son suddenly developed a high fever and was rushed to the hospital. Agèou appeared in Philo's head (the first time he had possessed her) and ordered the woman to retrieve her son from the hospital. "Lady," the spirit ordered, "go get your child. Go get him quickly! If you don't, that child is going to die tonight.

[3] Agèou, originally a Dominican spirit, should not be confused with the Vodou spirit Agàou. Alourdes says that, in Haiti, Agèou is served only in her family. Philo's relationship with Agèou was a product of her sojourn in Santo Domingo. She brought him to Haiti and subsequently merged him with the group of spirits known as Ogou. My impression is that the connection between Agèou (or Agaju) and Ogou is not made in the Spanish-speaking Caribbean.

Go now! I am waiting for you!" The doctors did not want to release the boy, but Philo's friend was convinced that the spirit
should be heeded. She brought the feverish ten-year-old home
in the middle of the night and found Agèou still there.

The spirit directed the mother to go out in the yard and drop
one penny at the foot of the *vèvenn* tree, shake the tree hard,
and collect three leaves. With the leaves, Agèou made a tea, to
which he added a bit of salt and sugar. After drinking the tea,
the boy fell into a deep sleep. Agèou stayed in Philo's head and
sat with the child throughout the night. The next morning, the
boy opened his eyes, looked at his mother, and said, "Mama,
I'm hungry. Can you make me some soup?" A grateful mother
gave Philo the money for passage back to the Dominican Republic and back to Luc Charles. Philo's relationship with Luc
Charles, however, was over in less than a year.

Philo knew that performing healing work with Agèou as her
spirit guide could bring financial security, but she resisted the
loneliness, the heavy commitment of time and energy, and the
change in lifestyle such a decision would necessitate. She was
young then, barely twenty, and she still dreamed of finding a
good man to support her and her children. Instead of pursu-
ing her relationship with Agèou, Philo found a new lover-
companion and had two more children. But this man turned
out to be more difficult than Luc Charles; he even had a child
with another woman while he was living with Philo. His infidelity eventually drove Philo back to Port-au-Prince and, in
time, into the arms of the spirits.

Soon after Philo returned to Haiti, the spirits increased their
pressure on her, and they did so through a series of well-timed
dreams. Philo was struggling to provide for three children and
had just discovered she was pregnant with a fourth, Alourdes.
In these crucial dreams, the spirits promised Philo precisely
what the ideal husband should offer: "I will support you. I will
give you everything. I'll give you drink; I'll give you food."

Alourdes's story is similar. She decided to heed the call of the
spirits and return to Haiti to be initiated when she hit rock bottom in New York. She was separated from her children, sick,
unable to find a job, and dependent on the charity of a family
friend. After she came to the United States, Alourdes was no
longer willing to sell sexual favors. This time, she turned to the
spirits. Perhaps not surprisingly, the word *love* is frequently

used in Alourdes's accounts of her spiritual call. "Papa Ogou want me to *kouche* [to be initiated] because he love me." Ironically, it appears that the Marie-Jacques and the *manbo* have something in common: neither charges for her services; both depend, in theory at least, on unsolicited gifts from satisfied clients. Alourdes has found this way of making money easier now that it is her spiritual expertise that is being judged and rewarded.

Doing spirit work allows Alourdes to trade a variety of goods and services with a wide range of people. From one perspective, my friendship with Alourdes is also a barter relationship. She accepted me into her world, in spite of some initial resistance from her community, because she decided that it would pay off in the long run. This book has become an important factor in our exchange patterns. I visit her frequently, bring her small gifts, and routinely assist at her spirit birthday parties. In turn, Alourdes teaches me about many things. She has been especially generous in discussing her life and sharing her family stories as I have worked on this project; in return, she will share any profits of our enterprise.

Soon after the idea of the book was born, I realized I would need to visit Gros Morne and Jean Rabel, her rural family homesteads. I wanted to develop a general sense of these places, and I also wanted to meet the heirs of the Kouzen and Kouzinn Zaka types who appear in her ancestral stories. In the summer of 1979, I proposed a trip for the following January, explaining that I would pay travel and certain other expenses. Alourdes could visit her family in Port-au-Prince and take care of some ritual obligations, but the main purpose of our trip would be to visit Gros Morne and Jean Rabel. Alourdes readily agreed.

A TRIP TO THE PROVINCES

Alourdes and I arrived in Haiti on January 18, 1980. The plan was to leave for "the interior" early on the morning of January 21. We would go to Gros Morne and then, after a short visit, push on north to the more remote Jean Rabel. Preparing for a trip into "the provinces" raises anxieties for city folk, so we spent most of one day laying in provisions and most of another discussing with everyone we encountered the current condition of the roads and the most desirable routes. We also rented a minibus for the difficult trip, promising the driver approximately eighty dollars a day to forgo his usual taxi service. His brightly painted bus was named "The Gamble," a name that would be the source of many jokes on the trying Jean Rabel leg of our trip.

The Gamble was due to arrive at five in the morning at the home of Chantal, Alourdes's sister, who lived in Bizoton, just off the coast road south of Port-au-Prince. In my experience in Haiti, plan and reality rarely match, but this time the driver ascended the hill to the cluster of tiny houses where Chantal lived before dawn, beeping his horn all the way and calling out: "Look, Madame Albert! Look how I made the bus beautiful for you today!" (Most people called Chantal "Madame Albert," Albert being the first name of a long-gone husband. This is a common, respectful mode of address for any woman who has been married, no matter how briefly.)

Madame Rigaud, a *manbo* from the next town south and an old friend of Alourdes's, was going with us, as was Justin, Alourdes's current "boyfriend." The driver, who also owned the minibus, brought along a relief driver and another man to help with flat tires and the more serious problems that sometimes occur while ascending rocky mountain roads and fording rivers in Haiti's interior. Nervous excitement prevailed as we clambered onto the bus. For the first half hour, talk was fast and noisy, most of it about the adequacy of our supplies and the wisdom of the routes we had chosen.

Leaving Port-au-Prince and heading north is a journey with a distinctive rhythm. It is as if the city would hold on to you as long as possible and subject you to its most intense self just before spewing you out onto the wide north road with its long vistas—ocean on one side, mountains on the other. The congestion was thickest around the Iron Market at the far end of town. Many *taptap* (colorful buses like The Gamble, nicknamed and painted with sacred and secular scenes) vied for space with people, burros, cars, jeeps, and the enormous lorries that carry produce and passengers from the interior. In the chaotic traffic, the biggest and the most brazen vehicles bullied their way forward, while the rest waited for a chance opening to shimmy through. Together, we made up a passel of fish, large and small, brightly colored and drab, pushing through a narrow channel out into the vast sea of the countryside.

The road from Port-au-Prince to Croix-de-Mission was populated terrain, but much less intensely so than the city itself. In the morning hours, the roadsides were sprinkled with those who had to walk because they had no other choice. They were heading toward the city market. As it is mostly women who sell, it is mostly the heads of women that bear the weight of commerce. When men do the toting and hauling, they tend to commandeer the backs of beasts and the bellies of machines. As roads have begun to open the interior of Haiti, men have begun to carry more of the loads. No longer restricted by what the human body or the back of a mule can bear, the payloads increase, as does the power of the men who transport them.

The French, who designed and built the new road, reinforced this social hierarchy. A beautiful, modern highway that will eventually run from the southern tip of Haiti to Cap Haitian in the north, it is the only road outside the city on which it is possible to go faster than a few miles an hour. It is also clearly designed for machines, not people. There is no sidewalk, and for long stretches there is not even a berm to accommodate the thousands who walk it every day. At some spots, people carrying heavy loads must scramble up steep embankments to get onto the road. Truck drivers in Haiti have become a macho hybrid, an elite cadre of men who display their newfound power by barreling along like angry bulls, terrorizing all who walk. Pedestrians and peasants (the two being virtually the same) have no rights on the highway.

After the bridge at Croix-de-Mission, the road was more hospitable, and the contest between those who walked and those who drove more episodic. The road followed the coast to St. Marc, winding past thatch-roof huts as well as the incongruous—and, in this poor country, obscene—Club Méditerranée. As the road cut inland on a straight route to Gonaïves, the sun sat higher in the sky and the cool gold light of morning was gone. Shadows on the mountains had begun to sort themselves from bright patches of sunlight. At mid-morning, soft crevices appeared in the coastal mountains, like those between breasts and buttocks. The mountains in Haiti are not high, averaging only about twenty-five hundred feet, but they have a special soft beauty I have found nowhere else in the world.

Such easy reveries ended abruptly just beyond Gonaïves as we left the highway and started the long climb to Gros Morne. The Gamble rattled and jarred. During the most precipitous part of the uphill climb, I made the unpleasant discovery that if I relaxed even a little my head banged sharply against the window. We scaled the mountain during the hottest part of the day on a narrow, rocky road that ran through polka-dot cottonfields. Thick dust coated the bushes and trees abutting the road and obliterated the last trace of green from our field of vision. We were finally forced to tie handkerchiefs over our mouths to keep from choking on the grit that poured into the bus in a steady geyser through a hole in the floor over the right rear tire. Looking at my traveling companions, I had a quick fantasy of being in a hopelessly slow getaway car with a group of bandits gradually being turned into plaster statues.

Hours later, a cheer went up in the bus and handkerchiefs were removed as we entered the town of Gros Morne. The town consisted of a small market at one end of a street about two blocks long on which tiny pastel houses leaned on one another at the edge of the road. Most had handpainted picture-signs advertising goods and services for sale: bread, beer, tailoring, hair pressing. Here we stopped to check on the location of Alourdes's cousin's home. We were directed through the *bouk*, as rural town centers are called, and across a stream filled with people bathing or sudsing and pounding laundry. The driver of The Gamble stopped ten yards from the stream, backed up, and, without warning, charged through the water at high speed, dousing giggling children and causing women to rush toward colored patches of clothes drying on nearby rocks.

A quarter of a mile on the other side of the stream, we found the parcel of arid land purchased by Marie Noelsine Joseph, now home to Marie Thérèse, daughter of Gloria Macena and granddaughter of Marie Noelsine. The Gamble stopped by a low cactus hedge, and Marie Thérèse came to the side window. She was barefoot, painfully skinny, and wore a ragged black dress. She was then in her late thirties, but her face, stretched tight over the skull beneath, could have been that of a woman anywhere between twenty-five and sixty. There had been no way to let her know we were coming, yet Marie Thérèse showed no sign of surprise, pleasure, or even recognition as she spoke with Alourdes. Only when we began to unload our ample cargo did she come to life.

Whatever plans Marie Thérèse had for this day were set aside. Her time, her energy, and her modest home were placed immediately and completely at our disposal. Her *ti-kay* (little house) was meager: one small room, whose walls had been jury-rigged from bits of wood, banana leaves, cardboard, and corrugated tin. Gaps a foot or more wide appeared in the walls in several places. But the house did have a brand-new door and frame. Marie Thérèse announced proudly that Alphonse, her new *mennaj* (lover-companion), had hung it for her. She said it as if it were sufficient reason to love any man.

Marie Thérèse wore black because she was in mourning for Ilium, her husband of many years, then seven months in his grave. Alourdes said that Ilium had been "a good man . . . good, good, good!" Dropping her voice, she added: "That man she got now, he too young for her. I don't know, maybe he want to take the land. I don't like that!" Alphonse may not have been ideal for Marie Thérèse, but she may have had no choice. She was the sole survivor of her generation left on the family land. The only others in Gros Morne with a claim to the land were her five children, the oldest barely a teenager. Marie Thérèse grew beans, millet, and bananas; she kept a cow and some goats. She could not have handled the farm by herself.

Inside the *ti-kay* sat a double bed and two rickety tables used to hold cooking utensils and food. Clothes, such as they were, were stored under the mattress. The oldest daughter, like Marie Thérèse, showed the effects of hunger: she had the body of a seven- or eight-year-old, although she was twelve. This child, full of secrecy and big plans, had her own special corner of the mattress under which she stored private treasures. Other family possessions were kept in the rafters above the bed in a suitcase artfully fashioned from scavenged tin. In its colorful, crazy-quilt pattern could be seen the remnants of old motor-oil, margarine, and powdered-milk cans.

In front of the eight-by-ten-foot hut was the much larger *tonnèl*—a broad thatched roof, open to the air, supported at four corners and the center by irregular poles of stripped sapling. Family members spent their time here when they were not working in the fields or off to the market in Gonaïves. In back of the house and behind a second cactus fence was the *lakou* (yard) containing Alphonse Macena's broken-down rum-making apparatus and remnants of the brick oven in which Marie Noelsine had baked bread. There was also a well, used not only by Marie Thérèse's family but also by several neighbors. Marie Thérèse apologized to Alourdes for the unkempt yard and for the condition of her house. "You will see," she concluded in an eager voice. "When you come back, I am going to have a beautiful house, all closed!"

On one side of her *ti-kay*, Marie Thérèse had a cactus corral for goats. All but the kids wore ungainly triangular wooden collars that kept them inside the corral. On the other side of the hut was a pile of *pitimi* (millet), with the wooden paddle Marie Thérèse had been using to thresh the grain when we arrived. Strenuous labor is needed to extract the edible portion of millet; many consider it the last resort of the hungry. Marie Thérèse abandoned her threshing when we arrived, and the millet pile was trampled and chewed by the baby goats that wandered about freely. When we said our final good-byes two days later, most of it was gone. But on the day we arrived, we replaced what promised to be a scanty meal of millet gruel with a veritable banquet.

After our things were unloaded and placed under the *tonnèl*, food preparation began. The first order of business was coffee. As we sat drinking the tiny cups—half sugar, half coffee—people began to arrive, as if they had picked up the scent of food, possessions, and money. Those who knew Marie Thérèse well, including some distant cousins, came in under the *tonnèl*. Others stood outside the cactus fence and stared. Our presence and the late afternoon hour—the time when people returned from the fields—soon produced a steady stream along the road in front of the house: men in blue denim with straw hats and straw satchels, women smoking pipes and riding sidesaddle on burros. Most moved by slowly and without comment, examining us closely as they passed.

In between the silent Kouzen and Kouzinn Zakas were bands of noisy, curious children returning from school in the *bouk*, all dressed in identical red-checkered shirts, with navy blue pants for the boys and navy blue skirts for the girls. Marie Thérèse's children did not attend school and appeared to want little contact with those who did. (Even in the local church-run school, families had to purchase uniforms.) Her raggedy children hung their heads and scratched in the dirt at our feet as a swarm of checkered shirts examined The Gamble inch by inch and eyed our case of cola. These neighbor children nudged one another in the ribs and speculated in easily overheard voices about the *blan* sitting under Marie Thérèse's *tonnèl*. A brave one called out to me: "*Eh, blan!*" and Madame Albert reprimanded him sharply and without hesitation. "*Ti-moun malelve* [Badly reared child]!" she snapped. "Call her Madame."

Alourdes had not visited Gros Morne in more than a decade. As cousins and neighbors arrived, she reconnected with them by rehearsing family history. Among them was a man in his early thirties whom everyone called Tonton (Uncle). He was the nephew of Marie Thérèse's dead husband. Once Alourdes had placed him, she launched into a song for the *lwa* that had been composed by his father. Tonton's face, otherwise flat and expressionless beneath his worn straw hat, lit up when he heard the familiar refrain, and he soon joined in the singing. No one is more charming than Alourdes when she is in an expansive mood, and she charmed this hardscrabble farmer. Alourdes and Tonton ended the song locked in an embrace, rocking back and forth to the rhythm of the chorus. By that time, more than a dozen locals had come beneath the *tonnèl* to visit with the city people. Most sat on their haunches around Alourdes's short-legged wooden chair. She talked, laughed, sang, and generally entertained the folk of Gros Morne.

All afternoon, a portable radio blared away under the *tonnèl*. Radios are essential in mountain communities. We heard mostly music, but occasionally the announcer broke in with messages in Creole: "Marie Rose, who lives in Basin Bleu by the river, get in touch with Olina right away. She has a message for you from your family." "Madame Roger, who lives in the mountains behind Port-de-Paix, come home right away. Your child is ill."

Dozens of times during the afternoon, the disk jockey played the same song, one by a popular group called Tabou Combo. It was a simple ditty with two repetitive lines sung to an insistent, energizing beat: "New York City, New York City, New York City"; then, "Haiti, Haiti, Haiti." During the days we spent in Port-au-Prince, the song had been our constant companion, sallying forth from the doorways of countless shops in the heart of the city. It played repeatedly on the radio in Madame Albert's home in Bizoton, and we rarely rode a *taptap* without "New York City, New York City" banging around the interior of the packed bus. When we had set out, early that morning, Alourdes had larded the anxious conversation about provisions with the Tabou Combo line: "New York City, New York City, New York City." But she never sang the second line.

Alourdes was caught between New York and Haiti. For her,

our trip was a sentimental journey, a pilgrimage to her country, her family, and her ancestral land. She made the journey to strengthen the bonds between New York City and Haiti. But, paradoxically, she also needed to put distance between the two. She wanted to affirm how far she had come in the world and how different her current life was from the meager existence she had left behind. A desire to distance herself showed in the constant comparisons she made. Sitting around her sister's house, for example, she commented to no one in particular, "Everything in Haiti so little. Houses in Haiti real little. In New York, houses got plenty room, room for whatever you want."

I became another means for Alourdes to distinguish herself from the local people. When she introduced me to her father, she mentioned right away that I was writing a book about her. She demonstrated how thick the book would be (a good three inches!) and announced: "After she finish, they going to mount a film on that book!"

Language was also an important area of self-definition. In New York, Alourdes and I switch back and forth between Haitian Creole and English as the topic demands. We routinely speak English and tend to fall into Creole when we discuss spiritual matters or human relationships. (Creole is far better for talking about people.) Although Alourdes's English is ordinarily quite good, after only a few days in Haiti I noticed that she was becoming less and less facile, stumbling over the most ordinary words and expressions. That seemed understandable, and so during the trip we spoke to each other almost exclusively in Creole.

The notable exceptions to our use of Creole were public situations in which we might have been overheard. Boarding a *taptap* for the half-hour ride from Port-au-Prince to Alourdes's sister's home in Bizoton signaled a switch to English. Climbing onto the bus, Alourdes observed the Haitian custom of greeting the other passengers, but she did so in English. "How are you?" she asked, with a big, lipsticked smile. Then she started a conversation with me in English, making many references to New York. I was a willing collaborator in this game. I have sometimes done the same thing on *taptap* rides, only in reverse; speaking Creole with a companion is a ploy to avoid being mistaken for a tourist. Alourdes, in contrast, did not want to be mistaken for an ordinary Haitian. The market woman in the next seat wearing a headrag and dangling three live chickens between her knees seemed to me far removed from Alourdes; but Alourdes herself could not be so sanguine, and I could understand that, too. Yet at times on that trip with her, empathy failed me and judgment intruded.

One such time came early in the evening of the day we arrived in Gros Morne. The sun had not set, and dinner was under way. A good-sized chunk of goat meat purchased in the *bouk* had been transformed into sizzling, bite-sized morsels, and the smell was attracting a growing crowd of Gros Morne's hungry and curious. At this moment, Alourdes chose to announce that she could not eat until she had her bath. Although it meant postponing the meal for everyone, Alourdes's wish had the status of a command in this group. Water was hauled up from the well, and, when all was ready, Alourdes took herself behind the house with several of Marie Thérèse's children in tow. After some time, I got up and followed.

When I rounded the corner of the *ti-kay*, I saw, against the backdrop of a crimson and ocher sky, a naked Alourdes, looking for all the world like the Venus of Willendorf come to life, her skin glistening with moisture. Her legs were planted wide apart, and her arms were held straight out from her sides. One child was working on each limb, smoothing in the contents of a bottle of lotion, which they passed from hand to hand. ("Queen bee!" I thought.) "Have a good bath?" I asked. "Yes!" she smiled lazily. "That feel good!"

The Dance of Reciprocity

In time, I would better understand the subtleties of exchange in that scene, and I would come to see her behavior with a less judgmental eye. The lesson came in stages, with an important piece of the puzzle falling into my hands two days later. We had returned to Gros Morne after an abortive attempt to get to Jean Rabel. It was mid-afternoon, and we were preparing to go back to Port-au-Prince. I had little to pack and decided to take a short walk. By the time I sauntered back into Marie Thérèse's yard, The Gamble was loaded, and the driver was leaning on the horn, anxious to get back to Port-au-Prince before dark. Driving on the coast road after sunset is dangerous; pedestrians and animals appear in the headlights without warning, and truck drivers often turn off their lights when they stop along the road. With The Gamble's horn urging me on, I ran toward the *ti-kay* to fetch my things.

As I opened the door, Marie Thérèse froze. My duffle bag was open on her bed, and she had my bottle of Ammens Medicated Powder in her hand. She had been shaking its contents into a small round box with a fluffy purple powder puff, an incongruous object in this spare setting. Her matchstick arm stopped in mid-air, and powder dribbled from the half-open holes in the lid. Her whole body communicated shame at being caught in this act of pilfering.

Discussing logistics is sometimes helpful in awkward moments. "You have to open it all the way," I said in a matter-of-fact tone. I took the bottle from her, twisted the cap open, and poured half its contents into her powder box. (I held some back because Ammens powder is one of the few things I find essential when traveling in Haiti. It eases insect bites and, in a pinch, is a reasonable substitute for a bath.) Marie Thérèse responded to my half-gift with embarrassingly genuine gratitude. "Don't tell Alourdes," she whispered like a child. I gave her money, a skirt, and a purple T-shirt. Then I ran.

As I took my place in The Gamble, I was awash in discomfiting memories of the surprisingly cold night when we, the guests, had been given the only bed in her *ti-kay*, while Marie Thérèse curled up with her children on a pile of rags on the floor. One of her girls had a hacking cough that erupted periodically throughout the night; all her children had red and brittle hair, indicating advanced malnutrition. Standing beside the bus as we pulled away, Marie Thérèse mouthed the words: "*Manman*, don't forget me." "How could I ever forget?" I thought.

It is never possible to give enough in Haiti. Gifts of money are like water in the desert. They are badly needed, but what I have to give is not enough to make a real difference. I have been going to Haiti since 1973, and over the years I have made an uneasy peace with the more or less constant guilt and inadequacy I feel when I am there. But this trip taught me how my own behavior exacerbated the situation. I grew up in the United States, a country founded by rebels against peerage and privilege, and I am well schooled in what constitutes pretension (the "queen bee" syndrome, for example) and what is appropriately humble, I'm-just-one-of-the-folks behavior. In Gros Morne, I cheerfully attended to my own luggage and amiably turned aside Marie

Thérèse's inquiries about favorite foods and the way I like things cooked. By doing this, I also unwittingly moved my gifts to her out of the realm of reciprocity and into that of charity. I also forced her to take from me what she could not justify asking for but craved nonetheless. A dollop of the mystique of a foreign woman? A sprinkling of femininity?

It was such a small thing, that bit of powder, but it made an old truth concrete. Charity breeds thievery, and both are deeply flawed human exchanges because both lack reciprocity. Marie Thérèse pointed to such a lack of balance when she called me, a woman of her own age, "*manman*." As The Gamble clattered along the mountain road, I began to see Alourdes's predinner bath in a new light. With four limbs to be dried and rubbed with lotion, Alourdes had placed herself four times in the debt of Marie Thérèse's family, balancing at least partially the gift of a case of cola, sacks of vegetables, and the left hindquarter of a goat.

Alourdes works hard to keep her relations with family in the arena of reciprocity. It is not always easy, however, to achieve even the appearance of balance. The morning after we arrived in Haiti, Marie Carmelle, Madame Albert's daughter, came to visit. She sat on the pallet where Alourdes and I had slept and rummaged eagerly through Alourdes's suitcase. "Make me a present of this white dress!" she said. "No," Alourdes replied, and then softened a little: "When I finish wearing it, I give it to you." By scaling down her demands, Marie Carmelle got a half-slip from me and another from Alourdes. She then found a bar of deodorant soap and claimed it without protest. Before long, she tried again for the object she coveted: "You got to give me that dress!" "I give it to you tomorrow," Alourdes said.

Marie Carmelle dug further in the suitcase and found a package of Rolaids. "I'm going to take these mints," she announced. "That not mint," Alourdes retorted, "that medicine." "Oh, medicine!" cried Marie Carmelle, "I need that." Alourdes said brusquely: "Organize that suitcase for me. Everything inside a mess!"

Marie Carmelle would meet this demand later, but for the moment something else caught her attention. Raising the lid of Alourdes's other suitcase, she whooped in delight: "Oh, look! Look at the little market! I'm going to take this towel. Who's this perfume for? Oh, what a beautiful blouse!"

"I pay six dollar for that!" Alourdes said, grabbing the blouse from her hand. "You hear me? Six dollar!" Then Alourdes inspected the garment and added, "But it don't even got a button. What you say? Can you put a button for me?"

Before we left Haiti, Marie Carmelle had the white dress, several other articles of clothing, and some cash, all of which Alourdes doled out in careful installments over our three-week stay. A similar process went on with half a dozen other relatives. Marie Carmelle carefully repacked the suitcases and sewed a button on the blouse. Madame Albert organized the trips to Gros Morne and Jean Rabel and supervised the ritual feeding of the poor. Such services in return for gifts maintained the appearance of family exchange, but, in truth, the atmosphere was strained. Family members were treated like children from time to time, and Alourdes sometimes became petulant and demanding.

The deep love of family and the complex pull toward its orbit are natural to Alourdes's temperament, as well as being the products of her religion and culture. Given these stressful conditions, however, she tends to feel clearer about that love from a distance. On our Haitian sojourn, Alourdes periodically became depressed about missing Maggie and the children left behind in New York. She called home four times, the last a lengthy call placed less than a day before our return. "There so many people at my house! I had to talk to everybody. Everybody asking for me. Everybody miss me so much!" Alourdes pouted: "I miss my bed. I miss my house. I miss my children."

But the airplane was not thirty minutes out of Port-au-Prince when she began to talk about going back to Haiti to live. It was not possible now, of course; she would need more money. Perhaps when she was sixty-five, she would return to Haiti. Then Alourdes got lost in a frequent fantasy: she would tear down her mother's old house on Oswald Durand and build a better one . . . put a little shop in the front . . . sell beautiful skirts and blouses.

Maggie came to the United States when she was an adolescent, and her ties to Haiti, though deep, are largely spiritual and sentimental. But Alourdes's commitments to the family of spirits are grounded in commitments to a human family, most of whom still live in Haiti. And so her hunger for family persists, in spite of the frustrations that escalate every time she deals with her family, frustrations arising from their poverty and the high expectations they have attached to her. My picture of Alourdes's life in New York includes the afternoon the rat ran over my foot in her downstairs bathroom. But when members of her family in Haiti picture her in New York, they see food, wealth, ease. Neither of us is more correct than the other; we simply start from different places.

With progress in life comes responsibility. When a Haitian emigrates, the family back home is full of expectations. Sending one of their number abroad is a cooperative family enterprise; everyone who can contributes to the sizable fund needed to get someone out of the country. Sometimes the family is forced to borrow from freelance moneylenders who prey on poor people. (In 1980 their annual interest rates hovered around 30 percent.) Alourdes came to the United States legally in the early 1960s, but in the 1970s and 1980s large numbers of Haitians have come illegally, with considerably higher expenses. A black-market tourist visa, the most popular means of escape for urban Haitians, cost two thousand dollars in 1980. Add to this the price of a roundtrip airplane ticket and several hundred dollars in pocket money, both of which may have to be shown to U.S. immigration agents at the airport. Family members who stay behind rightly expect to benefit from such a substantial investment. Many do—in fact, a significant percentage of the money and goods that circulate in Haiti each year comes from Haitians living abroad.

Unfortunately, people on both sides of this arrangement have a vested interest in preserving fanciful stories of the opportunities available in New York. For those who stay behind, stories of the good life in the United States justify their sacrifice. Those who emigrate do not challenge these stories, for fear the disparity between dream and reality will be attributed to a lack of effort or caring on their part. Caught in a rhythm of abusive, low-paying, short-term jobs alternating with periods of unemployment, many immigrants become so depressed that they stop communicating with their families in Haiti, as Alourdes did at first. During her long illness shortly after her arrival in New York, she broke off all contact with her mother. And she was especially hurt when a letter from her mother arrived accusing her of being so busy having a good time that she had forgotten her family back home.

As a rule, Haitian immigrants do not push their families away out of a simple desire to shed the responsibility of having relatives in the poorest country in the Western Hemisphere. They do so because they are ashamed. Their emigration puts them in a place of privilege, one from which it is not acceptable to ask for help or even understanding from those who have less. A letter home accurately describing the struggles of a Haitian immigrant in New York City threatens definitions of reality and self-worth on both sides. In most cases, such truthful letters are never written. A web of lies, promises, and rationalizations is required to explain a letter or telephone call that maintains the fiction but is not accompanied by a money order through Hatrexco, the funds-transferring agency whose main business is handling the flow of expatriate money to Haiti. Many initially try this approach, but if they do not find steady and profitable work, the strain of such posturing quickly becomes too great. The slender threads on which communication and the hope of responsibility rest snap.

Alourdes managed to avoid a rupture with her family largely because her early problems in New York were interpreted as spiritual ones and remedied in spiritual terms. Once her illness was defined as spirit-caused and her ties to family and country were reframed (and thus reinforced) as spiritual obligations, the pressure was relieved and the door opened for a creative renegotiation of debts. The burden of reciprocity shifted from the living family to a broader arena, one including the ancestors and the spirits. A penniless and bedraggled Alourdes could then present herself at the gate to her mother's house in Port-au-Prince. Both she and her mother understood that she was in this condition because the spirits were after her. If her mother could help her meet their demands, in time they would both benefit. And this, in fact, is what happened. "I got to go back to Haiti," Alourdes said not too long ago. "Two year since I go to Haiti. Two year! Who me? But you can't go back with no money in your hand. I need one thousand dollar, then I go to Haiti in January. I tell Papa Ogou, 'You give me that money, then I going back to Haiti.'"

Storytelling

In 1980, I was the vehicle the spirits had apparently chosen to finance a trip to Haiti. That was how Alourdes, freshly bathed and creamed, came to be in Gros Morne under Marie Thérèse's *tonnèl* that first day. She and I sat with her family and friends around an oil lamp made from an ancient Right Guard deodorant can, watching the last of the color disappear from the evening sky. We were eating spicy goat, boiled plantain, and rice with a delicious, thick black bean sauce. Marie Thérèse hunkered on the ground, her long skinny legs folded like those of a grasshopper. She ate with her hands from a bowl in which she had mixed the ingredients of our meal.

Whether from the habit of her personality, the dulling effects of years of hunger and hardship, or the strains of the moment—the social distance in this group being too great for her to traverse—Marie Thérèse withdrew into herself. Her face was blank and her eyes unfocused as she took small handfuls of food and tossed them toward her mouth. A few grains of rice fell back into the dish with each motion. When the meal was over, Alourdes convinced Marie Thérèse to sit with me and my tape recorder for an interview on family history.

In anticipating this trip, I had imagined an evening of listening to story after story about Manman Marasa, Joseph Binbin Mauvant, and Marie Noelsine Joseph. Surely, I thought, there was bound to be at least one traditional storyteller among Alourdes's country relatives. That raconteur would change voices with characters, jump up to enact dramatic episodes, and weave the story together by circling back again and again to the single memorable line that would emerge as its lesson and leitmotif. This night, however, was not to be such an occasion.

In Gros Morne, Marie Thérèse was my only source for family history. She told bare-bones stories with few details to bring them alive, and she spoke in a small, quiet voice almost without inflection. "A long time ago, it rained. The water came up to the road." ("My god!" I thought. "That would mean the river rose more than two hundred feet above its current level!") "People put chairs on top of tables. They put children on top of chairs. One family watched the river take tables . . . chairs . . . children."

Ironically, it was Alourdes who told the best stories that night in the mountain. She told one about Gloria, Marie Noelsine's oldest child and Marie Thérèse's mother. The theme of Alourdes's story ("Gloria—that woman got a lot'a courage. Oh, boy!") was a repeated tribute to a mountain woman whose heroism lay in surviving a life of continuous hardship punctuated by phenomenal bad luck. Gloria's husband died and her house burned down, all on the same day. Shortly after these tragedies, Gloria converted to Protestantism, in a fit of pique with the Vodou spirits. She died in her forties after a long illness, during which she repeatedly refused Philo's plea to come to Port-au-Prince for help. Like most mountain people, Gloria was deeply suspicious of hospitals, and by then she wanted nothing to do with the Vodou healing arts.

Marie Thérèse had not followed her mother into the Protestant church, but neither did she serve the spirits. She said simply, "If they want me to serve them, they have to give me money to do it." Traditional religion nevertheless pervades Marie Thérèse's life, as it does for everyone in the mountains. For example, she told me she had a *gad* on her house. She offered no further information about this protective charm, but before the sun went down, I thought I saw it: suspended from a roofbeam in the *tonnèl*, only partially visible through the fringe of thatch, was a banana soda bottle with a small muslin bag bound to its neck. Marie Thérèse said she also had a *gad* in her body, a charm that would have been created by a healer rubbing herbal medicines into a small cut in her skin. Although such traditional Vodou elements are very much a part of Marie Thérèse's life, she does not think of herself as serving the spirits. The issue is not whether Marie Thérèse believes in the spirits. They are a fact of her life. The issue is that they are not her exchange partners. She cannot make demands on the spirits, because she cannot afford to feed them on the regular basis they require.

After an interview of less than an hour, Marie Thérèse fell into a silence from which neither Alourdes nor I could extricate her. The three of us sat around the flickering oil lamp, and the long-ignored sounds of a night in the mountains of Haiti came alive around us: the rustle of trees when a stray breeze wandered through, the clip-clop of a donkey going down the road in front of the house, the thunking and scritch-scratching of wooden collars as the goats settled in for the night, the crowing of a rooster a mile away, the loud whine of a mosquito careening past my ear.

The Bòkò *and the Tonton Makout*

"*Ki moun malad, Kouzinn* [Who is sick, Cousin]?" Cesaire asked, appearing suddenly in our small circle of light. "Nobody," Marie Thérèse said, rising to fetch a chair for him. "But you sent for me! I ran all the way!" Cesaire snarled. "It was not me," Marie Thérèse replied in her soft voice. "Alourdes sent for you."

Earlier in the day, Alourdes had indeed asked Tonton to pass the word that she wanted to speak with Cesaire, a distant relative who farmed a piece of land several miles from Gros Morne. In his youth he had lived in Jean Rabel, and Alourdes, who had not been there since she was seven years old, wanted him to be our guide on the trip. Cesaire was a *oungan*, and when he got the message that he was needed at Marie Thérèse's home, he assumed someone was sick or in trouble. He was more than a little annoyed when he realized there was no emergency.

Cesaire wore an airplane pilot's cap with a patent-leather visor, a red scarf knotted around his neck, dark blue denim trousers with a wide belt, and a denim shirt. His pants and shirt were more carefully tailored than the usual denim peasant clothing—a signal that Cesaire was not only a *oungan* but also a Tonton Makout. His clothes were the uniform of the civilian militia started by François Duvalier after he took power in 1957.[4] Because the history of politics in Haiti was replete with military coups, Duvalier armed the Tonton Makout to check the power of the army and also to strengthen his control over the provinces.

Tonton Makout (Uncle Strawsack) is the name of a bogeyman in Haitian children's stories. More to the point, the name, like the uniform, inevitably evokes the image of a simple peasant farmer and therefore of the Vodou spirit Kouzen Zaka.[5] Thus, in creating his private army, Papa Doc, a *oungan* himself, subtly used Vodou to play on the deepest loyalties of the Haitian people—loyalties to land, family, and ancestors. The stories of corruption, intimidation, and violence that surround the Makout make heavy irony of their identification with Kouzen Zaka, a gentle spirit whose power resides mainly in herbal knowledge.

[4] In February 1986, after the fall of Jean Claude Duvalier, the son and successor of François Duvalier, the Tonton Makout were supposedly disbanded. The most hated among them were hunted down and killed by groups of vigilantes; others were taken into the army. More recent events, however, indicate that the Makout are still to some extent a cohesive and effective ingredient in Haitian politics.

[5] Just as Duvalier dressed his henchmen to look like Kouzen Zaka, so he himself appeared in the garb of another Vodou spirit: he often wore a black suit and dark glasses, mimicking Baron Samdi, chief of the spirits of the dead.

In the countryside, those who became Makout were often established local leaders, heads of large families, Vodou priests.
The Oungan-Makout thus emerged as a distinct and familiar
type on Haiti's political stage.[6] These priest-soldiers, rural and
urban, ran the gamut from assassins for hire to local leaders
who used the added power of the Makout network to promote
the interests of their people. Alourdes's distant cousin Cesaire,
who carried no gun while we were with him, probably fell
somewhere in the middle of this spectrum. In fact, Cesaire appeared to be little more than a con artist, a type not unknown in
Haitian religious and political circles. It gradually became clear
that the presence of a white face in this group had piqued his
curiosity and stirred the scent of profit. It was also clear that he
was willing to make a show of his religion for the city folk,
whatever their color.

The card reading Cesaire prescribed was a good example of
his modus operandi. He announced that a reading was necessary to determine the will of the spirits concerning our trip to
Jean Rabel. Before beginning, Cesaire asked Alourdes if she
served the spirits. "No," she said, "I do not serve." Relieved of
the threat that she might see through him, Cesaire set out to
impress us with his power and arcane knowledge.

The first splash from a fresh bottle of rum was poured on the
ground as a libation for the spirits. (The rest was for Cesaire,
who punctuated his ritualizing with frequent gulps from the
bottle.) First, he requested that the oil lamp be extinguished.
Then, lighting a single white candle, he made a great show of
marking it with cabalistic signs. Slowly, he drew his thumbnail
three times around the candle and intersected those lines with
deep vertical grooves. Cesaire's opening prayers, standard Catholic ones, were accompanied by dramatic hand gestures and
more mumbo-jumbo with the candle.

Then he took two packs of cards, limp and dog-eared, from
his back pockets. He shuffled the cards by taking a few from the
bottom of the stack and slapping them onto the top. Slap, slap,
slap—pause—slap, slap, slap. The shuffling took a long time,
and his severe manner quickly let us know that he would allow

---

[6] The term *Oungan-Makout* is also used to refer to a priest who has no temple, no
altar, and no following. He operates out of his *makout*, his straw satchel, whose contents are his only ritual paraphernalia.

no casual conversation while it was going on. Finally, he asked Alourdes to cut the cards. He examined the six bottom ones with great care, staring at them, folding and unfolding them, grunting meaningfully, and nodding his head. The candlelight lent tangible drama to the scene. Each of Cesaire's eyes reflected a miniature candle flame as he locked them on Alourdes and began to question her.

The question-and-answer part of a Vodou card reading can be a delicate diagnostic tool. Little specific information is exchanged before readings begin. Taking his or her inspiration from the cards, the reader asks various questions that lead to a description of the situation under review. (For example, Cesaire might have asked: "Did you have an important dream last night? Someone told you not to go on this trip. Is that right?") The one for whom the reading is being done accepts some descriptions and rejects others. The card reader then follows the path indicated by the responses and, working on the issue at deeper and deeper levels, poses new diagnoses, and so on. Working in this manner, both parties can discover surprising truths.

Given Cesaire's elaborate scene-setting, it was a great disappointment when his questions turned out to be quite pedestrian. "What did you say your name was?" "Where do you live?" "Who is that white person with you?" In the midst of this exchange, Alourdes was outwardly respectful with Cesaire. She assumed the position of the junior member of the family, which she was; but she also lied, telling Cesaire not only that she did not serve the spirits but also that my name was Carmen.

When he had gathered all the information he wanted, Cesaire took a big slug of rum and announced without further ceremony that the spirits saw no problem with our proposed trip. Alourdes turned to me and whispered in English that she thought Cesaire was "full of shit." This was uncharacteristic language for Alourdes. Although I tended to agree with her, I suspected we had reached our conclusions for different reasons. After wheedling two dollars out of her for the card reading, Cesaire had then asked for an additional ten to accompany us to Jean Rabel. The attempt to charge for something she understood to be family business angered Alourdes.

As soon as we could gracefully excuse ourselves from the circle, Alourdes and I headed for bed. As I walked away, Ce-

saire called after me: "Before you leave, I am going to do a treatment for you—a thing! You know, magic!" At the urging of
Marie Thérèse, I responded: *"M'pa kon sèvi avèk bagay konn sa* [I
don't get involved with that sort of thing]." The offer was probably more of Cesaire's bravado, a calculated attempt to titillate
me with every stereotype of Vodou he assumed I held. Yet such
an offer, in another context, might not have been a sham.

Vodou priests and priestesses work with *fèy* (leaves), and
herbal knowledge, the domain of Kouzen and Kouzinn Zaka,
can be used to harm as well as heal.[7] Each person has a choice as
to how to use this power, and therein lies the morality of the
matter. Alourdes, for example, says she has been told how to
prepare several simple and deadly poisons, one from the common *kowosòl* (soursop) leaf. "They told me how to make that
poison, but I don't pay no attention. I just hear about it, and I
forget it." Her position is grounded in self-preservation: "When
you do bad to people, that return—right on your back!"

The term *maji* (magic) is quite flexible. It is often used, for example, by an in-group to characterize the practices of an out-
group. People in Port-au-Prince talk about the religion of the Ar-
tibonite Valley as *maji*, and people in one rural extended-family
compound in the south describe the religious practices of those
in a neighboring compound, people with whom they have a
history of land disputes, as *maji*. Sometimes, the word is even
used self-descriptively—as a slang term for the Petwo rites almost everyone practices. The period between Christmas and
New Year's is known as the season of *maji* throughout Haiti.
During this time, Vodou ceremonies are rife with Petwo imagery drawn from the days of slavery and from the eighteenth-
century French culture that dominated then. Most acknowledge
that working with these "magical" powers is somewhat dangerous, but ignoring such powers, which persist in contemporary

[7] The history of the word *dechoukaj* (uprooting) reinforces a point about constructive and destructive medicine. In the city, the term used to be common only in
Vodou contexts, where it referred to a means of collecting *fèy* with roots still attached. This method gave the practitioner control of the full power of the plant, but
it also required that a price be paid. Coins had to be left at the spot from which the
plant was removed. After Jean Claude Duvalier's departure, *dechoukaj* was the term
Haitians adopted to describe a brutal (and perhaps also costly) kind of "social weed-
ing" in which bands of people tracked down and murdered the worst of the Tonton
Makout and others in the Duvalier regime who had abused their power.

Haiti in new and subtler forms, would appear to be even more of a risk.

There is an important difference between such public, ceremonial *maji* and the kind of *maji* Cesaire seemed to offer me. The latter takes place in the interaction between a client and a practitioner who "works with both hands." It is impossible to know how much of this so-called black magic is actually practiced in Haiti, but it is much discussed, and some of the common understandings about it are instructive.

Women involved in magic are believed to be primarily concerned with love magic, an especially ambiguous moral realm in which helping one person inevitably involves controlling the will of another. *Bòkò* (professional magicians), however, are usually understood to be men. One must have power beyond that provided by ancestral traditions in order to practice this kind of *maji*. By default, building such power is largely an individual effort. The potential rewards are thought to be great, but so are the risks; and groups are not prone to gamble in this way with their spiritual well-being. Reaching for magical power thus means, to some extent, leaving the protective web of family and spirits.

Furthermore, the actual powers used in this kind of *maji* are not inherited family spirits but *pwen achte* (purchased power points). One common type of *pwen achte* is a rock or bottle in which a wandering soul is captured, the soul of someone who died without family or proper burial. Rites for the dead direct the energy of souls back toward the surviving family, but free-floating souls are up for grabs. They become minor spirits, troublesome, demanding, and in many ways powerful. Unlike a relationship with an inherited spirit, the relationship a magician has with his power point is inflexible and unforgiving. When he fails to provide faithful and copious service, the spirit becomes immediately and severely punitive, often targeting the youngest or most vulnerable member of the *bòkò*'s family. Women are usually intensely enmeshed in family and thus less likely to take these risks.

The power of the Tonton Makout is like that of the magician, and, for similar reasons, there are few female Makout. (Madame Max, head of the Makout in Port-au-Prince, was a notorious exception to this rule.) Makout power is not rooted in blood ties but in political networks that override and often conflict with family loyalties and obligations. Makout borrow the image of a familial Vodou spirit, but they filter out and exaggerate the most alienating forms of Kouzen Zaka's potency. The Makout are extended-family patriarchs exercising power over their group, rather than seeking empowerment within it for the good of the whole community. Like the *bòkò*, the average Tonton Makout, with a swaggering walk and a gun casually stuck in the front of denim trousers, has purchased his prestige on the open market and sells his talents to the highest bidder.

Feeding the Family Spirits

The gentle little ceremony that took place the following morning on the family land in Gros Morne represented values that were the opposite of those of the *bòkò* and the Tonton Makout. By six o'clock, the day was in full swing in Gros Morne. Cocks were crowing, donkeys braying, and farmers on the way to their fields. Inside Marie Thérèse's *ti-kay*, where neither the sun's heat nor its light had yet penetrated, Alourdes was squatting on the floor arranging twenty-one crude cotton wicks in as many fragments of coconut shell. Into each she poured a little of the thick, dark yellow oil called *maskriti* and then lighted the wick. Next she put together a mixed plate of grilled corn, popcorn, fragments of cookies and cassava bread, candies, and one-inch segments of a white candle. On the top of the pile she placed a raw egg. Alourdes was preparing this *manje-sèk* (a dry meal, one for which no animal blood had been shed) for the spirits who reside on her family land. She turned to Cesaire, who had been there since before dawn, and asked him to "say a little prayer for us."

Cesaire picked up a bowl of holy water, dipped in a few basil leaves, and baptized the offerings. "God, you know this little one . . . ," he began awkwardly. "You know what mother she has. This is Alourdes . . . the daughter of Philomise . . . the granddaughter of Marie Noelsine . . . who has come to visit." The magician of the night before had become the family priest, uttering a halting but sincere prayer that, except for the setting, sounded quite Protestant.

In a large white metal cup, crumbs from the *manje-sèk* were mixed with molasses-water, and Cesaire, Alourdes, and Madame Albert took turns orienting it to the four directions of the sacred crossroads. Then the plate was carried out to a calabash tree by the front gate. This was Legba's *repozwa*, the tree within which the Vodou guardian of doorways and entrances lodged. Libations were poured at the foot of the calabash, and the egg was broken among its tangled roots, near the spot where a coconut-shell lamp was already burning.

For the first time in a decade, Alourdes's family spirits were awakened and called to the table. She and her sister Chantal began to pray at the same time, their lips moving rapidly, their words barely audible. Before long, tears were coursing down their faces. Alourdes rarely cries, and her tears on this day gave me a quick stab of insight into the depth of her family feeling.

Eventually, we turned from Legba's calabash tree and, laden with offerings, made our way to the *lakou* behind the house, pausing just inside the cactus fence at a small *bwadòm*, a tree that was also a Legba *repozwa*. Next we stopped at the well to honor a spirit called Danzweyzo. A coconut-shell lamp and a candle stub were placed in crevices in the inner wall of the well and a bottle of banana soda emptied into its depths. "Speak, little one!" Cesaire urged, obviously enjoying his paternal role in this ritual. Alourdes perched on the edge of the well and in

Ancestral offerings at the well on Alourdes's family's land. Gros Morne, Haiti, 1980.

simple and direct language pleaded with the ancestors for the well-being of each member of her immediate family. Nearby, at the foot of a small *sitwon* (a type of citrus tree), we left offerings for Sen Jan Batist, a spirit associated with Simbi, the mercurial water-dwelling crab who once took over Alphonse Macena's body and went scuttling down the well to retrieve a lost tobacco pouch.

The whole group then moved to the back of the property, where there was a sudden drop of about two hundred feet to the rushing Grande Rivière du Nord. Clinging to the precipice were two *sabliye* trees bursting with dark red, umbrella-shaped medicinal fruits. These trees were dedicated to Metrès Manbo, a priestess spirit said to "serve with" Labalenn (the whale) and Lasyrenn (the mermaid). Moving back toward the house, we performed rituals at each of three trees standing in a row. The first was a banana, dedicated to Labalenn. The middle one was a tall *labapen* (breadfruit), Ezili's *repozwa*. Although no one had seen it for a very long time, I was told that a two-headed serpent lived in the top of this tree. The last was a small mango for Lasyrenn. We moved on to a *syrol* tree, home for Kouzen and Kouzinn Zaka, and to an enormous mango that dominated the *lakou*.

In this simple ritual, space and time coincided. As we made a wide loop around Alourdes's family land, we were rehearsing her ancestral history. The rites at each *repozwa* quickened the spirits of the ancestors by nourishing the *lwa* who shaped their characters and guided their lives. The presence of so many strong female spirits among those we fed was no accident, given the strong women at the center of Alourdes's family stories. The queen of all the *repozwa*, the giant mango, was the home of a Vodou spirit aptly named Manman Zenfan (Mother of Children). Towering over all the other trees in the *lakou*, she seemed about to gather up in her wide-reaching arms all the strong women in Alourdes's extended family, spirits and humans, all of them good Madan Sara and, as a result, all indefatigable caretakers and consummate survival artists.

Before we left the yard, brief rites were also performed at a *mango gwo po* (a thick-skinned mango), the *repozwa* for both Sen Jak Majè and the Marasa (the sacred twins). Our last stops were at an almond tree for Lenglessou and an orange dedicated to Agàou.

By mid-morning of the same day, we were off to Jean Rabel. Marie Thérèse and the young man who had hung her new door, Cesaire and his wife, and the distant cousin nicknamed Tonton joined our traveling party, bringing our number to thirteen. On the way to Port-de-Paix, a relatively easy four-hour trip, the river cut deep into the mountain on our left, providing one spectacular vista after another. We bounced down the northern side of the mountain through tobacco fields and small towns—Basin Bleu, Champagne, Chansolm—with picturesque little wooden houses painted in primary colors. There was a small cinema in one town and an army post in another, but none of the towns was either sizable or prosperous.

Our arrival in Port-de-Paix marked the turning point of our journey. Starting there, everything began to go wrong. First, we could not find gasoline. Repeated consultations with passersby brought us no closer to locating fuel. Our crew sat inside the parked van for two hours, during the hottest part of the day, noisily arguing about whether the *gaz* sold in the shops was the same as the *gazoyl* The Gamble used. This inconclusive debate quickly got mixed up with another, pointless one: Had we taken the wrong route? Should we have backtracked to Gonaïves and taken the coast road, where gas is always available?

We were all hot and tired. Alourdes, who had talked us into taking the shorter route through Port-de-Paix, now wanted to turn around and go back to Gros Morne. She broached the subject with me: "Jean Rabel is far, far away. Too many problem! The chauffeur can't get no gas. So what you say, Karen?"

Because I very much wanted to get to Jean Rabel and was uncertain how real the impediments were, I decided to assert myself. "*Malheureusement,*" I said to the driver, remembering that Haitians tend to throw a little French into their Creole when they want to appear authoritative, "I can't pay you for sitting here all day in the sun. I hired you to take us to Jean Rabel, and I can't pay you for what you did not do." I had underestimated my power. In five minutes, gas appeared, and we were on our way to Jean Rabel. From that point on, the driver persisted with a reckless determination that frightened us all.

It was four o'clock in the afternoon when we left Port-de-Paix and headed west. A half hour later, a farmer on the road said we could reach Jean Rabel by six o'clock. But another person, thirty minutes further down the road, said it would be seven, adding comfortingly that we could do it *"fasil, fasil* [easy, easy]." We probably could have if we had been on muleback, as he was. Traveling in The Gamble was another matter.

The mountains flattened out as lush, green tobacco fields mixed with stands of *bwapen,* the slender, resinous pine trees grown for kindling. Banana plantations began to appear, sending out thick umbrella leaves to brush along the sides and top of The Gamble. For two hours, we jounced along a rutted track through tunnels of green and patches of sunlight without seeing another vehicle or even a peasant farmer. When, in the long light of late afternoon, we broke through the last of the banana groves onto a wide, dry plain, anxiety had reached fever pitch.

The driver stopped the bus. From a flurry of talk, a plan somehow emerged. Most of us thought we stood a slightly better chance of eating and sleeping that night if we pushed on. The driver threw the van into gear. The road stretched in front of us, little more than a ribbon of jagged rocks headed toward the horizon. Because the plain was both flat and dry, we decided to "baptize" our own road and took a wide loop to the left, raising a great cloud of dust.

A consensus was growing that this rapidly developing calamity was all my fault. People were "sending the point" around me thick and fast. One favored method was to rehearse endlessly my conversation with the driver in Port-de-Paix, how I had insisted on continuing and threatened to cut off his money. Alourdes had her own way of making me feel responsible: "If I know when I was in New York this trip going to be like this, I never come. No, not me! Not for all the money anybody give me. My life worth more than that! I have four children. They all love me. What they going to do without me? When we get to Jean Rabel, what we going to do? After we get there, we got to walk long, long way up the mountain. We not even know if we going to find nobody. It going to be dark. They got assassins on the road. Oh! Oh! Ohhhhh! I'm hungry, and there is nothing to eat."

In the meantime, Alourdes was shoving bread with grapefruit preserves into her mouth, her *manbo* friend Madame Rigaud had her hand deep in the candy bag, and Marie Thérèse and

Alphonse were chewing sugarcane. No one offered me a thing. "God save us!" I thought, unsure whether this was a prayer or simply a statement of exasperation. I took a cigarette from one of the packs I always carry in Haiti and lit up for the first time in years.

We came over the top of a mountain just as the sun set. Amid exterior peace and serenity—the soft green of the mountains, the warm gold of the setting sun, the moon and the evening star already visible—our garishly painted bus bobbled along with its interior lights on, its radio blaring, and all its passengers talking at once, except the one hunched in a corner smoking. Night fell quickly, and the feeble lights of The Gamble did little to dispel anxiety as we hurtled forward into a darkness so thick it seemed tangible.

Shortly after ten o'clock, we entered a tiny town called Cabaret. A young girl, the only person on its deserted main street, told us that Jean Rabel was the very next town. (A map consulted later showed Cabaret only about halfway between Port-de-Paix and Jean Rabel; mercifully, we did not know that then.) "*Pa lwen, pa lwen* [Not far, not far]," the girl told us. About a mile out of Cabaret, we came to a river some twenty yards wide. With the engine racing and The Gamble throwing a great rooster-tail of water behind us, we had forded a dozen such rivers and streams that day, half of them larger than this. But in this one, we stuck fast in the mud.

The driver could do nothing. Gunning the engine and rocking the bus sent us further into the muck. The shore was only a few yards in front of us, and so it was decided that everyone should get out of the bus. Following the faint path of the headlights, we jumped from rock to rock where we could and otherwise slogged through water and viscous mud. The air was thick with crisis. People gathered on the shore in tight knots, discussing what we could do. I stood alone, smoking my third cigarette and rationalizing it by concluding that cigarette smoke was an effective mosquito repellant.

After a long time, a local farmer emerged from the darkness. He had a quick conversation with the driver and disappeared, returning in less than an hour with half a dozen men carrying machetes. Small trees were felled and stray bits of wood, dry banana leaves, and large rocks collected. Everything solid, portable, and expendable was placed under the bus's rear tires. Finally, with a great slurp and a gurgle, The Gamble lurched free of the mud hole and, in reverse, shot back to the far bank. It was too dark and the water too deep for us to cross over to the bus. So, amid cries of concern and encouragement, the driver gunned the engine, charged into the stream—and put The Gamble back into the same mud hole. No one said a word as the local farmers looked for new supplies of wood and rocks. This time, the bus was retrieved with all of us safely on board.

After two hours of fitful sleep wedged like a muddy sardine into one of the seats of the bus, which the driver had parked on the main street of Cabaret, I awoke with the taste of cigarettes in my mouth, the feel of sun on my face, and the vision of a grizzled, toothless farmer staring at me through the window. We were all exhausted, and the trip back to Gros Morne was a somber, mostly silent affair. Alourdes said nothing, but I could tell she was still angry with me. Usually I am content to treat Alourdes as my Vodou "mother," defer to her wishes, and let her be in charge. But sometimes we have trouble keeping our roles straight, as the scene in Port-de-Paix had shown. I had thrown our carefully constructed roles into confusion by reminding the driver that I was the one paying his salary. After that, neither Alourdes nor I knew how to act.

Back in Port-au-Prince, Alourdes alternated between ignoring me and looking for situations to assert her authority over me. She became especially inventive at finding things for me to fetch and carry whenever people were around to bear witness. Things came to a head on the third day back at her sister's home in Bizoton. About a dozen of us were sitting in Madame Albert's yard around the dying embers of a charcoal brazier used to cook that evening's dinner. Alourdes, who had been acting as if I were not present, said abruptly and without even looking at me: "Karen, I need my purse. Go get it for me."

Something snapped. I was so instantly beside myself that my Creole came out backward and upside down. "*Sa se pa bourik ou m'ye* [That is not your donkey I am]!" I snarled and then strode away from the circle of light out into a nearby field to pace, stare at the star-filled sky, and contemplate the muddle of my life. In the distance, I could hear animated conversation. Every now and then, a clear phrase emerged—"*Sa se pa bourik ou m'ye!*"— and everyone laughed uproariously. When I returned to the group a half hour later, I was still feeling sore and vulnerable, but Madame Albert was merciless. She wanted to demonstrate her imitation of me, complete with garbled Creole, flat American accent, and dramatic exit. I had to admit she was good. Although it took some time, she eventually had me laughing too.

That night Alourdes and I exchanged apologies. "You my daughter," she said, settling all questions about roles. And then she added, "You know I love you." "I love you, too," I replied, and we both began to laugh. Life in poverty-stricken Haiti is a tinderbox of emotion. Each day is stressful, and the stakes are high. Haitians, accustomed to living on the edge, know that humor is an important survival skill. Everyone loves a joke, and a good one spreads like a brush fire. Two days later, as I walked through the main market in Port-au-Prince, a dozen miles from the town of Bizoton, I heard one of the *machann* whisper: "*Sa se pa bourik ou m'ye.*"

FEEDING THE POOR

Just before we left Haiti, on a Friday, the day of the week dedicated to the spirits of the dead, Alourdes staged a *manje pòv* (a ritual feeding of the poor). Alourdes believed that this ceremony, intended to bring blessing to her entire extended family, was long overdue. Like the rites in Gros Morne, this ritual obligation had fallen to Alourdes by virtue of her spiritual and economic ascendancy in the family.

Early in the morning, at the main gate to the big cemetery in the center of Port-au-Prince, Alourdes, her boyfriend Justin, and I met the two women who had been hired to help with the ritual. We converged under a wide archway bearing a legend in eloquent French (which could be read by 10 percent of the population at most) stating that we were all dust and would return to dust. One assistant carried a large bucket of coffee and another a basket of white bread, cassava bread, and small hunks of the strong yellow soap Haitians use for both laundry and bathing.

Before entering the cemetery, we stopped to consult with the *prètsavann* who congregate around the main entrance to the cemetery, along with the limbless, eyeless beggars and the tattered *machann* selling flowers. *Prètsavann* specialize in saying Catholic prayers in French and Latin. One of them, instantly reading the idiom of the group, approached Alourdes. "A beautiful little prayer for the poor?" he queried in overarticulated French. Alourdes hired him on the spot for three dollars. Dressed in her best New York City clothes, with her hair coiffed and makeup freshly applied, Alourdes led the way into the vast city of the dead, with the rest of us following like baby ducks in a row.

Like the city itself, the cemetery of Port-au-Prince is an urban sprawl ordered by a logic of class and privilege. Toward the edges of the cemetery, where we were heading, were densely packed neighborhoods of simple above-ground tombs made of concrete and painted in pastel colors, many bearing wreaths of garish metal flowers. Our first stop, in a "middle-class" neighborhood in the northwestern corner of the cemetery, was at the *kavo* (grave) of Alourdes's mother, Philomise Macena. Alourdes is very proud of this family tomb, which can accommodate four coffins. She had it built shortly after her mother's death in 1973. The day after we arrived in Haiti, Alourdes and I had visited the cemetery to tend Philo's tomb and perform more elaborate rites there, so this stop was perfunctory. The *prètsavann* prayed in French and Latin and sprinkled the tomb with holy water, and our simple ritual ended with a Catholic hymn often heard in Vodou temples. Its concluding line pleads with the saints to "bless the suffering poor."

Then we moved to the *kwa* Baron, the large white cross in the center of the cemetery dedicated to Baron Samdi, the keeper of the cemetery and the head of all the Gede (spirits of the dead). Libations of coffee and rum were poured at the base of the cross, and small bits of bread and cassava were scattered there. While Alourdes's boyfriend performed these rituals, she stood in the shadow cast by the large, white, tile-covered Duvalier family tomb and handed out bread, coffee, soap, and small change to the beggars who were gradually collecting around her. Along with these small gifts came an invitation to a feast later that afternoon at her sister's home. Alourdes told the beggars how they could find the *taptap* she had hired to bring them to Bizoton. After arranging with the *prètsavann*, for an additional two dollars, to come on the same bus to bless the *manje pòv*, our group headed back toward the main cemetery gate.

Several hours later when we arrived in Bizoton, preparations for the *manje pòv*, which had been going on all morning under Madame Albert's direction, were almost complete. Madame Albert's home was one of eight small cinderblock houses gathered around a yard, about half of which was covered by a thatched roof open on all sides. The ground under this *tonnèl* was covered with huge containers of food: rice with red beans, rice with black beans, cornmeal with beans, plain cornmeal mush, white rice, red bean sauce, *militon* (a sweet, small green squash) mixed with vegetables and bits of beef, a white soup made from bread and herring, a plate of boiled potatoes and plantains, a mixture of chicken with okra and black mushrooms, and *chaka*, the favored dish of Kouzen and Kouzinn Zaka. In the center was a huge pot of pumpkin soup with noodles. Seven leaves from the sweet orange tree in the yard lay in a row in front of the food. Each held a cotton wick and a dollop of oil. There was also a bottle of holy water and a bunch of basil leaves.

A few of the destitute, drawn by the rumor of food, had already arrived. They were careful to stay out of the ritual arena and sat quietly on the dusty knoll just behind the *lakou.* One man was stretched out on his back, asleep in the hot sun. A child of two or three, bloated by hunger, also slept, his head resting on the man's knee. A woman in rags, her left breast exposed, hunkered down and smoked. A terribly thin, frantic little boy sat beside her on the paint can he had brought to collect his food. He teased her constantly, grabbing at her cigarette and poking her. Then his face suddenly contorted in silent laughter, and he threw up arms thin as broomstraws to cover his face. "Look at the good little poor people," Alourdes said warmly. "They stay outside, on the hill."

The *prètsavann* began by sprinkling holy water on the food. Then he prayed. "*Voici ce grand moun . . . ,*" he began. (*Gran moun,* a Creole term inserted into his French prayer, referred, in this context, both to an adult and an important person.) "See this important person, Alourdes, who came here today from another country to make this generous feast, so she and her family might be blessed." Alourdes was in her element. She had changed into a flowing orange caftan and bound her hair in a colorful print scarf. She stood in the midst of the evidence of her bounty, singing, in her strong and beautiful voice, the same hymn we had sung at the cemetery: "Bless the suffering poor..."

The bus arrived, bringing the number of the poor close to forty. Alourdes, Madame Albert, and Madame Rigaud moved among them, collecting their food containers. Plastic bowls,

Children of the poor eating during the opening rituals of Alourdes's *manje pòv*. Bizoton, outside Port-au-Prince, Haiti, 1980.

motor-oil cans, and calabash shells were placed beneath the *tonnèl*. Then the children of the poor, a group whose double social vulnerability put them at the center of this ritual, were invited to sit under the *tonnèl* while songs were sung for Legba and libations of water, rum, and pumpkin soup were poured at the entrance to the *lakou*. A large banana leaf, wiped clean of dust, was laid in front of the children. A dollop of food, taken from a pot in which the various dishes had been mixed together, was placed before each child. The beggars' children were clearly uncomfortable with their role. They were all swollen bellies, spindly limbs, and fearful eyes that darted around the crowd, anxious to find some clue as to how they should act. When the children were finally given the signal to eat, quick, dirty fingers made the food disappear into hungry mouths in seconds. The formal part of the ritual was over.

Amid confusion and good humor, generous amounts of food were then passed out to all the poor. Soup was poured into each container, and a bit of everything else was piled on top.

Alourdes's assistants carried the food to the poor people, who continued to keep their distance. After everyone had eaten, tobacco and rum were distributed, along with small change. Everyone was feeling good when the *taptap* driver arrived, complaining that after this job he would have to wash his bus to get rid of the smell. Alourdes reprimanded him for his bad manners: "You say thing like that, you going to hurt those poor people." And then she bargained him down to eight dollars for the job.

Just before the poor people left, all of them came under the *tonnèl* for the first and only time. They dipped their greasy hands in a basin of water to which rum had been added, as well as basil, *twapawòl*, and *kapab* leaves. Then they clustered around Alourdes and eagerly wiped their hands on her face, head, arms, and clothing. As they climbed onto the bus, she was smiling broadly and waving good-bye, her face dripping, her gown wet and wrinkled. Thus was the blessing only the poor can give passed on to Alourdes and her family. When the spirits accorded this special power to the poor, they placed in their hands a ticket to the dance of social reciprocity. By the inversionary logic of Vodou, only beggars (those who would not be beggars if they had family to cushion their suffering and bad luck) can stave off misfortune for intact families.

When the crowd was gone, a small plate of leftover food was prepared, covered, and set aside. Later it would be taken to the cemetery and placed at the foot of the Baron Cross. Alourdes was mellow and expansive as she sat among the remnants of the *manje pòv* and passed out *gourd* notes to those who had helped her and to family members who had special money problems. To Mimose, Marie Carmelle's sister and the second youngest of Madame Albert's children, went nearly twenty dollars for a prescription for her sick child, Manouchka. I wondered, as Alourdes handed Mimose the money, if she thought of the time she sat in a dark house with her feverish child in her arms, unable to afford the medicine that child so badly needed.

CHAPTER SEVEN

Dreams and Promises

Clement Rapelle's right hand fumbled at the top button of his starched white shirt, while his left reached for the door of Pharmacie Bouc. He had thought the work day would never end, the time would never come for the pharmacy to close. Now he could barely keep from running. Rapelle, a handsome man in his mid-thirties, quickly settled into a long, loping stride through the crowded streets of Port-au-Prince. Moving with the intensity and agility of a soccer player, he dodged black-suited businessmen and crisp khaki soldiers. He gave wide berth to elegant light-skinned women as well as to dark men, all sweat and sinew, straining against rumbling two-wheeled carts heavy with charcoal and sugarcane.

Once free of the crowd, Rapelle moved in a straight line through the park beside the massive National Palace, fiercely white in the late afternoon sun. In a few minutes, he reached the maze of narrow, shadowed streets and closely packed houses behind the Old Cathedral. But not until he got to the center of the Sans Fil district, a small open plaza with an incongruous little fountain, did he slow his pace. In fact, he stopped—Rapelle did not know where to go. Three times he turned around slowly, inspecting the spiderweb of streets and alleyways radiating from the fountain. He was trying to match reality with directions he had been given in a dream, and at the moment the dream was receding.

Fearing that he looked foolish, Rapelle abruptly sat down on the edge of the fountain and took out a cigarette. Before long, a name floated to the surface, and Rapelle held on to it. "Madame, good evening. Excuse me, please!" he called to a passerby. "Can you give me directions to the *lakou* people call Seven Stabs

◀ Temple wall painting of Ezili Dantò (Mater Salvatoris). Port-au-Prince, Haiti, 1980.

of the Knife?" "Good evening, *monsieur*," she replied. "Yes, I can explain that for you. But you are almost there. Do you know Rue Tiremasse?"

As instructed, Rapelle walked down Tiremasse for a distance and then turned left into an alley so narrow he could touch the buildings on either side without fully extending his arms. He made his way with care, for a moment surrounded by bare-bottomed toddlers, here forced to straddle a gutter running with raw sewage, there to duck beneath a clothesline hung with long curls of drying orange and grapefruit peel. In front of each open doorway along the alley, Rapelle offered a polite "Good evening." At the end of the passageway, he found himself in a *lakou*.

Many of these homesteads, typical of the countryside, are hidden amid Port-au-Prince's urban sprawl; and many of them, like this one, have degenerated from well-kept extended-family compounds to hodgepodge rental housing for the urban poor. Seven Stabs of the Knife consisted of about a dozen small wattle-and-daub houses gathered around a broad, dusty yard with a few stunted trees. "This is the place!" Rapelle realized with a shock of recognition, and good manners temporarily left him. He seized the arm of a young boy and cried: "Do you know a woman called Philo? Does she live here? I need to talk to her!"

Philo lived in a small room in the back of one of the houses in Seven Stabs of the Knife. These were hard times, but of course Philo did not speak of such things with Rapelle. Instead, she offered her guest a glass of water and invited him to sit with her in a corner of the yard. "Are you from the north?" Rapelle asked her. "Yes," she replied, "I come from Jean Rabel, almost the last point in the north, near Môle Saint Nicolas." "I want you to treat my son," Rapelle said abruptly. He rushed on: "He was a good student, first in his class. But now—oh! Now he has lost his head. He cannot even remember his name. You have to help me!"

"But I do not know how to treat him," Philo responded. "Why do you ask me to do this?" "I had a dream last night, an important dream. The spirits told me to come to this place. They told me to ask for a woman named Philo, a woman from the north."

"But I do not know . . .," Philo began. "Then read the cards for him—just read the cards," Rapelle urged. "How do you know I read cards?" asked Philo. "They told me in my dream," Rapelle replied. "You read cards, is that not true?" "From time to time," Philo answered in a small voice and then stood up to signal their conversation was at an end. "I am sorry," she said. "I cannot help you." "I will come back," declared a stubborn Rapelle. "I know I have found the person to treat my son."

Clement Rapelle did come back. In fact, he visited often, and in time the two became friends. Yet whenever he brought up his son's illness, Philo's response was the same: "It would make me happy, Monsieur Rapelle, if I could treat your child, but truly I do not know how." One day, Rapelle would not let the matter drop: "But you treat other people. I have seen them when I come to visit you. They sit in the courtyard, and they wait for you." "That is true," admitted Philo, "but I treat them only when the spirits come in my dreams and tell me exactly what to do. They have told me nothing about your son's situation." "They will!" Rapelle insisted. "I have confidence in you. I have confidence in the spirits."

Gradually Philo opened up to her new friend. "My life is hard," Philo said to him one day. "I am not at ease working with the spirits. It is difficult. Do you understand what I am saying to you?" "Yes," Rapelle replied, "I can understand that. Give me the story, little Philo. Tell me how you started to treat people."

"It was a long time I lived in Santo Domingo," Philo began. "My three babies were made there. In Santo Domingo, there was a woman, a *manbo*. Madame Gilbert was her name, and she had a very strong spirit named Agèou. He worked, worked, worked. People came from all over the Dominicain to see Madame Gilbert and her Agèou. Any problem—any problem!—Agèou could treat it.

"But Agèou became angry with Madame Gilbert. She was . . . you know . . . a lesbian," Philo said, dropping her voice, "and she was always buying things for women. She bought them clothes . . . perfume . . . jewelry. All her money she spent on those women. She did not give Agèou even one candle! She expected him to work, but she gave him nothing! There was one day Agèou came in Madame Gilbert's head, and he got so mad, he made her cut off her finger. He did that!" Philo sighed, and, for the first time since she began talking, she looked Rapelle in the eye. "That woman—so stupid!"

Philo's voice quickly fell back to its somber cadence, and her eyes locked on the cup of herbal tea she held in her hand. "Madame Gilbert changed nothing. She went right on buying, buying, buying for all those women. She did not offer one little thing to Agèou. So he made her sick. She got tuberculosis . . . consumption. She started to vomit blood. They took her to the hospital. Finally she died—and do you know what happened?" Rapelle did not attempt to answer. "Not one of those women came to see her in the hospital. Not one came to her funeral. Not one."

Philo stretched in her chair like a cat waking from a nap and then swirled her finger absentmindedly through the thick mass of leaves at the bottom of her tin cup. After a lengthy silence, she continued her story.

"One night after Madame Gilbert died, I had to make pee-pee. I lighted the lamp. I went out to the yard. When I came back inside, there it was! A rock—black . . . shiny . . . round . . . in my house! On the floor, by my bed. That made me afraid! I did not put it there; I did not know how it got there. So I took it to someone, someone who works with that kind of thing, and I asked her, 'What is it?' She said that rock was a devil spirit and I had to pay her seven hundred dollars to get rid of it. I was so naïve! I paid her.

"Then a handsome man came in my dream. He wore khaki and a panama hat, and he had a beautiful mustache. He said, 'I am Msye Agèou Hantor Dahomey,' and he told me that rock was him. And he was angry at me for giving him away, but he said it didn't matter, because he loved me anyway and he was going to come to me now."

"Agèou comes in your dreams and he tells you how to make treatments?" Rapelle asked. "He can," said Philo quietly. "And he comes in your head, too?" her friend persisted. "He can," Philo replied. "But that's fantastic!" cried Rapelle.

"That's hard!" retorted Philo. "Too much responsibility. My children go to bed hungry. I don't have the money to send them to school. Now these people come to me, and they tell me I have to treat them. But the only thing I know about treatments is what I see in my dreams. How can I live like that? How can I make money like that? How? And let me tell you, when I came back from the Dominicain, four years ago, 1930, there were no jobs anywhere. I had so much trouble, so much suffering. One day, I had a little problem with my eyes; then after three days I

could not see. I was blind! Yes. They made me blind. The spirits
did that.

"I went to a *oungan*. I asked him to read the cards for me.
When the spirit came in his head, he told me what I had to do.
He said I had to *ranmase espri mwen* [gather up my spirits]. He
told me like this: 'You must go back to Jean Rabel, where your
navel cord is buried. You must go back there and give your family spirits a big feast.' 'How am I going to do that?' I asked him.
'I have no money!' The spirit said, 'Put on a *karabel* [blue denim]
dress, put a *makout* over your shoulder, and go out in the street
and beg for charity. Beg! That is how you will find the money.'

"'Not me!' I said. 'Not me! Nobody in my family ever asked
for charity, and I am not going to be the first.' Then the spirit
just looked at me, and he smiled. '*Sa va* [so be it],' he said. '*Sa
va*. But if you do not do this, then you will die—or one of your
children will die.' I was afraid, so I said, 'Okay, I will do it.'

"That night I went home, and I twisted seven cotton wicks
and put them on a white plate. I put a little oil. I lighted them.
I got on my knees, and I prayed to God. And I prayed to the
spirits, to Msye Agèou. I said, 'I am blind. You know that! You
are the one who made me blind. How am I going to walk in the
street and ask people for money when I cannot see?' Agèou
came in my head, and he told my son: 'Tell Philo to go to sleep.
She will wake up seeing.' And that is what happened. The next
morning when I woke up, I could see. Then I began to trust
him . . . to trust a little.

"So I put on a *karabel* dress, I took a *makout*, and I went out.
I walked in the streets. Up and down, up and down. I went to
the market, too. All day long, I begged. Me? Hah! Me! By the
time the sun went to sleep, I had three hundred and eighty
gourd in my hand. It was not enough to go to Jean Rabel and
buy the animals for the feast, too, but I gave the spirits a big
party here in Port-au-Prince and I said to them, 'Okay, now I
will serve you, but you have to tell me what to do. You have to
come in my dreams and tell me what to do. You have to!'"

"Things got better after that?" Rapelle asked, his voice full of
concern. "Better? Yes . . . but not good," Philo sighed. "Some
people come. Sometimes I dream, and when they come I know
already what to do for them. Sometimes. Not always. When I
have the dream first, the treatment is always successful, and
then they are happy. They give me money—two dollars, three.

Ten dollars if they are really happy. But let me tell you, I pay seven dollars a month for this room and I have not paid the rent in three months." That evening, Rapelle, a clerk in a pharmacy run by expatriate Germans, left in Philo's hand all the money he had with him, a little more than six dollars.

Philo hid five dollars in a secret place. The next morning, she took one dollar and twenty cents into town, to the Iron Market near the bay. She had in mind buying rice, oil, spices, and a few beans to feed her family, but she could have done that at a market closer to home. Her real reason for making the trip to the middle of town was to visit the herbalists at the biggest market in the city. She sought advice. If they had nothing new to tell her, she could at least buy more of the broad, prickly green leaves called *chapo kare*. Several friends had told her that *chapo kare* tea would "put that baby down . . . fast!" Philo was desperate. She had consumed quantities of the bitter tea in the past three weeks, but its only effects had been to increase the gas in her stomach and the ache in her head, discomforts that had been her constant companions since the morning after Alphonse Margaux had lain in her bed.

"Take a little beer," one herbalist said. "Put in a handful of salt the size of an egg and boil it. Let it sit overnight. First thing in the morning, before you eat anything or drink anything— even a glass of water—drink that." "I tried it," said Philo. "*Pa bon* [No good]." In fact, Philo had tried every recipe suggested to her. She had also jumped off chairs, pummeled her stomach, prayed until she had calluses on her knees, and burned enough candles to light the homes in her entire *lakou* for a month. None of it had worked, and this day's outing proved no more successful. Philo left the market with a bit of food and a bunch of *chapo kare*. Then she trudged back up the hill to Seven Stabs of the Knife, feeling sicker than usual.

That night, Philo slept badly. Her three children heard her groaning in her sleep. "And the night?" a neighbor called out cheerily, as Philo headed for the outhouse the next morning. "Not good," Philo responded, "but I had a dream." "What dream?" queried the neighbor.

"I dreamed an old woman, a white woman, very old—very, very, very old. The old lady called out: 'Philo! *Vin pale ou* [Come talk to me].' She asked me: 'You are pregnant?' And I put my head down . . . because I was ashamed . . . and I said to her,

'Yes, I am pregnant.' The old lady asked me: 'Why do you drink things to put that baby down? Why do you do that? That baby is going to be born, and that baby is going to be a girl.' 'How do you know?' I asked. She said, 'I know.' Then the old lady said to me: 'Stop what you are doing. Don't take anything more. I will support you. I will give you everything. *M'ap ba ou bwè; m'ap ba ou manje* [I'll give you drink; I'll give you food].' And I said, 'How are you going to do that?' And the old lady just turned and walked away."

"Ehhhhh!" said the neighbor, stretching her neck like a cock about to crow. "You were sleeping hungry. That's why you had that dream." Then she began to laugh: "Cawk! Cawk! Cawk!" Philo grew hot with shame. The awful sound of her neighbor's laughter followed Philo into the outhouse. While she hunkered over the latrine, she muttered to herself: "That old lady in my dream had on rags. All her clothes full of holes! She can't support herself. How is she going to support me?" "She's a liar!" Philo said out loud as she slammed the outhouse door and marched off to prepare a batch of *chapo kare* tea.

Weeks passed and little changed. Friends offered new recipes, and Philo tried them. No luck. Each time she relieved herself she searched for traces of blood, but none appeared, and the headaches got worse. Philo was often forced to stop what she was doing and lie down with a wet cloth over her eyes.

When she was two, almost three months pregnant, Philo had another dream. In this dream she was standing on the corner of Rue Macajoux, near the Iron Market. The street was very crowded, and she was hurrying to get home. In front of her were two men, each holding one end of a rope looped around a coffin suspended between them. Philo realized she would have to walk beneath the coffin to get across the street. "Excuse me, please," she said to the men. "May I pass under there? I have to get home." One of the men curled his lip and snarled: "You are not going home. You are too evil. You are going in this coffin." Philo said, "No!" Both men said, "Yes! Get in the coffin!" Philo said, "No!" They said, "Yes! Get in the coffin." Philo said, "No!" and she looked around desperately for a way to escape. No place to run! Her legs felt like lead.

Then Philo raised her eyes to the sky and saw the old woman from her first dream. This time, she was wearing beautiful clothes—a wide-brimmed hat and a long white dress with a beautiful blue belt. "Say '*Anmwe nèg*,'" the old woman urgently instructed Philo, and Philo quickly repeated, "*Anmwe nèg*." The old woman gave the order again: "Say '*Anmwe nèg*,'" and Philo shouted, "*Anmwe nèg!*" Before the sound of the password had died away, Philo felt herself lifted up, up, up, over the heads of the two men carrying the coffin. Philo wafted upward as if she were a piece of paper drifting on currents of air, and then slowly she settled onto the shoulders of the old woman. The two of them flew through the sky back to Seven Stabs of the Knife.

Philo spoke to no one about that dream. But she did stop trying to abort her child. She decided to take one day at a time. Neighbors occasionally shared their food, and clients and friends sometimes put a few dollars in her hand. When the pregnancy was in its fifth month, the mysterious old woman appeared again in a dream. As soon as she saw her, Philo got very upset. "You again!" she yelled. "I don't want to see you!" But the old woman put up her hand and said, "Hush, child. Close your mouth. Listen. I have an important message." "What message?" Philo asked. "I have come to tell you: Do not come to my house to have that baby. If you come to my house, you are going to die," the old woman said. "Where do you live?" Philo asked. "I live in the hospital," the old woman responded.

"Philo! Philo!" the old woman said. "It is all right. You are going to have a baby. That baby is going to be a girl. Call her Alourdes." In her dream, Philo sputtered and beat her hands on the air in impotent fury: "You promised to take care of me! Where is the money to eat? Where is it?" "Philo, Philo," soothed the old woman, "the money is coming." "You say the money is coming! You say! Do you think I believe you?" Philo was just about to utter an oath when the old woman turned and walked away.

When she woke up, Philo was still upset. But she needed no more ridicule, and so she shared the dream only with Ma'Nini, her one good friend in the *lakou*, a woman who lived in the front of the house where Philo had her room. Ma'Nini said, "Ahh! I understand. That was Our Lady of Lourdes who came to you. There is a chapel for Our Lady of Lourdes in the hospital. That is why she said she lived there. This is a serious dream. If I were you, I would not go to the hospital to have that baby."

"But I do not have money for a *fanm-saj* [midwife], and you know you do not have to pay in the hospital," Philo moaned. "I know a *fanm-saj*," said Ma'Nini. "She does not have a license, but she is very good. You can pay her later. I will call her as soon as you have your first pain." After that, Ma'Nini gave food to Philo every day and checked on her frequently.

Early one morning in her ninth month, Philo was getting ready to go to mass. It had become her habit to go to the six o'clock mass every day. Philo was all dressed and on her way across the yard when she felt an urgent need to urinate. She turned back to her house, unlocked the door, and went to the basin she kept beside her bed. As she squatted over it, Philo felt odd . . . dizzy. There was a sudden pressure in her stomach, and before she knew what was happening—without a single pain—the baby slid out of her and plopped into the shallow metal pan. Philo was a woman from the countryside, a person of the old school. She believed that a woman who has just given birth should not speak. The wind might come inside her. So she fell back against the wall, the afterbirth still in place, the umbilical cord still connecting her to her child, and she pounded with both fists.

Ma'Nini was there in no time. She snatched up a sheet and wrapped the infant in it, right where she lay in the chamber pot. "How beautiful you are, little Alourdes," Ma'Nini crooned as she tucked the cover around the newborn. Then, in a flash, she was gone to fetch the midwife. The *fanm-saj* cut the umbilical cord and massaged Philo's belly until the afterbirth came out. She cleaned Philo and the baby and put them both to bed. Together, Ma'Nini and the *fanm-saj* buried Alourdes's umbilical cord in the *blaïye,* the pile of smooth rocks where freshly washed clothes were left to whiten in the tropical sun.

Little Alourdes was fine. But Philo was not. The morning after she gave birth, she began to feel feverish and nauseated. A black fever epidemic had spread rapidly in Port-au-Prince; twenty-five people had died in the city hospital that very week. And now Philo had it. She lay on her bed day and night, soaked in sweat, hallucinating, unable to eat or feed her infant. Luckily, a wet nurse was found in the *lakou,* a crazy woman whose baby had died three weeks after it was born. This dirty, disheveled woman never sat still. She roamed the *lakou* talking endlessly, giving unsolicited advice on how to make baby food, how to discipline children, how to grow cassava without water. Ma'Nini put the deranged woman in her own house, gave her clean clothes and food, and washed her swollen breasts with strong yellow soap. Then she laid Philo's infant on her bosom. Alourdes would survive. But what to do for Philo? What to do?

Help came in the person of Clement Rapelle. His boss, the old German pharmacist, refused Rapelle's polite request, so Rapelle simply waited until the pharmacy was closed. Then he let himself in with his key and "borrowed" the big black book that described diseases and their cures. Rapelle figured out what Philo needed and bought the medicine for her. Ma'Nini nursed her back to health. In less than a month she was out of danger. But she could not breastfeed her child, and by then the crazy woman was beginning to push the infant away. So Philo asked a friend who had just had a baby if she would feed Alourdes. For several months, Alourdes lived in the home of Madame Frederic and sucked contentedly at a breast that did not smell of laundry soap. Alourdes was, for this short time at least, quite unaware of how precarious the world was and how fragile was her place in it.

Philo slowly regained her strength, and eventually she began to dream again. One night, a tall and handsome military man came riding into her dream. "I have come to tell you how to treat the son of Clement Rapelle," Agèou announced. That next morning was the first day in a long, long time that Philo awakened feeling happy to be alive.

"I do not want you to become discouraged," she later told Rapelle. "Your son's problem is serious. The treatment will take a long time." "I don't care how long it takes," Rapelle responded. "If you heal my son, I am going to give you a lot of money. When my father died, he left me a small piece of land. It is my inheritance, but if you treat him successfully, I am going to sell that land and give you the money." Philo replied, "All I need from you is one hundred dollars to buy the things for the treatment." The next day Rapelle brought his ten-year-old son to Seven Stabs of the Knife for the first of many, many visits. Over the course of the treatment, Philo became so close to the Rapelle family that, when Alourdes was baptized, Clement Rapelle and his teenage daughter were named as godparents.

The work for Rapelle's son took more than a year to complete. When Philo concluded it with a good-luck bath made from flowers, fruits, perfumes, and champagne, Rapelle, true to his word, gave her one thousand dollars. This was more money than Philo had ever held in her hand, and it marked a turning point in her life. The first thing she did was purchase a home in the Belair section of Port-au-Prince, not far from Seven Stabs of the Knife. Philo and her children soon settled into her little blue house with three rooms and its own latrine.

The years that followed were good ones. Philo had money to buy food and to send her children to school. Clients were coming to her in ever greater numbers. And she now had enough self-confidence and experience to treat people without specific instructions from the spirits. Life was so secure that an important promise was forgotten—until the day something happened to make Philo remember.

That day started in an ordinary way. Alourdes was seven years old, and her sister Chantal was just entering adolescence. Chantal had borrowed a hot comb from a neighbor. When she finished pressing her hair, she gave the comb to her younger sister and told her to return it to Marguerite. Alourdes stopped dead in her tracks when she reached the front gate of Marguerite's home. There was a dog lying inside. "Come here, little girl," called Marguerite from her chair on the porch. "I'm afraid of the dog," said Alourdes. "Come, dear, come. I am sitting right here. Do you think I am going to let that dog bite you?"

Alourdes was not convinced, and so she reached through the gate, grabbed a handful of the dog's hair, and gave it a hefty tug. The dog did nothing. Alourdes pulled its hair again, and again the dog did nothing. So the child opened the gate, jumped over the dog, and ran to Marguerite. She still had her hand out with the hot comb in it when she felt the dog's teeth sink into the back of her leg.

Alourdes dropped the comb and ran. *"Manman, Manman, Manman!"* she screamed all the way home. Philo met her at the door. "The dog bit me!" Alourdes sniffled, and she pointed to blood running down her left leg. Philo cleaned and wrapped her wound and put the child to bed. Exhausted from the trauma, Alourdes slept. But when she awoke two hours later, something was dreadfully wrong. Her mother had told her to stay in bed. She wanted to obey her mother, but an awful anxiety was rushing through her body, building toward panic. She began to shake, and her head was spinning. Aware only that she had to move, Alourdes got up, left the house, and began to walk. She walked and walked and walked. A frantic need to escape was the last thing Alourdes would ever remember of this incident.

Alourdes was lost for three days and three nights. Philo was beside herself with worry the entire time. She spent the first day checking in every place she thought Alourdes might go. At the end of that day, she went to the police station and reported her daughter missing. On the second and the third days, Philo sought help from friends. Rapelle took two afternoons off from his job at the pharmacy to search the northern areas of Belair and Sans Fil, which seemed to be likely places, but he had no luck. Madame Jacques read the cards for Philo and expressed her fear that Alourdes was dead. The *oungan* Cesaire consulted his head spirit, who announced that Alourdes had gone off with an older woman who was now keeping the child hidden in her house. Philo's friend Laline misjudged the extent of the crisis and attempted to make a joke of it all: "Perhaps the spirits have taken Alourdes below the water. Maybe they want to make her a *manbo*."

Another friend, Madame Victoir, also read the cards, and it was she who told Philo that Alourdes was all right. "Tell the police they will find nothing if they look in the north. They are going to find her only if they look in the south," Madame Victoir said. And then she gave Philo a long, searching look: "Was there something you were supposed to do for the spirits? Did you promise something and then not do it?" Philo's body jerked to attention. "Yes! There was something," she said, "a long time ago. I told Ezili Dantò I would kill a pig for her, and I have not done that." "Go home," Madame Victoir said. "You don't have to do anything more to find Alourdes. Just stop by the police and tell them to look in the south. But tonight light a candle, call Ezili, and tell her—promise her!—you are going to make the feast right away."

As darkness fell that third night, Philo went to her altar. She lit a candle, and she prayed hard. Then she lay in her bed, eyes wide open, and let the candle burn itself out. It seemed to her that the moment the candle sputtered out, the sun began to rise. Or perhaps she had fallen asleep in between. Philo was still trying to figure out if she had slept when she heard a knock at her door. It was a policeman with the news Alourdes had been found. "Where did you find her?" Philo demanded. "In the south, as you said we would," the policeman responded, "near the reservoir in Carrefour Feuilles. She was playing with some children. She had been there three days. None of them knew her name or where she came from. No one could say where she slept or what she ate. Come, your child is waiting for you. We think you should take her to the hospital. We are not sure what might have happened to her."

When Alourdes saw her mother come through the door of the police station, she ran to her and grabbed her waist so hard Philo caught her breath, but the child said nothing. Not until the doctors had finished their intimate poking and prodding and had given her a shot and rebandaged her leg did Alourdes begin to speak. She wanted to know where she was, what had happened to her. She remembered nothing of the last three days. "You don't have to remember," said Philo. "Everything is okay now."

That evening, Philo sat in her backyard drinking coffee with her good friend Clement Rapelle. "Thank you for your help, Rapelle, my dear," she said. "I know you don't get paid when you take off from work." "It is not a problem," said Rapelle simply. Then he added with real feeling: "I was so happy when I came by today and saw Alourdes in the house." "I know you were. I know," smiled Philo and gave him a warm embrace. "Now you can help me again. I need a strong man to tie up this bundle. It is for the journey. Tomorrow Alourdes and I are going to Jean Rabel. It is time for me to gather up my family spirits. It is time for me to kill a pig for Ezili Dantò."

And so it was that in the summer of 1942, on the land where Joseph Binbin Mauvant had grown tobacco leaves as long as his arm, just a few yards from the pile of rocks in which Philo's umbilical cord had been buried, she held a feast for her family spirits that lasted seven days and seven nights. For this considerable undertaking, all the members of her extended family still living in Jean Rabel were pressed into service as well as many of the neighbors. In addition to Ezili Dantò's pig, one cow, two goats, and six chickens were also offered to Philo's hungry family spirits. Drummers played throughout the week, and people danced so energetically that a dust cloud that could be seen a mile away rose over the Mauvant land.

During the early morning hours of one of the days when the drums were beaten from sunset until sunrise, Ezili Dantò possessed Philo's cousin, a woman known for her spiritual powers. "*Dey-dey-dey-dey*," Dantò said. "Look at the table we have made for you," a proud Philo responded. "There is *griyo* [grilled pork]. There is *selebride* [liqueur]. There is *rapadou* [brown-sugar

candy]. All kinds of fruit." "*Dey-dey-dey*," the spirit responded
with satisfaction. In gratitude, Ezili Dantò tipped the bottle of
selebride up to Philo's mouth, and she also took some of the liqueur in her hand and wiped it over Alourdes's face. Then she
hugged the seven-year-old to her with a fierce and passionate
"*dey-dey-dey-dey-dey*." "I know, mother, I know," said Philo, obviously moved by the spirit's show of affection for her child.
Forgetting that she was exposing very private information,
Philo continued: "You gave me this child. You kept me from
getting rid of my baby. Thank you. Thank you." The Vodou
spirit Ezili Dantò, who is also known as Our Lady of Lourdes,
looked at Philo, and her eyes communicated an acceptance that
was absolute and without illusions.

Then, with a sudden urgency in her manner, Dantò pointed
at Philo and then at Alourdes . . . at Philo and at Alourdes. Back
and forth, back and forth she went, appealing to the gathered family for an interpretation of her earnest "*dey-dey-dey*."
"Alourdes is going to replace you," a wise old uncle said. "Philomise, Dantò is telling you that Alourdes is the one to take
your place, to serve the family spirits after you." "That is okay,"
said Philo. "That is good."

Then the wrinkled old farmer took his pipe out of his mouth
and stared intently into Alourdes's face. "You are so young,
little girl. Already the spirits are choosing you. That is a big responsibility. You must never forget what Dantò has said to you
this night. Do you understand?" The wide-eyed little girl with a
bandage on her left leg and a solemn look on her face simply
nodded.

✳

CHAPTER EIGHT

Ezili

Several female spirits belong to the group called the Ezili. The three most important are Lasyrenn, the mermaid who links ancient African senses of woman power and water power; Ezili Dantò, the hardworking, solitary, sometimes raging mother; and Ezili Freda, the sensual and elegant, flirtatious and frustrated one. This chapter focuses on each of these powerful women spirits, in turn; all three are discussed in one chapter because each is more understandable in relation to the others. Taken together, they give a remarkably accurate and detailed portrait of the forces that shape women's lives both in contemporary Haiti and in Haitian immigrant communities such as the one in which Alourdes lives.[1]

Haitian culture is a misogynist culture. The ideology of male supremacy is fierce. Haitian humor is rife with anti-woman jokes, and domestic violence is a frequent occurrence. Vodou has not escaped the influence of this attitude. Certain *oungan*, for example, are notorious for mistreating, in various ways, the women who become *ounsi* (ritual assistants) in their temples. Yet, in spite of this, Vodou empowers women to a larger extent than the great majority of the world's religious traditions. As Haitians struggled to survive and adapt both during and after slavery, women gained social and economic power, gains that are mirrored in the influence of women within Vodou.

The role of women in Vodou is greatest where there has been the greatest change. Rural women can gain respect as herbalists

---

[1] Some of the central ideas presented in this chapter first appeared in Karen McCarthy Brown, "Mama Lola and the Ezilis: Themes of Mothering and Loving in Haitian Vodou," in *Unspoken Worlds: Women's Religious Lives*, ed. Nancy Auer Falk and Rita M. Gross (Belmont, Calif.: Wadsworth, 1989), 235–45.

◀ Mother combing her daughter's hair. Gros Morne, Haiti, 1980.

and *fanm-saj* (midwives), and in certain places in the country-side they can even be initiated as priestesses; but nowhere do they challenge the religious hegemony of the rural male. In the cities, however, the picture is quite different. There are no statistics, but my strong impression is that at least half of the urban Vodou leaders are women. Furthermore, the mood of the women's temples is markedly different from the atmosphere in temples headed by men. Generally speaking, the issue is flexibility. The ethos within a woman's temple is like that inside the home, where the mother moves in and out of her role as an authority figure as the situation demands; whereas a man's temple usually reflects the more rigid role definitions of the public arena.

The question of women and Vodou is broader than the question of leadership, however. Consideration of the three Ezili opens up this larger dimension. The adaptability of Vodou over time, and its responsiveness to other cultures and religions; the fact that it has no canon, creed, or pope; the multiplicity of its spirits; and the intimate detail in which those spirits reflect the lives of the faithful—all these characteristics make women's lives visible within Vodou in ways they are not in other religious traditions, including those of the African homeland. This visibility can give women a way of working realistically and creatively with the forces that define and confine them.

Lasyrenn, Ezili Dantò, and Ezili Freda are each conflated with particular manifestations of the Virgin Mary: Nuestra Señora de la Caridad del Cobre, Mater Salvatoris, and Maria Dolorosa. But unlike the Mary of mainstream Catholicism, who offers an impossible ideal of perfectly submissive (and virginal) motherhood for emulation, the Ezili are much closer to the human drama. In addition to providing examples of love, care, and hard work, they model anger—righteous and raging—power and effectivity, sensuality, sexuality, fear, frustration, need, and loneliness. In so doing, they become mirrors that give objective reality to what would otherwise remain, as it does in so many cultures, women's silent pain and unhonored power.

These female spirits are both mirrors and maps, making the present comprehensible and offering direction for the future. In the caricaturelike clarity of Vodou possession-performances, the Ezili sort out, by acting out, the conflicting feelings and values in a given life situation. By interacting with the faithful as individuals and groups, all the Vodou spirits clarify the options in people's lives; and the Ezili do this especially well for women.

When Alourdes says that Ezili Dantò is her "mother," she both describes key circumstances of her life and identifies some of her most important values. Yet, in her house, Lasyrenn is also saluted from time to time, and Ezili Freda is even more frequently honored, although neither is given the attention and service that Dantò receives. Thus although Ezili Dantò is Alourdes's major female spirit, her life as a woman is actually choreographed through a dynamic balancing of the three.

The individual and the spirits who love and protect that individual are in a mutually responsive relationship. The three Ezili, individually and in relation to one another, provide a template for Alourdes's life. But the circumstances of her life also cause the personalities of Lasyrenn, Dantò, and Freda to emerge in particular ways. Alourdes and her spirits create one another, a relationship recognized within her Vodou family, where someone is as likely to speak about "Alourdes's Dantò" as about Ezili Dantò in general.

Alourdes is a heterosexual woman, in mid-life, who grew up in Port-au-Prince and has lived in the United States for twenty-five years. Her situation as a woman relating to the three Ezili is naturally different from that of a man relating to mother and lover figures. Her heterosexuality suppresses the acknowledged lesbian dimension of Ezili Dantò, a part of the *lwa*'s character that could be very important for other women. Her age crystalizes an Ezili Freda who may act like an ingenue but certainly is not one. And her life in the New York Haitian immigrant community and earlier in Port-au-Prince—both places in which many, if not most, families are headed by women—mutes Dantò's identity as the mysterious tree-dwelling serpent and brings her status as single mother to the fore. These urban and immigrant dimensions of Alourdes's life are most likely also responsible for making Lasyrenn retreat even further into the depths than she usually does.

LASYRENN

Lasyrenn, Labalenn,
Chapo'm tonbe nan lanmè.
M'ap fè karès ak Lasyrenn,

Chapo'm tonbe nan lanmè.
M'ap fè dodo ak Lasyrenn,
Chapo'm tonbe nan lanmè.

The mermaid, the whale,
My hat falls into the sea.
I caress the mermaid,
My hat falls into the sea.
I lie down with the mermaid,
My hat falls into the sea.

Thus goes one of Alourdes's favorite songs for this watery Ezili sister. As both mermaid and whale (the two sometimes appear as separate spirits), she is an elusive creature of the deep sea. She is a fleeting presence, never fully seen, hinting at something monumental—huge, deep, sudden, and powerful. When people catch a glimpse of Lasyrenn beneath the water, they feel her beckoning them to come with her back to Ginen, to Africa, the ancestral home and the dwelling place of the *lwa, anba dlo* (beneath the water). She hovers large and dark and silent just below the surface of the water, a place Haitians call "the back of the mirror." Gazing at her is like gazing at your own reflection. It is seductive because she gives a deeper and truer picture of self than is likely to be found in the mirrors of everyday life. But it is also dangerous to try to get too close or hold on too tightly to the vision. A person who reaches out to stroke her or tries to lie close by her broad and comforting side may, quite simply, drown. First the hat falls into the sea, and the person follows quickly after.

Lasyrenn's elusive character is captured in Alourdes's description: "She's black, not white. Black, black. Her hair go down to her feet. Shiny, shiny, shiny, shiny, long hair! Sometime you see her a blonde . . . long, long, long hair. If you see her with your eyes in the sea, she's white; when you dream her, she's black, because they say she got one side white, one side black. A big fish with two color. Lasyrenn, Labalenn . . . always got a comb, to comb her hair."

Lasyrenn is connected to Mammy Water, whose shrines are found throughout West Africa. Some suggest that the mermaid persona, also common for Mammy Water, was derived from the carved figures on the bows of the ships of European traders and slavers. Thus the Vodou *lwa* Lasyrenn may have roots that connect, like nerves, to the deepest and most painful parts of the loss of homeland and the trauma of slavery. It is therefore fitting that she also reconnects people to Africa and its wisdom. In many stories, people are captured by Lasyrenn and pulled under the water, down to Ginen. Sometimes these stories are descriptions of tragic drownings or of suicides. But as often as not such tales are strategies used by the poor and otherwise disenfranchised to gain access to the prestigious role of healer.

The stories have a common pattern. A person, usually a woman, disappears for a time—three days, three months, three years. When she returns, she is a changed person. Her skin has become fairer, her hair longer and straighter. Most important, she has gained sacred knowledge. Immediately after her return, she is disoriented, does not talk, and does not remember what happened to her. But gradually a story emerges, a story of living for a time "below the water," where the spirits instructed her in the arts of diagnosis and healing.[2] A person who can make a convincing claim to receiving instruction in the priestly arts "below the water" need not go through expensive initiation ceremonies or a time-consuming apprenticeship. I once met such a rural priestess. She was called Sansami, a nickname meaning without friends. When I asked who had initiated her, she responded that no one had. Her instruction, she said simply, had come *anba dlo.*

Alourdes makes no such claim. Because her grandfather, Alphonse Macena, came from the south of Haiti where people go through formal and expensive initiation ceremonies to attain the role of healer, and because she inherited obligations to Macena's spirits, Alourdes also went through the rituals to take the *ason.* Ogou demanded it, and she was the first woman in her family to do so. This initiation gives her an official and widely recognized right to claim the role of priestess. Alourdes says, however, that she serves both her grandfather's and her grandmother's spirits. Her fidelity to the line of Marie Noelsine Joseph, daughter of the old African Joseph Binbin Mauvant, brings

---

[2]See Max Benoit, "Symbi—loi des eaux," *Bulletin du Bureau d'ethnologie* (Port-au-Prince) 3, nos. 20–22 (June—December 1959): 12–22.

claims to other sources of wisdom—Mauvant had the spirits "on him" all the time, and he healed the natural way, the simple way, without *ason* or elaborate ritualizing.

Quite unconsciously, Alourdes describes a time of instruction *anba dlo* when she connects her call to the priesthood with the time she was lost at age seven. The object that occasioned her adventure was a borrowed comb, and the comb is Lasyrenn's most common accoutrement. It was Ezili Dantò, Lasyrenn's dark sister, who caused the disappearance. And it was Dantò who, when Alourdes was found, made an appearance to convey the message that Alourdes was to inherit her mother's healing practice. Alourdes was gone for three days (the ritual number), was found next to the city reservoir (an urban transformation of the sea), and, when found, was disoriented and could remember nothing of what had transpired. Alourdes's story deviates from the pattern only in that she still claims amnesia about what occurred during those three days.

The events of Alourdes's life gravitated like barnacles to the back of the whale—Labalenn, Lasyrenn. Myth provided the template for life. Yet when Alourdes tells that story, she never says that she received religious instruction *anba dlo*. Like the elusive whale, the interpretive framework of her childhood experience hovers seductively just below the surface of the waters of consciousness.

EZILI DANTÒ

In 1965 Alourdes was finally able to bring her three children—Jean-Pierre, Maggie, and William—to New York. They arrived during midsummer's heat, two months before school began. By this time, Alourdes thought of herself primarily as a healer, and her practice was growing rapidly. Nevertheless, she had taken an outside job to cover the expense of reuniting her family, working from four in the afternoon until midnight doing laundry at the Hotel National on Seventh Avenue and Forty-second Street in Manhattan. While she was at work, the children fended for themselves in Brooklyn.

Maggie was twelve years old, about to turn thirteen. Some afternoons when Alourdes had gone to work, Maggie would sit on the front stoop watching the neighborhood children. She sometimes ventured, in her halting English, to join games of tag or skip-rope, but, in the beginning, she was not often successful. Her first weeks in New York were hard and lonely. On most days, like a dutiful Haitian girl-child, she did housework.

> One day when Mommie went to work, you know, being in the house, the only girl, I work a lot, right? So what I did, I wash all those clothes, Jean' clothes, William' clothes, my clothes, sheets—everything in the house, I wash by hand. And then when I finish (I don't know . . . I must'a thought I was in Haiti. . . .), I put my iron board and my iron. I start ironing, and I iron everything. Then I took a bath and from there—I got sick! I had trembling, fever, and the next morning Mommie took me to the doctor, and the doctor say that I was real sick!

The emergency-room physician suspected Maggie had tuberculosis, a disease common among Haitians, or perhaps pneumonia; but he could not be sure and wanted to hospitalize her for further testing. Maggie was afraid to be separated from her family and begged to go home. The doctor said that would be all right if she promised to come back the next day for more tests, and Maggie went home to bed. When Alourdes returned from work that night, Maggie got up, and the family ate, talked, and watched television together. It was after two in the morning when they turned off the lights. Maggie's bed was in the living room, and, when she lay down, the light from the streetlamp at the corner of Utica Avenue and Jane Street fell directly across her pillow.

> We just went to bed, and then I saw, like a shadow, coming to the light. . . . Next minute, I actually saw a lady standing in front of me. But I could not see her face real clear. I saw a lady standing in front of me with a blue dress, and she have a veil covering her head and her face. I wasn't scared of that lady, and I was saying, "Who are you? Who are you?" And then she said, "You don't know who I am?" I said, "I don't know who you are."
> And then she pull up the veil, and I could see it was her with the two mark. Ezili Dantò with the two mark on her

cheek. Whooooo! Yeah! And then I start to get scared. She told me, "Don't get scared, I'm your mother."

Then she told me to turn my back around, she was going to heal me; I wasn't going to be sick no more. She turned me around. She rubbed my back. She rubbed my lungs and everything; she rub it, and then she said, "Now you know what to do for me. Just light up a candle and thank me." I say, "Okay," and then she say, "I'm going now, I'm going," and I say, "Let me call my mother, tell my mother you here." It's strange . . . you know, just like a visitor . . . somebody come to visit. I said, "Let me call my mother—Don't! Wait! Let me call—" She said, "No, no, your mother don't have to come."

I have heard this important family story many times. When Alourdes is present, the story emerges antiphonally. When that happens, Alourdes invariably breaks in at this point, as she did once when my tape recorder was running: "When Maggie call,

Altar constructed for Ezili Dantò's birthday party. Alourdes's home, Fort Greene, Brooklyn, 1980.

she say, 'Mommie, come, come, come! Did you see?' And I see the veil going. . . ." Maggie's voice came in over the top of Alourdes's: "I saw her! She come into my house. I spoke to her just like I'm talking to you now. She was pretty—and black, black, black." Alourdes's voice folded into Maggie's: "I see the veil, but I don't saw the lady." And then Maggie's into Alourdes's: "I went back to the doctor, and the doctor say, 'What's wrong with you? I thought you was sick!'" Maggie and Alourdes agreed that after the visit from Ezili Dantò Maggie was no longer ill. The rest of the summer passed without incident, and in the fall Maggie and the other children started to school.

The chromolithograph Haitians most often use to represent Ezili Dantò is a particular manifestation of Mater Salvatoris: a Polish black Virgin known as Our Lady of Czestochowa. On her right cheek are two parallel vertical scars. (Many Haitians, perhaps projecting from an African ancestral memory, refer to Dantò's *twa màk* [three scars].) Her head is draped with a gold-edged blue veil. In her arms she holds the Christ child. In this image, Haitians identify her child as a girl. The child is the most important iconographic detail, for Ezili Dantò is above all else the mother, the one who bears children. This explains why certain white Virgins depicted with children, especially Our Lady of Lourdes and Our Lady of Mount Carmel, are also said to be Ezili Dantò.

Several of the male spirits are known to be Dantò's lovers and the fathers of one or more of her seven children. Ogou is the one mentioned most frequently as her lover. But when people are talking in an intimate, gossipy way, they point to Ti-Jan Petwo (her own son) as her favorite lover. It is well known that Ezili Dantò has not married any of the spirits who are her sexual partners. Being a single mother who raises children on her own is an important part of her identity. Dantò is, however, a frequent participant in marriages with *vivan-yo* (the living). In these rituals, individuals pledge loyalty, service, and even sexual fidelity for one night each week (sleeping with no human on that night and waiting to receive the spirit in their dreams) in return for the spirit's increased care and protection. And again, when gossip is the mode, people in Alourdes's community admit that some of these marriages are with women. Thus the portrait emerges of an independent, childbearing woman with an unconventional sexuality that, on several counts, flouts the authority of the patriarchal family.

Alourdes describes Ezili Dantò as substantial, "not fat, but heavy." She has dark black skin and, like Lasyrenn, long, shiny hair. Her eyes are "big, white, and shiny," the ever-watchful eyes of the mother. Maggie claims that when she talks with Dantò in Alourdes's altar room she can see the beautiful eyes in the chromolithograph moving. "Dantò is elegant, but not too elegant," Alourdes told me once, explaining that Ezili Dantò is not too proud to work—in fact, "she love to work." She works hard, and she works fast. If someone is in trouble or there is an emergency, Alourdes said, Dantò is the kind of woman who will forget about herself and her appearance, throw on her clothes, and rush to the side of the person in trouble. Maggie also connects her to crisis situations: "It seem like each time I'm gonna be sick, if it's something bad going to happen, she always the one coming to tell me." Both Maggie and Alourdes frequently refer to Ezili Dantò as "my mother." Hardworking, responsive, present in times of trouble, pretty but not vain— these are the qualities of the ideal mother.

Ezili Dantò fought fiercely beside her "children" in the Haitian slave revolution. In Maggie's words: "That lady is from Africa, and during the time we had slave back home in Haiti, during the eighteen-hundred . . . or the seventeen-hundred . . . she was the one that help my country to fight with the white people. She helped them to win that war." She was wounded, Haitians say, and they point to the scars on Our Lady of Czestochowa's right cheek as evidence. But those are not the only scars Dantò bears. Again, in Maggie's words: "In that war, she was going to talk, to tell something, and then they go over and cut out her tongue because they don't want her to talk." It seems that Dantò was rendered speechless by her own people, people fighting on the same side, people who could not trust her to guard their secrets. When Ezili Dantò possesses someone these days, she cannot speak. The only sound the spirit can utter is a uniform "*dey-dey-dey.*"

Alourdes and Maggie claim that the Ezili who says "*dey-dey-dey*" comes from Jean Rabel and that she belongs to their family. Other Ezili Dantò make a sound that Alourdes describes as a repeated "kuh" or a sound produced, ironically, by sucking the tongue up against the roof of the mouth, a kind of "thwap." Whatever the form, Dantò's inarticulate sounds gain meaning in a Vodou ceremony only through her body language and the interpretive efforts of the gathered community. Her appearance in Jean Rabel to indicate that Alourdes was to inherit her mother's healing practice was typical of the somber games of charades that surround her visits.

Dantò's inability to speak emphasizes something that is true of all the Vodou spirits: their messages are enigmatic. Terse, multireferential language works in similar ways with other spirits. Whether a given spirit uses articulate speech or not, the participants, individually and collectively, interpret and apply what is said. Vodou spirits do not often make authoritative pronouncements. Their presence in the thick social weave of a ritual is a catalyst activating group wisdom and group resources. Vodou ceremonies are accurately described as group healing sessions in which both individual and collective problems surface and are addressed. The community is therefore both the subject and the product of Vodou ritualizing.

On a hot July night in 1987, I saw how practical and specific this process can be. Some months earlier, Alourdes had taken in a family of recent immigrants from Haiti, and they had been living in her basement apartment. She was concerned about the three children in this family because they were listless and scrawny. Good manners prohibited Alourdes from challenging the quality of parental care the children were receiving—but when Ezili Dantò arrived, she was not so restricted. *"Dey-dey-dey-dey,"* said Dantò over and over. Eventually, the family was called to join the ritual, and Dantò put the children in the center of the group. She circled skinny wrists with thumb and finger and tugged at baggy clothes. Then she called in healthy children of approximately the same ages and had them stand together for comparison.

The community went into action. Older women in the group queried the mother about the general health of her children and then asked what she had fed them for dinner that evening. When she replied, "Hot dogs," several older women clucked their tongues and sucked their teeth. "She gives them American food," they repeated knowingly to one another, and they turned back to the mother with a step-by-step recipe for a watercress soup that is both cheap and nutritious. The women lectured the children's mother on the importance of putting in the extra time and effort to make "real food." Ezili Dantò spares no effort to see that her children are well cared-for.

But anger and even rage are often found on the flip side of a mother's self-sacrifice, and these emotions also appear in the Petwo spirit Ezili Dantò. The maternal anger that is called into play when a mother must defend her children turned Dantò into a woman warrior during the slave revolution. Another sort of anger turns against the children themselves. Those such as Alourdes, who serve Dantò, become her "children." "Ezili Dantò is my mother, but she very tough lady," Alourdes said. "Oh, boy, she's tough! You have to treat her very nice. You know what you suppose to do. You know what you don't suppose to do. Ezili Dantò—when you got her, she strict with you."

Dantò's anger can exceed what is required for strict discipline. At times, it explodes from her with an irrational, violent force. Ezili Dantò, like Lasyrenn, has connections with water. A gentle rainfall during the festivities at Saut d'Eau, a mountain pilgrimage site for Ezili Dantò (Our Lady of Mount Carmel), is readily interpreted as a sign of her presence; but so is a sudden deluge resulting in mudslides, traffic accidents, and even deaths. One of Alourdes's favorite songs for Dantò has the line: *"Lè ou wè Dantò pase, ou di se loray-o* [When you see Dantò pass by, you say it is a thunderstorm]." Thus Dantò's rage can emerge with the elemental force of a torrential rain, which sweeps away just and unjust alike. This aspect of Ezili Dantò might be described as an infant's-eye view of the omnipotent mother.

Some people call Dantò a *baka* (evil spirit). But Alourdes explains that some people have a good Dantò and others have an evil one. The evil ones are never inherited in families; rather, they are powers "purchased" by the envious and the greedy. Yet even a good Dantò, such as the one Alourdes inherited from her mother, has the potential if not to become a *baka* then at least to behave like one. "Some people have Dantò," Alourdes said, "they have good Dantò, but if you kill any animal in front of her . . . she see blood . . . she might turn." Among Haitians, killing an animal for a feast, Vodou or otherwise, marks the meal as prestigious. When the spirits are being honored, they usually do the killing. But not Dantò! She cannot be allowed to do that. At the sight of blood, Dantò goes wild.

"Dantò can be evil, too," Maggie said. "She kills a lot. If you put her upside down, you tell her to go and get somebody, she will go and get that person. If that person don't want to come, she break that person neck and bring that person to you." "Lot'a people scared of her—most people scared of her!" Alourdes said and then quickly added, "But I love her, even she tough. When she's behind you, sweetheart, nothing can attack you. Nothing!"

Alourdes's philosophy in working with Ezili Dantò is to treat her well and with caution. Any gift presented to Ezili Dantò— money, clothing, dolls (which the spirit loves)—stays right on her altar and is never used by any member of the family. With care and respect, the constructive parts of Dantò's anger and energy can be put to good use and the destructive parts kept in check. Alourdes believes that if she were to take the large tawny doll that represents Dantò on her altar and turn it upside down in an attempt to take vengeance on an enemy, the energy unleashed would eventually come back to destroy her. She leaves the doll upright and lets the part of Dantò that is sometimes called a *baka* slumber in the shadows where it serves a function. It fuels the engine of the hardworking single mother who must sometimes turn the world upside down to protect and provide for her children.

The following song, one Alourdes sings for Dantò every time she calls the spirit, indicates that disobedient children are not the only source of Dantò's problems. Relationships with men can be equally disturbing. This song takes blood, the trigger for violence in Dantò, and transforms it into an image of the spirit's own fierce suffering.

> *Di ye!*
> *Set kou'd kouto, set kou'd ponya.*
> *Prete'm terinn-nan, m'al vomi san ye.*
> *Set kou'd kouto, set kou'd ponya.*
> *Prete'm terinn-nan, m'al vomi san ye.* [repeat]
>
> *Men san màke pou li.*
>
> *Set kou'd kouto, set kou'd ponya.*
> *Prete'm terinn-nan, m'al vomi san ye.*
> *Mwen di ye, m'pral vomi san, se vre.*
> *Set kou'd kouto, set kou'd ponya.*

Prete'm terinn-nan, m'al vomi san ye. [repeat]
San m'ape koule, Dantò, m'pral vomi san ye.
San m'ape koule, Ezili, m'pral vomi san ye.
San mwen ape koule, Je Wouj, ou pral vomi san ye.

Say hey!
Seven stabs of the knife, seven stabs of the sword.
Hand me that basin, I'm going to vomit blood.
Seven stabs of the knife, seven stabs of the sword.
Hand me that basin, I'm going to vomit blood. [repeat]
But the blood is marked for him.

Seven stabs of the knife, seven stabs of the sword.
Hand me that basin, I'm going to vomit blood.
I say hey! I'm going to vomit blood, it's true.
Seven stabs of the knife, seven stabs of the sword.
Hand me that basin, I'm going to vomit blood. [repeat]
My blood is flowing, Dantò, I'm going to vomit blood.
My blood is flowing, Ezili, I'm going to vomit blood.
My blood is flowing, Red-Eyes, you're going to vomit blood.

Haitians have a talent for capturing history in terse images. Seven Stabs of the Knife was the name of the compound in Port-au-Prince where Philomise lived at the time Alourdes was born. It was named after an infamous event that occurred there not long before Philo moved in. A fight began in the compound with words between a man and his female partner. Their anger escalated, and the man rushed into the house for a knife. In front of their neighbors, he killed the woman by stabbing her seven times. People probably did not have to think too long or too hard to realize that this event belonged in the domain of Ezili Je Wouj (Ezili of the Red Eyes), another name for Dantò.

Ezili Dantò is a woman on her own. She is fiercely independent. But the brutal honesty of Vodou does not allow any woman who follows in Dantò's path to claim that she does so easily or entirely by choice. Dantò is independent, but she also craves connections with men for the new life they produce. In this need lies her greatest vulnerability. Dantò rages and destroys, but she also suffers. She vomits blood. In 1985, when Dantò appeared at Alourdes's annual July birthday party for her, she asked for a basin and vomited blood. I did not attend the party, but Maggie, who was moved by the event, called the next day to tell me about it. I did not know then and I still do not know (how would I phrase the question?) how Dantò's horse—that is, Alourdes—managed to vomit blood. Or, perhaps more to the point, I do not know what was going on in Alourdes's life or the life of her community that provoked this extreme gesture from Ezili Dantò.

Relationships between poor men and women in urban Haiti are often troubled and transitory. After the slave revolution (and in many rural areas today), the patriarchal, multigenerational extended family held sway in Haiti. Men who had sufficient resources could form relationships with more than one woman. Women had their own households in which they bore and raised their children. Men followed a circuit, moving among the households of wives and girlfriends, while often continuing to rely on their mothers as well as their women to feed and lodge them. When the big extended families began to break up under the combined pressures of depleted soil, overpopulation, and corrupt politics, large numbers of rural people moved to the cities.

Haitian women have fared better than men in the shift from rural to urban life. In the cities, the family has shrunk to the size of the individual household, an arena in which women have traditionally been in charge. Furthermore, women's skill at small-scale commerce, an aptitude passed on through generations of rural market women, has allowed them to adapt to life in urban Haiti, where the income of a household usually must be patched together. In contrast, men living in the cities have often been too proud to exploit small and erratic sources of income, even when their chances of finding a full-time job are slim.

Currently, unemployment among young urban males hovers around 80 percent. Many young men in the city follow the old pattern, circulating among the households of their girlfriends and families to be fed, enjoy some intimacy, and get their laundry done. But life is hard and resources scarce. With the land gone, it is no longer clear how essential particular men are to the survival of particular women and children. As a result, relationships between urban men and women have become brittle and, too often, violent.

Men are caught in a double bind. They are still reared to expect to exercise power and authority, although they have few resources with which to do so. When their expectations run up against a wall of social impossibility, men often veer off in unproductive directions. The least harmful is manifested in a national preoccupation with soccer. The most damaging involve the military, the domestic police force of Haiti, and a vast, complicated, many-headed male patronage system that provides the one road to upward social mobility for desperate, poor young men. Drinking and gambling fall somewhere in the middle of this spectrum. Alcoholism is a big problem throughout Haiti and an even bigger problem in Port-au-Prince, where a bottle of Johnny Walker is thought to be indispensable to the image of a young man who likes to *flannen* (hang out) with his buddies. Gambling is also pervasive among poor men. The many lotteries, large and small, that can be played every day in Port-au-Prince offer one outlet for the fever. Rue du Dr. Dehoux, a main artery that skirts the city cemetery, is clogged with rickety gambling concessions, roulette wheels, and dice games, which appear only after dark, garishly lighted by Coleman lanterns. Many of the players are men so poor their feet are bare and their clothes ragged.

Ezili Dantò's lover Ogou is a warrior spirit pictured as a hero, a breathtakingly handsome and dedicated soldier. But, just as often, Ogou is portrayed as vain and swaggering, untrustworthy, wantonly violent, and self-destructive. In one of his manifestations, Ogou is a drunk. Ezili Dantò will take this man into her bed, but she knows she cannot depend on him, and she would never dream of marrying him. The relationship between Ezili Dantò and Ogou thus takes up and comments on much of the actual life experience of Haitian women.

Ezili Dantò also mirrors many of the specifics of Alourdes's own life and the lives of other women in her family. Marie Noelsine Joseph and Alphonse Macena, Alourdes's maternal grandparents, fought constantly. Alourdes's mother, Philo, knew her own father only when she was a child, and what Philo remembered most clearly about Macena was her fear of him. Philo's life was also full of problems with lovers. The first man she was involved with, Luc Charles, was jealous, possessive, and violent. The second, like Charles a Haitian residing in Santo Domingo, fathered a child with another woman while living with Philo. Philo left each of them in turn and moved on, but a return to Port-au-Prince did not change her luck. Alourdes's father was a brief presence who disappeared from Philo's life before Alourdes was born. He stopped coming by as soon as Philo asked him for a minimal financial contribution to the family. And then, according to Alourdes, the spirits said, "That's enough!" Philo's menstrual periods stopped before she turned forty, and after Alourdes's father, she never had a sexual relationship with a man again. "The spirit make my mother stop. They want no interference."

In one intimate, late-night conversation, Maggie, Alourdes, and I discussed what it was like to be women on our own, an experience we shared. Maggie spoke with real energy: "My grandmother taught us to be strong as woman. You don't need man, to be the father of this, the father of that. Like . . . we woman . . . we could do *everything!* Like Wonderwoman!" (Like Ezili Dantò, she might have said.) Alourdes, as she so often does, responded with a more nuanced view that qualified Maggie's fantasy: "To give me food, to give me clothes—I don't need man for that. I can work!" But, Alourdes said, "Some thing you can't do for yourself. You need a man to love . . . to make love to you."

Now in mid-life, Alourdes is certain she is not cut out for a traditional marriage. She is far too independent and strong-willed. "I can't do that for nobody—cook and clean and take care of him. Not me!" But neither is she open to casual relationships with men. "I don't like boyfriend. When you deeply in trouble, it not his day to come! I like my one man." The problem is finding that one man. "You want company, right?" Alourdes asked one day. "You want somebody to talk, to make love? If you lucky, you find a good man. If you not so lucky, you find a bad man. Man is a lottery, right? You play it, you win or you lose. If you don't lose, you win."

Like so many of the older Haitian women I know, Alourdes has an irreverent humor about men that steals the sting from otherwise painful situations. For more than a year, there was a running joke in Alourdes's household about a mythical man named Joe. When there was no food in the refrigerator, it was because Joe got there first. He came by for breakfast and ate three dozen eggs, two loaves of bread, a pound of butter, and so forth. As the list got longer and longer, the laughter got louder and louder. When a child misbehaved, he or she was threatened with being punished by Joe, who would ask no questions before throwing the child out on the street. Maggie characterized him this way: "Joe say, 'I could beat a child until I kill them.'" When Alourdes was miffed because I had not come around in several weeks, she told all her friends that Joe had left her and gone off with me and now I was "too busy" to come and visit.

Alourdes did not always have a sense of humor about men. A good part of her life was spent searching for a man who would rescue her if not from who she was then at least from where she was. But Alourdes was not able to form a lasting union with a man. At fourteen, she fell in love with Abner, the only son of a struggling but not desperately poor Port-au-Prince family. He was sixteen and beginning his studies at the university when he met the vibrant young Alourdes. When Abner's family learned Alourdes was pregnant, they acted swiftly. He arrived home one day to find a large suitcase on the front porch. "Whose suitcase is that?" he asked. "Never mind," said his father. "We are going for a ride." And with that Abner was taken to the airport and sent to Chicago. He did not even have time to say good-bye. Some months later, Jean-Pierre, Alourdes's first child, was born. For a while, letters arrived from Chicago, some containing a little money. But soon the mail stopped. Alourdes was heartbroken and quite depressed for many months. The outsized emotions of adolescence magnified the real social and economic constraints that began to shape her life with the birth of her first child, at age fourteen.

When Alourdes was fifteen, she got her job with the Troupe Folklorique, and things began to improve. She was beautiful, naturally sensual, and I suspect that even then she had a strong and compelling personality. When the group was on tour in Cuba, she got to know Charles Desinor, a photographer who worked for the Haitian tourist bureau and traveled with the Troupe Folklorique. Although he was forty years old and married, he courted Alourdes with energy and great perseverance. At first, Philo was reluctant to allow Alourdes even to invite him to their home, but in the end Charles won out. His success may have had something to do with his considerable style. One day when Alourdes and Philo were sitting at home, a big truck arrived at the house on Oswald Durand, bringing furniture—complete sets for a living room, dining room, and bedroom. Philo's three-room wooden house could not have accommodated this much furniture even if she had intended to do nothing more than store it. Charles soon arrived to announce that he was going to rent a big house for Alourdes, where she could put the furniture. In no time, they were living together—or at least they were together as often as Charles's otherwise full life allowed.

This man was Maggie's father, a man who turned out to be more responsible than many of the men in Alourdes's life. To this day, she can remember his old telephone number, 2002, at the Office National du Tourisme, "because that number in my mind all the time. I have to call that number if Maggie got something, if she sick—*de mil de* [two thousand two]. If I need something—*de mil de*. I got problem—*de mil de*."

During the time Alourdes was with Charles, she met Antoine Kowalski in the Church of Our Lady of Mount Carmel in Port-au-Prince.[3] She was eighteen, and Kowalski was thirty-four. Alourdes went to pray before the statue of the Virgin, and when she returned to her pew, Antoine came and sat beside her. As an opening line, he told Alourdes that he was the one who could give her what she had requested from Our Lady of Mount Carmel (Ezili Dantò). When Alourdes asked how he knew what her prayer had been, Kowalski countered with a proposal of marriage. Alourdes had not yet said a dozen words to Antoine Kowalski.

Alourdes had only recently connected with a father who had previously ignored her and had even denied her existence, and she was quite anxious to win the approval of this newfound "daddy." Alphonse Margaux, a small, fastidious man who was a lawyer in Haiti's tax office, did not hide his disapproval of Alourdes's arrangement with Charles. Here was his daughter, with two children, living with a man who was not her husband. It made him ashamed. So Alourdes decided to marry Kowalski, and she sent her suitor to her father to ask for her hand. Alourdes knew she was not in love, but she nevertheless felt compelled to marry by a teenage sensitivity to her father's upper-class pre-

[3] Polish names are not uncommon in Haiti. They can be traced to the sizable Polish legion included in the force Napoleon Bonaparte sent in 1802 to quell the slave revolt in Saint Domingue. These Polish soldiers, some of whom had been freedom fighters in their own country, had been pressed into military service against their will. Once in Saint Domingue, many Poles sided with the rebels and eventually received protection from rebel leaders. See Laurore St. Juste and Frère Enel Clérismé, *Présence polonaise en Haiti* (Port-au-Prince: n.p., 1983).

tensions. Describing her feelings at the time, Alourdes said, "I did that to save my family name."

Kowalski, a bachelor who had spent more than a decade waiting for the one woman he could love (knowing he could love only one), set out to win Alourdes's heart as well as her hand. He tried hard, perhaps too hard. At one point during their engagement, Kowalski won the lottery. With a ticket in his hand worth twenty thousand dollars, he showed up at Alourdes's door. He gave her the winning ticket and told her dramatically, "Rip it up! Do anything with it. I love you. I don't love that ticket." Alourdes asked him to buy her a house with the money, and he did.

Alourdes Margaux (she had recently taken her father's name) and Antoine Kowalski were married at ten o'clock in the morning on December 30, 1954, in the Church of the Sacred Heart in downtown Port-au-Prince. Alourdes was nineteen, and she wore a traditional wedding dress. Her children, Jean-Pierre and Maggie, sat in their stiff new clothes in the front pew of the cavernous church. Pèpe, as Alourdes's father was known to his friends, sat contentedly beside them. After the wedding, he even came to visit his newly married daughter from time to time.

Alourdes's husband had a shoemaking business, and he set her up in their new house with two servants. This situation is not as luxurious as it sounds; there are thousands of desperately poor people in Port-au-Prince who consider themselves lucky to get a job as a maid or house "guardian," even if their wages are little more than food and a place to sleep. But for Alourdes, who had often been hungry as a child, this union and its accoutrements were, for a while, the realization of a fantasy.

The fantasy did not last long. Kowalski was more obsessive as a husband than he had been as a suitor. He demanded that she quit singing with the Troupe Folklorique. He threw a jealous fit if she spoke to another man, even someone passing on the street. He was so possessive he sent spies to follow her when she visited her mother in the little house on Oswald Durand. Alourdes began to chafe under his control. "He too selfish. He don't need wife, he need slave . . . not wife," she told her friends. She reasoned with herself: "He's not tied the way I'm tied. Right?" Tensions between them escalated. Kowalski lectured. Alourdes retorted, "Shut up, old man. You talk too much."

One day, he came home from work early. Alourdes, five

months pregnant, had a craving for raw meat, and, like a self-conscious, naughty child, she had placed her arm on the shoulder of the maid, who was busy preparing dinner, and begged for a bite of raw steak. Kowalski saw only the two women touching. He flew into a rage and fired the maid on the spot. Alourdes objected loudly, and Kowalski got madder. Alourdes's volatile emotions erupted like a volcano. She slapped him. He kicked her, and she lost the baby. Not long after, she moved away from the house Kowalski had bought with his lottery winnings, telling him to keep it. She wanted nothing but her freedom.

Freedom proved to be very hard indeed. Soon she could no longer afford even the few dollars a month it cost to keep her faithful maid. For some months, she lived on her own. Then she was forced to move back with her mother. Philo was furious with Alourdes for throwing away the security that the relationship with Kowalski had represented, and the two were barely on speaking terms. Eventually, Alourdes found a job that paid almost enough to survive and established her own home once again. There were men and there were relationships during this long and difficult period, but none of them sustained Alourdes economically or emotionally.

With a man named René, she became pregnant a third time. But when René learned a baby was due, the relationship quickly ended. Alourdes feared that she could not support herself and her children during this pregnancy, and she reluctantly concluded that she would have to abort the child. She did just what her mother had done—ran up and down stairs, punched herself in the stomach, jumped repeatedly from a table to the floor, and drank teas, potions, and anything she had ever heard mentioned as a possible abortifacient. And, just as the spirits had intervened to stop her mother, so they appeared to warn her. In the midst of these desperate efforts, Alourdes had a dream in which a brightly painted *taptap* stopped in front of her house. Notre Dame du Mont Carmel (Ezili Dantò) emerged and handed her a baby. Friends counseled her that this dream was serious and that she should do nothing to harm the baby. Alourdes persisted nevertheless, but somehow so did the fetus. Alourdes had pain with William, her third child and second son, from the time he was conceived until a year after his birth.

Four years later, when Alourdes was living with Gabriel (a man who remains her close friend), she had a surgical abortion in a Port-au-Prince clinic. This time, Alourdes wanted the child but felt compelled to have the abortion. Her visa to immigrate to the United States had been granted at last, and someone told Alourdes she would not be allowed to leave Haiti if the authorities knew she was going to have a baby.

Haiti is a Catholic country. People who serve the spirits, including those like Alourdes who are priestesses and priests, consider themselves good Catholics. In 1984, I was seated at Maggie's kitchen table, reading her copy of the *New York Post* and lamenting the rhetoric of John Cardinal O'Connor on abortion. "He doesn't have to use the word *murder* all the time," I said. "It *is* murder!" shouted Alourdes and Maggie with one voice.

In spite of this opinion, Alourdes knew about and, at least to some extent, sympathized with Philo's attempt to abort her. Alourdes herself had tried to terminate one pregnancy and had succeeded in doing so with another. At the time we had this discussion, Maggie was employed as a nurse's aide in what can only be described as an abortion mill on Manhattan's Upper East Side. Furthermore, the Vodou spirit Ezili Dantò is understood to oppose abortion, as Alourdes's and Philo's dreams indicated. "It really make her mad!" Alourdes once said. "She don't like abortion because she really love children. But, you know, human being do everything. That's life! Right? Abortion something human created. Right?"

Vodou morality is not a morality of rule or law but a contextual one. It is tailored not only to the situation but also to the specific person or group involved. A moral person, in Vodou, is one who lives in tune with his or her character, a character defined by the spirits said to love that person. Flexibility is provided in the midst of moral dilemmas by the support these favorite spirits offer to different and sometimes contradictory values. When Alourdes was pregnant with William, Ezili Dantò urged her not to abort the child. In this case, the price for following the will of the spirits has been high: William will never be able to support himself and will be Alourdes's responsibility until she dies. Yet, in contrast, when Alourdes was pregnant with Gabriel's baby, Ogou, the great survival artist and risk taker, won the day, and Dantò went silent. Alourdes had the abortion. In Ogou's honor, Alourdes donned a red dress when she boarded the plane for New York. Abortion "is murder," but it is also the only choice to make in some situations.

Each spirit has a moral pull, but no one spirit prevails in every situation. In Vodou, there is no Golden Age in the past and no heaven in the future.[4] Consequently, no value is higher than survival—not only personal but also, and more often, group survival. A survival ethic is necessarily highly contextual. Furthermore, Vodou is not a religion that promises a deus ex machina. Whatever is wrong, whatever persons want to happen, the Vodou spirits do not fix it or do it for them as much as empower them to do it for themselves. Alourdes once said about Ezili Dantò: "She don't give money. What she do, she give you opportunity . . . opportunity to help yourself. Yes."

For Ezili Dantò and for Alourdes, as for so many poor Haitian women, children are the center of life, the main reason for being. Yet Dantò's anger and her suffering prove that Vodou does not present an unmixed, sentimental portrait of childbearing and motherhood. In some parts of Haiti, infant mortality is as high as 50 percent, and birth control is rarely available. Although a responsible father who contributes substantially and willingly to the upbringing of his child is the ideal, this ideal is rarely achieved. Poor Haitian women, both in Haiti and in the United States, assume that the children born to them belong to them and are their responsibility. And they shoulder this responsibility in precarious circumstances.

Perhaps the physical, social, and economic risks of having children explain the occurrence of a condition called *pa-pale* (not-speaking disease). Although it can befall others who have reasons for depression, *pa-pale* is said to be found most often among women who have just given birth. Such women take to their beds and literally do not speak, sometimes for months at a time. Like the mute Ezili Dantò, they have had their voices taken from them by the people closest to them. Philo was known thoughout Port-au-Prince for her ability to treat mental illness, especially this intractable condition. This talent has passed to Alourdes, who reported treating a Haitian woman found wandering the streets of Brooklyn suffering from *pa-pale*. Alourdes took the woman into her home and fed and clothed her. At the

---

[4] Although the souls of the dead continue to exist and to participate in human affairs, they are also notorious for complaining about the cold, hunger, and dampness that characterize their world. No living person would consider the "life" of an ancestor superior to his or her own.

beginning, she even took the woman into her bed, where she held her at night as if she were a child. After the woman was cured, her story emerged. She had not recently given birth when she stopped speaking, but she had just lost her children to New York City's child welfare system. Through the politics of illness, poor Haitian women wordlessly articulate their pain and anger: *dey-dey-dey-dey-dey*.

Another condition common among poor women of childbearing age is called *pèdisyon* (perdition). When a woman "falls into perdition," the child in her womb is said to have been "held" or "tied" to prevent it from growing. (Sorcery is often implicated.) If a woman misses one or more periods and then begins to menstruate again, she assumes she is pregnant but has fallen into perdition. In this state, the menstrual blood, which Haitians believe is ordinarily retained in the womb to nourish the baby, bypasses the fetus. But the baby does not die. Instead, it is held in a state of suspended growth. When a healer does something to "untie" the child, the blood flow stops, and the child begins to "work" again and grow. Pregnancies interrupted by perdition can go on for years.

One advantage of this condition is that a woman can claim anyone she has had relations with over the course of several years as the father of her child. The naming of a father is often an important part of a mother's survival strategy.[5] Alourdes has never fallen into perdition, but she did once try to trick a man into believing he was the father of the child she was carrying. Her ruse failed, yet she shows compassion for herself and awareness of the difficult circumstances of her life when she tells the story. "Women got to do all kind'a thing. I know, 'cause when I got William, I tell somebody, 'I pregnant for you,' but that not true. What I going to do? I got to eat, or that baby going to die!"

Through the politics of illness, women increase the chances of survival for themselves and for their children. These two maladies, *pa-pale* and *pèdisyon*, can be treated only by Vodou healers. They are diseases of that world. Their presence there, along with what they reveal about the stress of bearing and providing for children in a poverty-stricken country, is part of the back-

---

[5]See Gerald F. Murray, "Women in Perdition: Ritual Fertility Control in Haiti," in *Culture, Natality, and Family Planning*, ed. John F. Marshall and Steven Polgar (Chapel Hill: University of North Carolina Press, 1976), 59–78.

ground against which Ezili Dantò stands with her infant in her arms. In a real sense, the risks and the suffering of childbearing and child-rearing are part of what every Haitian mother sees when she gazes at the image of Mater Salvatoris.

Even greater risks are involved in not having children, however, which makes my Haitian friends shake their heads ruefully when they hear I have none. For Haitian women, even for those now living in New York, children represent the main hope for a financially viable household and the closest thing there is to a guarantee of care in old age. The mother-child relationship among Haitians is strong and essential. In a not unrelated way, it is also potentially volatile. In the countryside, children's labor is necessary for the survival of the family. Children begin to work at an early age, and physical punishment is often swift and severe if they are irresponsible or disrespectful. Although children stay in school longer and begin to contribute to the family later in the cities, similar attitudes toward child-rearing prevail in the urban environment.

Dantò's strict discipline with those who serve her has its parallel in Alourdes's strong hand in her own household. Alourdes, like Ezili Dantò, is a proud and hardworking woman who will not tolerate disrespect or indolence in her children. Although her anger is almost never directed at Maggie, who is now an adult and Alourdes's partner in running the household, it can sometimes sweep the smaller children off their feet. I have never seen Alourdes strike a child, but she can express her displeasure sharply and mete out severe punishments.

In woman-headed Haitian households, the bond between mother and daughter is the most charged and the most enduring. Women and their daughters form three- and sometimes four-generation networks in which gifts and services circulate according to needs and abilities. These tight female relational systems create a safety net in a society where hunger is common. Knowing that she would eventually be dependent on Alourdes probably fueled Philo's anger when her daughter walked away empty-handed from her marriage to Kowalski. Nevertheless, Philo took her in. When Alourdes lay in a clinic, penniless and in constant pain in the last weeks of her pregnancy with William, Philo borrowed what she could—twenty cents and some bread—and brought these things to her daughter. In return, during Philo's last few years of life, Alourdes sent her mother the money that sustained her. The strength of the mother-daughter bond is one explanation of why Haitians identify the child in Ezili Dantò's arms as a daughter. And the importance and precariousness of that bond add meaning to Dantò's fiery temper.

Alourdes and her daughter depend on each other emotionally, spiritually, socially, and economically. Without the child care Alourdes provides, Maggie could not work. Without the money Maggie brings in every week, Alourdes would have only the erratic income she draws from her healing work. Without Maggie's supporting role, Alourdes could not stage elaborate birthday parties for the spirits. Alourdes does not use religion to hold Maggie against her will, however. The affection between them is genuine and strong; they are each other's best friend and most trusted ally. Each reports she feels most comfortable when the other is present. When one is depressed or afraid, the other can alleviate the depression or calm the fear. "When she not near me," Alourdes said, "I feel something inside me disconnected . . . something missing in me."

When either travels, they both become anxious, and at times they appear to communicate telepathically. They dream for and about each other constantly. When Maggie traveled to Haiti in 1988 for her father's funeral, she dreamed that her mother was sick. When she called home, she found that Alourdes was suffering from a bad head cold. When Maggie was in the hospital in 1979, Alourdes dreamed about what her daughter had to do to heal herself. "It's more than a mother and child relationship," Maggie said. "We are like twin sister—Siamese twin!" Alourdes admits that she sometimes forgets she is Maggie's mother and agrees that it is more like having a sister.

Maggie's greatest fear is that Alourdes will die. And I suspect that the reverse is also true. Alourdes and Maggie once engaged in an extended fantasy, complete with sound effects, about dying side by side in a big earthquake. Alourdes then became suddenly serious when she remembered how she used to feel the same dread about Philo's death. When Philo died in 1973, for a while Alourdes felt as if everything had ended. "Now," she said, "I don't cry all the time. But I dream her . . . my mother come in my dream, a lot!" Philo comes in her dreams when Alourdes has serious problems or when she is treating an especially difficult case and cannot figure out what to do. And when Philo does not appear, Alourdes's other mother, Ezili Dantò, does.

Although Maggie maintains her own apartment in the house they share, she rarely eats alone or only with her own children. The children of the two women mix and mingle, and the evening meal moves from Maggie's kitchen one day to Alourdes's the next. Their home is a social center to which they draw a multigenerational group of shared friends. There is some division of labor, however. Maggie is the family's representative in the outside world; Alourdes is in charge inside the home, where persons and events tend to organize themselves around her.

Maggie and Alourdes are not mirror images, but they do have a deeply symbiotic relationship, one not unlike the relationship Alourdes reports having with her mother, Philo. In Ezili Dantò's arms is the girl-child whom Haitians call Anaïse. Every time a Haitian woman looks at Dantò's image, she sees there the potential for a daughter who will stick by her, one who will extend her life and expand her world.

EZILI FREDA

The chromolithograph of Maria Dolorosa del Monte Calvario depicts the Virgin Mary with a jewel-encrusted sword plunged into her heart. Her arms, crossed over her breasts, are dripping with gold chains. Her fingers—even the thumbs—are covered in rings. On her head is a jeweled tiara, and she wears heavy gold earrings and half a dozen weighty necklaces. The wall behind her and the table in front of her are almost obscured by scores of gold, pearl, and jeweled hearts. Haitians recognize this image as Ezili Freda.

Ezili Freda is a white woman. Her skin color and her love of fine clothes and jewelry are Freda's most distinctive characteristics. Whereas Ezili Dantò is a fierce Petwo spirit, Freda is a spirit from the Rada pantheon, a group characterized by sweetness and even tempers. Whereas Dantò is known for what she can do, Freda is known for what she is—beautiful, alluring, desirable. Whereas Dantò occasionally rages, Freda pouts from time to time and withdraws into herself. Whereas Dantò lives out women's sexuality in its childbearing mode, Freda concerns herself with love and romance.

Maggie's bedroom altar, with a statue of the Virgin representing Ezili Freda. Fort
Greene, Brooklyn, 1978.

Ezili Freda's connection to romance, like her light skin and
her jewelry, identifies her with upper-class Haitian women. As
Alourdes observed, "Poor people don't have no true love. They
just have affiliation." Romance—its language, its style, its ward-
robe, and its dance—belongs to the top 10 percent of the Haitian population that controls the lion's share of Haiti's wealth.
From one perspective, the women of the elite are the contemporary incarnations of the mulatto mistresses of the slave era, the
famed Creole beauties who lent erotic charm to the outsider's

image of colonial Haiti. Ezili Freda rides the current of this particular ideology of female beauty and worth.

Ezili Freda, Alourdes said, is "fancy, and she very glamorous." Pink is Freda's favorite color. Saturday is the night that male devotees who have married her sleep alone and wait for Freda to come in their dreams. In her possession-performances, Freda is decked out in satin and lace. She is given powder, perfume, sweet-smelling soaps, and rich creams. The one possessed by her moves through the gathered community, embracing one and then another and another. In time, this generous sexuality begins to look driven, manic, like an unquenchable thirst. Something in her searches and is never satisfied. There is never enough love, never enough wealth, never enough honor. Her visits sometimes end in tears and frustration. Freda's gaze turns inward, and her arms wrap protectively around her own body.[6]

Ezili Freda takes her identity and her worth from her relationships with men. She is both married (to Ogou and to Danbala) and eternally ripe for marriage. Although she is in fact most often addressed with the respectful title of a married woman of means, Maitresse, Alourdes says that "you always got to call her Mademoiselle. Freda like people to think she a teenager."

Conflicting stories are told about Freda and children. Some say she is barren; some say she had a child who died. Others say Ezili Freda has a child but wishes to hide that fact in order to appear fresher, younger, and more desirable to men. Those who hold this view often point out that in the chromolithograph used to represent Freda a portrait of a young boy appears, nearly obscured by the left elbow of Maria Dolorosa. This biographical detail picks up a fragment from Alourdes's life that hints at her larger connections with Freda. When Alourdes married Kowalski, she already had two children by two different men. She wanted a church wedding and, for her father's sake as much as her own, a respectable life. So she hid the children from her prospective in-laws. Not until the wedding, when Antoine Kowalski's parents asked about the little boy and girl

---

[6] Maya Deren has drawn a powerful portrait of this aspect of Ezili Freda in *Divine Horsemen: The Voodoo Gods of Haiti* (New York: Dell, 1970; reprint, New Paltz, N.Y.: Documentext, McPherson, 1983), 137–45.

seated in the front pew, did they find out their son's bride was already a mother.

When Alourdes married Kowalski, she was only one step away from an impoverished childhood and was still living in a city where only a small fraction of the people are not alarmingly poor. Women of the small elite class nevertheless had the power to structure her dreams. These women are light-skinned—some are actually blonde and blue-eyed—and they marry in white dresses in big Catholic churches and return to homes that have bedroom sets and dining-room furniture and servants. These women never have to work. They spend their days resting and visiting with friends; at night, they emerge on the arms of their men, dressed like elegant peacocks and affecting an air of haughty boredom. Although Alourdes's husband was not a member of the elite, he provided her with a facsimile of this dream. It stifled and confined her, but she still has not entirely let go of the fantasy.

As a model, Ezili Freda is hard to follow, and perhaps especially so for a Haitian living in the United States. In one afternoon of disjointed conversation in July 1979, Alourdes told me that she had been her mother's favorite child because she was light-skinned and fat. (Chantal, Philo's only other girl, was dark and scrawny.) Alourdes also claimed that Kowalski had been attracted to her because she was "light and heavy." Drawing on memories of the prestige of a well-rounded body in a starving country, she told me proudly that she weighed two hundred forty pounds when she first came to New York. Only about an hour later, however, she announced that she was on a diet. As we watched television that day, she sang along, full voice, with the ad that proclaimed, "She's drinking Diet Pepsi, and it shows." When I went into her bathroom, I discovered that someone had cut out magazine pictures of skinny white women in leotards and pasted them around the mirror.

It is not only hard for a woman of Alourdes's color and girth to look like Freda (or Freda's New World incarnation in the Pepsi ad); it is also very difficult to please this fastidious spirit. "When you have Freda," Alourdes said, "you always got to be clean—twenty-four hours a day! Perfume . . . jewelry . . . fancy!" She told me that once, when she called Freda, the spirit refused to stay because Alourdes had not yet taken a bath that day. This close connection between hygiene and beauty speaks more eloquently in a country where most people do hard physical labor and bathwater must be hauled from its source to a house with an earth floor. Even with modern plumbing, Freda's concern with appearances is more than the life of a hardworking woman like Alourdes can support. There are too many crises when Alourdes, like Dantò, has to throw on her clothes and get right to work. Yet there are times when Freda's is precisely the image Alourdes wants to project. There is no sight like Alourdes dressed for a party—vermilion lipstick, hair curled, and a flower behind one ear.

> *Ezili Banda, Ezili Banda,*
> *Ezili Banda pase sa'l vo.*
> *Ezili Banda, Ezili Banda,*
> *Ezili Banda pase kò-li.*

This Freda song says worlds in a few words and a rapid syncopated beat. Its sparse, suggestive language makes it especially difficult to translate, but a rather loose rendering would go like this:

> Pretentious Ezili, sexy Ezili,
> Sexy Ezili outdoes herself.
> Strutting Ezili, preening Ezili,
> Preening Ezili thinks she's something.

Ezili Freda drapes herself in romance, wealth, and social status and at the same time reminds Haitians how precarious and superficial such things are. Another song for her complicates the point: "*Yo pran Ezili Freda, yo met'l anndan kay. . . . Lapli tonbe, latè-a glise* [They take Ezili Freda, they put her in the house. . . . The rain falls, the ground is slippery]." This song reminds the listener that Freda is an Ezili, a watery woman spirit from Africa, who would not content herself with describing the mere surface of things. Here is the paradox. The song can be heard as saying that when Ezili Freda is inside the house, when sensuality and love are in place in the family (or perhaps when money and status are secure), the people inside are safe from the rain and slippery mud that surround them. But it can also be heard as a warning about the ability of rainwater to insinuate itself through and under the wattle-and-daub walls of a Haitian house. When that happens, the glossy hard-packed earth floor becomes dangerous. Hunger for wealth, status, or romance can undermine the foundations of a family. Freda's insatiable hunger, the need that can never be met, is the parallel to the irrational, raging *baka* in Dantò and the death-dealing siren in Lasyrenn. But Freda cannot be expelled from Alourdes's altar any more than Dantò and Lasyrenn can be rejected because of their deep shadows.

Alourdes does not have all of life's questions answered or all its tensions resolved. The tension between the Dantò and the Freda within her is one that is not resolved. For the most part, Alourdes accepts her life and the choices she made that brought her to where she is now. But there are also times when she longs for male companionship. She is therefore not immune to Freda's glamour or, for that matter, to the pull of the images of domesticity and nuclear families she sees every day on television. "Sometime I really, really, really get lonely," said Alourdes in the late spring of 1985. "Sometime I want to make love, and I'm by myself . . . and, let me tell you, I'm fifty years old. I have four children. I can't take anybody to come . . . just to make love. That's a shame. Yeah!"

Alourdes also gets tired of living at the edge of poverty, tired of being in charge of such a big and ungainly household. At times, she thinks about her past with regret. "If I was marry Kowalski now, we stay until . . . death do we part. One time, I want to go back with him. He tell me 'No,' too much happen! Let me tell you, when I marry Antoine, I was too young, I don't understand. . . . And he got money. . . ." Not entirely missing from Alourdes's voice is the sound of the poor woman selling her "land," her love, to guarantee her survival and the survival of her children. But here the finances of love are wound round with longing and dreams.

A little more than two years after this conversation, Alourdes fell in love. Her current man is a delightful and loyal lover, friend, and ally. Alourdes is a deeply sensual woman, and this part of her comes out strongly in the presence of Edner. She dresses up, becomes coquettish, and caters to her man. When describing his lovable traits, she always says in the first or second breath: "He help me so much. Every month, he pay the electric bill." Edner is now a regular visitor in Alourdes's home. He is present for all the Vodou birthday parties and on many other occasions as well. There is no question of their marrying or living together; Alourdes and Edner are mature people with their life patterns set. Yet within those patterns they have made room for one another.

And Alourdes has made more room for an Ezili Freda in her heart—not a frustrated and driven one, but one who does a bit of strutting and preening from time to time. Alourdes loves jewelry. She almost always wears four or five gold rings and as many chains around her neck. She loves nice clothes—colorful fabrics, dresses that swish and sparkle. Ezili Freda, you outdo yourself.

THE THREE EZILI

Several years ago, when large numbers of Haitian refugees (dubbed "boat people") were imprisoned by the U.S. Immigration and Naturalization Service, I was invited to visit the facility where unaccompanied minors were detained. The visit confirmed my suspicion that many of these children had not been traveling alone but in fact had been accompanied by adults, adults who may even have raised them but were not necessarily blood kin. Many children in Haiti are raised by "aunts" or godparents, but the INS did not recognize such ad hoc parenting, and agency bureaucrats had separated the children from their traveling companions and confined them in a minimum-security camp in upstate New York.

These children were alone and afraid. Several of them had responded to their fear by going into possession. In Haiti, children are rarely possessed; it is considered too dangerous. When a spirit threatens to possess a child during a ceremony, the priest or priestess in charge immediately takes steps to send it away. In the immigration detention center, there were no priests to call the spirits for the young people, and none to send them away from those who could not bear the spirit's weight. Nevertheless, some frightened teenagers had tried to call on the spirits for help. The staff had responded with a different kind of fear, and that was why I was called in to advise them. I did two things: I suggested that the dormitory counselor, a North American black man, immediately stop his efforts to perform exorcism rites in the mode of his own Protestant Christianity. And I arranged to take Alourdes to the facility to counsel the young people, a visit that was quite successful.

Months later, I realized that there might be a parallel between what I had seen among the children of the boat people and the behavior of slaves newly arrived in Haiti. It is a universal instinct, I suppose, to turn to religion in times of crisis. When the elders, the priests, the institutions, the musical instruments, the images, the altars, and the sacred objects are absent, where do you turn for spiritual aid? In an African-based religion, possession seems an obvious answer. In Yorubaland and Dahomey, two of the areas of origin for Haiti's slave population, most possession-performances were formulaic affairs with more or less predictable words and gestures. In the New World, however, in that early time when the body and the voice were the slaves' principal mnemonic devices, possession could well have received much greater emphasis, and possession-performances could have quickly become much more extemporaneous and expressive. In other words, cut loose from their African base and institutional moorings, the spirits may well have burst into flower.[7] Times of crisis are often times of high creativity.

Whether it happened this way or not, the African spirits did change their style when they came to the New World. They hunkered down, got close to the ground. They came right up in the faces of those who served them and began to imitate what they saw and heard there. The possession-performances of the spirits took on more of the specifics of time and place and more of the intimate detail of life. High liturgy became improvisational theater. This was a happy occurrence, I think, for it is a large part of what has enabled the Vodou spirits to work for the Haitian people through a great deal of hardship and rapid social change.

Such flexibility and such responsiveness have enabled the *lwa*

---

[7]Further research is needed to confirm this hypothesis. The work of Erika Bourguignon, who has done an extensive study of possession phenomena around the world, appears to support the point. In comparing Haitian Vodou possession with that of traditional West African cults, she characterizes Vodou spirit possession as less fixed and more innovative (Erika Bourguignon, *Possession* [San Francisco: Chandler and Sharp, 1976], 18).

to provide maps that chart the future and mirrors that reflect the past and the present. For example, Ezili Dantò's mute "*dey-dey-dey*" honors the mother of a new child, so depressed and fearful that she stops talking. Dantò honors her by making her visible. Dantò also vomits blood alongside the woman murdered by her partner in the compound that came to be called Seven Stabs of the Knife. Lasyrenn subtly shapes the story of the time Alourdes got lost when she was only seven years old. And every time Alourdes prepares to meet Edner, she checks the mirror one last time to see if Freda would approve—that is, to see how much her image matches the dominant norms of female beauty. Vodou spirits present the social world to those who serve them. They present it fully through all its representative types, male and female, empowered and disempowered. And they explore both the constructive and destructive dimensions of each type.

Because the Vodou spirits hover so close to the social ground, they have also been useful in sorting out the moral dilemmas faced by a people first enslaved by the French, then oppressed and starved by their own leaders, and finally shoved to the margins in immigrant communities throughout the United States. Talk of ethical norms or moral absolutes is for those who have power and a wide range of choices, unlike the great majority of the Haitian people now or in the past. Haitians view life as a sea turbulent with moral crosscurrents. You do well in Vodou if you choose to ride the currents that flow in the constructive directions set by your basic character. The Vodou spirits help people to name the most important aspects of their character and then to hold on to this vision when the ride gets rough. Vodou is a religion of survival, and it counsels what it must to ensure survival. Dantò counseled Alourdes to keep one baby, and Ogou gave her sufficient reason to abort another.

Those who serve the spirits do not fall on their knees and implore a god to solve their problems for them. A Vodou spirit is not a deus ex machina but a catalyst who mobilizes the will and energy of human beings. Vodou spirits do not often deliver proclamations. They speak in lean, enigmatic ways that call forth the voice of the community. "*Dey-dey-dey-dey-dey,*" says Ezili Dantò, and the people say, "Yes, we will do it for you."

Slavery broke the African family. Drought, corruption, and poverty broke the patriarchal extended family that reconstituted itself after Haiti's slave revolution. From the wreckage, women's previously muted voices began to emerge. Women's *"dey-dey-dey"* is now becoming articulate in Haiti. Few other places in the world rival Haiti in recognizing women's religious leadership. In part, this is an inheritance of the African homeland where women could be cult leaders, even though the religious institutions with social status were led by men, as were the public ceremonies. But the more significant source of women's religious power in Haiti is, I believe, the recent shift in family structure brought on by the movement of large numbers of people from the countryside to the cities.

When women's religious leadership is unfettered by male control, that religion begins to take account of the circumstances of women's lives. Women become visible. In Vodou, the female spirits have begun to tell the stories of women's lives from their point of view, in striking contrast to religious systems in which goddess figures function largely as the carriers of male projections about women.

Yet Haiti is a place in transition. Women's voices are strong, but they do not dominate. Perhaps they never will, and perhaps they never should. For example, when men serve the female Vodou spirits, the vision can still be a thoroughly androcentric one. Alourdes's childhood friend Big Daddy once reported this dream: "I saw this lady, this white lady; and she have hair that come down to here." He traced a line below his buttocks. "And she was tall, maybe six foot three. I never seen no lady like that, and she was walking like this . . ." Big Daddy imitated a mincing step combined with a very sexy over-the-shoulder glance. "And I'm thinking to myself, you know . . . Oh, boy! How I'm going to get that lady? You know . . . take her to bed. And that was Ezili Freda! She my wife, and I didn't even know. The spirit is real, let me tell you!" Ezili Freda imitates ideas of beauty that have social power and prestige. For men, she can function as the target for dreams of conquest. Speaking for women, she reminds all people that these values can be superficial and even dangerous.

Dantò, in contrast, does not imitate the socially empowered woman. She tells poor women's stories, and, what is more, she does it from their perspective. Whatever her previous role—a role hinted at by multiple, currently unelaborated references to her as a tree-dwelling serpent—in contemporary urban Haiti she is a prism focusing light on the single mother and head of household. Ezili Dantò functions these days to bring hidden lives and hidden truths to the surface.

There is a story about conflict between Ezili Dantò and Ezili Freda. Most people, most of the time, say that the scars on Dantò's cheek come from wounds sustained in the slave revolt. But there is an alternative explanation. Sometimes it is said that, because Dantò was sleeping with her man, Maria Dolorosa (Ezili Freda) took the jeweled sword from her heart and slashed the face of her rival.

In the tension between Freda and Dantò, Haitians explore questions of race as well as those of class and gender. Freda is a white woman and, as a result, a privileged woman who has the power to draw to herself both men and wealth. She marries, and her status as wife and partner is legal and public. It has financial and social solidity. Dantò is black, "black, black, black," and, as a result, she is poor and must work hard. Dantò does not marry. The men in her life are as poor as she is, and they cannot be counted on. But Dantò is fertile. Her best hope for security and care in her old age lies with her children, especially her girl children.

In Vodou, blackness and whiteness carry within them complete life scenarios, as they do on a wider social scale in Haiti and in New York. In Port-au-Prince and in Brooklyn, Alourdes has wavered between these scenarios. She is light-skinned, which contributed to making her Philo's favorite child as well as the object of desire for both Charles Desinor and Antoine Kowalski. With these two men, Alourdes played out important parts of the Ezili Freda fantasy. She had a house, furniture, and servants. The circumstances of her life, however, combined with her indomitable personality to push her much more in the direction of Ezili Dantò. There is another way to say this. Life in urban Haiti and, probably to an even greater extent, life in New York have pushed Alourdes to embrace who she is—a black woman, born in poverty. Alourdes's strength lies in this rootedness and honesty. In a sense, Dantò has won. She is the one Alourdes calls "mother."

From another perspective, neither Dantò nor Freda can entirely vanquish the other, because the tension between them speaks to a tension in women's lives. Women, especially poor women, are still being forced to make choices between essential parts of themselves. Freda's image of womanhood is powerful partly because it promises Haitian women who can meet its standards the social support that makes a stable union with a man possible. Until Dantò finds her match and mate, Freda will continue to appear in the dreams of women like Alourdes. Only when reality is spiced with dreams, when survival skills are larded with sensuality and play does life move forward. Dreams alone lead to endless and fruitless searching. Freda acts that out. Yet a life geared entirely toward survival also has problems. It can become brittle and threatened by inner rage. Dantò occasionally lets this rage escape into the open.

Alourdes lives at the nexus of several spirit energies; Ezili Freda and Ezili Dantò are only two. Lasyrenn, half black and half white, is a submerged third who hints at an elemental womanness in which what society now declares opposites can somehow come together. But Vodou allows no such easy syntheses, no neat or abstract resolution of the race, class, and gender politics of the Ezili sisters. It must be remembered that Lasyrenn is also the spirit who turns poor, ordinary women into community leaders and healers. She pulls them beneath the waters and gives them boons and spiritual instruction to which they would otherwise have no access. And, irony of ironies, lest the community miss the effectiveness of the transformation carried out below the water, Lasyrenn sends them back with longer, straighter hair and fairer skin.

CHAPTER NINE

Sojème, Sojème

At nine o'clock in the morning on July 16, 1979, Alourdes Margaux lay unmoving, eyes wide open. The ornate headboard of her bed was draped with an enormous plastic rosary. Images of Santa Clara and an impassive, pretty Jesus gazed out from the wall above. The noises of children playing in the hallway drifted into her darkened room. She cleared her throat, rolled over, spat into the chamber pot beside the bed, and mumbled, "How come those children got to make so much noise?" "Oh, Lawd!" she sighed, using the burst of breath to carry her body to a sitting position.

In a few minutes, she came padding out the door of her bedroom wearing a long nightgown and floppy slippers. Alourdes turned a haggard face toward the offending children. "What happen?" she asked. "Nothing, Mommie Lola," nine-year-old Kumar chirped. "Michael and me was playing Batman!"

"How come you still got pi'jama on you?" Alourdes demanded. "Eleven o'clock, we going to the hospital to see Maggie. You know that! If you not ready when Karen come, you not going." Michael, just a toddler, began to cry: "I wanna see Maggieeeeee!"

"So, go get clothes on you. Kumar, you help Mikey. You understand?" "Yes, Mommie Lola," Kumar replied as he took the child's hand and pulled him up the stairs. Alourdes watched her son and grandson until they reached the second-floor landing, and then she went down the staircase to the basement.

Small windows in the rear admitted only faint light to the basement floor. Moving with care, Alourdes made her way toward her altar room at the opposite end of the house. In the dim light, she fumbled with a ring of keys, finally locating the right

◀ A *manbo* kisses a *veve* (cornmeal ground drawing) for Danbala. Port-au-Prince, Haiti, 1989.

one and unlocking the door. Three times she knocked, and then she opened the door to the tiny room, pausing on the threshold to breathe in its comforting, familiar odors.

Alourdes lighted a large votive candle on the table in the center of the room and then eased her ample body down onto a low stool between Gede's altar and the tall metal cabinet that held the accoutrements of her Rada spirits. She lit a stick of incense and secured it in the coin slot of Papa Gede's money box. The small, bright flame quickly disappeared, and a tendril of smoke began to climb the three steps of Gede's altar, curling around grotesque wax skulls, a metal crucifix, an old black top hat, and a huge phallic cane. As the smoke diffused, Alourdes reached up, opened the Rada altar, and fanned clouds of incense into its densely packed shelves. Her family of Rada spirits rested in shadow. The light from the candle picked out only an occasional object: a white porcelain cup with a lid and a girdle of colored beads, an image of Saint Patrick, a tiny bottle of a French perfume called Rêve d'Or.

She offered libations to her ancestral spirits. A splash of Babancourt rum activated the spirit of Papa Ogou; a dollop of sugary òjat called to the slumbering serpent Danbala. A mist of perfume enticed Ezili Freda to grace the company with her presence. A pungent bath of pepper-laced gin returned the shine to smooth black rocks in a dish at the foot of Papa Gede's altar.

Alourdes rose from her seat and sprayed perfume liberally into the closet on the opposite side of the room, the home of her Petwo spirits. The dark-skinned doll representing Ezili Dantò wore a faint smile, and Alourdes smiled back at her. As the odors of the room awoke, so did its spirits, and Alourdes drew them around her. She would need their protection more on this day than on others. Breathing deeply and slowly, Alourdes settled back onto her stool, closed her eyes, and made the sign of the cross. Putting her hands together as if she were holding a delicate flower, she kissed her fingertips and bowed her head in prayer.

Maggie Sanchez had been awake since six o'clock when the nurses had come to take her temperature, give her medication, and check the bottle into which her stomach tube was draining. The tube in her nose made her sound as if she had a bad cold, but she was otherwise her usual exuberant self. Maggie was explaining to her roommate, Mrs. Gonzales, that she had to be out of the hospital by Saturday because her new boyfriend had tickets for the Bob Marley concert.

"Somebody offer him two hundred dollar for those ticket, but he say no. Everybody want to hear Bob Marley. You think I'm going to stay in this bed and let him take somebody else to that concert? No way José! I got me some new Sergio Valente jeans, just a little bit tight, but they look goooooood! Besides, I think it is good to wear tight jean now, because, you know, I got hernia, strangulated hernia, whatever. . . . If I wear something tight, that mean it don't move. Me and Barnett—he's Jamaican . . . he got some Sergio Valente, too—we going to be like twin! We going to hear Marley and dance *all night!*" Maggie giggled and moved her hips seductively beneath the hospital sheets.

High clouds were scudding across the sky and a surprisingly cool breeze was blowing on that Monday morning as Karen Brown approached Alourdes's door shortly after ten-thirty. She carried a small offering, two ripe avocados in a paper bag. She knocked, waited several minutes, and then knocked more loudly. There was no response, so she went down to the basement door and kocked again. Finally, she returned to the front door to knock one last time, just as a puffy-eyed Alourdes appeared, blinking in the sun. Alourdes was dressed in a two-piece, blue and white polka-dot outfit. The top had a flared waist, puffed sleeves, and a Peter Pan collar. When she moved, a glimpse of bare stomach appeared between top and skirt. Muttering only "I'm all right" in response to Karen's solicitous query, Alourdes led the way down the hall to the bedroom.

She had been watching television, and, without saying anything, she returned to it. In silence, the two women sat side by side on the end of the bed watching the last few minutes of a lurid documentary on plastic surgery.

The phone rang. "Hello," Alourdes answered in a small, tired voice. She listened for a long time before sputtering: "Why you don't tell them? Why you don't tell me? How come he do that? Nobody don't say nothing? That not fair! Yes, we coming. Karen just get here. She going to drive us. Yes, we going to bring the children. Okay. Okay."

This large woman, stuffed into a frilly girlish dress, sat in her shadow-filled bedroom and curled into a ball of depression. Her features sagged, her shoulders rounded over until her head looked like a boulder lodged between them. She sat staring at the pink princess phone in her hand, idly punching its lighted buttons, sending it meaningless messages, a random series of numbers. The phone began to protest: birrup . . . birrup . . . birrup. The sound was hypnotic, and it seemed to go on and on.

And then from beneath it another sound emerged: women giggling and squealing. The television program had changed. It was the daytime version of "The Price Is Right." The voice of the announcer rose and fell in well-practiced, dulcet tones: "Now, Sally, if you can guess the price of this showcase without going over, the whole thing is yours. The trip to the Caribbean islands, the waterbed, the home recreation center, the whole thing! Sally, how much do you say this beautiful showcase is worth?" Birrup . . . birrup . . . birrup; the telephone continued to signal distress.

Alourdes turned to Karen, her face showing fear as well as fatigue. "How come somebody do that? Doctor suppose to take care of people. That not right! Maggie say her doctor put that tube in her and he go on vacation. He forget to tell . . . he don't tell nobody what to do. So nobody don't do nothing. She have that tube inside her one week—more than one week—and now she got some kind'a infection. They don't know how they going to make that tube come out. Oh, boy! Karen, I don't know. Maybe I love Maggie too much. I don't sleep last night. I don't know what happen. I don't sleep at all. I think too much . . . think about Maggie."

After a few minutes, Alourdes rallied. She stood up, straightened her clothes, and began to apply lipstick. "You know, this not ordinary sickness. Those doctor never figure out what Maggie got, not really. The spirit make Maggie sick. You know that, right? When they want you, there is no way you say no!"

"I imagine it's hard for Maggie to think about becoming a *manbo*," Karen suggested. "She has other things on her mind. She's young, she's in love, she wants to get married, have a house of her own. . . ."

Alourdes was quick to respond: "If she get marry again, that make me glad! That what I want for her—a good life. She need husband who understand her. That be good!"

"Are you afraid of losing her?" Karen asked. "Mmmm . . . no," Alourdes replied, "I just worry about the sickness."

Karen asked one more question: "Is it important to you that Maggie serve the spirits . . . that she carry on for you?" "No, that not important," Alourdes said. And then, almost as an afterthought, she added, "But I know they go after her."

That evening, back from visiting Maggie in the hospital, Alourdes cooked dinner, fed the children, and put them to bed. Then she worked with two clients, one a young man who had just lost his job, the other a woman trying to get a visa to bring her grown son to the United States. When the clients had gone and the house was quiet, Alourdes returned to her sanctuary. The doors of the spirits' altars were open; the votive candle still burned. Alourdes sat down on the low stool and picked up her *ason*. China beads and snake vertebrae slithered across the surface of the gourd. First they whispered. Then they rustled. Finally they pounded until the walls of the small room echoed with urgent sound. With her free hand, Alourdes picked up a bottle of rum, took a mouthful, and sprayed it in a fine mist over the Gede and Rada altars.

"*Papa Gede!*" she called. "*Ale! Ale nan pitit-mwen pou mwen. Papa Gede! Ale jwen Maggie nan lopital-la. M'pral fè trètmen pou li* [Papa Gede! Go! Go to my little one for me. Papa Gede! Go find Maggie in that hospital. I am going to make a treatment for her]. Papa Danbala . . . Papa Ogou . . . *ou tout* [all of you]!" While shaking the *ason* with her right hand, Alourdes began to rap on the altars with her left. She was calling her spirits to action.

"*M'jete ti dlo pou Maggie* [I am pouring a libation for Maggie]," she said. "*Kite baton pase nan men mwen* [Let the club pass into my hand]. *Ale jwen pitit-mwen nan lopital* [Go find my little one in the hospital]." Alourdes began to knock harder on the altar walls and to shake the *ason* faster and faster. She badgered the spirits and pleaded with them in a jumble of Creole and English. "Come on, *mistè-a* [spirits]! Come on! Help *pitit-mwen* [my little one]. *Ale nan lopital-la* [Go to that hospital]. Come on, Papa Danbala! *Maggie se ti-moun ou* [Maggie is your child]. Bring *li* [her] to me." In time, the *ason* fell silent and dangled from her limp hand. There was no more knocking, no more pleading. For a long while Alourdes sat, quiet and attentive, trying to discern the will of the spirits in the rushing of her own blood.

Maggie lay restless in her hospital bed, tethered by her stomach tube and a board strapped to her right arm holding an intravenous needle in place. Her back ached. Her body itched, first in one place and then another. Her mind raced with images, memories, plans.

"It all start when I lose that *po-tèt*.[1] That is when all the trouble start. I just finish *kouche*. . . . Those stupid people in the airport—Puerto Rican! Hah! Take my suitcase. 'We are going to call you when we find it.' Hah! They don't even look! I don't know, maybe they think they going to find jewelry, money, shoes. It's my fault. I should not put something so important in my suitcase. I think sometimes I'm going crazy, and I think that the reason . . . because they took my *po-tèt*. Next time, I am going to keep it right in my hand. Even if they tell me I cannot take that on the airplane—even if they think that some kind'a bomb—nobody going to take that out of my hand. Nobody . . . nobody. . . . I know it run in the family. In some family, men do that. Not my family. In my family, only women. That mean me! I know they want me, those spirit. It's a strain. . . . I'm trying to push myself, saying no. I don't want to be like them . . . like my mother . . . like my grandmother. Life is so hard. New York is different. . . . People here they don't care, they don't give a damn! I can do it for special people, people that I know. . . . If my children get sick, I can . . . but I don't want. . . . They come all hour of the day and night: 'Mommie Lola, I got this; Mommie Lola, I got that; you got to help me.' Not me! I got my own life. I could do it, *kouche*. I know they want it. . . . Lot'a people who *kouche*, they don't work as *manbo*. I won't be working as *manbo* full-time. . . . I just go and do it. . . . Maybe then they will leave me alone!"

Maggie's eyes snapped open. The room was eerie and unfamiliar. Stripes of light pulsated on the walls—street lamps shining through venetian blinds. Her roommate groaned in her sleep. Maggie raised her legs, one after the other, and let each drop back onto the bed with a dull thud. She heaved a sigh and rolled her head from side to side. Slowly, her eyes closed.

---

[1] A *po-tèt* (head pot) is the most important product of Vodou initiation rituals. Usually a white porcelain cup with a lid, it provides an external home for the spirits, who would otherwise dwell in the heads of the initiates. After the initiation is complete, the *po-tèt* becomes a focal point for personal ritualizing. When an initiate feels agitated or troubled, for example, he or she can bathe the *po-tèt* in cool water and spray it with perfume. Maggie went through the first stages of initiation in Haiti in 1977, completing all of the rituals except the final one that would have made her a *manbo* with an *ason*. For her return to New York, Maggie packed her head pot in her suitcase and checked the bag at the Port-au-Prince airport. When Alourdes and Maggie arrived in San Juan, Puerto Rico, where they were to change planes, the bag was nowhere to be found.

"It's just that I am tired of doing everything alone. The plumbing break, I fix it. I'm the one who paint my kitchen. Anything happen, I'm the one responsible! The children! I am tired. . . . It's just that I am tired. I got to sleep. It is hard being alone. . . . The first time I see Barnett, I know something going to happen, when he interview me for that job at Nedick's. He look at me hard, and then he say, 'How do I know you can work?' 'You just watch me!' I say, and I grab that rag and start to clean the table. All the time he watching me—and I can tell which part he watching! Heh, heh, heh. So I move like this . . . and like this. . . . When I turn around, Barnett got this big smile on his face. He say, 'Okay, you got the job.' I got to get out by Friday. Everybody want to hear Bob Marley. I got to put a hem in those Sergio Valente. . . ." At last Maggie slept.

In the middle of the night, she dreamed that she stood by the *labapen* tree on her family property in Gros Morne, a place she had never visited. "Come, come, little one," the spirits called, and Maggie followed the sound of their voices to a spot beneath the tree. Then snakes, little green snakes, began to fall from its branches. They were all around her! One fell down the front of her shirt and got caught in her brassiere. She began to scream and jump and tear at her clothes. No, no, no!

Alourdes lay on her back and stared at a cockroach making its way across the ceiling. It was three o'clock in the morning, and she had yet to close her eyes. A small votive candle burned on her dresser before an image of Our Lady of Lourdes. She was thinking about Maggie again, remembering her birth. Alourdes had been at a soccer match when her water broke. She stood up to cheer for the home team and discovered that the back of her dress was soaked. She and Charles, Maggie's father, left the stadium right away. Her bag was already packed, and they went right to the clinic. For three long days, she lay in that clinic waiting for something to happen. There was no real pain, just pressure, awful pressure, and a throbbing ache in her back. The doctor could not figure out what to do.

Around six o'clock in the evening on the third day, Philo came to see her daughter. Papa Ogou was riding Philo, but of course Alourdes was the only one who knew that, and even she was only dimly aware of what was happening. Papa Ogou brought something to help Alourdes—a bottle. He put it behind her bed before he left. At midnight, the bottle exploded—

bwaaaaam! The night nurse jumped and dropped a beaker of urine she was carrying, and, at the same moment, Alourdes felt the first stab of pain. Labor began in earnest. By noon the next day, the baby's head had crowned. But hours later, the baby had moved no further down the birth canal.

Her doctor was becoming nervous. He tried to pull the baby out with forceps. He tried eight, nine, ten, eleven, twelve times. Alourdes began to hemorrhage. The front of the doctor's coat was soaked in blood; Alourdes saw hands and clothing red with blood. She was going in and out of consciousness. The doctor put her in the back of his car and took her to the city hospital. At ten o'clock that night, Maggie was born by cesarean section, weighing an astonishing seventeen pounds and ten ounces. As he cleaned out Alourdes's womb, the doctor also removed the partially formed fetus of a dead twin brother.

The pain was hard to recall in detail; Alourdes remembered only that there had been a lot of it when Maggie was born. She could accept this suffering. When she made any effort to explain it, she simply referred to the biblical mandate that women are supposed to suffer in childbirth. "That what God say, 'Women, they got to have pain. Men work and sweat, but women, they got to have pain when they get a baby.'" The pain children could bring later in their lives was harder for Alourdes to explain and much harder for her to bear—what vulnerability came with loving them, needing them, depending on them! This was what she could not make peace with on that lonely, sleepless night. "What if she die! What if? What if she marry Barnett and leave? What if . . .?" These were unaskable questions. Alourdes blinked hard and decided to think of something unrelated to pain.

She remembered staying in the hospital for more than two weeks after Maggie was born. On September 14, a national holiday in Haiti, the president of the country, Paul Magloire, visited the city hospital. When he saw Maggie in the nursery (easily twice as large as any other baby there), yelling at the top of her lungs and waving her little clenched fists, he smiled, "Ah," he thought to himself, "there is some life left in the youth of this country. I will give the mother of this one a reward." President Magloire presented Alourdes with a check for three hundred dollars.

More than a quarter of a century later, Alourdes lay in her bed in Fort Greene, thinking about how good things sometimes can come out of bad. She smiled. Yet when she drifted briefly into sleep, Alourdes dreamed she had to move to a new house, a smaller one. She had no money to hire professional movers, and the furniture was too big for her to carry by herself. She could find no one to help her carry it.

The nurses arrived at Maggie's beside very early the next morning. They gave her a shot to make her drowsy and relaxed. Six men in white coats soon surrounded her bed. They were here to remove the tube that they feared had become imbedded in her stomach wall. The last thing Maggie remembered was hearing one of them whisper: "The chief is going to have your ass in a sling for this one!" Then she was deep in a dream.

She had been away. Traveling. When she came in the front door of her house, no one was there to greet her. She set her suitcase beside the door and went down to the basement. "Mommie, Mommie! Where are you?" she called. Several women she did not know were busy in the kitchen preparing what looked like food for a banquet. The basement living room was all white. Sheet canopies were draped from the ceiling. White sheets covered the walls and the floor. A large sleeping pallet had been arranged in the center of the floor, with space for several people. Alourdes, dressed all in white, was shaking out a billowing white sheet and spreading it over the bed.

"Mommie, why did you make a big bed like that?" Maggie asked. "I made it large," Alourdes said nonchalantly, "because it is not only one person who is going to *kouche*. There is going to be more than one who is going to *kouche*." Maggie said, "Oh, yeah?" And then she turned and tried to make a break for the doorway.

Somehow, she went in the wrong direction and ended up in the kitchen dodging women carrying huge plates of food. Things tipped—spilled—broke. Maggie spun around, skidded on the linoleum floor, and ran back toward the door. She stumbled, her feet entangled in sheets. By then, she was so panicked she failed to notice the creature occupying the doorway. "Excuse me, please," she said breathlessly and made a movement as if to shove it aside. "Where do you think you are going?" the creature said in a deep, resonating voice.

"I am trying to save myself. I am not going to *kouche*. I do not want to *kouche*," Maggie panted. The creature expanded to fill the entire doorway, and Maggie realized for the first time that it was a giant cobra. Its head reared up, its hood flared, and its upper body swelled to gigantic proportions. Maggie backed away. The cobra began to speak again. Maggie felt its voice before she heard it. The floor was vibrating, and the vibration was traveling up her legs. It took a while before she could decipher words. Everything was in slow motion . . . the voice a roar in her ears, in her body.

"Get on your knees! Right now! Swear three times! If you don't do it, I am going to swallow you!" And then the cobra opened its mouth wider and wider, until Maggie could see nothing but a huge cavern of moist, pale white meat. Maggie dropped to her knees and raised her right hand. Three times she raised her hand, and three times she said: "*Sojème, sojème, sojème.*[2] I will do it. I will take the *ason.*"

"*Sojème, sojème, sojème . . .*," Maggie mumbled as the doctors worked the tube loose and pulled it up through her esophagus. "Miss Sanchez, Miss Sanchez!" One of the doctors shook her gently. "It's all over now. You can sit up." "*Sojème, sojème . . .* I swear I will do it," Maggie whispered. "You don't have to do anything more, Miss Sanchez. It's over."

At approximately the same time, the pink princess telephone by Alourdes's bed rang, waking her from the first sound sleep she had had in two days. Her voice was thick and foggy as she picked it up and collapsed back onto the pillow with the phone cradled next to her ear.

"No, that's all right, sweetheart. I got to get up. Huh . . . ? Oh, Maggie going to be okay. No, I don't talk to her today. But I got a dream about her. Just when you call, I was dream about Gabriel. You don't remember him? He my old boyfriend. In Haiti, you know. He my boyfriend long time . . . long time. Gabriel come to see me. I say, 'Come in, sit down.' He say, 'I can't. My girlfriend in the hospital. I have to go see her.' I say, 'Oh, Gabby, you going to that girlfriend to give me trouble?' I say, 'You too old to let woman run you like that!' And then he mad. He say, 'I'm not going to pay you no mind.' And he left.

[2] *Sojème* is an African word that has been preserved in Vodou *langay*, where it is employed for swearing serious oaths.

Everytime I dream Gabriel, I know that Papa Gede.[3] Papa Gede going to the hospital to see Maggie. When I dream that, I know everything going to be okay."

[3]Saint Gabriel is one of the Catholic saints conflated with Gede, the spirit of humor, sex, and death and the protector of small children. This Vodou spirit is also the master of the healing arts.

CHAPTER TEN

Danbala

In 1931, Melville Herskovits noted that the Fon of Dahomey (the modern West African republic of Benin) still mourned the loss of kin to the trans-Atlantic slave trade. Herskovits recorded this remarkable prayer, which was chanted as blood was poured over an altar to the unknown dead: "Oh, ancestors, do all in your power that princes and nobles who today rule never be sent away from here as slaves to Ame'ika, . . . We pray you to do all in your power to punish the people who bought our kinsmen, whom we shall never see again."[1]

Such long-held sentiment is more than a historical grudge. Although there is in Dahomey a public cult with deities recognized by all, the heart of Dahomean religious life is ancestor veneration. These rites necessarily occur within specific lineages. Dahomeans depend on the day-to-day protection of their lineage ancestors, and they fear the anger of any of their family dead who might be neglected. They also believe in a form of intralineage reincarnation. For all these reasons, the loss of kin to the European slave trade diminished every family represented on the slave ships. This loss did not dissipate with time, and it continues to threaten the well-being of the living on both sides of the Atlantic. In the popular naïve painting of Haiti, a blighted, leafless tree whose branches have been lopped off is a recurrent motif. Like the Dahomean prayer, it testifies to the persistent sense of loss occasioned by slavery.

[1] Melville J. Herskovits, *Dahomey: An Ancient West African Kingdom* (Evanston, Ill.: Northwestern University Press, 1967), 2:64.

◄ Temple wall painting of Saint Patrick (Danbala) and Saint Peter (Legba). Port-au-Prince, Haiti, 1980. Photograph by Judith Gleason.

In Dahomey, an area from which many Haitian slaves were taken, Dambada Hwedo is the most ancient of the ancestral spirits. He stands collectively for the powerful dead who lived too long ago to be remembered, those in the deep past, the members of any particular lineage who lived before the ancestral cult was in place, perhaps even before the mythic time of the founding ancestors claimed by each group. Thus Dambada Hwedo has a key role in the elaborate and expensive ceremonies to establish the lineage dead in their role as accessible, protective spirits for the living.[2] Decades may pass between these enormous ritual undertakings, but the name of each one of the dead must be called, and ceremonies must be performed to retrieve each soul and to enshrine each one first in its own "house" and then in the family altar. In this ritual, Dambada Hwedo also represents the more recent anonymous lineage dead, those such as the descendants of slaves, who were never known to their African kin.

Da is a spirit—or *vodu*[3] as the Dahomeans say—that represents what might be called life force or, perhaps more accurately, the coiling, sinuous movement that is life's movement. In the words of one of Herskovits's teachers:

All snakes are called Da, but all snakes are not respected. The *vodu* Da is more than a snake. It is a living quality expressed in all things that are flexible, sinuous and moist; all things that fold and refold and coil, and do not move on feet, though sometimes those things that are Da go through the air. The rainbow has these qualities, and smoke, and so have the umbilical cord, and some say the nerves, too.[4]

Around Da is gathered a group of other spirits who have similar qualities. Among them are Dambada Hwedo and Aido Hwedo.

---

[2] Ibid., 1:194–208.

[3] The Fon word *vodu* is the source of the name currently given to Haitian Vodou. The name Vodou is applied by outsiders to the whole of Haitian traditional religion. In Haiti, however, the term *vodou* more commonly refers to a particular drum rhythm. The religion is usually referred to with a verb rather than a noun; Haitians talk of "serving the spirits."

[4] Herskovits, *Dahomey*, 2:248.

Aido Hwedo, a male, is sometimes depicted as a creature, both snake and rainbow, that swallows its own tail.

In urban Haiti, where ancestral rites and the public cultus have merged, Dambada Hwedo has become Danbala Wèdo, and he has moved to the top rank of the spirit hierarchy. He has become the oldest and the most respected of all the Vodou *lwa*. In Haiti, Aido Hwedo has become Ayida Wèdo, the wife of Danbala. Together, the two (both are serpents and rainbows) arch over the broad ocean. Alternately, the rainbow and its reflection in the water below turn the serpent into a circle. Some say Danbala has one foot—that is, one end of the rainbow—on the ocean where he draws up moisture, which he then deposits in the form of life-giving water through the other foot planted firmly in the mountains of Haiti. Danbala thus moves between the opposites of land and water, as snakes do, uniting them in his coiling, uroboric movements, generating life. Danbala also tunnels through the earth, as snakes do, connecting the land above with the waters below.

The sacred center pole in Vodou temples, a pathway on which the *lwa* travel between Ginen, their watery subterranean home, and the land of the living is called the *poto-mitan*, the middle doorway, or the *poto*-Danbala. Like a snake, which can survive in even the hottest and most arid landscape, Danbala also models the persistent will to live that will not surrender to an inhospitable environment. The merciless and unrelenting sun is a powerful and recurring metaphor for all the sufferings endured by African slaves and their descendants in the New World. *"Papa Danbala, m'pa ka sipòte solèy sou do mwen"*—this popular Vodou song cries out for Papa Danbala's help because "I cannot abide the sun on my back."

In the Vodou temple, the serpent spirit Danbala receives all the care and respect routinely accorded the elderly in Haiti, magnified in his case to suit his extreme age and his status as *lwa*. Papa Danbala is so old that, in possession-performances, he cannot speak. His horse hisses or makes a *"ke-ke-ke"* sound. Danbala's food is natural, raw, and white. He is given *òjat* (a thick almond and sugar syrup) and an uncracked and unblemished raw egg that has been balanced in a mound of *farin frans* (refined flour). Danbala is so pure that he instinctively avoids touching anything dirty, and thus he never does any direct healing work. He does not involve himself in the jealousy, hatred, and fear that lard the human drama and are at the root of so much suffering. Instead, he stands above the human tug-of-war, shedding luck on all who come into his presence with appropriate love and respect.

To let Danbala slither between your legs or, alternatively, to walk his length straddling his writhing body is to give birth and be reborn at the same time. Danbala plays tricks with time. As a coiling, sinuous serpent, he is a persistent, unquenchable life force that unites past and present and turns both into a future that is and is not different from the past. The serpent, who gives up its skin in order to recreate itself and thus remain what it is, connects Haitians to their lost African ancestors and, at the same time, shows them how to be flexible enough to adapt to whatever the future brings. The serpent part of Danbala's identity carries, in the most condensed form, the many messages of this *lwa*'s character, and it also accounts for his identification with Saint Patrick. In the chromolithograph of Saint Patrick preferred by Haitians, he is shown standing at a point where land meets water, in a tangle of writhing snakes.

Alourdes's New York birthday parties for the Vodou spirits, like those celebrated in Haiti, have a prologue known as the Priyè Deyò (Outside Prayers). Although Danbala is not directly named in this prologue except where his name naturally occurs in lists of the *lwa*, he nevertheless insinuates himself into the text throughout this opening segment of Vodou ritualizing. The Priyè Deyò, whose form is the same no matter which spirit is the guest of honor, begin with standard Catholic prayers and hymns. By their end, however, a thoroughly Catholic ethos has gradually shed its skin and emerged as a thoroughly African one.

PRIYÈ DEYÒ

There is no single, dramatic moment at which a Vodou ceremony in Alourdes's home begins. At some point, without calling attention to herself, Alourdes sinks down onto the low wooden stool in front of her elaborate altar tables, makes the sign of the cross, and begins. It usually takes a little time for all the people in the room to notice she has started. The Catholicism Alourdes celebrates in her home in Brooklyn is the Catholicism of gesture, rhythm, and intonation more than that of creed. She leads her people in the Our Father, the Hail Mary, and the Apostles' Creed, all in French, in a rapid, low murmur that quite accurately reproduces a Catholic mood. Yet the content of these prayers and songs—and, specifically, their emphasis on sin, salvation, and incarnation—cannot in the end be easily assimilated into a Vodou worldview.

First, the older women, the steadiest and most responsible of Alourdes's ritual helpers, take up the singing. Then the other guests gradually join in. "Come, my God, come; come, my sweet Savior," Alourdes sings in French, and the people join in:

> Come, my God, come;
> Come, my sweet Savior.
> Come reign within me,
> In the center of my heart.
> Come, my God, come.

Alourdes sings through a second song rapidly, sotto voce, and the people pick it up:

> The angel of the Lord said to Mary
> That she would conceive Jesus Christ,
> The Trinity having chosen.
> And she conceived, by the Holy Spirit.

Many Haitians who serve the spirits have been baptized and have received their First Communion in the Catholic church. It is doubtful, nevertheless, that they have ever understood their Catholicism to be about beliefs or concepts such as those contained in these songs.

I gained an important insight into the Vodou attitude toward Catholicism in 1975, when I participated in a popular Vodou-Catholic pilgrimage in Saut d'Eau, a small mountain town northeast of Port-au-Prince. Vodou ceremonies for Ezili Dantò, which drew large crowds, were held every day a short distance from the Church of Our Lady of Mount Carmel, which supposedly hosted the event. Each morning for a week preceding the feast day of Our Lady of Mount Carmel, before going to the Vodou ceremonies, I attended mass at this church with my traveling companion, a woman who was both a *manbo* and a baptized Catholic. Toward the end of the week, when my curiosity could no longer contain itself, I asked her how she felt about the Catholic priest's repeated insistence that those who serve the Vodou spirits would go to hell. She laughed at my question: "Oh, didn't you know, Karen? That's the way priests talk!"

I did not hear this as a sign of my friend's ignorance or naïveté but rather, on one level, as a wonderful example of the skill with which Haitians turn the power of oppressors back against them. On a deeper level, I heard it as a claim that words, especially ideological ones, can appear frivolous and even expendable when compared to the complex comment on the world that goes on in a full ritual context, including that of the mass. In other words, the mass continued to be effective for her, regardless of what was said during it.

Once Alourdes is well into the Priyè Deyò, her voice begins to pick up momentum. The opening segment of a Vodou ceremony tunnels slowly through the archaeological strata of Haitian history. The first part comes from the most recent layer, the Catholic one derived largely from eighteenth-century French plantation society. But the ceremony quickly moves by gradual increments of sound, energy, and rhythm toward songs that assemble the group and summon the *lwa* in Creole and in *langay*, the sacred language of Vodou composed of partially remembered African words and disguised Creole.

Things start to heat up before the Catholic segment is completed. Alourdes begins the first line of a new song before the last line of the previous one has died away. When her energy rises, so does that of the entire room. By the time she introduces songs for Saint Peter, a Catholic counterpart (along with Lazarus) of Legba, guardian of doorways and barriers, the group is attentive and has found its full voice.

> Saint Peter, open the door.
> Saint Peter, open the door to grace.

Saint Peter, open the door,
The door to Paradise.

Danbala   The rhythms rise and fall, rise and fall as we move through one
hymn or chant after another.

> Grace, Mary, grace.
> Grace, Mary, grace.
> Grace, Mary, grace.
> Jesus, forgive us.

At the end of the sequence of Catholic prayers and songs,
Alourdes usually signals a break in the Priyè Deyò. She may
simply stop singing, heave a sigh, and reach for a drink of
water. In response to her signal, small conversations begin to
break out around the room. Someone makes a joke. Alourdes
guffaws. The conversation picks up, and for a few minutes the
room is abuzz.

Then suddenly the ritualizing begins again as Alourdes picks
up the *ason*, which has been lying at her feet, and shakes it
softly. Once the *ason* is introduced, she begins to take the community rapidly down into the first layers of the ceremony with a
distinct African flavor. The bead mesh gently rustles over the
surface of the small gourd rattle. Yet the dominant sound, for
the moment, is made by the small bell attached to the handle of
the *ason*. Alourdes begins a litany of the saints with a line in
langay: "*Zo li mache, li mache, li mache. . . . Kouran li mache, li mache, li mache. . . .*"

Theoretically, *langay* cannot be translated by common folk.
Alourdes says that even many *oungan* and *manbo* do not know
what it means. Nevertheless, I can sometimes decipher at least
those parts of it that are simple distortions of Creole. These distortions follow some general patterns in which, for example,
kouman (how) becomes *kouran*. The opening lines of the litany
for the saints appear to say: "The bone, it walks, it walks. How
it walks, it walks." This translation, if accurate, can be heard as
an arcane comment on the life energy that persists in the bones
of the ancestors. Alourdes's *ason* is covered in a mesh of many

multicolored glass beads and a few snake vertebrae, the most common type these days. But some older ones I have seen in Haiti have mesh covers made entirely of delicate snake vertebrae. In these vertebrae sleep the sparks of Danbala's life energy, sparks that ignite when the bones dance over the surface of the gourd rattle.

The litany of the saints continues. *"Zo li mache, li mache* [The bone, it walks, it walks],"* Alourdes sings. And the voices of the people follow, rising from these first two lines in *langay* to rest for a moment on one in Creole—*"Lavi'm nan men Bondye e sen-yo* [My life in the hands of God and the saints]"*—before moving on to name, in French, each of the important saints. The litany of the saints is sung midway through the Priyè Deyò. The continuous soft shaking of the *ason* as well as the mixture of languages hint at what is to come, for this is the first clear shift from the solemn Catholic beginnings of the Priyè Deyò to the energizing cross-rhythms of Vodou with which they end.

The litany begins by invoking each of the most important male saints, starting with the great Eternal Father. In French, Alourdes sings, *"Il y a le grand Père Éternel,"* and the people respond in *langay,* *"Sen djo-e."* Alourdes repeats the line, and people respond again in *langay,* *"Sen djo, dogou agwe."* She repeats it a third and final time, and the people reply in Creole, "My life in the hands of God and the saints." After calling Christ, Saint Anthony, Saint Joseph, Saint Isidore, and a dozen others in similar fashion, Alourdes ends the first half of the litany: "There are all the sainted men in heaven and on earth, all those I do not know and do not remember." Three times this is repeated, and the people give the traditional responses, twice in *langay,* once in Creole. Then the same process is carried out for the female saints, starting with the Virgin Mary and ending with "All those I do not know and do not remember." Thus Haitian immigrants in Brooklyn begin their ritualizing by reciting a sacred lineage in a manner not unrelated to what the Dahomean priest must do at a ceremony to establish his lineage dead. Like that priest, Alourdes includes an extra invocation for all those not remembered or never known.

At the conclusion of the litany of the female saints, the sound of the *ason* picks up to a feverish intensity as Alourdes breaks into line after line of rapid *langay,* an urgent jumble of sounds in which African words and fragments of Creole tumble over each other as if drawn toward a climax by the energy of the *ason*. "*Lisa dole zo,*"[5] she chants, and the people, clapping softly and rapidly, say, "*Zo, zo, zo.*" Alourdes continues over the top of their response: "*Lisa dole zo, kouran agwaysa ongansi, ila lele, o zo li mache, li mache, li mache.*"

In Haiti, where drums almost always accompany the ceremonies, the *langay* crescendo ending the litany of the saints is the signal for drumming to begin. When the complex polyrhythms of the drums come rolling in over the end of this rapid chanting, the effect is stunning and paradoxical. The drumming raises the energy level dramatically and, at the same time, gives order to the frenzy of *ason*, handclapping, and *langay*, each of which had seemed about to dissolve into chaos. After the drums enter, the *ason*, which is used to direct ritual action and never simply as a musical instrument, slows to a steady beat and then, after a time, is silent. The handclapping gradually finds its own rhythm to enter into conversation with the cross-rhythms of the drums, and the *langay* transmutes into the familiar Creole of the first of the Vodou songs. In New York, Alourdes has no drums at her ceremonies. Here, the excess energy raised by the crescendo of the litany dissipates slowly through social exchange: people lean back in their chairs, talk and laugh with their friends.

After a short period of socializing, Alourdes begins the Creole part of the Priyè Deyò, in which the group is called together and reminded of who they are and where they come from.

> *Lafanmi sanble,*
> *Sanble nan.*
> *Se Kreyòl nou ye,*
> *Pa genyen Ginen ankò.*

---

[5]Dahomean religion contains an important androgynous spirit called Mawu-Lisa. This figure, who is sometimes spoken of as two separate entities, Mawu (a female) and Lisa (a male), is the creator of the world, the so-called high god. In Haiti, Bondye has taken over the role of high god, and Mawu-Lisa has been largely forgotten. The enigmatic reference to Lisa in this line of *langay* ("Lisa gives bones") seems to be the only instance in which Alourdes's community retains even a shard of memory of the Dahomean creator spirit.

The family is assembled,
Gathered in.
We are Creoles,
Who have Africa no longer.

Haitians who serve the spirits seem to have accepted that they "have Africa no longer." For those who serve the spirits in New York, having Haiti—in the sense of having actual memories of life in Haiti—is the more poignant issue. Haitians started coming to the United States in large numbers after François Duvalier came to power in 1957, but most of the nearly half million who live in the New York area arrived within the past ten to fifteen years. Thus, among the group gathered in Alourdes's home, virtually every adult Haitian has active, living memories of Haiti. And many have earlier rural memories overlaid with later urban ones.

As they participate in these New York rituals, they can reach back in their minds to touch memories of candle-lit cemetery rituals and dancing beneath an open-air *tonnèl*. When they sing in Creole, they sing in their first language. With the power of memory, they can add the sound of drums to the handclapping that goes on in Alourdes's basement. When they gather to sing Vodou songs in New York, wearing their new double-knits, some with car keys in their pockets, the imagery of these songs still resonates with their deepest sense of who they are. The sugarcane and cassava bread on Azaka's altar, the *òjat* on Danbala's, the hot-pepper sauce on Ogou's are foods with tastes tied to the primal memories of childhood.

This is not so for the first generation born in this country, for children such as Alourdes's son Kumar and her grandson Michael, who prefer potato chips to cassava bread. And it is not so for those of us with other cultural backgrounds who have been drawn into Alourdes's circle. Marj probably brings memories of life in her native Grenada to match, where and when they can, with her experience of the ceremonies in Alourdes's home. Robert brings even scantier memories of a poor childhood in rural Georgia. When taking his first ritual bath, he commented: "This is just how we use'ta do it! I remember we always takin' baths out'a these little metal pans. I know how to do it. Don't you worry!" A small but steady stream of North American blacks moves in and out of Alourdes's world, most of them searching for roots that are even more idea and less memory than those Robert seeks to affirm through his connection to Haitian Vodou. And I am here, the anomalous white person, almost always the only white to attend Alourdes's Vodou parties. Lacking links of blood or memory, I challenge myself to take the risks of intellect, empathy, and imagination that enable me to weave, with Alourdes, a slender bridge over the chasm that separates my childhood memories and hers, my current world and hers.

The separation between those who have active memories of Haiti and those who do not at times feels like a fault line running deep and dangerous beneath the united surface of New York Vodou families, threatening to divide them. The majority of participants have lived in Haiti, and they come to ceremonies to activate former parts of themselves. And yet, I remind myself, they are also activating memories carried only in the "genetic" structure of their culture, memories of Africa passed on through many generations of people who had no lived experience of that place. I remind myself of this when I start to think that Vodou in New York might disappear when the responsibilities of leadership pass to the generations born in this country.

The group sings:

> *Janmè, janmè,*
> *M'pa bliye Ginen ray-o.*
> *Janmè, janmè,*
> *M'pa bliye zenfan-la yo.*

> Never, never,
> I'll not forget the ranks of Africa.
> Never, never,
> I'll not forget their children.

The movement from French to Creole, from Catholicism to Vodou, from the soft sing-song of European Christian liturgy to the energetic contrapuntal clapping that accompanies African rhythms also marks a change in imagery. Images of transcendence are replaced by images of family. The awe-inspiring distance between a Catholic heaven and earth transmutes to an im-

age of a bloodline continuous throughout time, one running
along the spine of Danbala and extending further back in time
than memory can reach. The image of a single savior figure, at
once human and divine, gives way to one of a family continu-
ally present in the form of the ancestors and the spirits inherited through them, spirits who, theoretically at least, can possess any human body they choose and make of that person the
bridge between this world and Ginen, Africa, the home of the
spirits.

With steady rhythmic clapping, the New World family assembled in Alourdes's Brooklyn row house sings:

> *Depi anwo, jouk anba,*
> *Nan Ginen, tande la.*
> *Mezanmi, tout sa m'ape fè-a*
> *Nan Ginen tande.*
>> *Bo manman mwen,*
>> *Bo papa mwen,*
> *Nan Ginen tande.*
> *Mezanmi, tout sa m'ape fè-a*
> *Nan Ginen tande.*
>> *Bo marenn mwen,*
>> *Bo parenn mwen,*
> *Nan Ginen tande.*

> From on high, right down below,
> Africa listens.
> My friends, everything I am doing
> Is heard in Africa.
>> The family of my mother,
>> The family of my father,
> In Africa, they hear.
> My friends, everything I am doing
> Is heard in Ginen.
>> The family of my godmother,
>> The family of my godfather,
> In Ginen, they hear.

After several of these introductory Creole songs are completed, Alourdes begins a song that she will eventually transform into yet another litany of the saints. This time, however,
she will call the "saints" by their African names.

　Anonse o zanj nan dlo,
　Bak odsu miwa.
　O, l'a wè, l'a wè.
　Nou pral nan Vil-o-Kan ye.
　Kreyòl mande chanjmen, vre.

　Alert the angels down in the water,
　Beneath the mirror.
　Oh, he will see, he will see.
　We're going to Ville-aux-Camps.
　Creoles ask for change, truly.

The first lines of this song speak of the *zanj* (angels), or spirits, down in Ginen, below the water, and call on the participants to sing loudly to notify them that the ceremonies are
about to begin. The spirits live on the back side of the mirror
surface of the water. In Dahomey, mirrors are used for divination, and mirror gazing is thus one way to tap the wisdom of
the ancestors. In Vodou, the mirror is the principal accoutrement of Agwe, the male sea spirit, although I am not aware of it
being used for divination. Vodou water-mirrors, however, can
be seen as a route even more direct than divination to the wisdom of those who have gone before.

The connection of mirrors, water, and Ginen, the home of the
spirits, makes a complex, uroboric point. Gazing into the water,
a woman sees her own reflection, and through it, simultaneously, she sees the *lwa*. Superimposed on the faces of the *lwa*,
she sees the faces of her ancestors, because an ancestor returns
to the living in the form of the *lwa* he or she revered most during life. Thus, Haitians gazing into the mirror surface of the
ocean that separates them from Africa see in intermingled reflections the *lwa*, the ancestors, and themselves.

The last two lines of the song talk about going to Ville-aux-

Camps. This town, located in the remote Northwest Department of Haiti, is an actual town with a mythic function. It is thought of as a sort of embassy for Ginen in the New World, a place for the *lwa* to stop on their long journeys back and forth from Africa. Members of the Vodou community sing of going there to ask for changes in the circumstances of their lives— a remarkably clear and direct statement of the intention of all Vodou ritualizing. It is a practical matter: people call the ancestors and the *lwa*, give them gifts, and sing and dance for them in order to better their lives.

After this song has been sung two or three times in a standard call-and-response format, Alourdes begins to improvise. "*M'ape anonse Papa Danbala Wèdo, m'ape anonse* [I am announcing Papa Danbala Wèdo, I am announcing]," Alourdes sings. And the people respond, "He will see, he will see." Then, together, all sing: "We're going to Ville-aux-Camps. . . ." Alourdes moves her statements in over the end of the community responses faster and faster, at times naming two or three *lwa* before giving people a chance to reply.

Running rapidly through the list of the most important *lwa*, male and then female, she continues without a pause to her own ancestors: "*M'ape anonse moun Jean Rabel, m'ape anonse* [I am announcing Jean Rabel people, I am announcing]. *M'ape anonse moun Gonaïves, m'ape anonse.*" (Alourdes's maternal great-grandfather, Joseph Binbin Mauvant, settled in Jean Rabel, and her maternal grandmother lived in Gros Morne–Gonaïves.) The litany of spirits thus moves seamlessly into a litany of ancestors, an extension that would not be possible in the two-story universe of Catholicism, where the human and the divine do not mix.

When this litany is finished, the Outside Prayers are complete, and the group moves immediately into the call to Legba to open the door for all the spirits. The mood of solemnity and control that characterizes the Priyè Deyò is dispelled. People are not allowed to smoke or drink during the opening prayers, but once they are completed, the atmosphere becomes more expansive, tolerant, and playful. From this point on, the ritualizers are frequently on their feet, turning, kissing the ground, raising offerings, lighting candles, pouring libations, and dancing for each of the *lwa* in turn. Conversation, joking, and ordinary social exchange flow freely in and out of the ritualizing.

Through Danbala's sinuous, timeless body run the narrow veins of blood and memory. In the earlier discussion of Azaka (Chapter 2), it became evident that just as African slaves in the New World were forced to redefine the group of people they called "family," so their descendants in contemporary urban Haiti and in immigrant communities in New York employ a similar, creative survival strategy. Discussing Danbala again raises the question of family, but here the issue is not weaving a social safety net from a collection of friends and neighbors. Danbala operates from the territory of blood and memory, where the questions are of a deeper, more existential sort: Who am I? Who are we?

The answer demanded by these questions begins by naming the lineage dead. No one knows the stories of people whose names have been forgotten. And these stories are needed to provide answers to the root questions of identity and meaning. Round and round is the movement of time, like the serpentine coils of Danbala. It can be said that history repeats itself and the ancestors return, because their life experiences tend to be repeated in subsequent generations. The wisdom of the ancestors can make contemporary lives easier.

Alourdes was told how Sina resisted the call of the spirits until the day she encountered Ezili's whistling rock, and Alourdes knew Philo's story of how the spirits temporarily blinded her when at first she refused their call. These stories made the illness that plagued Alourdes shortly after she arrived in New York more comprehensible. And, coil upon coil, the spiritual crises experienced by Sina, Philo, and Alourdes provided the interpretive framework for Maggie's struggle. The lineage is a chain, each generation a link. Spiritual leaders in each generation shoulder the heavy responsibility of maintaining that chain. If it were to be broken, all future generations would be impoverished, losing their ancestral stories and therefore their deepest connections to who they are.

For her entire adult life, Alourdes has had to work at maintaining ties with her blood kin. In the midst of the poverty and social fragmentation of Port-au-Prince and Brooklyn, this has not been easy. Her father, Alphonse Margaux, for example, denied paternity until Alourdes was in her late teens.

The last time I saw Alphonse Margaux was in January 1984 in Port-au-Prince, where he lived. Pèpe, as his friends called him, had been ill with liver problems and was confined to bed. The day before I was to leave Haiti, I stopped by his house in the center of town to see how he was. I had also promised Alourdes I would pick up some papers and small gifts he had for her. I arrived, damp and wrinkled, during the hottest part of the day, only to find Pèpe looking dry as a lizard, perched on the edge of his bed in freshly pressed yellow pajamas. He was holding the telephone, one of his prized possessions, with one hand over the mouthpiece, listening in on a party-line call. With his active eyes, which were always on alert, he beckoned me to a chair beside the bed. (If he had not been ill, Alphonse Margaux would never have entertained me in his bedroom.)

The house Pèpe rented in Haiti was not grand. True, he had several rooms and even a shower and a flush toilet (marks of privilege in Haiti), but not one of his rooms was fully furnished. The airy parlor that took up the whole street level of the house seemed the most finished, but even that was more impression than reality. Three large, tinted photographs of family members hung on the wall, somber frontal shots. Beneath the portraits were two dinette chairs, a small sofa, and a boxy armchair, each covered in a dark plastic that stubbornly refused to absorb per-spiration. In the middle of this formal circle was a coffee table, on which sat a single object—a "Gemini" ashtray with a picture of two cherubs in a creative sexual embrace. It was a sign of Pèpe's powerful presence that even in such a home visitors sat nervously on the edge of their chairs for fear of breaking one of the unspoken rules of the house.

Alphonse Margaux had been retired from his job with the Haitian tax bureau for some time. Nevertheless, on most days he put on a business suit and starched white shirt. Perhaps these clothes had once fit him, but by the time I met him they were much too large for his tiny, frail, and wrinkled body. Pèpe usually spent the cooler morning hours bustling around the city with the air of someone who had important business to trans-act. What he actually did was anyone's guess.

Although Pèpe was by then on the threshold of his tenth decade, something of the womanizer who had fathered twenty-five children by almost as many different women persisted. When I hadn't seen him for a while, he would put his skinny arms around me and try to kiss me on the mouth.

I had known Alourdes for a long time before she said much about her father. She talked about him at length on our first trip together to Haiti in January 1980. We were staying at Pèpe's house. He had made a pallet for us on the floor of a room normally used for storage, placing clean white sheets and fluffy pillows on top of layers of mats and blankets. We had just arrived in Haiti and were tired from traveling. The bed was comfortable, and we slept well. The sun was already burning a white rectangle around the closed wooden shutters in the room, when I heard Alourdes whisper, "You sleeping?" "No," I said, "I'm awake."

"We going to my sister' house today," Alourdes said. "We going to sleep there." I was confused: "Why, Alourdes? We just got here last night." "I know," she replied. "I don't like to stay at my father' house too long." Again I asked why. Instead of rebuking me with her usual "You ask too many question!" Alourdes began to talk.

"You know, you got family . . . you got to love that family. I love my father because he my father, but . . . when I was grow up, you know, when I just a little girl, I don't even know who is my father. . . . Nobody don't tell me. Sometime I ask my mother, but she don't say nothing." After a short silence, Alourdes continued: "One day, I was walking in the street with a lady, my mother' friend, and she say, 'Oh, here come your daddy.' And I say, 'Who? I don't know that man.' I don't remember I ever see that man before."

"Did you talk to him?" I asked, still whispering. "Yeah, I talk to him," she whispered back. "And you know what he do? He don't say nothing. He just put the hand in the pocket, and he take fifty *santim*—you know, ten cent—and he buy little thing. He give it to me. Yeah. He just buy a little box of powder from a *machann* on the street. That what he give me!"

"But did he admit he was your father?" I asked as gently as I could. "No," she sighed, "not that time. That time, he don't say nothing. . . . Long time I don't talk to my mother about that. But when I do, you know what she tell me? She say, when I was grow up, he don't give her one penny. Not one penny! She don't even see him."

Another silence followed, and then Alourdes began to talk again: "He use to come by her house, talk nice . . . you know. But she don't do nothing; she just talk to him. One day, he come to the house and she say to him, 'Can you give me some money to buy uniform for my children?' 'Cause, you know, she got Frank and Jean in school, and when you go to school in Haiti, you got to wear uniform. If you don't have no uniform, they don't let you come. Pèpe say, 'Yes,' he going help her. So she . . . you know . . . they . . . they make love. One time, and that's it! She pregnant for him. She got me.

"But after that, he don't come back. He just don't come back. And . . . you know . . . same time my mother pregnant for him, another lady pregnant for him, too. And she live close to my mother' house. Not too far, no. That how come he always walking around that *katye* [quarter]. That how come he always talking to my mother before . . . you know. . . ."

Alourdes seemed about to sink into her own private thoughts, and I was afraid of losing her, so I risked one more question. "Well, when did it happen, Alourdes? When did you two start to be, to have—I mean, when did you really get to know each other?"

"Long time that don't happen. Long time," Alourdes said softly. "When I really, really, really get to know my father, I was already grow up. That time I was singer in Troupe Folklorique—you know that, right?—and before I was marry Kowalski, we got lottery ticket. He got—he won that lottery. Then I get to know my father."

Impulsively, I exclaimed, "Alourdes! You don't mean he admitted he was your father just because you won the lottery!" "I don't say that, Karen. I don't say that. . . ." Two heads, one dark, one light, lay back on the pillows in a room fast losing its battle to keep out the light and heat of a tropical day. Our conspiratorial whispering was silenced, and for a long time there was nothing the old man outside might overhear.

The relationship between Alourdes and her father was complex. Alourdes tried to love him in her way, and he, in his, tried to make up for his earlier neglect. But the years when he had not acknowledged her as his daughter had left bitterness and hurt, and Alourdes tended to hold him at arm's length. When Pèpe died in the fall of 1985, however, Alourdes's actions showed none of this ambivalence. She immediately went to Haiti for the funeral and the wake and also paid a substantial portion of the funeral expenses. As an ancestor, Alphonse Margaux is less problematic than when he was among the living.

Philomise Macena

Alourdes never speaks about her mother with ambivalence:

I love my mother so *much!* Up til now, my mother the one always coming to help me. Sometime somebody come . . . they got a problem, and I don't know how I going to help that person. Then I sleep and I dream my mother, and she tell me what to do. Yes, she the one that help me. She tell me do this, do that. Next day, I do this, do that, and plop! The person just get up and gone. No more problem! She the one always coming to help me. Something going to happen in my life, some kind'a problem, my mother always come. I dream my mother, and she tell me about that. You know, when I come to New York, I think about my children, my three children I left in Haiti, but my mother!—she the one who the real headache. I think about her every day—*every day!* That what make it hard. Let me tell you something. I'm afraid of ghost, but if I see my mother right now, standing up over there, I just open my arm!

Just outside Alourdes's altar room, in the area where birthday parties for the spirits are held, hangs a blurry enlargement of a black-and-white photograph of Philomise Macena. It shows up in the background of many photos I have taken of Alourdes's Vodou ceremonies over the years. Whether the party is for Azaka, Ezili, Ogou, or Danbala, there is Philo, watching over the drama.

During the early years I worked with Alourdes on her biography, a portrait of her childhood with Philo emerged, a portrait of a poor and hardworking *manbo* with a headstrong child who was perhaps spoiled and surely indulged. Alourdes claimed that she could sweettalk her mother into almost anything. Yet

Impromptu kitchen-cabinet altar for Philo created by Maggie and Alourdes on Mother's Day. Fort Greene, Brooklyn, 1978.

poverty seemed to have set limits on Philo's ability to meet her child's needs. Alourdes remembered many times when she was sent to school without breakfast and then came home to find there was still no food. But Philo must have instilled considerable pride in her, because Alourdes also claimed that when school friends asked what she had eaten, she would reply: "Oh, bread . . . chocolate . . . ham."

Philo's work as a healer earned her a substantial reputation in Port-au-Prince, even though she did not make much money from this work. Alourdes said that when she was growing up, Philo's house was often overflowing with clients who came seeking help. Many of them lived there while they were being cured; and when there was not enough room indoors, some camped out in Philo's yard. Philo's charitable spirit was legendary and is illustrated by a multitude of stories. Once, when Philo went to church, she found a poor woman who was on her knees, crying and begging the saints to help her find the money to pay seven months of overdue rent. Her landlord was about to evict her and her children. Philo befriended the woman, gave her the rent money, and even added a little extra to buy food for the children.

How much Alourdes must have learned by having Philo as her role model, I often thought, and how much knowledge she must have gained by growing up in what amounted to a Vodou healing center. Alourdes resisted these images of mine, but she did so indirectly, claiming that as a young child she slept through most of the ceremonies and that as a teenager she preferred secular dances to those for the spirits. When Philo called the drummers into her small backyard, Alourdes said, she would leave for an evening with her friends. She said that when she was an adult living on her own, she sometimes asked her mother to pray for her if she had problems, but she never engaged the spirits herself. "Sometime I say, 'Mommie, light a candle for me,' but I don't do nothing for myself." Something in the notion of Alourdes willfully holding herself apart from the center of her mother's life seemed unlikely to me, but by the time these doubts became clear, I knew better than to push with direct questions.

In March of 1984, six years after we met, Alourdes gave me the missing piece of the puzzle, the piece that caused all the others to realign themselves. I had spent the night at her home, where I slept in the children's room, adjacent to hers. Alourdes called to me when she heard the first sounds of my stirring. I went and sat beside her on her big double bed. I pulled the blankets over my legs and leaned up against the headboard with the king-size rosary draped over one post. We had a sleepy, intimate discussion, focusing at first on the dreams we had each had the night before. Then, in a very small voice preceded by a big sigh, Alourdes said, "I don't ever tell you my mommie don't raise me."

The story that followed made me ache, as much for the shame its telling caused Alourdes as for the actual experience. I tell this story now because of an attitude I have come to know and admire in Alourdes. Earlier, when she first told me about the period when she worked as a Marie-Jacques, she had spoken in the same small voice. But then she had added in a much stronger tone: "You got to put that in the book. Because that's the truth. Right? Women got to do all kind'a thing. Right? I do that to feed my children. I'm not ashame. Right?" The story about her mother was longer in coming, yet she told it to me just as purposefully.

It seems that the same *manbo* who would deplete her savings to help a stranger pay overdue rent and feed children did not think she had the resources to raise a fourth child on her own. Alourdes had not participated in her mother's spirit work because, for most of her childhood, she had observed it from a distance. As a toddler, Alourdes was given into the care of a childless woman friend who was an occasional recipient of Philo's charity. Leah Clemence was delighted to have a child to raise. When Alourdes was seven years old, however, Philo heard rumors that she was being mistreated by Madame Clemence, and the mother reclaimed her daughter. I do not know what went on in the Clemence household when Alourdes lived there, but I do know that Alourdes made a point of not inviting Leah to her wedding years later.

Alourdes and her mother lived together for a year in the house in Belair, the one Philo eventually lost to a treacherous friend and the fraudulent legal system. It was during this time that Alourdes wandered off for three long days. After she was found, she and Philo traveled to Jean Rabel to kill a pig for Ezili Dantò, and Dantò announced that Alourdes would serve the family spirits after Philo. All this happened in one short year. By Alourdes's eighth birthday, she was living with her older brother Frank and his wife, Rita. There she stayed until she became pregnant with her first child at the age of fourteen.

Rita then declared the precocious Alourdes too much to handle and sent her back home. For a second time, Alourdes and Philo were reunited—but again for only a brief period. Less than two years later, Alourdes began to live with Charles, the man who eventually became Maggie's father. Furthermore, the relationship between Alourdes and her mother was apparently not always smooth, whether or not Alourdes was living at home. Small comments have led me to conclude that Philo had a fearsome temper; in spite of Alourdes's status as a favored child, it seems that this temper sometimes erupted in her direction.

Nevertheless, when Alourdes talks about her mother with great love, it does not sound false. I can detect no underlying bitterness. "Women got to do all kind'a thing," Alourdes says, referring to herself, and it seems that applying this same attitude to her mother has enabled her both to understand and to forgive. Even if, in a manner of speaking, Philo gave Alourdes away, the bond between them seems to have been forged deep and strong. When Alourdes had difficulty giving birth to Maggie, Philo rushed to her side with spiritual help and motherly comfort. And later, when Alourdes suffered so much during her pregnancy with William, Philo came to the clinic and gave her what little food and money she could scrape together. Philo often fed Alourdes's children during the difficult period after she left Kowalski, and, when Alourdes went to the United States, Philo kept the children for nearly two years. By the time Alourdes was an adult, she and her mother were so psychically connected that when communication broke down between them, Philo's dreams informed her of her daughter's illness and hospitalization in New York. Alourdes's decision to serve the spirits after that illness was inseparable from her decision to remain tied to her mother. So it is fitting that her mother is the one who now appears in Alourdes's dreams to help her in her healing work.

BLOOD AND MEMORY: MAGGIE

Margaret Georgette Margaux Sanchez has different kinds of problems to face in maintaining the lines of blood and memory.[6] Maggie came to the United States before she had her first menstrual period. In New York, she became an adult and learned most of what she knows about the world. Maggie has spent a lot of her time outside the home, going to school and working. Consequently, she has constructed a larger world than has Alourdes and has developed more public skills.

This independence, which was more or less forced on Maggie, can create conflicts when she thinks about the future. In 1979, responding to a question about her hopes for the future, Maggie said, "Well, my future dream is—since I have that degree in dental technician—if I have enough money, I think I would open my own lab where I could be my own boss . . . you

---

[6] Maggie was briefly married to a Puerto Rican man named Sanchez, who is Michael's father. In certain circumstances, Maggie still uses the name Sanchez.

know, working whenever I feel like it."[7] But then she thought a minute and added, "Or, if I could get a husband to support me enough . . . I could stay home, do a little housework, and let him take care of me."

When Maggie was thinking of settling down with the Jamaican man named Barnett, that was how she spoke about her dreams. Since she has become a *manbo*, however, her mood has changed. The Haitian man who is now her frequent companion and the father of her daughter Betty does not dream of carrying Maggie off to their own home or expect her to play the role of a traditional wife. Maggie and Alourdes have the primary bond; they are the heads of the house, and he knows better than to try to exert his authority there.

The Vodou spirits are an important part of Maggie's life. But even after her initiation they have remained only one part of her large and complex world. Furthermore, this is a part that must often be hidden. Maggie tells an amusing story about taking an important lab exam at the technical school where she received a certificate in dental mechanics. Papa Gede showed up to give her some help with the test, signaling his presence with the strong odor of cigar smoke. Maggie said to him, "Don't do that! You going to get me in trouble!" "Who are you talking to?" asked her lab partner. "And what's that awful smell?" This is one of the more benign stories Maggie tells about the clash she often experiences between her different worlds. A patient in the gynecologist's office where she once worked refused to let Maggie touch her when she found out she was Haitian. The reasons the hysterical woman offered were "Vodou and AIDS." Maggie rarely lets anyone outside her immediate community know how important the Vodou spirits actually are in her life.

Maggie has been marked from early childhood as the one to inherit her mother's altar and, along with it, the responsibility of serving the family spirits. Prescient dreams, starting when she was quite young, indicated that the spirits favored her. Alourdes also had such dreams, beginning when she was little

---

[7] Maggie took vocational training to become a dental technician. She found out about the vocational school through an advertisement on the subway. The program was long and expensive, and when she completed the course, the school reneged on its commitment to find her a job.

more than a toddler. For both of them, dreams continue to be significant life events, sometimes diagnosing current situations and sometimes foretelling important future events.

Dreams

The story of the last stage of Maggie's struggle in taking on the identity and responsibilities of a *manbo* can be told through a sequence of such dreams. The dreams, both interpretive and predictive, occurred during the first six months of 1981, a time when the family was beset by a serious and extended period of bad luck. Bad luck,[8] the broadest diagnostic category in the lexicon of the Vodou healing system, can be a one-time thing such as a car accident, a lost job, or an illness; or it can be a shift in the quality of life that affects everything—which was how Alourdes and Maggie diagnosed their situation in early 1981.

Everything went wrong, small things (lost keys, jammed doors, mail that did not arrive) and big ones. The trouble started when the heating pipes froze and burst in January. Less than two weeks later, Maggie lost her job and contracted chicken pox. The bad luck then began to spread, as it is known to do, to vulnerable others (those not spiritually protected) who were connected to them. Gabriel, Alourdes's former boyfriend, who was living with them at the time, was mugged. Alourdes's son William was arrested for purse snatching.

When bad luck is pervasive, "you got to pay attention to that," as Alourdes put it. But in order to pay attention, a person has to be centered and calm enough to sleep well, dream frequently, and remember those dreams. By early March, the anxiety level in the house had risen so high that when the spirits sent Maggie a dream warning her about the next link in the chain of bad luck, she did not remember it right away, and, when she did remember, she misinterpreted a key element:

They warn me. They tell me about that. I just have too many thing in my head. I forget about it. I just been running around trying to do too many thing. But I dream. . . . I dream that I

---

[8]Strictly speaking, Haitians refer to an absence of luck: *"M'pa genyen chans* [I don't have any luck]."

come home one night and find my door open, and I go in there and look, and there are four horses looking at me right from the fire escape. They just standing there looking at me, and then I hear something in the front of my apartment, you know, in the bedroom, and I go in there . . . and there is Joe. You know Joe? Aileen's son. And I say to him, 'What you doing in here? What you doing in my apartment?' And he tell me he just come in looking for something. And I get real mad and just sock him, beat him up! And throw him out!

In mid-March, a few days after this dream, the row house in Fort Greene was robbed, the first burglary they had experienced in nearly twenty years of living there. Maggie occupies the second-floor apartment, below the one rented out to Aileen and her son, Joe. The burglar got onto the fire escape in back and came in through Maggie's kitchen window, where the horses were standing in her dream. Maggie lost the engagement ring that Raphael Sanchez, Michael's father, had given her; a jar full of quarters; a collection of foreign money; and a new camera for which she had yet to make her first payment.

After the robbery, Maggie was hard on herself: "They trying to tell me somebody going to break into my house. I don't pay no attention." I asked what difference it would have made if she had remembered the dream, and Maggie replied that the spirits might have been telling her to confront the robber and fight with him. When the robbery happened, Maggie had been on the first floor in her mother's bedroom, tending a sick child. She heard the thief leave her apartment and descend to the basement.

"I should have just open that door and spray something right in his eye," Maggie said, "perfume . . . Lysol . . . Comet cleanser." She also criticized herself for initially misinterpreting the dream, for reading the presence of Joe, a mulatto, merely as a signal that the thief was a light-skinned man. (Skin color is a significant part of the message in any dream from the spirits.) She soon learned through neighborhood gossip that Joe had actually committed the robbery. Maggie had not realized how directly the spirits were speaking to her.

The robbery clinched Maggie's diagnosis about the cause of the period of bad luck. She decided it was definitely a result of harassment by the spirits, who were demanding that she stop postponing her initiation. It had been almost two years since the important dream in which she had sworn to Danbala that she would return to Haiti to take the *ason*. Work and financial troubles, she said, had prevented her from fulfilling her promise right away. Now, she felt the spirits were increasing their pressure. "That's just what those spirit do. That's how they are! I'm just thankful they don't make me sick again."

It seems fair to speculate that Maggie's delay in making the trip to Haiti was not entirely a result of external circumstances. Family spirits do not often molest people who are the victims of things they cannot control. In fact, during the two years since her promise to Papa Danbala, Maggie had been struggling mightily with the consequences of taking on the responsibilities of a *manbo*.

In 1963 Alourdes, on her way to board the plane that would take her to the United States, had said to Philo, "I don't think I'm going to need no spirit in New York." Sixteen years later, in 1979, when I asked Maggie if she planned to become a *manbo* like her mother, Maggie had said something similar: "I don't think I'll be working as a *manbo*, because my mother is living. Plus, I'm right here in the U.S., and so I don't think I'll need to work as a *manbo*." Maggie had concluded that she could not live the life of her *manbo* grandmother here in New York. "New York is much different than any place that my grandmother ever live. Like here, people don't care. They just don't give a damn! Because I came here when I was young, and I seen New York City. . . . I think it's New York teach me a lot'a thing—New York so tough! That's the big experience that I have in New York that make me realize I can't be like my grandmother." When I pointed out to Maggie that Alourdes was also living in New York and working full-time as a *manbo*, Maggie said simply, "She grow up in different ways than me."

Yet at no point did Maggie's reluctance about becoming a *manbo* signal ambivalence about Vodou itself. She has always been a staunch defender of her mother's work and has appreciated what the spirits bring into her life. "You know, maybe if I wasn't part of Vodou, I would not know so much about people. Maybe if I did not grow up in it, I would be just, you know, just like ordinary people . . . walking . . . like everybody else walking on the streets, up and down . . . and don't know right from wrong."

In 1981, when the spirits increased their pressure on her, the conflict Maggie felt about becoming a professional healer intensified. On the third Saturday in March, Alourdes was scheduled to hold her annual birthday party for Papa Danbala, Maggie's main spirit. On the Friday night before the ceremony, Maggie had a terrifying dream, which woke her up and kept her up for the rest of the night. "I dream all these snakes coming from everywhere, big ones, little ones—all green, coming after me and chasing me. And I turn and say to them, 'Leave me alone. I'm going to kill you. I'm going to kill all of you!' And they say to me, 'If only you could. . . . If you could just find us.'"

This dream occurred when the streak of bad luck was well under way. Maggie had recovered from chicken pox, but she did not yet have another job. The house had been robbed the week before, and William had been arraigned in court the previous Wednesday. At the ceremony that Saturday night, when Papa Danbala came to ride Alourdes, the usual ritual forms were observed. Danbala inched across the floor on his belly like a snake. When he arrived at the foot of the altar table, a white sheet canopy held at the corners by four participants was lowered over him so he could consume his raw egg in privacy.

William, whose plight was by then known to many in the community, was the first one called up to greet the *lwa* as he lay under the canopy. William was directed to offer his little fingers to Danbala in the discreet and proper handshake this ancient spirit prefers. Then he was told to bend over and straddle Danbala's body, under the protective cover of the sheet, and slowly walk its length. He emerged from the other end of the cloth tunnel looking dazed and aroused at the same time.

This selection from my field notes picks up the description of the ceremony after several other people had greeted the spirit and Danbala had finally released his horse. Alourdes was being helped to her feet when

all of a sudden, Maggie is down. Danbala has mounted her! Her body, prone on the floor, curls like the body of a paralytic. Her hands knot up. She looks like an old, old person lying, self-protectively, in a fetal position. She screams as if

A *manbo* possessed by Danbala. Port-au-Prince, Haiti, 1989.

in real pain, several times—unwilling, unable to let go. The people in the room move protectively around her. Maggie's possession passes quickly, never emerging into articulateness. Before long, Maggie jumps up, uttering obscenities. "Shit! That's just shit! *Kaka!*" There is something both moving

and painful in this, and also something quite expressive of
Maggie's ambivalence about the world of the spirits. She can't
move away from it, but she can't quite get into it either.

A few days later, when Maggie and I were talking on the
phone, I laughed and said, "Well! That was the first time I have
seen you get a *lwa*."

"That was scary, Karen!" she replied quickly. "I don't want it
to happen. I don't like that. I was flying. It's the fly I don't like! I
can't take that sensation. I have to be able to stand on my foot,
to feel my legs. I don't like that flying. That's why I'm scared of
heights. Like, I'm up there, and my foot cannot touch the
ground. Like, I'm scared I'm going to fall." But then, without a
pause, she began to speak about her initiation: "I know this is
what I have to do, and when I do it, things will get better. I'm
not going to say no 'if' . . . not no more!"

Maggie went on to say that there were still problems with the
trip to Haiti, tentatively set for July, four months hence. Ogou
had told her she had to go out and beg to raise money for the
things she would need for her initiation. Ritual begging is a lesson in humility often prescribed by the spirits. (They had forced
Philo to beg.) In Haiti everyone recognizes that the person begging in the market, the one who wears blue denim or clothing
pieced together from fabrics of different patterns, is such a ritual beggar. But, in New York, Maggie wailed, "nobody gonna
know why I do that thing!"

Two weeks later, at a Danbala feast given by Madame François, the serpent spirit appeared and counseled Maggie that
begging can mean different things in different contexts. Maggie
had already approached friends for loans to meet the expenses
of her initiation, and Danbala judged this sufficient to meet her
spiritual obligations. Maggie was tremendously relieved. She
also acknowledged that asking friends for loans had been quite
a blow to her pride.

In early April, Maggie had a dream that signaled an end to
her bad luck and indicated that Danbala was content with the
good intentions of his devotee. In the dream, she was in some
sort of factory. "There were two men come in, one black and one
white. And I was sharing cake with a lot of people, and I think
one of them—at least one of them—was Papa Danbala," she
laughed. "Because I say to him"—she laughed once more—"I

tell Papa Danbala if he come to me looking like a snake again, I'm going to reject him!" Then Maggie added: "Any time you dream you eating cake, that mean you going to have success throughout the year."

Fear and Protection

A desire for personal safety—or "protection," as Maggie more often puts it—is perhaps the main reason she was finally willing to serve the spirits despite the toll in time and energy and despite the prejudice against Vodou she encounters outside her Haitian community. She once put it this way:

> I know New York City is hard. But, thank God, nothing ever happen to me. I don't have the fear. The reason why is that I know my spirit are around me, all the time, and if there should be danger, you know, somewhere I'm going, I just have a feeling of something pulling me back not to go. I'm not afraid to go to the store, say, at eleven o'clock at night, or afraid to go to school, or afraid to go to work real early in the morning. I don't have no fears, I just get up and go . . . and I know that nothing will happen to me.

Maggie fears concrete situations, violence at the hands of people she does not know, whereas Alourdes fears less tangible evils such as the ambition, jealousy, or general malevolence of people she does know. Alourdes's fears almost always have a spiritual dimension. Maggie's are more rooted in the realities of everyday life in a tough Brooklyn neighborhood. The two women also handle their fears differently. After the robbery, both felt insecure, but each handled that insecurity in her own way. After the break-in, Maggie bought some rough lumber and built narrow, haphazard shelves over the window where Joe had entered and the one in the basement where he had exited. Alourdes constructed a *gad*. She submerged a doll, with a mirror bound to its breast, in a bottle filled with water. ("Alert the angels down in the water, Beneath the mirror. . . .") She placed this protective charm on one of the shelves in the basement window, where it gazed out over the rear yard.

In keeping with her tendency to fear the duplicity of persons known to her, Alourdes made her own diagnosis of the period of bad luck in 1981, claiming that it was the work of a distant relative, one descended from her grandfather, Alphonse Macena. On her last trip to Haiti, this man had approached Alourdes and asked her to take over his recently deceased father's altar and, along with it, the service of the spirits housed there. Alourdes did not want to do this, because the *oungan* had "practiced with both hands." Some of the spirits he served were not family spirits at all but "purchased spirits," free-floating souls of those who had died without family or proper burial, souls that had subsequently been captured and "tied" in a bottle or stone. Alourdes wanted nothing to do with this sort of spirit work, and she avoided further contact with this part of her extended family. During the period of bad luck, she came to believe that these relatives had been offended by her behavior and had done "work" against her.

Somewhat surprisingly, Maggie did not disagree with this reading. In fact, she talked about it as much as Alourdes did. At the same time, however, Maggie held to her own parallel explanation about the spirits wanting her to become a *manbo*. And Alourdes did not disagree with Maggie's theory, either. Both seemed to be accurate explanations of their protracted spell of bad luck. They knew both diagnoses were accurate because the spirits spoke to both scenarios in their dreams. And when the bad luck had run its course, more dreams signaled the return of good times.

Just a few days after Maggie's dream about sharing cake with Danbala, Alourdes had a dream in which Ogou spoke to her, telling her that she had nothing to fear from the family of Alphonse Macena. "The trouble over," the spirit announced. "Everybody back to work!" And a day or two after that dream, Maggie had one that also indicated that her mother's problems with Macena's descendants were at an end. In Maggie's dream, uncharacteristically, God himself intervened.

I don't think nothing more going to happen, because I have a dream. Those people been bothering Mommie, God going to fix them. I dream like I was walking up this mountain, like a big mountain, and something coming out of the sky, like fog . . . or cloud . . . like white smoke . . . and they talk to me. They tell me He going to lock them up. I was in this house—but it was not my house—like a Haitian house, and they tell me to clean it, to get it ready, because God going to bring them people there and lock them up. They had given me the front room of that house to open up a store, and I tell them I don't want it. There was a lot of leaf, a lot of dirt in that house, and they just say, 'Clean it. Get ready. We are going to lock them up.' Mommie tell me that was a good dream.

After these dreams, Maggie and Alourdes breathed a mutual sigh of relief. It had been a time of testing, and they had emerged stronger. Maggie had strengthened her ties to her kin, and Alourdes had done some necessary pruning on her family tree. After that, the two began serious planning for a trip to Haiti in July, a trip from which Maggie would return a full-fledged *manbo*, with *ason*. The bones of Danbala could continue to be shaken alive, and the veins of the serpent spirit would flow with the bright red blood of another generation. The stories would not be forgotten.

BEYOND BLOOD AND MEMORY

What made the events of the first half of 1981 so poignant was that both Maggie and Alourdes were confronted with the most basic of questions: who are my people? Maggie discovered that she could not slough off her family identity and responsibilities. With those connections in doubt, her sense of security in the world had been placed in jeopardy. Alourdes discovered that blood ties are sometimes binding in the wrong ways. Family is never as clear-cut as the ethnographers would make it, especially for Haitians, who have been through cycle after cycle of social upheaval. Although Alourdes seeks to honor the ties of blood and memory, she insists on doing so selectively. Her argument against taking over the altar of Macena's descendant—that he served spirits who were not family spirits—was understandable, but she does not apply this rule systematically. Technically, Philo did not meet this standard, either. Alourdes's mother did not traffic in purchased spirits, but her head spirit, Agèou, was not inherited from her forebears; rather, he was a Dominican spirit acquired while she was living in Santo Domingo.

Alourdes also flouts official definitions of family when she presents the stories of her people as a matrilineage. To some extent, she rewrites history when she says, "In my family, men don't serve no spirit; only women serve spirit." Alourdes makes this claim in spite of Joseph Binbin Mauvant and Alphonse Macena, both of whom had considerable, if not always benevolent, religious power. Alourdes chooses the women as the main branches on her family tree, and the mother-daughter link forges the chain of generations for her.

In refusing to assume the spiritual obligations of the extended Macena family, Alourdes in part revealed the consistency with which she defines family and makes the connections between duty to family and religious duty. Alphonse Macena had greater spiritual power, but it was Marie Noelsine Joseph who sustained the family as best she could. Thus Sina's whistling rock rests on Alourdes's Brooklyn altar, not Macena's sword. Among Alourdes's people, time and again, the women have shouldered the responsibility of the generations, caring for the young, the old, and the ancestors. They have fed the spirits of the dead and the hungry babies as well. Alourdes's religious responsibilities devolve from this lineage of mothers who survived and nurtured as best they could. These are her people, and it is their spirits she keeps alive with her ritual feeding.

Alourdes's loyalty to family spirits is clear. But equally clear is a pull toward working with a wider clientele. When I asked her if most of the people who came to her for help were Haitians, she responded, "All of them not Haitian. Noooooo! Canadian, Barbadian, Italian, Jamaican—you know. I work for lot'a white people. Chinese, too." Although it remains my impression that most of her clients are Haitian, Alourdes does do her healing work at a cultural crossroads. But describing the relationship between a non-Haitian client and the Vodou spirits is complex. If the mutual obligations between the spirits and the living are inherited within families, how can a person who encounters the Vodou spirits in Alourdes's altar room, perhaps for the first time, expect them to respond to a request for help?

Although I did not originally come to Alourdes as a client, her attitude toward me is instructive on this issue. Alourdes takes different approaches with me. One day, she looked closely at me and asked, "What color your eyes?" "Blue," I answered, and she responded: "You a real honky, aren't you? Oh, boy! A real honky." Yet, when reading the cards for me, she began to talk about the black ancestor somewhere in my past. "Even you don't see that . . . people look like you, sometime they got that in their family," she explained. And, during the same period, I also noticed that she used another, more comprehensive explanatory scheme. This theory, articulated by Alourdes several times and in different ways, holds that there is only one religion, one God, and one group of spirits. People simply call God and the spirits by different names. Overall, Alourdes's attitude toward my involvement in Vodou has been pragmatic: "Try it and see if it work for you." In the summer of 1980, I decided to do just that, with my marriage to Ogou (described in Chapter 4).

When I told Alourdes that I was ready to marry Ogou, she responded, "Okay, but . . . you got to marry Danbala, too. Ogou too hot. You got to balance." I was familiar with the Vodou principle of dynamic balance, so the new requirement did not surprise me. It did not even occasion much thought. I was certain that the main event would be my marriage to Ogou. In the weeks before the two spirit weddings, I thought about the Danbala part of the rituals only when going over my mental checklist. Marrying two spirits meant I had to buy two complete sets of clothes (for Danbala, I needed a white dress with sleeves) and two wedding rings (Danbala's had to be in the shape of a snake).

Much to my surprise, the marriage to Danbala turned out to be the more powerful of the two. Ogou's behavior disappointed and frustrated me. I had wanted Ogou to open his arms and welcome me as one of his own. Instead, he kept trying to teach me lessons about self-assertion, and I ended up feeling rejected. It was Danbala who fed the deeper hunger, the one beneath the anger I had wanted to "marry," to own up to, by marrying Ogou.

The Danbala possession came on fast that July night. The spirit did not descend first on Alourdes, but rather on Andre, a pleasant young man and a relative of Alourdes's whom I knew only superficially. Andre fell and wiggled across the floor like a snake, his eyes wide, his tongue darting—the only sound he made was a hiss. I was quickly directed to lie beside Danbala, and the two of us were covered with a sheet canopy held in place by several of the devotees. Someone put Danbala's egg— the traditional offering—under the canopy, along with a small white dish containing the wedding ring I had purchased.

Sweet-smelling Florida Water was sprayed over the sheet, and its edge was lifted briefly to allow each of us a drink of almond-sugar syrup. Our translucent, private bower bloomed with pungent odors, and Danbala gently hissed his gratitude. Singing surrounded us. Then, with his lips, Danbala picked up the ring, a tiny coiled silver serpent. Holding it in his mouth, he bit into the raw egg. Somehow, he maneuvered the slippery, egg-coated ring onto the first finger of my right hand. Next, Danbala traced, with his darting tongue, a trail of albumen up my right arm to the shoulder bone, and then he hissed gently in my ear.

A curiously asexual sensuality overtook me. I was floating. Danbala stopped time for me. He stopped the voice of the commander in my head, the one who wanted to take charge, make lists, get things done—set things right in my life. His presence was pure sensation—timeless, purposeless pleasure. This part of the ritual accomplished something Alourdes had often tried but never quite managed even with her oft-repeated: "Karen, you think too much!"

Then the singing intensified, and I heard scuffling and thumping a few feet from where Danbala and I lay side by side. The sheet was whipped away, and hands picked me up (I remember being limp) and carried me to lie beside Alourdes, now mounted by a second Danbala. Hers emitted an urgent "*ke-ke-ke-ke-ke*." When the marriage license was brought, this Danbala signed it with a big X and then crumpled the document against his heart: "*Ke-ke-ke-ke*," he crooned. Then he pressed the crumpled sheet of paper against my heart: "*Ke-ke-ke-ke*." Back and forth the paper went between us. Finally, Danbala threw it aside and hugged me tightly to his breast.

I had never seen two Danbala appear at once. Both Maggie and Alourdes later described it as unusual. "They both come for you, the white one and the black one." The first, they said, had been the white Danbala, Saint Patrick. The second was the black one, Moses. Alourdes reminded me that Moses carried a stick that could turn into a snake. During the last stage of the possession, Alourdes's Danbala leaned on a stick with a carved snake wound around its entire length.

With hindsight, I understand the Danbala marriage to have marked my acceptance in Alourdes's Vodou family. Some people in her community had been uncertain and tense about including a white person, particularly one who used a tape recorder and a camera. After the July marriages in 1980, however, the question was closed. It seems significant that it was Danbala who opened the family to me. I remembered Joseph Binbin Mauvant's African legacy: "You in, you in. You out, you stay out."

Much of the social and religious energy of rural Haitians has gone into defining their family over and against other families. In Mauvant's time, his powerful African words were probably understood on that level. The many Haitians who were forced to migrate to the cities had to expand their definitions of family. The sense of the in-group and the out-group shifted, but Mauvant's words persisted. In Port-au-Prince, Alourdes's family used them to cast the line between those who could be trusted and called on in times of trouble and those who could not. Immigrating to the United States caused further shifts, but the drive to define an inner core group that stands together against a larger outside group remains.

In the early 1980s, when I became involved in the plight of the Haitian boat people, refugees who arrived on U.S. shores in leaky vessels and were immediately imprisoned by the Immigration and Naturalization Service, Alourdes responded to my talk about this effort by observing: "Karen, you always talking about the Haitian people, the Haitian people. . . . I don't understand. You don't know those boat people. Why you got to get involve?" Abstractions do not provoke loyalty in Alourdes. She continues, in the spirit of Joseph Binbin Mauvant, to locate those individuals who can be called her people because she knows them and because they have earned the title.

But these days she casts her net more widely, and the group she includes in it is more diverse. Alourdes has always shown courage and creativity in taking on the new and the foreign. Through her, at my marriage ceremony, Danbala moved her whole community to a broader response to the question, Who are my people? This may be the way of the future for Vodou in the immigrant communities. But such a path leads to both gains and losses. Vodou can share its wisdom and its healing techniques with a larger and more varied group; but as the group of potential devotees expands, the spirits will also become more universalizable, the faces of the spirits less transparent to those of the ancestors, and the stories that carry the wisdom of the religion more abstract.

The spark that keeps Vodou alive dances along Danbala's backbone. As the religion changes to respond to its new environments, Danbala must change. On a trip to Haiti in March

1988, I found a whole nation suffering from depression. The hated dictator Jean Claude Duvalier had departed in February 1986. Hope and energy had risen among Haitians, only to be smashed when voters, lined up for the first democratic election in several decades, were machine-gunned on the spot. I arrived in Haiti less than four months after this tragedy. What intrigued me was that several Vodou leaders spoke about their current suffering in terms of the anger of Danbala.

Danbala used to stand with one foot on the water and one on the land, they said. But not now. Now Danbala is so angry that he has withdrawn his foot from the land. He is angry about the abuses of Duvalier and about the Duvalierists, who remain in control. These are people who turn on their own, on the "families" for whom they are father figures. As punishment, Danbala has withdrawn his foot from the land, and Haiti is withering and dying. Even members of the Haitian elite talked this way, though they would never use the name of Danbala. One woman, light enough to be my sister, told me that when she took her usual morning walk in the woods near her mountain home, she felt that all the spirits of the trees had departed. In her words, Haiti was "losing its life force."

Vodou has never included a notion of a Golden Age in either the past or the future. There is no heaven or hell, and no apocalypse is anticipated. At least, there had been no apocalyptic vision—until recently. When such a vision forces itself upon the people of Haiti, it is significant that they feel it in terms of the retreat of Danbala. What Danbala is doing in Haiti and what he is doing in New York are good indices of the well-being and the future direction of the families who serve him in both places.

CHAPTER ELEVEN

Plenty Confidence

April 24, 1981—3:00 P.M.

Mimose sat in her home in Bizoton, a home that was really only a room. The concrete floor had been swept. The dishes had been washed and arranged carefully on top of the bureau: two plates, one bowl, three jelly glasses, and a cooking pot. The pretty flowered sheets had been smoothed out, stretched tight, and tucked in neatly around the edges of the bed. Mimose, freshly bathed and dressed in pale lavender, sat on the edge of her bed staring at an expressionless face in a mirror she held in her right hand. On a mat beside the open door, little Manouchka slept on her stomach, her thumb in her mouth. Mimose thought she heard something—a small indecipherable noise . . . maybe a baby's cough . . . maybe a spider dropping from the thatch. She glanced away from her reflection, turned her head toward her child, and, seeing nothing, looked back in the mirror.

Mimose was bored; that was what she told herself. But it was more than boredom she felt. This was a complex feeling without a name. Call it dread. Deep hunger. Hopelessness. Earlier in the day, when the all-too-familiar feeling had begun to stir in her, Mimose had written Jacques a passionate love note. Then she ran down to the Carrefour road and waited on pins and needles for his bus to appear on one leg of its regular circuit. When she saw the brightly painted van with "La Vie Belle" written across the front in fat red letters and blinking lights, she raced to it, pushed the note at Jacques through the driver's window, put a hand on her lips to forestall his questions, and pranced away, giggling.

After that, Mimose felt much worse. All day, the dread had

◀ The author emerging from the initiation chamber. Outside of Port-au-Prince, 1981. Photograph by Jerry Gordon.

been growing steadily, like a boil. Her mind searched for something that could make her feel less precarious. "If we could get married . . . if I could find a job and pay someone to take care of Manouchka. . . . Mama doesn't even have a home right now. She can't do it. If I could take the *ason* . . . start to work as a *manbo* . . ." Each attempt to find an escape route led her into the same cul-de-sac, the one marked *money*. Well, if the problems could not be solved, it was at least time to make the fear go away. Her hand moved automatically toward Jacques's rum bottle.

"*Sa pa bon pou ou, ti cheri* [That isn't good for you, dearie]," said Chantal as she walked through the door. Sitting down on the bed next to her daughter, Chantal withdrew a grease-stained packet of fried pork from the pocket of her housedress and offered it to Mimose. Mimose shook her head; she preferred to let the fire burn in her belly pure and unadulterated. Methodically and in silence, Chantal ate the four nuggets of meat. Then, while picking her teeth with the nail on her little finger, she asked her daughter for a glass of water. Mimose pointed to a plastic jug on the edge of the bureau; but, catching her mother's disapproving look, she quickly rose to fetch the water herself. Chantal watched her beautiful young daughter and shook her head ruefully. In another minute, Mimose was standing before her, holding out a tray with a brimming glass of water balanced in the middle. Chantal took the glass, raised it to her lips, and emptied it down her throat.

"Alourdes called last night," said Chantal. "She called at Madame Jesnair's, and by chance I was there. I talked with her. Maggie is going to *kouche* in July. Alourdes said you can go in, too. She is going to pay for everything." Mimose's face lit up. She jumped from the bed and danced around the room. "Tant Alourdes! Tant Alourdes! I love you!"

May 3, 1981—11:00 A.M.

Karen Brown stood at the front door of her loft in lower Manhattan, giving it an appreciative look. It was a bright Sunday morning, and this was the day Alourdes would bless her new home. "Mine, all mine!" she thought to herself as she breathed in the odors of sawdust, fresh paint, and polyurethane. "Brace yourself, friends," she whispered to her brick walls and shiny wood floor, "our peace and quiet are about to disappear." Then she got into her battered Volvo and pointed it toward Brooklyn.

All five members of the Brooklyn household were dressed and ready to go. And when Alourdes's gregarious friend Big Daddy arrived just as they were about to leave, he was persuaded to come along as well. Spirits were high on the trip to Manhattan. Karen let the stories, the laughter, and the teasing swirl around her, paying no attention to the antiphonal shouts of the two young boys in the back of her station wagon: "You cow!" "You horse!" "You truck!" "You airplane!" "You—you—you Haitian!" Karen was trying to plot the best route, through street fairs and road construction, back to the area New Yorkers call TriBeCa, an acronym for the Triangle Below Canal Street. "I'll cut through Chinatown," she thought and took a sudden left on Mott Street.

In less than two blocks, it was clear this had been a mistake. Even on Sunday, the streets of Chinatown were filled with people, and traffic inched along. Small-scale commerce—shoes spread out on the sidewalk, fish on ice in the back of a truck—intensified the congestion. As the Volvo came to a stop alongside a car with a young Chinese woman in the passenger seat, Alourdes leaned across Karen and greeted the woman with a nod and a bright smile: "*O wang gi nichi pi.*" Then she and the other passengers burst into laughter, while Karen was left to face the woman's disgusted look and respond with a helpless shrug of her shoulders.

"Beauteeeful!" cried Alourdes as the crowd finally pushed through Karen's front door. Standing at the top of the staircase leading to the lower level of the loft, Alourdes exclaimed: "*Woy!* That stair too high. I going fall." She picked her way carefully down the stairs, swaying from side to side in a pair of blue jeans so tight she had had to be helped in and out of the car. Reaching the bottom, Alourdes plunked herself into a wicker rocking chair and heaved a sigh of contentment. "If I got a place like this . . . so quiet! I don't need nothing. I sleep. Nobody don't bother me. If I got party for spirit, nobody don't hear. Nobody don't know my business." Then she turned to Karen with a sly smile. "You going give me this apartment?" "No way!" Karen cried. "But you can come and visit me whenever you want."

"Where you born . . . Florida?" Big Daddy asked Karen.

"No," she said, "I was born in Pennsylvania." "Your parents Jewish?" Big Daddy asked. "No," Karen replied. "Italian?" "No," she laughed. Big Daddy persisted: "What are they?" "Well, my father's family is Irish," said Karen. "Oh!" Big Daddy exclaimed. "That explain why Papa Danbala love you so much. Saint Patrick is Irish."

Alourdes, who had been rummaging in her bag for things she would need for the house blessing, continued to dig, but her voice became suddenly earnest. "Some people say to me, 'Why Karen got to marry spirit? She can't have no spirit. She white!' I say to them, 'What you think Papa Ogou is? He a white man, you know.'"

She stopped searching through her purse, looked straight at Big Daddy, and declared, "Those people say, 'Why you have to spend so much time with Karen?' I don't pay them no mind. I just do what I want. Nobody don't tell me my business! What they mean? White people can't have no spirit? Spirit for everybody!" Having said her piece, Alourdes returned her attention to the handbag open on her lap. In a few minutes, she had retrieved two white candles, a small bottle of holy water, and a plastic sack containing bits of charcoal and frankincense.

After Maggie managed to improvise an incense burner from kitchen utensils, the group gathered upstairs near the front door of the loft. Karen was directed to put a glass of water beside her door and light a candle next to it. Maggie was handed the bottle of holy water and Big Daddy the smoking incense pot. After Alourdes lighted the second candle, a few Catholic prayers were quickly recited. Then Alourdes turned to Karen, handed her the candle, and told her to "talk."

Karen looked uncertain. "What's the matter with you?" Maggie asked sharply. Alourdes stepped in to help: "Talk . . . like, you say you don't want no evil people coming in the door. Come on, Karen!" "Okay, okay. I'm going to do it," said Karen, clearing her throat.

"Let no unfriendly people come through this door," she began. "Good!" cried Alourdes. "But let lots of friends come!" Karen continued firmly. "And let me always feel good about coming through this door. And keep my home safe . . . ." Everyone chimed in: "Make Karen' house safe!"

"No evil people—" Alourdes started to say, and Maggie shouted: "That's right! No burglar, no rapist, no murderer,

no thief, no man with gun, no—" "That's enough!" broke in
Alourdes. She instructed Maggie to sprinkle holy water around
the door and told Big Daddy to pass incense all over the area.
"Don't forget that little corner," Maggie urged. "I don't want no
bad spirit hanging around."

In this manner, the group moved through the loft, stopping
at the bathrooms, the bedroom, the windows, the kitchen. As
the rite continued, Karen's tongue loosened. Standing in the
kitchen, she waxed eloquent about good food, about the importance of food in creating community, about how she wanted
many people to gather around her table. . . . Maggie staunched
the flow of rhetoric with a practical wish: "And don't let that
stove explode!"

At the end of the ritual, Alourdes suggested that Karen buy
a small statue of Lazarus (Legba, guardian of doorways and
barriers) to put next to her front door. "Just a little one," she
said, spreading her thumb and middle finger about three inches
apart. "Somebody see that, they don't think nothing about it."
Big Daddy suggested an image of Ezili Dantò as well.

An hour later, after drinks and snacks, everyone but Karen
and Alourdes disappeared downstairs to watch television. The
two women sat at the round oak table, sipping iced tea, which,
in Alourdes's case, was nearly half sugar. "I love your apartment," Alourdes said. "Very, very pretty! Only thing I don't like
is you here alone. It not good to be alone. You need somebody,
and I don't mean just to have a good time." "I know," replied
Karen.

"Beside, Karen, you getting older. Right?" "Right," Karen answered glumly. "Nobody don't get younger," observed Alourdes
without a trace of humor. "What you going do—something
happen to you, you sick, you can't work? You going go into that
store and say, 'I'm Karen Brown, give me some food?' They don't
care if you Karen Brown! That don't mean nothing." "Well . . . ,"
said Karen, "it's not that bad. I've got some protection." She
was thinking about the retirement fund and disability insurance
her university provided, but Alourdes heard something else.

"I know you got protection, because those spirit love you. But
you need somebody and . . . you got to fight for that. Let
me tell you, life is a war. You got to fight from the time you
leave your mother' belly. You got to fight for what you need!"
"I know," Karen sighed, wishing the conversation would end.

But Alourdes was not ready to drop the topic: "What you think? You can leave everything to God? You think God going watch out for you? God got too many problem for hisself. He too busy to take care of you. You got to help yourself." "Sometimes it's hard to figure out how to do that," Karen observed.

Alourdes started to say something, hesitated, and gave Karen a long, searching look. "If you find somebody, he not married and you love him—I mean really love him—you don't want to do something . . . you know . . . fix him?" Karen laughed nervously. "No," she said, "I don't like to use my will against anybody, not like that. I want a man to choose to be with me, out of his own free will—not because I did some 'work' against him."

"Look," said Alourdes, in a tone she might use with a child, "you too naïve. Nobody don't get hurt." Lowering her voice to a conspirator's whisper, she added, "Let me tell you, if I find somebody—if I really love him, I'm going bind him from top to bottom! I'm going tie him right to the floor! That's right, sweetheart. You got to help yourself; not just for man—for your job, for everything."

"Maggie going *kouche* in July," Alourdes said, apparently changing the subject. "In two month, we going to Haiti. You coming?" Karen raised her eyebrows in surprise but said nothing. Alourdes continued, "You could come inside . . . *kouche* . . . with Maggie . . . at the same time. That not going cost you a lot. I going charge you just what that cost me . . . only a little more. So, what you say, Karen? It's time you do something to protect yourself!"

"I don't know, Alourdes," Karen responded cautiously. "I'm not a Haitian . . . and I'm not sure what it would mean for me to be initiated. Do you really think I should do it?" "That up to you," Alourdes said, with a impatient shrug. Then she leaned back in her chair and opened her ample arms.

"Look at me, Karen," she said. "I got plenty confidence in myself. You want some, too?" Karen nodded her head and gave a bemused smile. "Yes . . . ," she said slowly, "yes, I do."

May 15, 1981—9:30 A.M.

Robert Gerard had been at his workbench for an hour. His SONY Walkman was on its fourth trip through his favorite

Aretha Franklin tape. His left leg jiggled up and down, but he was not keeping time to the music. His body was following some other urgent rhythm. Robert's eyes shifted from the piece of equipment in front of him to sweet, brown Carmelita seated two stations away. She had on a bright purple blouse, and he could see just the top of her cleavage.

"Plug in the calculator. Turn it on. Twenty-four times seventy-eight." Encouraging little green numbers flashed on the display panel. Carmelita shifted position, and more of her cleavage loomed into view. "Five hundred and eighty-six plus three hundred and five." Aretha picked up the beat. "Unplug the calculator. Flip it over. Check the screws on the back panel." Putting on the back panel was Carmelita's job. Robert's leg moved faster.

"Oops! A smudge." Robert removed it with a clean white cloth. He slipped the calculator into its plastic sleeve, tucked in a small slip of paper ("Inspected by No. 26"), and replaced it in a box with twenty other calculators, each in its own styrofoam slot. Then Robert removed his headset, spun himself around once on his swivel chair, and headed for the men's room. Passing Carmelita, he bent and whispered in her ear: "Lookin' gooood!" She giggled.

Robert, a black man in his early thirties, has a short, muscled body with a firm pot belly. He grew up in rural Georgia in a large family, and he was encouraged to strike out on his own when he was barely a teenager. Robert followed an older sister to New York City, where, at seventeen, he married and began his own family. He now has three children, all with names that are variations of his first name.

Alone in the bathroom, Robert risked a long look in the mirror. His face went slack for a moment but quickly recomposed itself. "Everythin' gonna be okay," he said out loud, giving himself an authoritative nod. "This is the right decision. No question about that. When a man see somethin' he wants, he got'a go for it. Better believe it! Nothin' ventured, nothin' gained. Bein' afraid never got nobody nothin'. No, sir!"

But he had clearly felt fear two months earlier when he had awakened from that dream. He had dreamed about a woman, a beautiful woman with long hair, standing by a river. She beckoned to him, saying, "You have to come in the water. You have to!" Then came the strange part. Even though he was trying to run away, he felt himself moving steadily toward her. Robert discussed the dream with Mama Lola, and Alourdes said simply, "Robert, you not going to have no peace until you wash your head. You know that, right? I going take care of that for you. Don't you worry. When Maggie go to Haiti, when she *kouche*, you coming, too."

At first, Robert had worried about the cost. But he soon figured out a way to handle the money problem, taking on a night job for the month of June. Ordinarily, he could not have worked nights, because of school, but there was no school this summer. The extra job would pay for his airplane ticket and the things he had to buy for the initiation. What he owed Alourdes, he could come up with later.

As for his other fears, Robert held them at bay with well-practiced techniques of positive thinking he had learned in a course taken several years ago. In fact, he had taken a number of self-improvement courses—yoga, est, karate—before he decided to get serious about earning his degrees. He had spent three years earning his high school equivalency certificate, and he was almost finished with a two-year college degree in business administration.

"This is the real thing! That lady know what she doin'. Lola don't fool around!" Robert assured himself as he pushed through the men's room door. Back at his bench, he replaced the Aretha Franklin tape with one that had a blank label. Robert had made this tape from the radio, and no one else was ever allowed to listen to it. It began with the 1812 Overture. Before long, Robert was lost in a clash of cymbals and another box of calculators. Only once did a fleeting memory of Maggie's voice intrude. The night before, she had called to say, "We are going July seven. I already make that reservation for you. So you better get yourself ready. You hear me, Mister Gerard?"

June 12, 1981—6:30 P.M.

Karen and Maggie sat in the little altar room in the basement of the Fort Greene house, waiting for Robert to arrive. Instruction for their initiation was to begin that night. Robert ambled in nearly an hour late, and, despite Maggie's efforts to make him feel guilty, he refused to apologize. "I was sleepin'. Everybody have to sleep some time, right?" "Besides," Robert added, "Lola is talkin' on the phone. I'm not the one holdin' things up."

"You are holding me up," Maggie announced. "Mommie going to be on the phone a long time. Since I *kouche* once before, I can just start and tell you some thing before Mommie come." "All right," said Robert, settling onto the stool by Papa Gede's altar, "you got my attention." "We going July seven," Maggie began. "American Airline. We got to be at the airport at six in the morning. Nobody better be late!" "Calm down," Robert said, "nobody gonna be late."

Maggie passed out paper and pencils. "We got to write things down, so nobody don't make no mistake! Karen, this is what you got to bring: three white scarf; two white dress, long sleeve; one white nightgown; one rosary; one thimble—" "Wait a minute!" Karen cried, "I can't write that fast."

Maggie plunged ahead: "Robert got to bring the same thing as Karen—but no dress." She giggled. "And, Robert, don't forget a little plastic bag." "What for?" he asked. "To put your *koudok* [penis] in!" Maggie shouted, and then added with a snicker, "Maybe after you go in there you going to get one." "Take it easy," Robert cautioned, "this is serious business."

Maggie ignored him and continued: "I don't want nobody to get out of line, 'cause then they got to spank you. They got a switch they keep inside that room." "Don't you worry about me," Robert said truculently. "Mommie going to be your mother, so you got to do what she say," Maggie added. "When you in that little room, you got two mother. There is the inside mother and the outside mother. Mommie is going to stay outside, but we got someone in there with us. When you go pee-pee, she is the one who empty the bucket and bring it back. She give you food. She the one got the whip, too. *Kouche* is like a . . . like a rebirth . . . like you get reborn. We going to be like baby—smell like baby, too! heh, heh—so we got to behave."

"That's right!" said Alourdes, who had just appeared at the door of the altar room. "I'm not going to spoil nobody!" She settled herself in the big, overstuffed armchair, and the instruction of the candidates began in earnest. "This is a very big step, very big decision. But don't think, when you do it, you not going need nobody. Even me . . . I need people. I can't do everything by myself. No! And don't think, when you finish, then everything going to be okay . . . you just sit down, wait for luck to come. I don't got no luck to give you. You still got to help yourself. This one big, big, big, long step; but every day after that you still got to shuwa . . . shuwa . . . shuwa." Alourdes made a shuffling sound and moved her hands like feet stepping along a path. "Even me, I'm not finish. I got to walk every day just like you . . . shuwa . . . shuwa . . . shuwa. And don't think that going make you a wealthy person. Oh, no! Do I got a lot'a money?"

"Everybody who go in together, they brother and sister," Alourdes said. "I am your mother—not your real mother, you don't come from the stomach—but I your mother . . . by spirit . . . by God. So after we finish, when I have a party for spirit, I call you. Everybody come and help me. When Robert need something, he call Karen. It like one hand wash the other hand. And when we finish, everybody got to make a *mèsi*—like you say thank you . . . like you a slave and those spirit give you freedom."

"After you finish *kouche*, you keep the head covered, forty day from the day you go inside," she instructed. "And don't let nobody put the hands on your head! And no *chou-chou*! You hear me? No *chou-chou*! I mean that." "What's *chou-chou*?" Karen asked. Maggie jumped up from her chair. "You know . . . you are together with your boyfriend, you two go *chou-chou-chou-chou*," she said, giggling and pumping her hips.

Alourdes leaned forward in her chair and looked directly at Karen. "And don't tell nobody what go on when you in there. That your secret. Even they give you money, don't say nothing!" "I'm not going to tell the secrets," Karen said defensively. "That's right!" said Alourdes, sitting back in her chair. "You do that— you going die."

July 7, 1981—7:45 P.M.

In the long light of early evening, the mountains surrounding Port-au-Prince on three sides had flattened out like stage sets. In the cemetery, above-ground tombs cast long lavender shadows. The dead seemed to be as crowded as passengers on a *taptap*. In the center of the cemetery, countless monuments to individuals and families pushed up out of a single mass of concrete—the individual and the group, the one and the many, perennial human dilemmas as unresolved in cemetery architecture as they were in the minds of four struggling initiates.

Alourdes and two helpers were leading the way through the vast necropolis. Trailing behind were Robert and Karen, Maggie and Mimose. Maggie was wearing culottes, an off-the-shoulder blouse, and stiletto heels. From the moment the group had boarded the plane early that morning, she had been resisting her mother's authority. But once inside the cemetery, the sharp tongue and chaotic energy had given way to a cleaner expression of fear. Maggie whined and sniffled as she moved awkwardly on the narrow, uneven paths between the tombs. Once she stumbled and fell. Before long, she was at the tag end of the parade, and she was crying.

Alourdes glanced back at Maggie, shrugged her shoulders in disgust, and pushed on with a rapid, determined step. After twice heading down blind alleys and doubling back, Alourdes finally located her mother's tomb. Libations of *kleren* were poured by Philo's grave, and candles were lit in the niches at its base. On the ground in front of the tomb, the first of three baths for the initiates was prepared. Four calabash shell bowls were filled with *kleren* and water. Alourdes carried two bundles of leaves, one a bunch of glossy green marigold leaves and the other powdery grey wormwood. Alourdes's helpers, Mimose's brother Sonny and his friend Yves, were pressed into service mixing the baths. Plunging their hands into the bowls, they mashed the leaves and rubbed them together until the liquid turned dark green and the herbs were reduced to a sodden pulp. Alourdes then led one initiate after another behind Philo's tomb.

"Quick! Take off your clothes," she said to Karen. "We don't got all day!" Karen winced at the thought of her glaringly white body so exposed in this busy city of the dead. Nevertheless, she took a deep breath and began to peel off her dress. "Oh, well," she said to herself, "I can write about this part. It will be worth it." Karen's field journal had begun to serve the same function as Maggie's flamboyant clothing. In clinging to it, she clung to an adult identity that she hoped would arrest a perilous slide toward helpless infancy. Robert had been using his masculinity in much the same way. All day, he had been under Alourdes's feet, helping with this, giving unsolicited advice about that. Mimose was handling the role of obedient child more gracefully than any of them.

"Take this," Alourdes said, shoving a lighted candle toward Karen, "and pray. Ask Philo to help you. Hurry up! Somebody coming." Painfully aware of a man lingering in the shadow of a tomb less than twenty yards away, and shivering despite the warm air, Karen managed to concentrate her mind on Philo for all of one minute.

"Haven't you got nothing raggedy, something you can throw away?" demanded Alourdes. Karen picked up her red underpants, tugged at them until they ripped in two places, and handed them to Alourdes. Alourdes put them in the gourd containing the remnants of the herbal bath, and then she sent the whole thing sailing far from Philo's overgrown tomb, up in the air and away, into an intense mauve sky. In flight, the gourd turned slowly round and round like a saucer. It disappeared behind a glowing alabaster tomb without spilling any of its liquid contents. But the underpants, once free of the gourd, continued to fly away, a small red bird headed straight for the setting sun.

It was almost dark by the time the four initiates left the cemetery. Damp clothing clung to their bodies. Maggie was walking barefoot, her high heels dangling from one hand. Bits of leaves and tiny twigs were visible on their cheeks and collarbones. Heady aromas filled their nostrils, making them light-headed and a little giddy.

July 8, 1981—5:00 P.M.

Karen was in her room at the Toussaint L'Ouverture Guest House, sleeping soundly for the first time in two days. Alourdes suddenly burst through the door. "The drums already start. Hurry up! Hurry up!" Alourdes threw a box of cotton balls and some nail polish remover onto the bed. "Get that nail polish off—toes, too! You can't wear no nail polish inside." So suddenly awakened from a sleep padded by tropical heat, Karen felt her heart pounding. Clumsy fingers refused to cooperate as she tried to remove the polish from her fingers and toes. Her blouse was only half tucked into her skirt and perspiration trickled down her face as she climbed into the taxi that would carry them the short distance to Madame Rigaud's temple, where the ceremonies were to take place.

As the taxi edged into the dusty swarm of vehicles on the

Carrefour road, Alourdes was still discussing price with the driver. He said four dollars; she said three. The initiates, wedged into the back seat, talked in stage whispers. Alourdes, fearing that the group might appear to be tourists, who would be charged more as a matter of course, tried a covert warning. "Ta-da, de-da, la, la, la," she sang in her rich, full voice, "don't speak Engleeesh!" Karen, sensing the possibility of a problem larger than the language they spoke, responded with a song made up on the spot:

> *O, manman'm se nwa, papa'm se nwa.*
> *Kouman yo sezi, lè'm sòti blan.*

> Oh, my mother was black, my father was black.
> How surprised they were, when I came out white.

Mimose and Maggie quickly picked up the song. Robert, who could not understand the words, nevertheless joined in, even adding a little syncopated thigh-slapping. Soon the taxi was rolling into the narrow rutted lane leading to Madame Rigaud's temple. Alourdes was still laughing as she handed the driver four dollars and waved him off.

The mood in the temple was in stark contrast to their frivolity. As they cleared the door, Madame Rigaud's assistant cracked a writhing bull whip within inches of their toes. The whip cracked three times. The ritual called *bat gè* (fighting the war) was in full swing. From the drums at the far end of the *peristil* (temple) came urgent Petwo rhythms.

A dozen people were clustered around the entrance to the Petwo altar room. Inside, four of Madame Rigaud's *ounsi* (ritual assistants) were seated on a white sheet. Each held a knife and a fork, and they kept time to the music by beating the utensils on metal plates. In their midst sat a curious animated bottle wrapped in red sequined cloth. A cork had been impaled on a spindle emerging from the bottle. The tines of two forks had been stuck into the cork; their handles sloped downward. One of the *ounsi* kept the forks constantly spinning, like a miniature airplane ride at a carnival. Two men with red scarves tied tightly around their biceps stood in the center of the Petwo chamber, each wielding a sword. Their swords clanged together on every third beat of the knives and forks.

Madame Rigaud leaned into the Petwo chamber and blew a fine mist of hot-pepper rum over the ritualizers. The *ounsi* squinted and ducked, trying to protect their eyes from its pungent fire. With lightning speed, the whip, a good ten feet long, slithered across the floor of the *peristil* and delivered a loud crack just in front of the drums. The hands of the lead drummer exploded in a burst of energy and sound. The war had begun, and it was being fought for Maggie and Mimose, Karen and Robert.

July 9, 1981—11:00 P.M.

The initiates, dressed in white, were sequestered in a back room of Madame Rigaud's temple. They were unable to participate in, or even see, the elaborate ritual called *chire ayizan* (shredding the *ayizan*), which was being performed in the *peristil*. But they could hear the drums and, beneath their sound, the soft slapping of dancers' bare feet on a beaten earth floor. Outside, six *ounsi*, all in white, swirled around the sacred center pole, shredding a single, gigantic palm leaf as they danced. The final product of their ritual labors was the *ayizan*, a protective palm fringe hung over the door to the initiation chamber.

Just before midnight, Maggie and Mimose, Karen and Robert were brought out and lined up at one end of the temple before a crowd of fifty or sixty people. Many of them approached the initiates to say good-bye. It was as if these four were about to die. Family and friends hugged and kissed them. Tears were rolling down the cheeks of many. Then the initiates were directed, through the words of a song, to swear allegiance seven times before their mother. Alourdes stood before them, surveying her children with a somber eye. Four right hands were raised palm outward, seven times, and then darkness suddenly descended. From behind them, blindfolds were whipped out and bound tightly over their eyes.

Karen was grabbed from behind by a woman whose bosom felt as wide and soft as a river delta. Mimose was grasped about the waist by someone with sinewy arms that felt like steel.

Maggie and Robert each had their doubles pressed hard up against their backs. The drums quickened. Intricate, intoxicating Petwo rhythms were pounding in the ears of the initiates as each began to dance with his or her shadow. Mimose did not need to see in order to dance. Her slender body moved instinctively into the complex polyrhythms. Her feet, not touching but in perfect union with the feet of her shadow, moved rapidly forward and backward to a staccato beat, while her shoulders pulsed to another beat, folding inward and stretching back as if they were attached to giant butterfly wings and she were trying to fly away.

Karen was in a cold sweat. She knew she could not do this dance. She had tried many times, but she had always ended up feeling like an elephant in its death throes. In the excitement of the moment, however, she forgot these failures, and suddenly she was dancing . . . though not through her own efforts. Her body was like a rag doll bound to the body of her partner. The woman's legs moved, hers moved. The woman's shoulders moved, hers moved.

"Not bad!" Karen thought. "But I had better pay attention." As soon as the thought entered her head, the two of them veered to one side, and Karen banged her shin painfully on a chair. Karen understood the situation perfectly. She knew exactly what she must do. "Let go! Let go! Let go!" the inner voice shouted, as she and her dancing partner hobbled and lurched around and around and around the center pole. After a very long time, someone shouted in her ear: "*Leve pye ou* [Lift your feet]!" and she and the others were whisked into the aromatic rock-hard, leaf-soft bower where they would *kouche*—lie down, sleep, make love, die—and be reborn.

Sometime later that night . . . or perhaps it was early the next morning. . . . It was hard to keep track of time when the drums kept pounding and candles provided the only light. Day and night got mixed up . . . and so did dream and reality. Still, this occurrence seems likely enough. Karen opened her eyes and saw a hairy black spider the width of a teacup making its way down the wall. Suppressing a shudder, she tried to make a joke. "Look there," she whispered, poking Maggie in the arm. "Papa Gede has come for a visit!" "That is just a spider!" Maggie hissed. "You know Papa Gede cannot come in here! He is not allowed."

The initiates, carrying red roses and dressed in white, with strings of multicolored beads crisscrossed on their chests like bandoliers, stepped backward out of the initiation chamber and then turned in confusing spirals as they made their way into the *peristil*. They were at once newborn babies and gangly adolescents on a too-rapid path to adulthood. Their heads were doubly covered in scarves and straw hats, as if to protect vulnerable soft spots on the top of the skull. Their faces, not yet ready for the full light of day, were obscured with palm fringe.

Cheers and applause greeted them. They had survived their trials. They had faced the fire and learned that one could choose to call it strong rather than hot. They had drunk from the mouth of death. They had tasted the sword of justice. They had been changed. They were changing. The final forms that would emerge were not yet clear. In other words, they had been reborn into the human family, this time better equipped to pit will and strength against fate. That was the most that could have been done. Life would go on, and, as always, fate remained the joker in the deck of cards.

November 2, 1987—3:00 A.M.

Fifteen people were gathered in Alourdes's basement in Brooklyn to honor Papa Gede. The walls were peppered with dancing skeletons, all Hallmark Halloween decorations. Orange and black crepe paper defined the niche. The altar table was draped in more traditional Gede colors, purple and black. It looked like funeral bunting. Alourdes's ritual assistants, Maggie, Karen, and Robert, were dipping and turning before the altars, pouring libations for Papa Gede. The group offered song after song in an attempt to draw Gede into their company. Then they launched a new song for a Gede called Nan Mitan Kay (In the Midst of the Home). It was a simple song with a haunting lyric: "Nan Mitan Kay, how are you? How are you? Nan Mitan Kay, I know you are there."

Suddenly Maggie began to cry. Robert and Karen instinctively moved toward her. "I'm okay," she said, sniffing back her tears and giving her head a definitive shake. "I was just now thinking about Mimose. When we was little kids, playing together, me and Mimose, we used to make food for Nan Mitan Kay. Put some cookie on a plate, leave it for him. You know . . . just kids playing. We thought we made him up. Later, my mother tell me someone way back in our family, they got a Gede called Nan Mitan Kay."

"I miss Mimose . . . ," said Maggie, tears again appearing in her eyes. "Me too," said Karen. "Me too," said Robert. The three stood, their arms around one another, singing, "Nan Mitan Kay, I know you are there."

Gede, trickster and spirit of death, had no place in the initiation chamber in 1981, but four years later he dropped stealthily into the midst of Mimose's humble home and sent the place reeling. In the fall of 1985, in the turbulent months preceding the downfall of Jean Claude Duvalier, Jacques, the father of Mimose's child, had been arrested on a charge of distributing anti-Duvalier leaflets. It had taken six agonizing months for Mimose to learn that he had been killed within hours of his arrest. In the spring of 1987, when most Haitians were busy nourishing a flickering flame of hope for their country, a drunken Mimose stumbled onto the Carrefour road, directly into the path of an oncoming vehicle. Several days later, she died in her mother's arms. The family is still not certain whether it was internal injuries from the accident or the ravages of alcohol that killed this gentle, hungry priestess . . . the best dancer of them all.

CHAPTER TWELVE

Gede

When asked to describe Gede, Vodou spirit of death, Alourdes said, "Papa Gede is a cemetery man. He live in the cemetery, but that not mean he's bad. He very good man. He love children a lot. He love woman a lot. He a very sexy man. Sometime he say a bad word, but . . . he love everybody. He love to help people. When people sick—all kind'a sickness—that's his job to help."

Gede is Alourdes's main helper in the healing work she performs. All the Vodou spirits get involved in healing in one way or another, but only Gede claims it as his main job description. And even when Papa Gede does not make an appearance (through dream or trance) in the course of a particular treatment, his spirit pervades the situation.

Two different chromolithographs are commonly used to represent Gede, one of Saint Gabriel and the other of Saint Gerard. In both, handsome young men in black clerical dress contemplate a human skull juxtaposed to a sprig of fresh flowers. But in Gabriel's image, the more popular of the two, the saint's gaze actually falls just beside the skull, onto the framed picture of an appealing young woman.

Papa Gede, as Alourdes usually calls him, is a trickster spirit. Through his randy, playful, childish, and childlike personality Gede raises life energy and redefines the most painful situation—even death itself—as one worth a good laugh. Gede is a transformation artist, and this is the reason he is also the principal healer among the Vodou *lwa*.

The Gede (there are many of them) are different from other Vodou spirits. They are neither Rada nor Petwo. In fact, they do not even form a *nanchon* (nation), as the other spirits do. Their aggregate is described by the more intimate term *fanmi* (family).

◄ Temple wall painting of Saint Gerard (Gede). Port-au-Prince, 1980.

No other group of spirits is described this way. Papa Gede sits at the center of the thick weave of relationships that make up a family—an ideal place for a healer to be, because all Vodou healing is the healing of relationships.[1]

This concluding chapter first discusses healing as Alourdes practices it within the Vodou system. In this section, Papa Gede's presence will be more implicit than explicit. In a paradoxical way, which Gede himself would relish, the appropriateness of his presiding over the healing arts emerges clearly in the second half of the chapter, where attention is actually focused on his other areas of expertise: sex, satire, children, and cemeteries. The discussion of healing begins, in Papa Gede's mode, with a story.

JAMAICA

Early on the morning of January 12, 1980, Alourdes and I met inside the international building at Kennedy Airport. We were traveling together, first to Jamaica and then Haiti. We had been planning the trip to Haiti—our visit to Alourdes's ancestral homes—for some time, but Jamaica had been added to our itinerary at the last moment. When the possibility first arose, a week before our departure, Alourdes seemed to assume that I would go to Jamaica with her. She had been hired to do some healing work for a woman who owned a dairy farm near Kingston. The farm was big, Alourdes said, and there was plenty of room for both of us to stay. The work would not take long, and after that we would fly directly to Port-au-Prince. Forty-eight hours before our departure, Alourdes began to hedge. She suggested it might be better if I met her in Haiti. I persisted, telling her I really wanted to see the "treatment" she was going to do. Alourdes finally agreed to my going, but with something short

[1] For further discussion of healing within the Haitian Vodou system, see two articles by Karen McCarthy Brown: "Afro-Caribbean Spirituality: A Haitian Case Study," in Healing and Restoring: Medicine and Health in the World's Religious Traditions, ed. Lawrence Sullivan (New York: Macmillan, 1989), 255–85; and "The Power to Heal: Reflections on Women, Religion, and Medicine," in Shaping New Vision: Gender and Values in American Culture, ed. Clarissa W. Atkinson, Constance H. Buchanan, and Margaret R. Miles, Harvard Women's Studies in Religion Series (Ann Arbor, Mich.: UMI Research Press, 1987), 123–41.

of full enthusiasm. We were in line at the check-in counter when the reason for her reluctance appeared on the scene.

Mabel Wycliff, breathless and complaining, bustled through the automatic doors under the sign marked Pan American Airways. She had enough distance on her husband, who was dragging two overstuffed suitcases, for the doors to close and open again before he made it into the terminal. Mabel plunked down two bulging handbags at our feet. Her greeting was a continuation of a rant apparently begun long before she arrived at the airport. "No cross, no crown," Mabel announced in her Jamaican lilt. Ever so quickly, her eye flicked over me, and she raised a quizzical brow but said nothing. Her verbal train was running on a well-oiled track.

"Always doin' for me family. Up since four o'clock makin' chicken wings and rice, so there be food in the refrigerator. That man just lay in bed, too lazy to get himself up and help. And him forget me little blue bag. It got all me things for the Haiti business in it, and that man forget! Lola, the white dress you tell me to buy, the sheet—all in that bag. That man is full'a dust! Full'a donkey dust." Her husband, Oswald, had joined the group by then, and from a jumble of opinions a decision somehow emerged that Oswald would race home for the missing grip. He might make it back before our plane left; if not, he would put the bag on the next Kingston flight, and we could collect it at the airport.

Mabel is a toffee-colored woman in her early fifties. She has a short, squat body and a no-nonsense, high-energy personality. Mabel fancies herself the only pole in a one-pole tent. In relation to her family, at least, there is some truth to this. Her husband always seems a little dazed; and, if Mabel is to be believed, her children generate one crisis after another to which she must apply her heroic and self-sacrificing energy. Her work life may be more rewarding, but it is not less demanding. Five days a week, she commutes from New Jersey to Long Island, where she works in a hospital geriatric ward. Mabel must be a lively presence for the old people she talks about with genuine affection.

As we headed down the ramp to the plane, I whispered a rhetorical question to Alourdes: "Mabel is going with us?" "Of course Mabel going!" Alourdes responded, full voice. "Mabel going to get her head wash' in Haiti. She got a lot of problem.

She got to do that so she can help herself. But first we going to Kingston, because I got a little thing to do for her son." "What about the woman with the dairy farm?" I asked. "That the real reason we going, but I just tell Mabel I do this little thing for her, too," Alourdes responded.

"Where are we going to stay?" I whispered. "We going to stay with Mabel' family. Okay, Karen?" She sounded annoyed. "But did you tell Mabel I was coming?" I persisted. "No . . . ," Alourdes answered slowly, as if she had to think about the question. "I forget. But that don't matter. Caribbean people not like that. You come to stay in their house, they always gonna be glad to see you coming. Don't you worry, sweetheart."

We sat three abreast in the smoking section. Alourdes and Mabel kept their hats on throughout the flight. Mabel leafed through a copy of *American Woman*, and both ordered double Tia Marias. Each slipped one small bottle of the sweet liqueur into her purse, along with packages of crackers and cheese from the snack tray. "That Tia Maria for Sonny," Alourdes said, referring to her nephew, who lives in Philo's old house in downtown Port-au-Prince.

Inside the Kingston airport, Alourdes turned to me and said, "Jamaicans not like us. They don't talk like us. They don't dress nice like us. They the biggest thief." "*Un, de, twa,*" she added, dropping into the privacy of Creole, "*yo vòlè ou* [One, two, three, they rob you]." Then, seeing a man with dreadlocks across the way, Alourdes turned up her nose and observed that "Rastas" do not take baths.

Alourdes's anxiety at being away from home and in a place she had never visited before took the form of strong Haitian chauvinism. On the way into town from the airport, she pointed to various trees. "Mango. We got mango in Haiti, plenty mango. . . . Breadfruit. We got big breadfruit in Haiti." The only tree Alourdes had never seen was the *ackee*. The taxi driver stopped so we could get out and inspect one, and Mabel promised that we would soon taste Jamaica's national dish, *ackee* with cod fish. Alourdes looked at the hard red fruit suspiciously.

Among the local plants, most were familiar to Alourdes, though not by their Jamaican names. An orange spaghettilike creeper that slowly kills the shrubs it covers is called love bush in Jamaica. "In Haiti, we call that *lamitye* [friendship]," Alourdes announced with a self-satisfied smile. I identified some plants as African violets, but the Jamaican driver told me they were Russian violets; Alourdes responded that neither name was right, but she had forgotten the "real name."

Then the competition turned from nature to commerce. Alourdes asked: "In Jamaica, you have Bank of Nova Scotia? You have Bank of Canada? You have Citibank?" The driver responded affirmatively to the first two but was uncertain about Citibank. "In Haiti, we got big, big Citibank. New building . . . beautiful," Alourdes said as she leaned back, contented for a while to let the striking scenery of the Kingston Bay mountain range roll past. Not far from the airport, white sand beaches backed by soft lavender mountains began to sprout oil refineries: Esso, Texaco, Shell. I noticed that Esso gas sold for the equivalent of more than two dollars a gallon at a service station within sight of the pier where the huge Esso tankers loaded and unloaded.

When we were finally settled in with Mabel's aunt in her tiny, neat-as-a-pin house in the Ligaunae section of Saint Andrew's parish outside Kingston, I mentioned my shock at the high gasoline prices. That comment opened a conversational floodgate. Jamaicans—unlike Haitians, who are well schooled in the value of silence on any matter relating to the government—are habitually, persistently political. No conversation of any duration is without its political dimension.

That evening, when we gathered in the parlor around a kerosene lamp (a blackout was in effect), Mabel's extended family held forth on a wide variety of topics ranging from the role of the World Bank in Jamaica's economy to the upcoming elections. Aunt Emma was unhappy with the socialist tendencies of the current government led by Michael Manley; by way of protest, she spoke warmly and often of the United States: "Americans are good people. Good Christian people. Them always helpin' the poor." In this crowd, most of whom lived with hard-won if precarious dignity, only Mabel's twenty-three-year-old son, Edmund, sounded a different note: "Them say the capitalists sabotagin' the economic reforms Manley been tryin'." Mabel later said to me in confidence and, I suspect, as an attempt to explain her son: "Edmund not a Rasta, but him Rasta-minded."

Aunt Emma, who had lived in Cuba for thirteen years, where she had cooked and cleaned for the American commander at Guantánamo Bay, was a vigorous eighty-three years old when

Alourdes and I met her in 1980. She remembered Marcus Garvey, "a small man." "Me can just see the little man walkin' up King Road. Everybody was jumpin' and pushin', just to see Garvey." Aunt Emma had even owned shares in the Black Star Line, which Garvey started in the 1940s to take blacks back to Africa. In her old age, however, she had apparently lost her taste for radical politics and did not care to analyze the larger causes of the backbreaking inflation Jamaica was experiencing. She knew it had started with Manley, and she wanted Manley out so it would end.

If the truth be told, the core of Emma George's life was not politics but religion, and perhaps this had always been the case. Aunt Emma (in deference to her age and experience, Alourdes and I also called her Aunt Emma) had sung in the choir of Saint Margaret's Episcopal Church for decades. She kept her starched white collar and her red cap fresh and ready; on Sunday mornings, she put them on before she left the house. She was one of the first members of Saint Margaret's and remembers when they met in a lean-to and sat on the floor while Reverend Gilmartin, an Englishman, led the service. She proudly showed us an anniversary publication of the church containing a picture of her 1924 wedding. She wore a wonderful flapper-style wedding dress (purchased in Havana, "in the French store"), and her young husband wore a solemn face, a dark suit, and a high collar.

Aunt Emma lived in a turquoise and white house at the downhill end of a community that became more and more slumlike as it climbed the mountain behind. Her home was filled with crocheted doilies, starched to stand-up firmness, and lots of pictures—pictures cut from greeting cards, wedding pictures, family portraits, pictures of Queen Elizabeth, Robert Kennedy, and Bustamante (Jamaica's first prime minister after the island gained its independence from Britain). Her china cabinet was filled with shiny treasures that looked like silver or crystal but might as easily have been plastic or aluminum. Beneath Aunt Emma's bed was a rack of shoes. Three pairs were freshly coated with shoewhite, ready to complete her Sunday-morning outfit. At the time I met her, church was about the only thing that took Aunt Emma away from Barbicon Road. And when she was at home, she listened to radio evangelists. She did not like Billy Graham: "If you do not send fifty dollars, forget it!" But she thought Oral Roberts was better: "Him good. Him always send you right to the Bible."

In deference to her religious beliefs, no one told Aunt Emma that Alourdes was there to perform Vodou healing ceremonies or that one of them was for Edmund, a member of her own family. When Alourdes asked her for milk one evening, Aunt Emma assumed she wanted to drink it before retiring. Instead, Alourdes dumped it into a shallow tin basin, added some cinnamon, and put the concoction on the stove to boil. When it was hot, she poured in most of a bottle of Florida Water. Aunt Emma turned her back and went to bed.

The milk bath was the second of three good-luck baths prescribed by Alourdes to help Edmund get a visa to travel to the United States. Alourdes mixed the baths in either the kitchen or the bathroom and administered them in a small wooden structure in the side yard, which served as a shower stall. On three occasions, Alourdes and Edmund went outdoors late at night carrying a candle, a basin, and a large towel. A half hour later, Edmund came back inside wearing only the towel, his body glistening, small bits of leaves still visible on his skin. Nothing was really hidden from Aunt Emma, but the treatments were carried out discreetly enough that she did not have to acknowledge what was going on. The tension in the house grew nevertheless. By our last night in Jamaica, Alourdes realized she had some repair work to do.

There was another blackout, and we gathered in candlelight around the kitchen table. Alourdes looked wonderful that evening. She was wearing a lavender caftan and large gold hoop earrings, with her hair tied in a colorful scarf. Alourdes had dressed up and turned on the charm. At first, the talk was casual, but before long she deftly turned the conversation to religion. Soon Aunt Emma was talking enthusiastically about her "strong spirit." She said that she had an instant sense of people, that she knew the minute she set foot in a house if she was going to like the people there and if they were going to like her. She claimed she could sleep alone, walk anywhere, and never be afraid.

Her niece Mabel, a Catholic, told how her religion had always prevented her from having anything to do with the African religions still practiced in Jamaica. But she did admit going to the Sundial once when she was a child. The Sundial, she explained, was a dance that went on for twenty-one days. The participants did not eat for the entire time. They just danced and danced until "them fall down." Mabel said nothing about having changed her attitude toward these religions.

Alourdes chose this moment to tell a tale of her own, a strategic one that gave her the opportunity to establish her Christian credentials before Aunt Emma. She told of a potential client who had once been a dues-paying member of a satanic group. "Listen," Alourdes reported saying to the troubled young woman, "you going to pay 'til you die. Even you don't send them money, you going pay. Satan more powerful than me. I am a Christian; I don't have nothing to do with him." Alourdes concluded her story with a vehement: "I sent her home!" Then, almost as an afterthought, she mentioned that the Book of Daniel in the Bible tells how to identify the children of Satan.

Aunt Emma's ears perked up at the mention of her beloved Bible. She described her favorite little paperback of the psalms, "printed in America," that she kept with her wherever she went. It told her what the lines of each psalm meant, what life problems each addressed, and what time of day was best for reading each one. "You have to believe what you read, mon," Aunt Emma said with real feeling. "You have to believe and keep on believin'. You have to believe in God." "And in yourself," Alourdes added. "And in yourself."

After this conversation, the differences between Aunt Emma's spirituality and that of Alourdes were both less and more apparent. More than once, I have heard Alourdes and Maggie describe the protection afforded by the Vodou spirits in practically the same words Aunt Emma had used about her "strong spirit"; and Aunt Emma's use of the little book of psalms suggested what might be loosely called a magical attitude toward the scriptures. But in other ways the gap between Aunt Emma's Anglican piety and Alourdes's commitment to Vodou yawned wider and deeper than ever. Aunt Emma lived a scrupulously moral life and each night humbly surrendered herself into God's hands, accepting whatever happened as "God's will." Although Alourdes had been too polite to say so that evening, she thought God was far too busy to set the terms of each individual life. For her, spiritual labor was only one kind of labor that all people who were not either foolish or lazy performed for themselves and their families. Furthermore, Alourdes surrendered to no one and had no problem using her will in the spiritual arena or in any other.

Three days before this conversation, when two of Edmund's

three good-luck baths were finished, Alourdes had turned to the treatment that had been the original reason for our trip to Jamaica. On January 16, we hired a taxi and headed out to Cecile Shepherd's dairy farm. Cecile, a shy and appealing mulatto woman in her mid-thirties with a light scatter of freckles on her nose and soft curly hair, was in the middle of a crisis the day we arrived. She ran a large farm in Bushy Park, which she had inherited from her parents. The electricity had been out in the area for more than twenty-four hours, and Cecile had two hundred cows who needed milking. It appeared that somehow she would have to milk them by hand—and even then she probably would have to throw the milk away, because she had no refrigeration. In the midst of all this Alourdes arrived, clearly signaling that she expected Cecile to drop everything and extend her the hospitality due someone of her stature.

Alourdes had been hired to "treat" a thirty-acre parcel of land for which Cecile could find no buyer. Alourdes had been called in on this case by one of her own apprentices, a woman she had initiated, who had begun the job but had not been able to complete it. A card reading by the apprentice had indicated that someone had done "work" against Cecile. That person's influence needed to be removed to clear the way for the sale. For such serious business, the apprentice had deferred to her "mother," Alourdes. As it turned out, the land problem was only the most superficial layer of the deep trouble that beset Cecile Shepherd.

At their first meeting, Alourdes spent most of her time talking with Cecile. She did not perform the customary diagnostic card reading, I suspect, because her apprentice had already done one, and she did not want to appear to undercut that effort. Alourdes often uses a preliminary card reading to get people to open up and begin to tell their life stories. ("They have to tell me all those story if I going help them.") With Cecile, she accomplished the same purpose with a few hours of questions and empathic listening. When the time came to deal more directly with business, Alourdes offered Cecile strong assurances: "When I do that work for you, you going sell that property— bam! Just like that."

Before leaving, Alourdes carefully instructed Cecile about the materials she would need for the treatment of the land, including several kinds of plants. Alourdes also used this opportunity to get "leaves"—marigold (*sowosi*) and congo bean—she needed for Edmund's last good-luck bath. But she wanted a particular plant for Cecile's treatment and could not remember either the Creole or the English name. Cecile and Alourdes, two people who clearly lived on more familiar terms with the plant world than I could begin to comprehend, put their heads together.

"It just a little thing. You don't eat it." Alourdes searched for a way to describe what she knew so well. "Don't make tea with it. No, no tea. It grow on the ground. You walk right by it. You not even going see it. It little, real little, but you look, you see it got leaf like that," she said, pointing upward to the leaves of the large mimosa we were sitting under. Cecile's face lit up, and she cried out eagerly: "And when you touch it, it curls up!" Alourdes beamed, "That the one!" "We call that shimalady," Cecile said with satisfaction, explaining that the name derived from the phrase "Shame, my lady." "I saw some just the other day by the stream that cut across the back'a me land," Cecile added. "Good!" said Alourdes. "You get that one, too."

As we stood by the taxi with its motor running, Alourdes dropped her voice to a whisper and said to Cecile, "I going to help you with your man, too. I need that plant 'cause that the way your husband going to be with you. He going to bow the head in front of you, just like that plant." Then she added special instructions: "When you pick it, you take it with the root. And you got to leave something when you do that. It don't got to be a lot, but you got to leave something. One penny . . . two penny." As we got into the taxi, Alourdes leaned out the window and said: "The plant—call it by his name. Don't forget!"

The next day, Alourdes, Mabel, and I arrived early. Cecile provided a large pail of water, to which, after candles were lit and prayers offered, seven limes, a handful of ashes, Florida Water, and molasses were added.[2] After the pail of water was ritually treated, the remaining half-bottle of Florida Water was infused with indigo powder, which turned it a deep blue.

[2]Limes are valued for their prophylactic properties; Haitians use them, for example, to "clean" meat before marinating and cooking it. Alourdes explained that limes were included in the treatment to deal with the malevolent influence of outsiders. The ashes were those of a piece of paper on which a "prayer," a statement of intent concerning the land sale, had been written. Molasses is a sweetener of both business deals and individuals, and Florida Water is a libation frequently offered to the spirits.

After lunch, the four of us loaded Cecile's truck with the materials for the *trètmen* (treatment) and headed for the parcel of land. We began at a spot where prospective buyers entered the property. Alourdes made the sign of the cross and raised an egg to each of the four directions. She repeated this with a cup of molasses. Next, she broke the egg and, walking into the field, dribbled its contents in a line pointing toward the center of the property. A trail of thick molasses was laid on top of the egg. And finally a dipper of the treated water was added on top of that.

Then Alourdes walked to the furthest corner of the property. The original plan was to treat all four corners, but this proved too difficult in the overgrown field. Vodou rituals, like all other elements of Haitian life, easily bend to the exigencies of the moment. After treating one corner, we pushed on to the center of the field, getting tangled up in plenty of devil's horsewhip on the way. As we waded through the undergrowth, Alourdes tossed out dipper after dipper of the brew from the pail in a neat, straight line in front of her, tracing a path from the far corner to the middle of the plot, where the vegetation was waist-high. She scattered most of the rest of the treated water there, along with about half of the indigo Florida Water. "Let's go back," Alourdes said, dropping the cap to the Florida Water. Always the teacher when in the company of budding apprentices, she added: "See, I don't pick up nothing I drop." The dipper was also discarded in the middle of the field.

We fought our way back to the road and were about to get into the truck when Alourdes remembered that one more thing must be done. Cecile was instructed to throw seven bright copper pennies into the field, saying, "I buy this land and I pay for it. Now I'm going to sell it." With this action, Cecile defined the sale of the field as a purely monetary transaction and therefore one from which she could walk away free and clear. When exercising the will, an action that lies at the heart of all Vodou treatments, it is important that certain exchanges be clean and well defined, with no troubling entanglements that could pull a person back to a prior state. This is also why Alourdes left behind the containers and implements used in her ritualizing and why she had earlier instructed Cecile to leave a few pennies when she picked the shimalady.

We got back into the truck and drove down a narrow dirt

track to the property's water source, another place where prospective buyers were taken. Here, we completely emptied the pail and also dumped the last of the blue Florida Water into a clear, shallow pool formed at the point where water emerged from rock. Alourdes turned, threw the empty Florida Water bottle over her shoulder, and walked to the truck without looking back.

As Cecile talked about her problem that afternoon, I noticed she had already begun to turn away from seeing it as a simple matter of being unable to sell some land. "Everything I put my hand to, it just go wrong," she complained. "Your luck no good," Alourdes said, "but don't you worry, we going to find the source of that problem."

Cecile mused aloud: "The business about me husband . . . I don't know. . . . All of a sudden, he just get bored with his family. Now he like to spend all his time in Florida. He call, he call. He want to see us. When we get there, he doesn't want anything to do with us." She volunteered that a woman had answered the telephone several times when she called her husband in Miami. In fact, she said, there were several different women, but one in particular—a stewardess—was the likely source of her trouble. Somehow Cecile had heard that the stewardess had gone to Haiti and hired someone to "do something" against her.

Alourdes smiled but said nothing when she received this crucial bit of information. Other Caribbean peoples tend to look down on impoverished and illiterate Haitians, but there is also a widespread belief that you must go to Haiti for the most powerful medicines. This attitude may explain not only the action of the stewardess but also why Cecile turned for help to a Haitian healer.

On the drive back to the main house, I asked Cecile how she felt about other women staying at her husband's Miami apartment. She replied with remarkable equanimity, "They always move out when I come." When I asked if she had ever had other lovers, she admitted, "Yes, once." She also said she had told her husband about it afterward and then endured weeks of his anger. She said simply, "I am always honest, you know." Cecile seemed to accept her husband's infidelity and even the double standard that condemned hers. But she could not accept his absence: "I want me family back together." With this conversation, the problem with the plot of land was at last seen in its proper context. It was a by-product of a much deeper disturbance in Cecile Shepherd's family.

When we returned to Cecile's house, the long shadows of afternoon had turned her yard into a cool haven. Alourdes, Mabel, and I rested under the trees. We treated the welts raised on our legs by devil's horsewhip with handfuls of Chivas Regal (the only alcohol Cecile had in the house), while Cecile went to gather the things needed for the second, and by now clearly more important, stage of the treatment. As we waited, Cecile's two youngest children ran around the yard, shouting nursery rhymes at each other: "Georgie Porgie, puddin' and pie, kissed the girls and made them cry. . . ." Their noise did not deter us from analyzing the situation.

"She too naïve," Alourdes said softly. "Too naïve, yes, mon!" Mabel echoed loudly. "Cecile, she too trusting . . . too nice," Alourdes said, sucking her teeth. "That girl trust too much!" Mabel fairly shouted. "Look at her," observed Alourdes. "She got no *gad* on herself. She got no *gad* on the house. She got those little children. They got nothing on them! She too naïve."

"Look, girl, you too naïve," announced Mabel as soon as Cecile returned. But Alourdes simply said, "Never mind. We got thing to do. The sun almost gone. Soon, we got to get back to Aunt Emma' house. I'm hungry."

Cecile had produced a clay pot with earth in it, two shimalady plants in wet paper (which we tested to be sure they would curl up when touched), some pennies, and two candles. At Alourdes's direction, Cecile took a piece of lined white paper from her daughter's school notebook and carefully wrote her husband's name twenty-one times, ten times on one side of the paper and eleven on the other. She was shaking as she wrote in large block letters that covered the sheet: Joseph Shepherd, Joseph Shepherd, Joseph Shepherd. . . . Then, with the ingredients in hand, we all went inside to Cecile's bedroom.

From a hubbub of activity, our small group slipped suddenly into a pocket of calm. The low angle of the sun caused splotches of light and fluttery shadows of leaves to dance across the walls of the spacious and airy bedroom. The voices of the children seemed far away and insignificant. Alourdes plunged us into the ritual action. She made the sign of the cross and lit a candle.

With the candle in one hand and the pot and the paper in the other, she slowly and deliberately saluted each of the four directions, ritually tracing the shape that is both cross and crossroads and thus a point of historic confluence between Christianity and the religions of West Africa. Her face was very serious. She held the instruments of her cure out in front of her, at a level considerably higher than her head. At each of the four directions, her lips moved in inaudible, sincere prayer for the well-being of Cecile Shepherd.

When she finished, Alourdes folded the paper with Joseph Shepherd's name on it and tore it slowly in half. Then she tore each of the halves in half again. A third time, she stacked the pieces and tore them in half. Then she handed them to Cecile and directed her to tear them three more times. "When you tear it, you talk. Say what you want," Alourdes directed. "Talk, girl!" Mabel coached from the sidelines. Cecile was embarrassed. Three times she mumbled something like, "For make him come back to me. Make him come on home."

Alourdes mixed the tiny pieces of paper into the soil and buried a penny in the bottom of the pot. Then she handed the pot to Cecile with instructions to plant the shimalady. When that was done, a candle was lit and pushed down into the soil. Cecile was told to take the pot of shimalady in both hands and orient it, just as Alourdes had done earlier with the other materials. "You hold it up to each side like this . . . this . . . this . . . this. And you talk!" Alourdes told her in a firm but gentle voice.

Cecile, an Anglican from birth, dug deep in herself and produced a small voice that said, "Lord, please let him come back to me." "Don't beg," said Alourdes. "Say what you want. You got to say, 'I want him come back.' Come on now, you can do it." "That girl too weak," Mabel mumbled loud enough for all of us to hear.

Cecile reverted to her earlier, ambiguous formulation: "For make him come back to me." Her lower lip was trembling now, and she was trying to hold the pot up and hug her arms protectively close to her body at the same time. With the downward pull of her elbows toward her waist, it looked as if the little potted plant weighed a hundred pounds. On the third direction of the crossroads, Cecile broke down and sobbed.

Mabel exploded. She danced around the room as if fire ants

were climbing up her legs. "Her weak! Me knew it! That lady not only naïve, her weak. Shiiiiiiit, mon!" Alourdes had a different response. She moved in quickly, put an arm around Cecile, and said, "That's okay, sweetheart." Then she gently guided Cecile through the end of the ritual.

When it was done, Alourdes took the plant and put it in a puddle of sun on Cecile's dresser. "You going leave it there. Nobody going know nothing. Even your husband come, he don't know. So you got a plant? So what? That nobody' business but you. But every day you got to 'work that point.' Light a candle. Talk. Okay, sweetheart? Don't you worry. Everything going be all right. I do that work for you. I know. Now you can go and be peaceful."

When Alourdes left the room, Mabel moved in for the kill. She was still jumping and sputtering: "Shit, girl, you weak! Listen, me speak straight. That crying don't do you no good. You got to be strong. Listen to me, girl! Some lady and . . . her . . . her in the geriatric ward . . . her say her goin' to leave me fifty thousand dollars, and that woman's sister stand there, take that money away from me. You think me cry? Not me, mon! That don't do no good, and look here . . . me tellin' *you* about it!" By this time, there were tears in Mabel's eyes.

On the way home, Mabel slowly transformed tears into anger. All the way back from Bushy Park to Barbicon Road and Aunt Emma's prim little pastel house, Mabel muttered and mumbled. Every once in a while, she would turn full around in the front seat, look at Alourdes and me, and say something like: "Crying never did nobody no good! Shiiiiit!" Out the windows of the car, the sunset turned the parasitic creeper the Jamaicans call love bush and the Haitians call friendship to a glowing, pulsating orange.

HEALING, THE VODOU WAY

The healing work Alourdes performed in Jamaica is more easily understood when set within the context of the Vodou view of person and the Vodou philosophy of life. In the Vodou understanding of personhood, the individual is given identity, solidity, and safety in a precarious world by a thick weave of relationships with other human beings as well as with spirits and ancestors. That the world is precarious is the core of the Vodou philosophy of life.

"*Moun fèt pou mouri* [People are born to die]," Haitians are fond of saying, usually with a casual shrug of the shoulders. This proverb gives voice to both the pain of life in poverty-stricken Haiti and the stoic acceptance that, on one level at least, characterizes the Haitian attitude toward this life. *Mizè* (suffering, and, more precisely, the suffering of poverty) is an expected and recurrent condition. Haitians face this, and they accept it. Neither experience nor religion gives them a way out. The notion of progress is of no help in making sense of their history, and they have seen little upward social mobility, either in their own lives or in those of their children. Furthermore, Haitians do not believe that the human condition has degenerated from an ideal state any more than that it leads to one; in Vodou, there is neither an Eden nor a heaven. Because, for the great majority of Haitians, it is a given that life is filled with struggle and suffering, it is not inaccurate to say that problem-free periods are pervaded with an anxiety that anticipates crises just around the corner. Life, in the Vodou view of things, is thus characterized by alternating cycles of suffering and the transient relief from suffering that is called "having luck."

Luck (*chans*) is, however, not entirely a matter of chance in Vodou philosophy. Maintaining and enhancing good luck and, when necessary, fending off and removing bad luck are forms of labor as necessary to life as the labor of the peasant farmer in his fields or the urban pieceworker at her factory bench. A person who expects that life will run smoothly without spiritual effort is "naïve," the word Alourdes used to describe Cecile. Vodou healers such as Alourdes are for-hire specialists in the spiritual labor required to orchestrate luck.

Raising luck is the general rubric under which all kinds of Vodou healing can be grouped, and healing is the main purpose of all types of Vodou ritualizing. Whether Alourdes is treating clients one-on-one in her altar room, an activity that goes on nearly every day in her Brooklyn home, or staging elaborate birthday parties for the Vodou spirits, which happens six to eight times a year, what she is doing is healing—healing individuals and healing groups. Both in public rituals and in private sessions, Alourdes heals by exercising, strengthening, and mending relationships among the living, the dead, and the spirits. In the final analysis, the only effective means of controlling luck is the care and feeding of family, in the largest sense of that term.

Many different kinds of problems are amenable to treatment within the Vodou system—love, family, work, and money problems as well as physical maladies. The immediate problem that brings a "client" to Alourdes's door, however, gives little indication of its true origin. A problem with a neighbor's jealousy, for instance, can be manifested in boils, a lost job, or difficulty with one's children. Alourdes does pay attention to the presenting problem. For example, she may treat a minor physical ailment herbally. For a more serious problem, she may recommend that the client see a medical doctor. But the main focus of her healing energy is directed to the deeper issues uncovered in the course of treatment. Cecile's case was typical. Alourdes treated the parcel of land, but she quickly moved to the more significant relational issues in Cecile's life. The diagnosis of the underlying or root problem often comes as a surprise to the client.

Alourdes invariably diagnoses the origins of her clients' problems as disturbances in relationships of one sort or another. Because relational networks extend beyond the living to include the dead and the *lwa*, the Vodou healer must explore a vast, tangled web of relations to find the troubled strand putting stress on the whole fabric. And because the dead and, to some extent, the *lwa* are as susceptible to destructive emotions as living persons are, the problems Alourdes treats can be traced to neglected spirits or hungry ancestors as well as to jealous, angry, or malicious human beings.

The first thing Alourdes must do with new clients is ascertain whether the problems they have are "natural" or "supernatural" in origin. She usually does a card reading to determine this. The diagnosis of a natural problem indicates that the malady is "from God," and this means that neither Alourdes nor any other Vodou healer can do anything about it. Alourdes sends such clients away. "Why I got to take those people' money if I can't help them?" she asks. Virtually all natural problems seem to be physical maladies. The reverse is not true, however; many physical afflictions are diagnosed as supernatural in origin. Resistance to diagnosis and cure by scientific medicine is taken as a sure sign that a problem is supernatural. Most problems are diagnosed as supernatural, and, because they fall into the realm of the spirits, something can be done about them.

In spite of using terminology such as *natural* and *supernatural*, Vodou does not assume the existence of a two-story universe. Both God and the spirits operate in dimensions that permeate ordinary human life, but the two operate in different ways. "Between God and the spirit is two different thing," Alourdes said. "You don't see God to talk to God. No. You are born. You see the sky. You see the earth. You don't know who put it there. But that's God. . . . God you don't see. God you talk about. You go to church, they talk about God. You read the Bible, you read about God. But spirit you don't read about. The spirit come in people' head, and you see them, you talk to them. They help you." Alourdes can treat supernatural illnesses, which are within the spirits' purview, because the spirits are directly available to her. The spirits have come to depend on Alourdes's care, just as she depends on theirs. She has leverage with them. God is different. A problem that comes from God is natural; like a rock, it simply is. You cannot plead with a rock to change or coerce it into another state of being.

Relationships, the focus of Vodou healing rites, are complex and often fragile. The range of diagnostic categories in Vodou reflects the range of difficulties that can develop in relationships. On the mild end of the spectrum lies the diagnosis that a person is suffering from "eyes"—too many others are thinking and talking about the client, and all the attention has pushed that person spiritually off balance. With no prior knowledge of the situation, Alourdes diagnosed me as suffering from "eyes" during the time I was being considered for tenure at my university. A slightly more serious version of this condition is called a *djòk*, or "bad eyes," in which the attention focused on the client has a negative tone, involving, for example, jealousy. This diagnosis, however, does not indicate a conscious intent to harm the client.

Cecile's case, in which someone had "done work" against her, falls toward the far end of the spectrum. Such a diagnosis assumes that the damage is willful, and it usually means that another spiritual expert has been involved in focusing and directing that ill will. The most extreme cases involve deliberate harm that is more than the mere by-product of getting one's own way; such malice crosses over into the territory of pure revenge. Alourdes never initiates activity at this end of the spectrum, which is the domain of the *bòkò*, a specialist in "work of the left hand."

Vodou healing shows a penchant for "the science of the concrete."[3] In her cures, Alourdes puts problematic human relationships into a tangible, external form, where they can be worked on and ultimately transformed. When a love relationship is desired, she binds two dolls face-to-face. When the dissolution of a relationship is sought, she binds them back-to-back. For restive, "hungry" spirits, she prescribes a meal of their favorite foods. To treat a violent marriage, Alourdes makes a charm for the wife by filling a jar with ice ("to cool him down") and molasses ("to make him sweet"). Then she wraps the charm in some article of the husband's clothing and turns the whole thing upside down, a clear signal within the Vodou science of the concrete that a revolutionary change is desired. For Cecile, an upper-class Jamaican woman experiencing some conflict about her involvement with Vodou, Alourdes fashioned the unobtrusive potted shimalady. These charms are called *pwen* (points). They are condensations of complex social, psychological, and spiritual conditions.

Baths, a staple in Alourdes's healing repertoire, are also *pwen* of a sort. These mixtures of herbs, perfumes, milk, alcohol, fruits, and, in some situations, less agreeable things concretize troublesome as well as desired states in a variety of ways. Smell is among the most powerful instruments. After taking a ritual bath, the client is instructed not to wash for three days, leaving the heady odors of Alourdes's medicine chest on the skin for three long days, waking and sleeping. Our sense of smell connects with the limbic mind, a primordial, nonverbal self, and it is often this deeper self that is addressed by Alourdes's cures. Unlike psychiatrists, Vodou healers do not believe they must bring problems to the level of consciousness to work with them.

There are two types of baths: good-luck and bad-luck. In both cases, about two cups of viscous liquid are used. Bad-luck baths are applied from the top of the body down, whereas good-luck baths proceed from the bottom up. Many problems are treated with a simple series of three good-luck baths. But when the negativity is more palpable, a preliminary cleansing with a bath designed to remove the bad luck is required. If a healer pre-

---

[3] This phrase is taken from Claude Lévi-Strauss, "The Science of the Concrete," in his *The Savage Mind* (Chicago: University of Chicago Press, 1966), 1–33.

scribes a bad-luck bath, it does not necessarily mean that the client has been the object of malice. It may simply mean that the problem has been around for a long time and has infected many areas of the person's life.

Vodou healing operates according to traditional wisdom. For example, a great deal of solid herbal knowledge is available to healers such as Alourdes. They use it to treat successfully a variety of noncritical physical ailments. There are also standard ritual forms for treatments such as baths and standard recipes for concocting them. But there is room for inspired innovation, too. Alourdes told me that on several occasions when she was unsure how to treat a client, she had a dream in which one of the spirits—or, more often, her mother—told her to "take such and such a leaf, mix it with this fruit and this perfume," and so forth. At other times, she simply has an impulse to try something new. Part of what a healer must learn to do is identify and trust what might be labeled intuition, if this term is taken in its most serious sense. Strengthening *konesans* (intuitive knowledge) is one of the goals of Vodou initiation ceremonies.

Alourdes never refers to the persons she works for as patients, and for good reason. In Vodou, the one being healed remains active throughout the healing process—from the card reading, in which the client is free to agree or disagree with any diagnosis Alourdes suggests, to the manufacture of the *pwen*, in which the client has a direct hand. It was Cecile who picked and planted the shimalady. With the point in hand, the client's participation becomes crucial, for a point must be "worked": it must be prayed over daily, candles must be lit before it, refreshing water poured over it, sweet-smelling perfume sprayed on it.

In the months following our trip to Jamaica, I asked Alourdes several times if she had heard from Cecile, but she had nothing to tell me until nearly a year later. "Yeah, I hear from her," Alourdes said, in a matter-of-fact tone. "Everything okay." And then she added with a touch of impatience: "Of course everything okay. I do that work for her, don't I?" "The land was sold?" I queried. "I forget to ask," Alourdes responded.

In the beginning of my association with Alourdes, I tended to view her treatments as suspense stories, and I eagerly awaited their denouements. For Alourdes, however, the outcome of her healing work is rarely cause for suspense, and, furthermore, its value does not appear to depend on particular concrete results.

It took me some time to realize what motivated this attitude. Alourdes is confident in the effectiveness of her work, and she knows intuitively when it has been successful. In a non-contradictory way, she also knows that the most she can do is identify the root problems and then place the proper tools to deal with them in the hands of those who are in trouble. It is up to the clients to use these tools. Cecile had to learn to "talk." She had to stop begging and say what she wanted. She alone was responsible for working the point, that is, talking daily before the potted shimalady until she understood that she possessed the power to bend her husband's errant will. From what Alourdes had to say, Cecile learned this lesson.

Mabel's problems were not so easily resolved. Edmund's visa did come through but not for several years. The missing suitcase containing the ritual clothing and other things Mabel needed to undergo initiation in Haiti never showed up. It was just as well, because Mabel never made it to Haiti. Instead, she got side-tracked into multiple family problems. For the entire time we were in Jamaica, Mabel was in constant motion, doing everyone's laundry, running their errands, and troubleshooting in their lives. On the day Alourdes and I left for Port-au-Prince, she hardly took time to wave good-bye as she bustled off to town on yet one more mission.

"What do these people do when Mabel isn't around?" I asked Alourdes. "How do I know?" she responded peevishly. "I think she uses their problems to avoid her own," I observed. "I suppose so," said Alourdes.

"She's a tough one," I mused. "She makes people dependent on her and then gets mad at them for it." "Humph," said Alourdes, who has little taste for psychologizing. She simply re-iterated the opinion she had expressed in the airport: "Mabel got a lot'a problem. She got to wash her head . . . so she can help herself."

INITIATION AND THE SPIRITS IN THE HEAD

There are four levels of initiation into Vodou as it is practiced in Port-au-Prince. The first is a ritual headwashing aimed at the spirits lodged in the head. From one perspective, these are the particular Vodou spirits said to love that person. But, from another, the spirits in the head are the constituent parts of the self, principally the *gwo bònanj* (big guardian angel), which is roughly equivalent to the personality or consciousness of the individual. When someone is troubled, the big guardian angel becomes agitated, and, as a result, that person loses access to dreams as well as the waking powers of discrimination, insight, and understanding. Like a boat without a navigational system, such a person bobs perilously through life at the mercy of the currents. The headwashing ceremony "refreshes" and "feeds" restive head spirits. Once placated, they will function as conduits for the wisdom, ancestral and spiritual, that every person needs to negotiate daily life. Alourdes had prescribed this treatment for Mabel, and it is a required first step even for those who go on to higher levels of initiation during the same cycle of ceremonies.

The second level of initiation is called *kanzo*, a term referring to a rite of fire designed to transform suffering into power. The public, and therefore discussable, part of *kanzo* is a ritual called *boule zen* (the burning of the pots), in which the initiates are briefly removed from the inner chamber of the temple where they have been sequestered in order to undergo a sort of trial by fire. Small clay pots are placed in the center of specially prepared fires. Hard, hot dumplings are snatched from the boiling pots and pressed into the palm of the initiate's left hand and the sole of the left foot. When this ritual is complete, the initiates may be told, "Never say hot again; say strong!"

To *kouche*—to lie down, sleep, make love, give birth, and, less frequently, to die—is the verbal form used for all levels of initiation. To *kouche sou pwen* (to lie down on the point) is the third level of induction into the arts of Vodou. In this phrase, the word *point* (*pwen*) refers to a ritualized concentration of the power of the Vodou spirit said to be the master of the initiate's head, the *mèt tèt*. Through the *kouche sou pwen*, novices solidify their relationship with their *mèt tèt* and at the same time come to recognize that spirit's power as a dimension of their own character. The giving of the sacred rattle, the *ason*, is the final level of initiation. Possession of the *ason* qualifies a person to begin to do healing work.

No one undertakes these various levels of initiation idly or out of pure curiosity. They are expensive and taxing. Persons who take the *ason* do so because they have serious problems,

problems that, by a sort of circular reasoning, are interpreted as the harassment of spirits who desire that person to *kouche*. Initiation is thus an especially intense form of healing. All those who are empowered to heal in Vodou have received their training by first being healed themselves. Almost everyone who has taken the *ason* has a story to tell about suffering and instinctive resistance to the call of the spirits. In this respect, the experiences of Alourdes and Maggie were not extreme.

People resist the call to be a healer because, although such a life may provide prestige, it also requires considerable self-sacrifice. For example, when Alourdes's mother finally said yes to the spirits, it signaled the end of her relationships with men. Philo's house filled up with those in need of healing, and she no longer had space, time, energy, or money to raise her daughter Alourdes. *Manbo* and *oungan*, those who take on the most serious obligations in relation to the spirits, are prepared for these sacrifices by the initiation process itself. In a pattern common to such rites the world over, Vodou initiation rituals demand nothing less than a surrender of self. These rites force a rapid regression on the part of the initiate. They hammer a person back to a state of childlike uncertainty and dependence. In this vulnerable state of infancy, ritually revisited, Vodou teaches its potent lessons.

For the higher levels of initiation, one of the central surrender lessons has to do with possession. Through ritual means, an attempt is made to pull the initiate over the edge and into the deep waters of trance. Those who serve the Vodou spirits believe that, in possession, the *gwo bònanj* leaves the body and floats loose in the world. No one easily gives up consciousness and the control associated with it; even as practiced a horse of the spirits as Alourdes still shows signs of struggle as she is mounted by a spirit. But she no longer fears the experience as she most likely did when the spirits first sought to use her as their vehicle. When Alourdes was only thirteen, an ancient female spirit called Marienette "passed" through her head, a type of spirit contact that falls short of possession. Alourdes's first full possession came at the age of nineteen.

In 1980 Alourdes described possession in this way: "When the spirit going to come in you head, you feel very light, light like a piece of paper . . . very light in your head. You feel dizzy in your head. Then after, you pass out. But the spirit come, and he talk to people, and he look at the table you make for him . . . you know. Then he leaves and . . . and you come from very, very, very far. But when the spirit in your body, in your head, you don't know nothing. They have to tell you what the spirit say, what message he leave for you." In the matter-of-fact, almost clinical way Alourdes describes the descent into possession, the unconsciousness during it, and the amnesia that follows can be heard the voice of a *manbo* secure in her relationship with the Vodou spirits and trusting her own ability to pull herself back together after their temporarily fragmenting visits.

Maggie, who has absorbed a heavier dose of New York's hard lessons about the need for constant control, still fights against the surrender demanded by trance states. And she uses revealingly different language in describing possession. When she told me about her first possession experience, which occurred in Haiti at age ten, Maggie began with characteristic bravado: "I started to be Miss Invisible—the Invisible Woman!" But she soon switched to a different tone: "I'm losing my foot. . . . I'm losing my arm . . . losing my body, and it's just going. And I was much younger then, and I start calling, 'Mommie, Mommie, Mommie!' and then my mother—she doesn't come. . . . I don't know if she come or don't come. . . . Once it hits your head, that's it! It's black, and then I don't know nothing. Nothing!"

While describing a more recent brush with possession by the *lwa*, Maggie reiterated the language of loss that filled her account of that first experience, but she combined it with other threatening and paradoxical imagery: "It's the funniest feeling . . . like losing your toes. Your toes is gone, like you stand up and someone is pulling your blood out of you. You don't feel your head . . . like something running through your body, you know . . . like you taking a shower and the thing just running down all over you. You feel like your feet is not touching the ground. Your head is heavy. . . . Not heavy. It's like you are floating up, like high blood pressure . . . running down." Whether Maggie can eventually trust enough to welcome— even to seek out—the unconsciousness of trance has yet to be determined, but it is an important issue if she is to take over Alourdes's healing practice. In her role as healer, Alourdes must frequently, and more or less at will, go through the perilous ego-exchange with the *lwa* that is at the center of possession.

All persons who take the *ason* do not become practicing healers. Some choose not to, and others never gain the needed assent of the community. In urban contexts, those who function as priests or priestesses for Vodou families can do so because their skills (including the skill of being a good horse for the spirits) have been recognized and repeatedly proven. Some of these skills are taught in the initiation chamber, but others are inherited.

Alourdes's mother, Philomise, was a well-known healer in Port-au-Prince, with a substantial following. Everyone knows that Alourdes "replaced" her mother, that is, inherited her role. Alourdes's tangible inheritance from Philo is her altar, the aggregate of Philo's relationships with the Vodou spirits, made tangible in stones and pots and other ritual implements. The intangible inheritance involves extraordinary diagnostic and curative skills. Philo was known for her psychic abilities, but Alourdes resists the claim that she has these same gifts. "I'm not psychic like my mother . . . no," she says.

She does, however, admit to having the "gift of eyes." "When somebody come in—even three person come—I got the feel which one need me." When I asked if calling this the gift of eyes meant that she saw something such as light or color, she responded: "I don't see light. I got the feel in my body. The blood goes up and my hair start to stand up if there a spirit there that bothering somebody. I feel something inside that mean danger." In a related way, she claims to know when a treatment has been successful, because of how she feels. "After you treat people, you feel relieved, you feel happy. Then I feel in my body that the people going to be all right. Also, the people' face change. It not the same face any more."

Just as Alourdes routinely attributes greater psychic powers to her mother than to herself and greater ones still to her most distant remembered ancestor, the old African Joseph Binbin Mauvant, so Maggie declares that she does not have her mother's abilities. But she does admit to some extraordinary ways of knowing things. "Me and my ESP!" Maggie said. "Usually I dream something. I get a funny feeling, like a pressure. When I feel that pressure, that when I know what I dream going to happen."

The skills of the Vodou healer focus on the social drama, on relational problems that often fall through the cracks between the various specialists who do the healing in Western, technological society. This focus may be not only the most realistic but also the most helpful for the majority of Haitians, who lack any realistic expectation of gaining access to the powers that actually control the world—that is, to guns and money. Understanding people, maneuvering and even manipulating human relationships—these are the weapons of the disenfranchised, the survival skills of the oppressed.

Innumerable times I have heard Alourdes say: "I got plenty confidence in myself!" Emphasis on self-confidence as a relational and survival skill is one of Alourdes's most distinctive traits. This confidence enables her to take on the thorniest of problems, even those that involve pitting her will against that of another healer. And, on many occasions, the treatment Alourdes prescribes for a client includes attention to that person's need for more self-confidence.

Self-confidence, as Alourdes uses the term, is not to be confused with the heroic "I can do anything I want to" attitude valued in the United States, or even with simple pride. "Pride?" said Alourdes. "Pride never did nobody no good." The self-confidence Alourdes fosters in herself and encourages in others is not so much a sense of self-importance as it is basic self-respect. When Aunt Emma talked about the importance of believing in God and in the Bible, Alourdes added emphatically, "And in yourself." Self-respect is the antidote to the daily insults poor, urban Haitians experience when they see how members of the elite live. Self-respect is also the most important thing to have with you when standing in line in a New York welfare office or asking a white bureaucrat for a job.

Alourdes's challenge to imitate her in having "plenty confidence" is probably most resonant for women. It is not surprising that women healers (I doubt Alourdes is the only one) are quite sophisticated about the problems women face. Inattention to self—Mabel's frantic self-sacrifice in the service of her family, for example—is one of the greatest female problems. For wives and mothers, the self-caring Alourdes counsels is the necessary counterbalance to the push and pull of family claims. Healers, like mothers, define their life's work as the service of others. Thus when Alourdes, both a mother and a healer, urges self-confidence in the women she treats, she speaks with authority.

Alourdes works at maintaining a large and diverse Vodou family around her, and as a result she sits at the confluence of dense and powerful streams of human neediness. Her instinct is to want to help. "I love to make treatment. I love to help people. When they feel good, that make me feel good." But she has to be constantly vigilant to maintain her balance in the midst of her big needy "family," and she does so by insisting that her own needs be met as well as those of her clients. When I see Alourdes acting like a "queen bee," something she does from time to time, I try to remember what a difficult role it is that she occupies.

Priestly power is said to reside in *konesans*. This knowledge could be called psychic power, the gift of eyes, empathy, or intuition. It is any and all of these things. Above all, it is knowledge about people. Vodou provides a vast and complex symbol system for thinking about people. *Konesans* is the ability to read people, with or without cards; to diagnose and name their suffering, suffering that Haitians know comes not from God and usually not from chance but from others—the living, the dead, and the spirits. Finally, *konesans* is the ability to heal.

The initiation chamber is the alchemical oven in which suffering is transformed into knowledge, into experientially rooted priestly power. It is also the only ritual arena I know of that Papa Gede is forbidden to enter. If an initiate has Gede as his or her head spirit, that person will *kouche* on the point of Ogou, the patron of self-assertion and Gede's temporary stand-in during initiations. In the *djèvo*, the small room where initiates spend several days in seclusion, no songs are sung for Gede and no prayers are offered to him. Gede's presence in the initiation chamber would be a fearful redundancy that might snap the delicate balance between death and rebirth which these rituals orchestrate. Papa Gede must be excluded because he is so present.

A BIRTHDAY PARTY FOR PAPA GEDE

About twenty-five of us were gathered at Alourdes's home in the predawn hours of a Sunday in late October 1981. Gede was with us, holding forth in the center of the crowd. "Papa Gede," someone called out, trying to get his attention. Gede drew himself up, erect and proud, pulled down his black top hat with both hands, and stuck out his lower lip in an exaggerated pout.

Devotees gathered before a table made for Gede's birthday party. Bedford-Stuyvesant, Brooklyn, 1978.

"*Msye Gede, Ti Malis Kache Bo Lakwa, Papa'm Te Rekonèt Mwen, Gwo Zozo . . . sil vu ple* [Mister Gede, Little Mischief Hidden Near the Cross, My Father Acknowledged Me, Big Cock . . . if you please]!" he retorted. "If people don't remember my name," Gede whined, "I'm not going to stay!" And with that, he grabbed his walking stick—the one carved to look like a huge erect penis—and headed for the door. "No, no, Papa Gede, stay!" Maggie cried. Then she giggled and said in a rush of words: "I mean, Mister-Gede-Little-Mischief-Hidden-Near-the-Cross-My-Father-Acknowledged-Me-Big-Cock . . . stay!"

Halfway out the door, Gede wheeled around and planted his walking stick firmly on the floor. Spreading his legs to make the other two points of a tripod, Gede began to roll his hips in the lascivious dance step Haitians call the *gouyad*. "Little hole, little hole, little hole," he sang, "Big hole, big hole, big hole." The men whistled and hooted, and the women smiled. Soon everyone was swept into the simple, energetic song. With the roomful of people singing full voice, Gede took three little wide-legged jumps forward until the wooden phallus protruded directly from his crotch, and the song jumped to a new level, with a faster beat: "Little hole, little hole, little hole . . ." Just as abruptly as he had started, Gede stopped singing. He marched back into the center of the group, snapping his cane smartly under his arm. Then he poked it mischievously at a woman and asked her to hold his *zozo* (literally, bone-bone), a common slang term for penis.

Like a teacher poised to begin an important lesson, Papa Gede held his finger up in the air. "When a girl is little, little, little, like this"—Gede moved a flat hand within two feet of the floor—"what does she have?" "*Ti twou* [A little hole]!" people shouted. Gede made a tight circle with the thumb and finger of his left hand and began to push the first finger of his right in and out of it. "*Ti twou, ti twou, ti twou, . . .*" Gede kept the rollicking beat with his plunging finger. His hands moved together and apart, together and apart, and in counterpoint his hips went round and round. After seemingly endless repetitions of his childish ditty, Gede stopped the group by lifting his hand once more. He assumed a serious expression, adjusted his hat, and asked: "When she grows up, like this, like this, and like this"— he moved his palm from close to the floor to shoulder height— "what has she got?" "*Gwo twou!*" a dozen voices shouted, and we were off again: "*Gwo twou, gwo twou, gwo twou, . . .*"

Papa Gede had been late in arriving. Even though the party was for him, he had delayed his appearance until the early morning hours. It had been one of those situations that happen from time to time with Alourdes. She seemed tired and distracted, and she had a hard time remembering songs to "send" for the spirits. Her coterie of older women friends who often pick up the slack for her was not out in force that night. Madame François was the only one there, and, like Alourdes, she did not seem in the mood. Thus the early part of the ceremony had a struggling, desultory quality. We sang and sang, but nothing much happened. Two or three times, Alourdes's body shuddered, and when she was on her feet pouring libations for Gede, she temporarily lost her balance, but nothing came of these passes of the *lwa*.

Then we started to sing "Anba Gwo Wòch-o" (Underneath the Big Rock), the favorite song of her personal Gede, Ti Malis. This lively song with a simple lyric evokes a group of Gede connected with small pesky insects, little creeping and crawling things that bite and sting and live in dark, hidden places. Some inhabit the cracks and crevices of furniture and woven leaf mattresses. These tiny living things secreted in lifeless objects provide small but persistent reminders of the vulnerability of the flesh. Defying human efforts to control our environment, they insinuate themselves into our homes, our beds, our persons. Others churn away in the earth just beneath the deceptively unchanging rock, a layer of life that can be suddenly revealed in wiggling animation when the "big rock" is moved. Beneath the surface of things, these communal, hardworking creatures carry on constructive work (aerating the soil) as well as what might be called destructive work (devouring the flesh of corpses). In addition to Ti Malis, Ti Pis, a biting insect found in woven chair seats, and Gede Nibo, the spider, also fall into this category.

"Underneath the Big Rock" always works to bring on Alourdes's Ti Malis. But that October night in 1981, we sang and sang and sang, and Gede did not come. Depression descended on the small group. But then, just when it felt most impossible and I thought I was about to witness my first ceremony at Alourdes's home when the spirits failed to respond, Ti Malis arrived. His animation and energy were in stark contrast to Alourdes's mood, and his spark ignited the crowd. Alourdes is a subtle choreographer of her own moods and energies as well as those of a group. Rather than resisting negative feelings, her habit is to sink into them, plumb their depths, and then rebound through the other side. She has learned this transformational art form from Gede. It is the essence of his message, the point of his humor, the reason for locating this trickster in the middle of the cemetery and in the center of the practice of healing.

Toward the end of his visit, Gede asked who in the room had *kominyone* (communioned), that is, gone through their First Communion in the Catholic church. Almost all hands went up. "I communioned," Gede said earnestly. Everyone laughed. "I did that! I did that! I did that!" he asserted, looking wounded. "I, Mister Gede Little Mischief Hidden Near the Cross, myself, I did that! And I took the examination, too!"

"Oh, did you, Papa Gede?" Andre, Alourdes's nephew, asked. "Tell us the story." Gede pulled up a stool in front of the questioner, and everyone else gathered around them. "The priest did the examination," Gede said, leaning forward with his elbows on his knees and his face close to Andre's face. "What kind of examination?" Andre asked. And then Madame Arnold, who had been through this routine many times before, intervened: "What questions did he ask you, Papa Gede, dear?"

"*Li di langèt. M'te reponn se pa bagèt! Li di zozo. M'te reponn se pa kouto!*" In this series of rhyming statements and responses, Gede casts the priest as the one with the foul mouth. The priest said *langèt* (female genitalia), and Gede responded, "It's not a loaf of bread." The priest said *zozo* (penis), and Gede answered, "It's not a knife." This exchange is more subtle than it appears. Vaginas are identified with a variety of edible things, and, although the penis is rarely called a knife, the most common slang term for sexual intercourse is to *koupe* (to cut).

Gede's report of this strange catechetical examination went on for some time, punctuated only by giggles and snorts from the group gathered around him. Then Gede paused and, with a pensive look on his face, asked: "When we finished, do you know what that priest did?" "No, Papa Gede, what did he do?" "He turned his back and . . . and . . . he did a little fart. Not a big one—you understand what I am saying to you?—just a little one." Andre jumped in eagerly, "I know, I know, Papa Gede, like this . . . ," and he bubbled his lips, making the sound of a motor boat starting. "No, no, no, no!" cried Papa Gede. Then he delicately pursed his lips and let a barely audible stream of air hiss through them. "Like that! Just a little one."

SEX, DEATH, AND HUMOR

Gede is the Vodou spirit who presides over the realms of sex, death, and humor. His possession-performances vary along a spectrum that tracks the path of a human life. He eats with his hands and sometimes throws his food like an infant. Like a two-year old, he delights in saying naughty words. He is horny and predatory with women, like a young man with raging hormones. Like a favorite uncle, he hunkers down with the faithful and listens with genuine care to the most homely of their complaints—an abscess on the buttocks, a disrespectful child, a car with a malfunctioning heater. As Baron Samdi (Baron Saturday), head of all the Gede, he arrives as a corpse; his body falls to the ground, stiff. In a mood of solemnity and sadness, the people surround him, bind his jaw with a white cloth, stuff his nostrils and ears with cotton, and powder his face to reproduce the pallor of a cadaver. When Baron Samdi possesses Alourdes, which he does infrequently, the tense psychodrama of death ends only when time doubles back on itself, when Ti Malis displaces Baron and a childish giggle escapes from the mouth of the corpse. Then, and only then, does the tension snap and the fun begin.

Gede has license to break all the social rules. The language that comes out of Gede's mouth is language Alourdes would never use when not possessed by him. Haitians are, in general, a discreet and proper people. Lacking physical privacy, they strongly emphasize good manners. It is, for example, highly insulting to call a person *malelve* (badly reared); were Gede not a spirit, he would be a prime candidate for this insult. He can say all the things that are forbidden in polite company, act out the impulses others must suppress. When Ti Malis arrives, he immediately greets the women with big puckering kisses. With his favorites (as well as with the occasional woman who is a bit too proper), he presses his pelvis up against them and rolls his hips. Gede steals food and money, stuffing his pockets full of other people's things with exaggerated gestures of secretiveness sure to catch the attention of anyone half-awake. He alone can satirize the powerful and the privileged; only Gede could get away with making fun of Catholic priests.

Sex, death, and humor: the great social levelers. In the presence of Papa Gede (at birth, making love, and in our coffins), we are all stripped down to our basic humanity. Once, I went with Alourdes to a Gede feast at the home of one of her protégés, a *manbo* in training. Alourdes's Ti Malis arrived to entertain us, and he was still there when it was time for me to leave. As I was saying good-bye, Papa Gede reminded me of another party for him two weeks hence. He wanted me to come. "I'll come," I answered and then added a polite question: "Is there something I could bring?" All the way across a room full of people I had just met Gede shouted, "Bring a clean cunt!"

Gede shows up at virtually every birthday party for the spirits. He comes late, and he stays long. He is always the last to arrive, and his gossipy informality, his sexual high jinks, and his penchant for telling satire work alchemical changes on the mood of a Vodou family. After a long night of deep spirit work, his presence entertains, eases tension, and soothes pain. Gede's arrival in the predawn hours facilitates the transition between the deep drama of Vodou and the everyday struggle of life in New York City. Gede takes people on a journey through their most out-of-control selves and, in so doing, prepares them to move back into the ordinary world where reserve and control must reign. Yet Gede's possession-performances should not be mistaken for mere entertainment.

Gede brings to the surface a connection between sexuality and life energy pervasive in Vodou spirituality. All Vodou rituals aim to *echofe* (heat things up). To raise heat, to raise luck, to raise life energy, to intensify sexuality in the broadest sense— these are all more or less the same process. The arrival of Gede at the end of a Vodou ceremony provides an extra, intense dose of the power needed to conquer life, to use it and enjoy it, rather than be conquered by it.

During late October and early November, the streets of Port-au-Prince are filled with roving bands of Gede. Gede possessions are lighter than those of the other spirits, and during Gede season many devotees spend several days caught up in the trickster spirit. The horses of Gede mill around in groups in public arenas, something the other spirits would never do. The dominant colors of their outrageous outfits are purple and black, and they have powdered faces. They wear top hats, bowler hats, airplane pilots' hats. They wear two or three hats at a time, and they often put on dark glasses with one lens missing. (The penis has only one eye, one *oungan* observed. But another person said Gede wears these strange glasses because he sees between the worlds of the dead and the living, and that is also why he jokes so much.) Around their necks the Gede hang pacifiers and baby rattles; in their hands they carry wooden phalluses. With a coffin hoisted on their shoulders, bands of Gede stage mock funeral processions through the heart of the city. Flocks of Gede, sometimes accompanied by musicians, accost innocent bystanders. Women are surrounded and not released until they have paid the toll—a kiss on the lips for every Gede. Awkward young boys are talked into spending five cents to have a look at the secret in the cigar box—a Barbie doll with real pubic hair.

During Gede season in 1980, in a big shed-like temple in La Saline (arguably the worst of Port-au-Prince's slums), five hundred people chanted, "Zozo, zozo, zozo," until they were hoarse. The atmosphere of the crowd teetered on the edge of riot. Most of the people were on their feet, more than half doing the *gouyad* to the sexy, energetic Banda drumbeat, Gede's rhythm. In a temple in Waney, on the coast road southwest of Port-au-Prince,

Gede, who wears glasses with one lens missing because he sees into the lands of both the living and the dead, possesses a female devotee. Port-au-Prince, Haiti, 1981. Photograph by Jerry Gordon.

a slender young *manbo* possessed by a Gede called The Inspector moved through a crowd of fifty or so, acting officious and insisting on examining the contents of pockets, purses, and wallets. In a larger temple a little further down the coast road, a ragtag bunch of Gede mimicked the pretenses of the military. One appointed himself commander and organized a dozen others into a dress parade. Penis-headed canes became firearms. And, although Gede himself is rarely present during Haiti's popular Carnival season, Gede-style political commentary prevails. In a country that has known severe and almost constant political repression, Gede's ambiguous, many-layered humor is often the only safe avenue of protest.

Haiti has been the recipient of a great deal of charity from the outside world, but little respect. Gede's humor can provide trenchant commentary on this as well. In 1980 in a *peristil* just outside Port-au-Prince, a man possessed by a Gede called Rubber on the Cross took on the Protestant missionaries. He donned a prim little dress, put a string of beads around his neck, and hung a short-handled pocketbook in the crook of his elbow. In one hand, he held an open, soft-backed Bible; in the other, a pornographic picture. In a singsong drone and with great earnestness, Gede led the group in a hymn:

> O Lord, if you free me,
> If it is you who sets me on my feet,
> Ordain the angels in the sky,
> To hold my hand,
> So my feet do not stumble,
> In the middle of the big rock. . . .

Rubber on the Cross winked at the crowd, switched to a syncopated rhythm, and began to transform the last line: "In the middle of the big rock. . . . In the middle of all the coconuts [vaginas]. . . . In the middle of all the whores. . . ." The performance dissolved into chaos as young men competed with one another to shout out new endings for the hymn.

THE DEAD RETURN

These raucous spirits of the dead are a far cry from the spirits of specific ancestors who return to complain of hunger and neglect and to advise their progeny in the countryside. In many areas in rural Haiti, and even in a few large, intact urban families, individual ancestors return through possession-performance. Although she was not safely lodged in such a large family, Philo, Alourdes's mother, used to be possessed by her ancestors. Her own mother, Marie Noelsine Joseph, appeared frequently; her father, Alphonse Macena, rarely. Alourdes, however, does not consult the ancestors in this way.

Alourdes's family dead are accessible by other means. There are dreams; Philo, for example, appears regularly in Alourdes's dreams. And the dead can also be ritually approached through their graves. Alourdes says that visiting her mother's tomb is the most important thing she does on her visits to Haiti. Petitionary prayers said in the cemetery are believed to be especially effective. On the first day we were in Haiti in 1980, Alourdes went directly to her mother's tomb in the main cemetery in Port-au-Prince. When the *prètsavann* she hired had completed their French and Latin prayers and the cemetery guardian had swept around the tomb as instructed, Alourdes took a bottle of clear water and poured it around the perimeter of the tomb. Then she knocked four times on her mother's grave: "Mama, it is me, Alourdes. Mama. Philo! Mama!" The others withdrew to a respectful distance as Alourdes told her mother all the family news and mumbled her earnest requests.

The dead also return in other ways. An ancestor who served the spirits in life can come back in the form of his or her *mèt tèt*. Understanding this makes it easier to grasp the significance of an unusual event that occurred at one of Alourdes's New Year's parties.

Maggie and Alourdes stage an annual New Year's Day dinner. By the time I arrived that day in 1981, the house was jumping. Alourdes and Maggie are happiest in the midst of a hubbub of guests, for this is noisy proof of their power to pull the community around them. Gregarious good humor and expansive hospitality peak in the midst of chaos, when no room can be entered without dislodging two or three persons from the doorway and when each trip in or out of the kitchen requires at least one mock-angry exchange. This one was initiated by Maggie: "Come on, Big Daddy, what you doin' standin' there drinkin' like some kind'a bum? What kind'a place you think this is? Move your butt out'a my way, this plate is heavy." She lifted a brimming platter of spicy, roasted turkey bits and walked through, swinging her hips in such a wide arc that she managed to bump into people on both sides. Alourdes would never do something like that, but there is always a little Gede at work in Maggie!

When the copious meal was at last on the tables, Maggie, without calling attention to herself, began a small and perfunctory ritual. She fixed a plate of turkey with rice and beans and a bowl of soup left over from their New Year's Eve dinner. Then she gestured with her head for me to follow. Together, we placed the food before the Legba shrine near the basement door. Even at non-Vodou events, the spirits are not forgotten.

Then the party began in earnest. Glasses of pink champagne and Asti Spumanti were offered to the twenty or so family members and friends gathered that day. We were surrounded by talk, laughter, kids screaming and haggling at our knees. Maggie, in high glow, yelled, "Okay, everybody, quiet! Shut up! Shut up!" Shyly, her brother Jean-Pierre, the family spokesman, lifted his glass and began a toast: "This is an annual event—"

"Yes!" Alourdes broke in before he finished one sentence.

"Every year we do that 'cause my mother ask me to do that. Agèou come, and he say my mother want that. Every year we make a big party, January first, invite everybody. . . ."

Jean-Pierre continued: "This is a very important party . . . the family all together . . . which we have every year on January first. And we hope everybody, er . . . lots of happiness and prosperity in the coming year!" His words were met with cheers.

It was Maggie's turn to speak. She singled out several people for special recognition, including Gertrude LeGrand, their long-time family friend. "My other mother! Everybody here know my other mother? Here she is, right here!" Next, Maggie raised her glass to me and to a friend I had introduced to this boister-ous family: "To my two sister, who have become such good friends!" Then Maggie started to say something, stopped, and, after a dramatic pause, went on: "Oh, well, I can say it. Every-body here is family."

She raised her glass toward the altar room door. "To all those spirit in there: Kouzen Zaka, and Papa Ogou, and Metrès Ezili, who bring us so much good luck this year. . . ." Everyone began to chime in their favorites. Alourdes cried, "And Papa Gede! Don't forgot Papa Gede!" And I added, "And Papa Danbala." Poupette, a playful young woman recently arrived from Haiti, and Big Daddy both echoed: "And Papa Danbala!" Poupette, carried away by the mood of the moment, executed a mock rit-ual salutation. Acting as if Big Daddy were possessed, she twirled, fell on her knees, and kissed the ground in front of him. Half-playfully, half-seriously, Big Daddy said, "Don't do that!" And at that very moment Agèou arrived.

From somewhere over my left shoulder, beneath the clatter of voices, I heard a strange, haunting sound. Frank, Alourdes's brother and the oldest member of the family present that day, was singing in a strained and urgent voice. The song was well known in this house—the song of Agèou, the head spirit of Alourdes's deceased mother, Ti Gran Philo (Little Grandmother Philo). Many took up the Creole song, which has a wonderful lilting melody.

> *Agèou, ou o!*
> *Agèou, ou hantor!*
> *Agèou, ou nèg Dahomey.*

Ou mande charite.
Ou fè di-set an,
T'ape manje youn sèl zepi de mayi.

Agèou, you, oh!
Agèou, you liar!
Agèou, you Dahomey man.

You beg for alms.
You spent seventeen years,
Eating only one ear of corn.

The mood of the crowd shifted with the arrival of Agèou in Frank's wrinkled old head. The noise level was just as high, and the people just as excited, but we were suddenly brought together by the song. We were welded into one powerful voice that sang its way up through the three stories of Alourdes's small Brooklyn row house and beyond into the dark winter sky.

After the song died away, Agèou offered the ritual handshake first to Alourdes, then to Maggie, then to the other family members: his right hand to their right, his left hand to their left. Then, with the weight of the *lwa* making his body lean heavily on Alourdes, Agèou wrapped his arms around her and offered an embrace cheek to cheek, first on one side and then the other. When Agèou had greeted all the members of the immediate family in this manner, he turned to the others present and extended his hand.

A bottle of rum appeared from the altar room. While Agèou took a long drink, Big Daddy moved through the dipping and turning steps Poupette had mimicked a short time before, a formal salutation used to honor the spirits as well as superiors in the priestly hierarchies. Not until Big Daddy executed the final moves, prostrating to kiss the ground in front of the spirit, did I notice how moved he was. There were tears in his eyes. People murmured: "You see, Philo has come." "Alourdes's mama, that's her Agèou." Frank, with Agèou still in his head, was led to the altar room, and we all moved hungrily toward the food. Alourdes's brother soon emerged, back to his old self, and sat down to an enormous plate of food.

Agèou's appearance at this family event was so welcome because it was so appropriate. In one sense, it was an appearance of Philo herself. Yet, for Alourdes, being visited by Agèou is not the same thing as being visited by Philo. When Agèou is needed, like the other *lwa*, he can be summoned by the sound of the *manbo's ason*. But Philo has slipped further away. Alourdes cannot summon her as Philo once summoned her own mother, Marie Noelsine. Dreams are the most direct contact left to Alourdes, but they cannot be commanded.

"Once, long time I don't dream my mother," Alourdes said. "*Long time* I don't see her. And I don't like that!" Alourdes said she prayed and prayed for her mother to come, and then one night Philo appeared. "What's the matter with you?" Philo scolded. "Don't you know I'm busy? Your sister sick. I got to take care of her first." So Alourdes must wait and allow Philo to determine when, where, and how she is needed. The loss of direct, and to some extent controlled, contact with the ancestors through possession-performance is a major way in which urban Vodou and Vodou in the immigrant communities differ from that of the rural extended-family compounds.

Just as Alourdes combines different senses of family—one family defined by blood ties, another gathered in by a wider net—so she combines different strategies in relation to her ancestors. On the one hand, she depends heavily on her mother's advice in her personal life and in her healing work, and she grows anxious when she does not dream about Philo. On the other hand, Gede, a generalized spirit of all the dead, has come to take over much of the day-to-day caretaking that, in former times and still in many rural areas, would be the domain of the spirits of influential ancestors. One New Year's Eve, for example, with no one in the house but the immediate family, it was Papa Gede, riding Alourdes, who came tripping up the stairs to Maggie's apartment at five minutes to twelve to give her a good-luck bath.

CEMETERIES

Gede stands at the point where the land of the living intersects the land of the dead. The cross, which is also the crossroads, is the central symbol in his iconography. And the cemetery, Gede's home, is a major ritual center in Vodou because it is the most charged and direct incarnation of this same crossroads.

In the countryside, cemeteries are family affairs. They are on family land and contain family graves. Cemeteries, along with small cult houses maintained on a part of the land referred to as the *eritay* (inheritance), are the main places where country people serve the Vodou spirits. In the cemetery, at a point where two paths intersect, the *kwa* Baron (Baron Samdi's cross) is located. The *kwa* Baron and the Baron grave (the grave of the first male buried in the cemetery) are focal points for cemetery rituals. The ground around them is littered with the remnants of Vodou ceremonies: dolls bound together, crumpled pieces of paper with magical imitations of writing, clumps of candle wax, mounds of peanuts and cassava bread, chicken feathers, flowers.

Prayers and offerings before the *kwa* Baron are incorporated in many healing rites in Haiti. For certain serious problems, a visit to the cemetery is absolutely mandatory. For example, when a family is threatened by the ill will of outsiders, any family member can go before the *kwa* Baron and request that a *mò* (a spirit of one of the dead) be sent against their enemy. By definition, this powerful spiritual resource can never be used by one family member against another. Baron Samdi takes revenge only in the name of the family united.

Urban cemeteries are quite different from rural ones. Though still a center for ritualizing, the main cemetery in Port-au-Prince is a huge government-owned city of the dead. Tombs, with compartments for several coffins, are built and owned by families, but the land on which these tombs stand is often rented, and the rent must be paid regularly or the bones of the ancestors will be thrown into the charnel house.

The *kwa* Baron in the Port-au-Prince cemetery also functions differently. It is not a point of access to the most powerful of one's own family dead; instead, it is the main shrine for Gede, representative of all the dead. When I first started going to Haiti in the early 1970s, a large cement cross that had been erected by the Catholic church to mark the section of the cemetery reserved for the burial of priests and nuns was being used as the *kwa* Baron. Needless to say, the church was not pleased to see poor people gathered at this cross whispering urgent messages to Baron Samdi and leaving behind small offerings for him. On several occasions, church officials put fences around this cross, but the people scaled each new barrier and eventually broke them all down. Finally, just a few years ago, the church demolished the putative *kwa* Baron. These days, another large cross,

The *kwa* Baron in the Port-au-Prince cemetery, 1980. Photograph by Judith Gleason.

at some distance from the church's burial ground, has taken over the function of the *kwa* Baron.

In the Port-au-Prince cemetery, a tug of war between Vodou and the modern world goes on on several levels, the dispute with the Catholic church representing only one. The class stratification of this cemetery, for example, is a condensed form of a much more pervasive conflict for urban Haitians. Narrow streets, paved only in prosperous sections, run between row upon row of aboveground tombs designed to look like small houses. The *kavo* of elite families have porches, interior altars, and arched windows. Some are covered in tile and surrounded by elaborate wrought-iron fences. Most of the graves, however, are densely packed cinderblock constructions, painted in pastel colors. These have the look of low-income housing. Thus the urban cemetery reiterates the city itself; all kinds of people are thrown together within its boundaries. Baron Samdi's partisan help is no longer available. If we take the Port-au-Prince cemetery as a measure, then the answer to the all-important question, Who are my people? has become elusive indeed.

In this regard, the most serious issue concerns the ownership of cemetery land. The urban poor are, by definition, landless. Their inability to purchase a cemetery plot in the city is redundant of their general condition. The poorest of them, and that is a great number, cannot even rent one. Many of their family dead end up in the charnel house, which sits off to one side in the cemetery. On any given day, crowds of the poor gather around this structure, trying to make contact with ancestors who lie buried in a great anonymous heap of bones.

Loss of land splits the tripartite root of Vodou: the ancestors, the land, and the spirits. Even in Alourdes's case, the roots of the system are endangered, because the bones of her ancestors rest, at the pleasure of the landlord, on rented land. To some degree, maintaining her generational line depends on timely payment of rent on an eight-by-ten-foot cemetery plot in Port-au-Prince, a hallowed spot she manages to visit only every year or two. In spite of this, Alourdes says that when she dies she wants to be returned to Haiti to rest next to her mother. Not surprisingly, Maggie has different ideas. She recently said she wants to be cremated and have her ashes scattered over the ocean.

Gede, a portable spirit of the collective dead, is important to Haitians in New York. He eases the immigrant's sense of loss and feelings of guilt, emotions that often attach themselves to the family land, and particularly to the ancestral graves left behind on that land. Although focusing on him does change the meaning of relating to the dead, Gede nevertheless preserves the sense that the dead are involved in ongoing human life.

Gede not only is helpful in dealing with ancestral links; he also keeps the families together in other ways. In addition to presiding over the realms of sex, death, and humor, Papa Gede is, by a series of obvious connections, also the protector of small children.

"YOU CAN'T DO NOTHING WITHOUT THE CHILDREN"

When Maggie was about to give birth to her daughter, Betty, Alourdes, who was with her in the delivery room, suddenly began to talk in Gede's nasal twang, a twang caused by the cotton stuffed in the nostrils of corpses. "*Bonswa, Moo-garet,*" he said. Maggie and Alourdes laughed about it afterward: "Those doctor never even know Papa Gede there." Gede had anxiously watched the development of this child from the beginning. Each time the spirit appeared during the pregnancy, he called for Maggie. He lifted her shirt, rubbed her aching back, stroked her expanding belly, and blew a fine mist of rum over its taut skin. After one such ministration, Maggie turned to me and whispered: "You see? That's why Mommie go to those natural childbirth classes with me. I want her to be my partner, not Henri [the baby's father]. I want her so Papa Gede can come. I want him to be my partner, so he can help me."

"The children," Maggie once said, "you can't do nothing without the children." Children are the center of home life, Gede's domain, and their presence is also crucial in certain Vodou rituals. For example, after Maggie, in her dream, swore a solemn oath to Danbala that she would take the *ason,* she held a small *pwomès* (a promise) to assure the spirits that, when time and resources permitted, she would fulfill this commitment. The form of the *pwomès* was a ritual known as a *manje* Marasa (a meal for the Marasa, the twin spirit children). In this ritual, the children of Maggie and Alourdes, as well as some others from the extended family, were stand-ins for the sacred twins. All the children sat together on a cloth Maggie had spread on the floor of the altar room. She laid before them all the foods Haitian children love. They were instructed to eat with their hands, the child's mode of consumption. At the end of the meal, Maggie stood in the center, and all the children wiped greasy fingers on her, just as the beggars did at Alourdes's ritual feeding of the poor in Haiti. With this act, they gave the special blessing that, in Vodou, can be given only by the socially vulnerable—children and the poor. At the same time, they acknowledged the spirits' acceptance of Maggie's promise.

Children are also a part of Vodou in less formal ways. No matter how late the hour or how long the event, children are included in the ritualizing. No matter how risqué the language of the spirits or how potentially volatile the possession-performance, children are witnesses. By age two, Betty seemed to know the difference between talking to Alourdes and talking to Papa Gede. Through interaction with the spirits, children absorb the social world and learn to distinguish among and interact with its various types, an education they begin at a very young age. In Haiti, sleeping infants ride on the hips of their dancing mothers. In New York, drowsy children are put to bed in the room where rituals are going on. As the spirits arrive, children are roused to greet them and be blessed by them. I remember seeing Ti Malis handle Betty (with the practiced hands of a mother!) when she was no more than two months old.

Haitian women have a rough, loving, good-humored way of dealing with infants. They seem to work from two assumptions: first, that children are not fragile; and, second, that things will not get out of hand. A crying child is roughly jounced and, at the same time, firmly held. Mothers communicate security, attention, and a lack of tolerance for crying all at once. It seems to work.

As children become less dependent, the strategy changes. With older children, a great deal of affection is expressed, but there is also an occasional bit of emotional jouncing. I have watched this process most closely in Maggie's relationship with her two children. Betty once came prancing into the room looking adorable: white knee socks, organdy dress, multicolored hair ribbons. "Get away from me!" Maggie cried. "You ugly! You too ugly. I don't want to see you." These moments made me wince until the day when Betty, age five, put her hands on her hips and said calmly but firmly: "I am not. I am not ugly." It made me remember the time, years earlier, when Maggie had done something similar with Michael and then grinned at me, saying, "Life is hard. You got to make them tough!" Intrinsic to Maggie's child-rearing strategy is the belief that if you push a child off-balance occasionally, that child will learn to locate the inner balance Alourdes calls "confidence in yourself."

A similar dynamic is at work in Vodou ritualizing. Vodou drumming is both polyrhythmic and polymetric. The resulting clash of rhythms and meters from the three drums used in most large ceremonies in Haiti demands that the dancer maintain yet another beat with his or her feet, a beat that integrates those of the drums.[4] As I learned from my own initiation, Vodou ritualizing also pushes at people, forcing them to find in themselves a way of staying steady in the midst of conflict. In child-rearing and in ritualizing, the same principle seems to be at work: both are aimed at creating a flexible centeredness, a dynamic balance.

BALANCE: GEDE'S ART FORM

In ordinary Creole, to *balanse* (balance) means to weigh choices. When asked about her plans for her day off, Maggie might respond that she is "balancing between" going to the movies and doing her laundry. In Vodou, the term has a more specific meaning: to *balanse* means to swing ritual objects from side to side or to hold them as you turn yourself around and around. Such balancing "heats up," or enlivens, the object.

Balancing in both these senses is an active, not a static, state of being; and in both it refers to a situation of conflict. (The side-to-side swinging motion is Vodou's kinesthetic rendition of conflict.) But there is one significant difference between the two usages. In ordinary speech, balancing merely refers to being caught in a dilemma not yet resolved. In the language of Vodou, balancing involves using forces that contradict each other to raise life energy.

Andre Pierre, a well-known Haitian artist and Vodou priest, once used the word *balanse* in a revealing way. We were discussing the recent death of someone we both had known. Andre

---

[4]For an excellent discussion of the dynamic relation between drummers and dancers in the African context, see John Miller Chernoff, *African Rhythm and African Sensibility: Aesthetics and Social Action in African Musical Idioms* (Chicago: University of Chicago Press, 1979), 48–49. For further discussion of the relation between musical structure and morality within Haitian Vodou, see Karen McCarthy Brown, "Alourdes: A Case Study of Moral Leadership in Haitian Vodou," in *Saints and Virtues*, ed. John Stratton Hawley (Berkeley and Los Angeles: University of California Press, 1987), 144–67.

Pierre commented, "*Baron Samdi te rive la* [Baron Samdi came there]." And then he paused and grinned, "*Ah! Li te balanse kay sa* [He balanced that house]!" Andre Pierre loves to teach about his religion, and he does so in typical Vodou style, in compact images. His macabre humor that day suggested that a close look into the face of death (Is there any larger affront to the living?) can actually raise our life energy. This point of view helps to explain why the spirit of death is such a randy character and why the one who lives with corpses also dotes on small children.

Most Haitians do not have the luxury of choosing to avoid confronting death. That Vodou deals so directly and frequently with death is no doubt related to this fact. Haiti is ravaged by diseases that were conquered long ago in industrialized societies. The average life expectancy is alarmingly low, and the infant mortality rate alarmingly high; in some parts of Haiti, half the children die before their first birthday. Furthermore, most people live in the countryside, where there are no funeral parlors. The people themselves handle the bodies of deceased family members and prepare them for burial. "*Moun fèt pou mouri* [People are born to die]," Haitians say. With this familiar proverb, they acknowledge the inevitability of death, much as they acknowledge the unpredictability of their lives when they refuse to make any plans without adding the disclaimer, "*Si Dye vle* [If God wills]." Yet those who serve the spirits are not without defenses in the face of death. Haitians are not, on the whole, a depressed or morose people. Gede's humor is their antidote.

I once learned an important lesson about Papa Gede's comic sensibility. Early on, when I was still feeling my way at Alourdes's Vodou parties, I risked joking with Ti Malis. "I like your hat," I said. "Do you like my *zozo?*" he asked, and everyone laughed. "I don't know your *zozo,*" I responded. People laughed again. "Oh, yes, you know it," said Gede. "If you know any man's *zozo,* you know my *zozo!*" More laughter. "Oh, Papa Gede," I said, feigning great earnestness, "maybe you did not know. I am a virgin." This time no one laughed, and Gede simply looked confused. Then someone leaned over and whispered in my ear, "You know, Papa Gede does not lie." Gede's humor denies no reality; he is funny precisely because he tells the truth. He is powerful because he works an alchemical change, not on the facts of life, but on our attitude toward them. Thus the mischievous laugh of Ti Malis emerges directly from the mouth of the Baron Samdi corpse.[5]

Gede's humor is an important survival strategy both in Haiti and in New York, because his powerful truth-telling relativizes the suffering and the vexation of daily life by balancing them against issues of greater weight. I have seen the quick transition between moods that marks Gede's comic sensibility hundreds of times in the marketplace, on the streets, and in homes. A tense situation is flipped on its back by a sudden laugh, a quick joke, or a bit of clowning. This kind of humor is never gratuitous, cruel, or untruthful, and it tends to work best when the stakes are high. "Some people got Ogou," said Alourdes. "Some got Papa Danbala . . . not everybody. But everybody got Gede. *Everybody!*" Everyone has Gede because death is a part of every human life.

GEDE TAKES ON NEW YORK

Gede's importance in immigrant communities such as New York's is based on several character traits. Chief among them are his flexibility and his fearlessness. Gede can guide people in adapting to almost anything, and he does not cower or pull back from the constant change of modern life. On the contrary, Gede, like a sponge, absorbs whatever is new on the social horizon.

Like all the *lwa*, Gede is both one and many; but his ranks are more populous than those of other spirits, and they grow more rapidly and more casually. New Gede persona appear every year around All Souls' Day. These new Gede are born at the forefront of social change, spawned by new occupations, new technologies, new social groups. There is a Gede who is a dentist, and one who is an auto mechanic; and now there is even a Protestant missionary.

---

[5] The frequency and honesty with which Vodou deals with death and sex is probably one reason people in the United States tend to caricature Vodou as a religion preoccupied with sex, evil, magic, and malice. In American culture, we work hard to suppress our knowledge of our own mortality, as we do to control our sexuality, and we are deeply threatened by anything that challenges these approaches.

Whereas spirits such as Danbala work as powerful conservative forces in Vodou, pulling individuals back to ancient loyalties and traditional forms of acting them out, Gede balances
these forces by modeling flexibility in the face of change. By
giving permission to be creative, even playful, in adapting to
the world, he eases situations in immigrant communities that
might otherwise lead to spiritual crisis. One such situation concerns Vodou's deep ties to the earth, ties that cannot be easily
maintained in New York.

Some of the slaves who were brought to Saint Domingue
from Africa, although able to carry away nothing else, brought
small sacks of earth. By holding onto a bit of the homeland, they
hoped to keep some contact, however tenuous, with the ancestors and spirits who sustained their lives. In greater New
York, where many of the descendants of these slaves now live,
immigrants have lost contact not only with both the African and
the Haitian homelands but also with the earth itself. They walk
on concrete streets and sidewalks covering an underground
labyrinth of subways, sewers, and water pipes. They live in
high-rise apartment buildings and row houses with concrete or
wooden floors covered in carpet or linoleum. When Haitians in
New York pour libations for the spirits, their offerings spill out
on hard, unreceptive surfaces. This problem of ritual logistics
has cosmological implications. In New York, it is difficult to continue believing that "from up here to down there, in Ginen they
hear," when Ginen has become so palpably inaccessible. In the
spirit of Papa Gede, Haitian immigrants are currently negotiat-
ing this shift in the cosmos.

One *manbo* in Bedford-Stuyvesant, who lives on the thirty-
seventh floor of a low-income housing project, carts a garbage
pail filled to the top with earth up to her apartment, and all libations are poured there. Alourdes handles this in another way.
When I asked her about the differences between serving the
spirits in Haiti and in New York, the problem of libations was
the first thing that came to her mind: "In Haiti, you got this big
yard, and you pour the rum on the earth for the spirit. But here,
you pour it on the floor, and you have to be careful to don't
pour too much." In everyday ritualizing, Alourdes pours eco-
nomical libations directly on her linoleum floor, where they
eventually evaporate. For large ceremonies involving many libations, she places a basin in front of her altars to collect the rum,

water, and perfume offered to the *lwa*. At the end of the ceremony, this mixture is often transformed into a ritual bath. Perhaps it is because all persons have Gede that human skin can now absorb libations for ancestral spirits, libations that once had to be poured out on the thirsty earth holding the bones of those ancestors.

Such cosmological shifts are still very much in process. Alourdes continues to refuse to initiate people in New York precisely because she feels these important ceremonies demand contact with the Haitian soil. And yet she does perform certain rituals in New York that require getting in touch with the earth. For some rituals, it is necessary to make a trip to Gran Bwa (Great Woods), the name of a Vodou spirit and also of the forest itself. Each neighborhood in Haiti has its own wooded patch that serves as the Gran Bwa for the people of that area. In Alourdes's Brooklyn, Gran Bwa is Prospect Park.

Other rituals require trips to cemeteries and crossroads. For the former, Alourdes, who has no family members buried in the United States, prefers a small Jewish cemetery in Brooklyn, because it has walls around it to provide some privacy. And if the only requirement is that the remnants of a healing ceremony be left in the cemetery, it is relatively easy to toss a plastic bag over the wall without having to risk entering the grounds themselves. Almost any crossroads will do for ritual purposes, even a paved one. But no crossroads in Brooklyn is truly private, and Alourdes and her clients have therefore become adept at unobtrusively scattering seven pennies at the corner of Nostrand and Church avenues or surreptitiously dropping a bag with the leftovers from an expeditionary bath (an extreme form of a bad-luck bath) in the gutter at one of the busy intersections on Empire Boulevard.

Gede's talent for hiding is also important to Haitians in New York. (Recall that Alourdes's Ti Malis is "Hidden Near the Cross.") By habit, Haitians live inconspicuous lives. Generations of political oppression in Haiti have taught them the need for this. Secrecy has also long been part of the practice of Vodou. A great deal of discretion was surely required during the days of slavery, and since then both the Haitian government and the Catholic church have intermittently opposed Vodou. During several periods of religious repression in Haitian history, sometimes accompanied by violent "anti-superstition campaigns," Vodou was forced underground.

In New York, where prejudice against Haitians and Vodou is rampant, these habits of secrecy about religion are reinforced. Maintaining two discrete worlds side by side is a skill even children must learn. When Kumar, Alourdes's youngest, was about ten years old, he asked if I thought he could discuss something Papa Gede had said with the priest at the local Catholic church. "Oh . . . ," I replied, "I don't think so." Kumar jumped up and down with glee. "I knew I shouldn't!" he cried. "I figured that out already!"

Alourdes and Maggie, like most others who serve the spirits in New York, keep their connections to Vodou hidden from the larger world. Nevertheless, on stressful or significant occasions, the barrier between the worlds is sometimes breached. In such situations, it is likely to be Papa Gede, traveling incognito, who makes an appearance in enemy territory—arriving in the hospital just as Maggie gave birth or appearing when she was taking an important exam at school. Papa Gede has even crossed the line between the worlds for me. Gede is the only spirit who would have risked making an entrance at my housewarming party. I was talking with Alourdes in the midst of a group of friends drawn from quite disparate social worlds when I noticed her eyelids begin to flicker and a slight tremor appear in one hand. Before I knew what was happening (the others in the room never did know), Papa Gede was giving his blessing to my new home and suggesting rituals I could perform to make it secure. Gede, whose nature it is to hide and who delights in making fun of life's contradictions, is the perfect one to venture into foreign territory when his children need him.

Among all the spirits, Gede stands out as the great survival artist. His adaptability, his skill at hiding and maneuvering in unfriendly territory, his penchant for making sense (by making fun) of the forces that impinge on people's lives, his expertise as a healer, and his role as a mobile, collective representative of all the dead—these characteristics make Gede an especially important spirit for Haitian immigrants. No spirit, not even Ogou, Alourdes's *mèt tèt*, rides her more frequently than Papa Gede.

MALE AND FEMALE, SPIRITS AND THE SOCIAL WORLD

Gede and Ogou are the quintessential males of the Vodou spirit world. Ogou's heroism and aggression make him very much the man, as do his versions of social irresponsibility and self-destructiveness: infidelity, drunkenness, and lying. But Papa Gede, in his exploration of rapacious sexuality, is even more un-relievedly male. Both the Gede persona and the cemetery rituals that fall within his domain reflect a somewhat anachronistic but still powerful patriarchal ideology. Papa Gede, like Kouzen Zaka, has a wife. But unlike Kouzinn, who is in many respects Azaka's peer, Gede's wife, Brijit, is clearly his inferior. Haitians pay special attention to the grave of the first female buried in every cemetery, calling it the Brijit grave. But ritual attention to Brijit is only a small and perfunctory part of rites intended mainly for Baron.

Brijit is not Gede's female counterpart outside the cemetery, either. Possessions by her are infrequent; I have never seen her ride Alourdes. In other contexts, she comes as an ancient, hobbled woman who can barely talk or walk. Gran Brijit (Grand-mother Brijit), as she is usually called, is an old woman who no longer has sexual power. Papa Gede's enlivening sexual energy, his infectious humor and telling satire, his childlike disregard for social control have no parallels in Gran Brijit. Gede's domi-nation of the realm of the dead reflects a time when male an-cestors, as well as living males, held all the power in Haitian families.

Clearly, this is no longer the case. Alourdes heads her own multigenerational family and traces her lineage through the women in her family. From among her many ancestors, she chooses to rely most heavily on the spirit of her deceased mother. Many Haitian families, perhaps the majority in urban Haiti and in the immigrant communities, no longer fit a patriarchal model. Why, then, has Gede, who is so flexible in other aspects of his character, held on so firmly to an ideology of male domi-nance? Perhaps gender roles are so fundamental that changes within them are more threatening than other kinds of social change.

Gran Brijit is too ancillary a figure to provide a model for strong and independent women such as Alourdes. But an in-triguing chink has recently appeared in Gede's masculine ar-mor. At Papa Gede's birthday party in November 1982, after a long evening with Ti Malis, another Gede made a brief but tan-talizing appearance in Alourdes's head. Her name was Gedelia! She came in like a powerful burst of energy, sexiness, and humor. Unfortunately, she did not stay long enough for me to get to know her well, and I have not seen her since. Not long ago, however, I saw Gedelia's name written across the front of a bus in Haiti. Thus I suspect that Alourdes is not alone in recognizing the need for her.

Surely a full-blown Gedelia will be more than a Gede who happens to be female. Women's energy, their sexuality, and their humor have sources different from men's and are manifested in different ways. What will emerge when the energy of the indefatigable *madansara* bird that infuses Kouzinn is wed to the complex sexuality of Ezili Dantò and Ezili Freda, and then enlivened with the irreverent humor Haitian women use so well against men and other power figures in their lives? I anxiously await Gedelia's emergence from the cocoon of Haitian history and religion.

Agèou	An Ogou; Philo's principal spirit
ason	Sacred rattle of priests and priestesses
Ayida Wèdo	Wife of the rainbow serpent Danbala
Azaka	Peasant farmer spirit
baka	Evil spirit
Baron Samdi	Head of all the Gede
bat gè	Fighting the war, a Vodou ceremony
blan	"Whitey"; a white person
bòkò	A sorcerer; one who works with "both hands" or the "left hand"
Bondye	God
boule zen	Burning the pots, a Vodou ceremony
Brijit	Baron Samdi's female partner
chire ayizan	Shredding the palm leaf, a Vodou ceremony
chwal	Horse of the spirits; one who is possessed
Danbala Wèdo	Ancient spirit, serpent and rainbow
dechoukaj	Uprooting
djèvo	Initiation chamber
djòk	Bad influence from the feelings of others
echofe	To heat up
espri	Spirit
Ezili Dantò	Solitary mother spirit
Ezili Freda	Spirit of sensuality
fanm-saj	Midwife
fèy	Leaves, herbs

gad	Guard; a protective charm
Gede	Trickster spirit of death
Ginen	Africa; a watery realm under the earth
gouyad	Pelvic dance for Papa Gede
Gran Bwa	The ritual forest; a Vodou spirit
gwo bònanj	Big guardian angel; consciousness or personality
gwo nèg	An important or powerful man
kanzo	A level of Vodou initiation
karabel	Haitian denim
kay	House, usually wattle and daub with a thatched roof; a children's game
kleren	Raw rum
kombinayson	Combination; a creature of disparate parts made by magic
konesans	Spiritual knowledge; intuition; extrasensory perception
kouche	To lie down, sleep, make love, give birth, and, less frequently, to die; term used to describe Vodou initiation
kouche sou pwen	Lying down on the point; a level of Vodou initiation
Kouzen	Cousin; a common name for Azaka
Kouzinn	Female cousin; a rural market woman spirit who is Azaka's counterpart
kwa Baron	Baron Samdi's cross in the cemetery
Labalenn	The whale, closely associated with Lasyrenn
lakou	Yard; extended-family compound
langay	Arcane language used in Vodou, composed of African words and disguised Creole
langèt	Slang for female genitalia
Lasyrenn	The mermaid; an Ezili
lave tèt	Headwashing; first step in Vodou initiation
Legba	Spirit guardian of doorways and barriers
Loko	Spirit patron of the priesthood
lwa	Vodou spirit
machann	Market woman
Madan Sara	Market woman, especially a wholesaler

madansara	Noisy, hyperactive black finch
maji	Magic
makout	Straw satchel used by farmers
manbo	Vodou priestess
manje Marasa	Ritual meal for the spirit twins
manje pòv	Ritual feeding of the poor
Marasa	Spirit twins, child spirits
Metrès	Mistress; title for Ezili Freda
mèt tèt	master of the head; principal protective spirit
mizè	Poverty; suffering; misfortune
nanchon	Nation; grouping of spirits
Ogou	Vodou warrior spirit
Ogou Badagri	Handsome soldier; Alourdes's main spirit
òjat	Almond-sugar syrup; favorite drink of Danbala
oungan	Vodou priest
ounsi	Ritual assistant in a Vodou temple
pa-pale	The not-speaking disease, frequently suffered by women who have recently given birth
pèdisyon	Perdition; condition that causes a fetus to stop growing
peristil	Vodou temple
Petwo	One of two spirit pantheons dominant in Port-au-Prince
poto-Danbala	Another name for the *poto-mitan*
poto-mitan	Sacred center pole in a Vodou temple
prètsavann	Vodou functionary who plays the role of Catholic priest in certain types of ritualizing; literally, "bush priest"
Priyè Deyò	Outside Prayers; prayers said at the beginning of Vodou ceremonies
pwen	Point; concentrated spiritual power
pwen achte	Purchased point; nonfamily spirit
pwomès	Promise; a ceremony to show good intentions
Rada	One of two spirit pantheons dominant in Port-au-Prince
rasin	Root
repozwa	A tree that houses a spirit

restavèk	Stay-with; a borrowed or purchased child
sen	Saint; spirit (pl. *sen-yo*)
Sen Jak Majè	Saint James the Elder, head of the Ogou
sojème	Oath-swearing word in *langay*, arcane language of Vodou, probably African
taptap	Brightly painted buses used for public transportation
ti feỳ	Little leaf, a "child of the house"; a Vodou initiate
Ti Malis	Little Mischief; Alourdes's Gede
tonnèl	A thatched-roof pavilion open to the air
Tonton Makout	Uncle Strawsack, a bogeyman in Haitian folklore; the name given to Duvalier's civilian militia
trètmen	Treatment; healing ceremony
Vil-o-kan, Ville-aux-Camps	A town in northern Haiti, the spiritual embassy of Africa in Haiti
vivan-yo	The living; persons who have not died (sing. *vivan*)
Vodou	The religion of the majority in Haiti; a particular drum rhythm used in that religion
zozo	Slang for penis

BIBLIOGRAPHY

Banks, Russell. *Continental Drift*. New York: Ballantine Books, 1985.

Barber, Karin. "How Man Makes God in West Africa: Yoruba Attitudes Towards the Orisa." *Africa* 51 (March 1981): 724–44.

Bastide, Roger. *African Civilisations in the New World*. New York: Harper Torchbooks, 1971.

——. *The African Religions of Brazil: Toward a Sociology of the Interpenetration of Civilizations*. Baltimore: Johns Hopkins University Press. 1960.

Bastide, Roger, Françoise Morin, and François Raveau. *Les Haïtiens en France*. Paris: Mouton, 1974.

Benoit, Max. "Symbi—loi des eaux." *Bulletin du Bureau d'ethnologie* (Port-au-Prince) 3, nos. 20–22 (June–December 1959): 12–22.

Bourguignon, Erika. *Possession*. San Francisco: Chandler and Sharp, 1976.

——, ed. *Religion, Altered States of Consciousness, and Social Change*. Columbus: Ohio State University Press, 1973.

Brown, Karen McCarthy. "Afro-Caribbean Spirituality: A Haitian Case Study." In *Healing and Restoring: Medicine and Health in the World's Religious Traditions*, edited by Lawrence Sullivan, 255–85. New York: Macmillan, 1989.

——. "Alourdes: A Case Study of Moral Leadership in Haitian Vodou." In *Saints and Virtues*, edited by John Stratton Hawley, 144–67. Berkeley and Los Angeles: University of California Press, 1987.

——. "Mama Lola and the Ezilis: Themes of Mothering and Loving in Haitian Vodou." In *Unspoken Worlds: Women's Religious Lives*, edited by Nancy Auer Falk and Rita M. Gross, 235–45. Belmont, Calif.: Wadsworth, 1989.

―――. "Olina and Erzulie: A Woman and a Goddess in Haitian Vodou." *Anima* 5 (Spring 1979): 110–16.

―――. "Plenty Confidence in Myself: The Initiation of a White Woman Scholar into Haitian Vodou." *Journal of Feminist Studies in Religion* 3, no. 1 (Spring 1987): 67–76.

―――. "The Power to Heal: Reflections on Women, Religion, and Medicine." In *Shaping New Vision: Gender and Values in American Culture,* Harvard Women's Studies in Religion Series, edited by Clarissa W. Atkinson, Constance H. Buchanan, and Margaret R. Miles, 123–41. Ann Arbor, Mich.: UMI Research Press, 1987.

―――. "Systematic Remembering, Systematic Forgetting: Ogou in Haiti." In *Africa's Ogun: Old World and New,* edited by Sandra T. Barnes, 65–89. Bloomington: Indiana University Press, 1989.

―――. "The *Vèvè* of Haitian Vodou: A Structural Analysis of Visual Imagery." Ph.D. dissertation, Temple University, 1976.

―――. "Women's Leadership in Haitian Vodou." In *Weaving the Visions: New Patterns in Feminist Spirituality,* edited by Judith Plaskow and Carol Christ, 226–34. San Francisco: Harper and Row, 1989.

Brown, Susan E. "Love Unites Them and Hunger Separates Them: Poor Women in the Dominican Republic." In *Toward an Anthropology of Women,* edited by Rayna R. Reiter, 322–32. New York: Monthly Review Press, 1975.

Chernoff, John Miller. *African Rhythm and African Sensibility: Aesthetics and Social Action in African Musical Idioms.* Chicago: University of Chicago Press, 1979.

Clifford, James, and George E. Marcus. *Writing Culture: The Poetics and Politics of Ethnography.* Berkeley and Los Angeles: University of California Press, 1986.

Comhaire-Sylvain, Suzanne. *Les contes Haïtiens: Origine immédiate et extension en Amérique, Afrique, et Europe occidentale.* Vol. 1, *Manman D'Leau.* Wetteren, Belgium: De Meester, 1937.

Courlander, Harold. *The Drum and the Hoe: Life and Lore of the Haitian People.* Berkeley and Los Angeles: University of California Press, 1960.

Deren, Maya. *Divine Horsemen: The Voodoo Gods of Haiti.* New York: Dell, 1970; reprint, New Paltz, N.Y.: Documentext, McPherson, 1983.

Farmer, Paul. "Bad Blood, Spoiled Milk: Bodily Fluids as

Moral Barometers in Rural Haiti." *American Ethnologist* 15, no. 1 (February 1988): 62–83.

Foster, Charles R., and Albert Valdman, eds. *Haiti—Today and Tomorrow: An Interdisciplinary Study*. New York: University Press of America, 1984.

Geertz, Clifford. *The Interpretation of Cultures*. New York: Basic Books, 1973.

Heinl, Robert D., and Nancy G. Heinl. *Written in Blood: The Story of the Haitian People, 1492–1971*. Boston: Houghton Mifflin, 1978.

Herskovits, Melville J. *Dahomey: An Ancient West African Kingdom*. 2 vols. Evanston, Ill.: Northwestern University Press, 1967.

———. *Life in a Haitian Valley*. Garden City, N.Y.: Anchor, Doubleday, 1971.

Hurbon, Laënnec. *Dieu dans le Vadou haïtien*. Paris: Payot, 1972.

Hurston, Zora Neale. *Tell My Horse*. Berkeley, Calif.: Turtle Island, 1981.

Kiev, Ari. "The Psychotherapeutic Value of Spirit-Possession in Haiti." In *Trance and Possession States*, edited by Raymond Prince, 143–48. Montreal: R. M. Bucke Memorial Society, 1968.

Laguerre, Michel S. *American Odyssey: Haitians in New York City*. Ithaca, N.Y.: Cornell University Press, 1984.

———. "Haitian Americans." In *Ethnicity and Medical Care*, edited by Alan Harwood, 172–210. Cambridge, Mass.: Harvard University Press, 1981.

———. "Ticouloute and His Kinfolk: The Study of a Haitian Extended Family." In *The Extended Family in Black Societies*, edited by Demitri B. Shimkin, Edith M. Shimkin, and Dennis A. Frate, 407–45. Paris: Mouton, 1978.

Landes, Ruth. *The City of Women*. New York: Macmillan, 1947.

Larose, Serge. "The Meaning of Africa in Haitian Vodu." In *Symbols and Sentiments: Cross-Cultural Studies in Symbolism*, edited by Ioan Lewis, 85–116. New York: Academic Press, 1977.

Lévi-Strauss, Claude. *The Savage Mind*. Chicago: University of Chicago Press, 1966.

Lewis, Gordon K. *Main Currents in Caribbean Thought: The Historical Evolution of Caribbean Society in Its Ideological Aspects, 1492–1900*. Baltimore: Johns Hopkins University Press, 1983.

Leyburn, James G. *The Haitian People*. New Haven, Conn.: Yale University Press, 1966.

Lowenthal, Ira P. "Labor, Sexuality, and the Conjugal Contract in Rural Haiti." In *Haiti—Today and Tomorrow: An Interdisciplinary Study,* edited by Charles R. Foster and Albert Valdman, 15–33. New York: University Press of America, 1984.

———. "Marriage Is 20, Children Are 21: The Cultural Construction of Conjugality and Family in Rural Haiti." Ph.D. dissertation, Johns Hopkins University, 1987.

———. "Ritual Performance and Religious Experience: A Service for the Gods in Southern Haiti." *Journal of Anthropological Research* 34, no. 5 (Fall 1978): 392–414.

Marcus, George E., and Michael M. J. Fischer. *Anthropology as Cultural Critique: An Experimental Moment in the Human Sciences.* Chicago: University of Chicago Press, 1986.

Métraux, Alfred. *Voodoo in Haiti.* New York: Schocken Books, 1972.

Mintz, Sidney W. *Caribbean Transformations.* Baltimore: Johns Hopkins University Press, 1974.

Mintz, Sidney, and Richard Price. *An Anthropological Approach to the Afro-American Past: A Caribbean Perspective.* Institute for the Study of Human Issues (ISHI), Occasional Papers in Social Change. Philadelphia: ISHI Publications, 1976.

Murray, Gerald F. "Population Pressure, Land Tenure, and Voodoo: The Economics of Haitian Peasant Ritual." In *Beyond the Myths of Culture: Essays in Cultural Materialism,* edited by Eric B. Ross, 295–321. New York: Academic Press, 1980.

———. "Women in Perdition: Ritual Fertility Control in Haiti." In *Culture, Natality, and Family Planning,* edited by John F. Marshall and Steven Polgar, 59–78. Chapel Hill: University of North Carolina Press, 1976.

Price-Mars, Jean. *Ainsi parla l'oncle.* Ottowa: Lemeac, Collection Caraïbes, 1973.

Rotberg, Robert. *Haiti: The Politics of Squalor.* Boston: Houghton Mifflin, 1971.

St. Juste, Laurore, and Frère Enel Clérismé. *Présence polonaise en Haiti.* Port-au-Prince: n.p., 1983.

Thoby-Marcelin, Philippe, and Pierre Marcelin. *The Beast of the Haitian Hills.* San Francisco: City Lights Books, 1986.

Thompson, Robert Farris. *Flash of the Spirit: African and Afro-American Art and Philosophy.* New York: Random House, 1983.

Wilentz, Amy. *The Rainy Season: Haiti Since Duvalier.* New York: Simon and Schuster, 1989.

Madan Sara, 157–63, 166–67, 192, 381

Madansara bird, 147, 158, 381

Maggie, 7–8, 17, 18, 71, 110, 244, 286; at Abimbola's visit, 102, 104, 107, 108; at Alourdes's wedding, 239; at Azaka's birthday party, 39–40, 41, 43, 49–50, 61–69; birth of, 43, 266–67; blood and memory, 294–304; and children, 372–73; cremation wanted by, 371; and Danbala, 269, 299–302; dreams of, 245, 268, 295–97, 299, 301–2, 303–4; and Ezili Dantò, 226–28, 229, 236; father of, 238, 293; and finances, 129–31; and Gede, 264, 270, 295, 357, 365, 368, 372; Haiti ties of, 180; in hospital, 260–70; initiation of, 50, 132, 135, 298, 301, 313, 317–28; job history of, 163; at Karen's house blessing, 315–16; and male dominance, 157; mother-daughter bonds with Alourdes, 245, 246; at New Year's Day dinner, 365, 366; in New York, 124–25, 127–28, 163, 225–26, 294, 298, 302; and Ogou, 46, 47, 119–20, 264, 266, 301; and possession, 299–300, 353; and psychic abilities, 354; spirits calling, 131–32, 263–69, 295–304, 372; vocational training, 295; and William, 115–25, 131

Magic (*maji*), 105–6, 188–90

Magloire, Paul, 267

Makout (straw satchel), 61, 186 n, 208

Makout forces. *See* Tonton Makout

Male dominance, 157, 220–21, 380. *See also* Patriarchy

Male saints: litany of, 279. *See also names of individual saints*

Male spirits, 3, 377–78; Agèou, 96, 110, 167–68, 206–8, 304, 366–68; Agwe, 284; Aido Hwedo, 274; Duvalier and, 95 n, 185 n; Ezili Dantò's lovers, 228; Kouzinn always paired with, 156; Loko, 55, 56–57; white, 315. *See also* Azaka; Gede; Kouzen; Legba; Ogou

Mama Lola. *See* Alourdes

Mammy Water, 223–24

Manbo (priestess), 4, 37, 50, 352; Alourdes becoming, 75–76, 77–78, 167, 224–25; *anba dlo* ("below the water"), 224; with "gift of eyes," 133–34; illustrated, 93, 259, 300; Madame Gilbert, 206–7; Maggie becoming, 131–32, 263–69, 298, 304; Philo, 75, 77–78, 304; rural, 221; urban Vodou families headed by, 157

Mandang, 100

Mandingo, 100

Ma'Nini, 211–13

Manje Marasa (feast for Vodou twin child spirits), 8, 372

Manje pòv (ritual feeding of poor), 197–201; illustrated, 200

Manje-sèk (dry meal), 190–92

Manley, Michael, 334, 335

Manman. See Mother

Manman Marasa, 22–27, 31–33, 81, 86

Manman Zenfan (Mother of Children), 192

Manouchka, 201, 312, 313

Marasa (sacred twins), 8, 55, 192, 372

Margaux, Alphonse, 209, 238–39, 286–90

Margaux Kowalski, Marie Thérèse Alourdes Macena (Mama Lola). *See* Alourdes

Marguerite, 214

Maria Dolorosa del Monte Calvario, 221, 246, 248, 256. *See also* Ezili Freda

Marie Carmelle, 179–80, 201

Marie Claire, 24–25, 26, 27

Marienette, 352

Marie Thérèse, 172–74, 178–79, 183–85, 188, 193–95

Marines, U.S., 95

Marjorie, 50, 281

Market women (*machann*), 156–57; in Haiti, 27, 63–64, 79, 84–85, 141, 143–44, 155, 156–64, 171; illustrated, 79, 141, 155, 161; Kouzinn as, 156, 157–63; as Madan Sara, 157–63; in Santo Domingo, 148–49

Marriage: Alourdes's, 238–40, 244, 248–49; Ezili Dantò and, 228; Ezili Freda and, 248; in Haiti, 83; Maggie and, 263; Vodou, 113, 133, 134–39, 306–8

Mary Magdalene, 56

Designer: Janet Wood
Compositor: G&S Typesetters, Inc.
Text: 10.5/13 Palatino
Display: Delphin I, Palatino
Printer: The Maple-Vail Book Manufacturing Group
Binder: The Maple-Vail Book Manufacturing Group